THE POLITICAL EC(
A CHRISTIAN S

By the same author:

The Christian Philosophy of Education Explained, 1992
Christianity and Law, 1993
The Nature, Government and Function of the Church, 1997
A Defence of the Christian State, 1998

THE POLITICAL ECONOMY OF
A CHRISTIAN SOCIETY

by

STEPHEN C. PERKS

KUYPER FOUNDATION
TAUNTON, ENGLAND
2001

Published in Great Britain by
THE KUYPER FOUNDATION
P. O. Box 2, Taunton, Somerset,
TA1 4ZD, England

British Library Cataloguing-in-Publication Data
A catalogue record for this book is available from
the British Library

Printed and bound in Great Britain

PREFACE

THE purpose of this book is to introduce the reader to the subject of Christian economics. What I have to say must of necessity be condensed, and much detail will be left out. My aim has been twofold: first, to give a general overview of the field of economics; to elucidate the general principles of economic concepts and the basic structures of economic institutions, and to provide a perspective that will enable the reader to assimilate the details of our modern economic system into an overall understanding of how the economy has developed and currently functions. Secondly, I have tried to indicate in what respects the economy needs to be reformed if it is to conform to Christian standards and so point the way to what the political economy of a Christian society should be like. Because I am attempting to approach this whole subject from a Christian—that is to say a biblically informed—perspective, there are a number of important qualifications and explanations to be made regarding subjects sensitive to Christian ethics, especially in certain areas where biblical teaching relevant to the subject in hand has been misunderstood, abused or neglected, and these are dealt with in the appendices.

A glossary of terms has been included at the end of the book. There is a certain amount of overlap with the main text in this glossary. Nevertheless, it seemed a good idea to summarise certain concepts and provide definitions for frequently used terms and make these available for quick reference in a glossary.

This book had its origins in a workshop originally given in October 1990. The workshop consisted of the substance of Chapter Four, with much of the material in Chapter Three being distributed as accompanying notes. These notes and the text of the workshop lecture were subsequently published in *Calvinism Today* Vol. I, Numbers 3 and 4 (July and October 1991). This material has been extensively revised and expanded since its original publication in *Calvinism Today*. Appendix A was originally given as a discussion paper at the 1993 Spring meeting of the Kuyper Association. Much of the material in the appendices was originally published in *Calvinism Today* also: Appendix D was originally published in the October 1992 issue (Vol. II, No. 4), Appendix E in the April 1991 issue (Vol. I, No.

2), Appendix F in the July 1993 issue (Vol. III, No. 3), and some of the material from Appendix C in the July 1991 issue (Vol. I, No. 3). Appendix B was originally published in the July 1994 issue of *Christianity and Society* (Vol. IV, No. 3). This material has been revised considerably since it was originally published, however.

I should like to express my thanks first of all to Michael G. Butcher, a trustee of the Kuyper Foundation, with whom I have spent many hours discussing and debating the issues raised in this book. That process of discussion and debate has made a valuable contribution to my understanding of the ideas that form the content of this book. A particular word of thanks must go to Colin W. Wright, also a trustee of the Kuyper Foundation, for the encouragement he has given me and for reading earlier drafts of the manuscript and making many helpful comments and suggestions. I should also like to thank Bob Graham and Chris Passerello for reading earlier drafts and Esmond Birnie, Paul Mills and Matthew Wright for reading parts of earlier drafts and making many helpful comments, suggestions and criticisms. Thanks are due also to Matthew Jenkinson for proofreading the book and to the members of Covenant Reformed Church, Leyton, East London, Dave and Ruth Paul and family, and Nick and Julie Pike, whose generous support has made the printing of this book possible. Finally, a very special word of thanks must go to my wife, Susan, whose help and support has been and continues to be vital to the work that this book is a result of.

STEPHEN C. PERKS
SEPTEMBER, 2000

TABLE OF CONTENTS

INTRODUCTION

ECONOMICS has been called the "dismal science." This is in a sense odd, since it affects us all in the most direct and pervasive manner and as a result arouses some of the most heated arguments and angry emotions that modern man experiences. And it has no claim to be a science, at least not in the modern sense—i.e. an exact science—as we shall see. Nonetheless, it is not difficult to understand why the subject has attracted this opprobrious appellation, which seems to be so universally affirmed by the general population. In spite of the fact that economics affects us all vitally and is of the very greatest concern to us in every detail of our lives the subject has suffered badly at the hands of professional economists. It seems always to be hedged about with ideas and arguments that are difficult to understand and that professional economists seem reluctant to explain in clear terms —assuming of course that they understand the arguments themselves and are not just repeating parrot-fashion the ideas of the latest school of economic mumbo-jumbo. Whenever one hears economists talking on the radio or television or reads about the subject in the paper, one is faced with an endless and bewildering mass of statistics, equations and arguments—or perhaps just assertions masquerading as arguments—that are hard to make sense of. It is, therefore, to some extent what econom*ists* have done to economics that has turned it into a dismal science. On top of this, however, economics seems inevitably to be linked with politics, and hence with the tedious and inane propaganda peddled by politicians who seem unable to answer a simple question in a direct manner. It is, perhaps, the association of economics with this latter fact as much as anything else that has rendered the subject so odious to the general population. Politicians so often hide behind a misleading screen of economic "doublespeak" when they know that to answer their critics honestly would make them unpopular and possibly even unelectable. As a result economics is abused by politicians and misunderstood by the general public.

This may be reason enough for a book that attempts to explain to those who have not been initiated into the abstruse craft of modern economics how the economy functions, what is wrong with the way it functions, and what should be done to reform it. But why, it may be asked, do we need a book purporting to explain these matters from a specifically *Christian* perspective? Why do Christians, of all people, need to understand how the economy works and how it should be reformed?

There are a number of answers to this question: first, as already stated, economics affects us all. What goes on in the economy, how politicians manipulate it for their own ends, or for political expediency permit other privileged groups to manipulate it, affects us all in the most pervasive manner, whether we find the subject interesting or not. The condition of the economy determines a great part of our lives, from where we can afford to go on holiday to whether we can get the kind of medical treatment we need or want when we are ill; from how much we can afford to give to charity and thereby help those less fortunate than ourselves to how much we can afford to give to church and thereby help to build the kingdom of God; from where we live to how we travel to work, or indeed whether we have any work at all. It affects how we raise and educate our children; and it affects not only whether they will be educated in private or State schools, but what kind and level of service is provided in both systems. And it affects how we provide for ourselves and how our children provide for us in retirement and old age. All these, and many more, are vitally important matters. How we respond to them will be determined in some measure by the extent of our knowledge—or ignorance—of economics. A better understanding of the economic realities upon which so much of life depends would affect the way many people act economically, and this would have a significant effect on the economy.

Second, economics is not a subject that is religiously neutral. Moral judgements are not irrelevant in economic matters. The way the economy works is intimately bound up with fundamental issues of right and wrong. The answers to the questions that the present state of the economy poses are not neutral from a religious point of view. What one judges to be right or wrong is itself intimately bound up with one's religious perspective. The economy concerns Christians urgently today since it is an area where vital issues of right and wrong and the consequences of society's response to those issues are played out.

Third, the Bible itself directly addresses this subject in the most uncompromising terms. Economics is an important area of concern to Christians since the Christian Scriptures give specific and abiding rules about how men are to behave economically. To be ignorant of at least the basic principles of economics is to some extent to cut oneself off from an important area of divine revelation and thus to be ignorant of God's will for man in an area in which he has commanded man's obedience. It is the calling and duty of the church to address *all* areas in which God has revealed ethical norms for human behaviour. Not to do so is to ignore God's law, God's will for man. This is so in economic matters just as much as in any other area. Immoral economic behaviour must be addressed and challenged by the church no less than immoral sexual behaviour. God has given laws to mankind governing both realms of activity. It is important that the church should teach God's laws for economic behaviour and call society back to obedience to those laws when it departs from them. It is necessary therefore that the church should bring the moral teaching of the Bible to bear on the economic issues that face modern society. If Christians are to do this effectively, however, they must be informed. Ignorance of the economic realities upon which so much of life depends will vitiate the church's ability to speak prophetically in this area and call the present generation back to faithfulness to God's word.

Fourth, the future of our culture and of our civilisation is also vitally affected by economic issues. A political system that systematically penalises the kinds of economic activity that lead to capitalisation and economic growth will obviously have far reaching effects on the general standard of living enjoyed by society. But it will also affect the long-term future of society by effectively making the civilising process itself impossible to sustain on a scale that would support the kind of culture and welfare that we have come to expect in the West. The effect of unleashing such a system on a culture can be seen from the history of the Soviet Union. Not until the early 1950s did the peasants of Soviet Russia attain the standard of living they had enjoyed under tsarist rule in 1913[1]—and this is no apologetic for tsarism. The systematic enforcing of socialist economics on Russia led to a drastic decrease in standards of living,[2] and this was in spite of the massive Western aid that was poured into Russia after the

---

[1] G. North, *An Introduction to Christian Economics* (The Craig Press, 1973), p. 81. North cites as his source Janet Chapman, *Real Wages in Soviet Russia Since 1928* (Cambridge Mass.: Harvard University Press, 1963), p. 150.

[2] See Wilhelm Röpke, *A Humane Economy: The Social Framework of the Free Market* (London: Oswald Wolff [Publishers] Ltd, 1960), p. 150f.; P. T. Bauer, *Reality and Rhetoric: Studies in the Economics of Development* (London: Weidenfeld and Nicolson, 1984),

Revolution and the fact that Russia is a country rich in natural resources.[3] Socialist economics, to put the matter succinctly, cripples economic growth and retards the technological advancement of civilisation, which on the physical level is made possible only by capitalisation (i.e. economic growth) on the scale that has been observed in Western Christendom since the Reformation. And of course such capitalisation was itself, historically, only made possible in the West because of the adoption of a Protestant world-view and the subsequent rationalisation of economic activity in accordance with the Protestant ethic.[4] As British culture increasingly moves away from the kind of political and economic system that made modern Western civilisation possible to a system that has already demonstrated its inability to advance civilisation and its inevitable link with economic crisis and decapitalisation, society will begin to decline economically. This has already happened in many ways. In spite of the attempt to create an "enterprise culture" under a Conservative government in the 1980s Britain is now intimately involved with and committed to membership in a pan-European super-State that is socialist through and through and, in order to achieve its goals, is strangling the nation economically. As a result the nation is slowly but systematically being reduced to economic servitude by means of bureaucratic legislation passed in Brussels, to which the British government must yield.

What is not so obvious is the fact that as the world-view that

---

p. 187f.; Carroll Quigley, *Tragedy and Hope: A History of the World in Our Time* (New York: The Macmillan Company, 1966), pp. 386–405.

[3] Ludwig von Mises stated the problem well: "Russia is the largest country in the world and is thinly inhabited. Within its borders it has the richest resources. It is much better endowed by nature than any other country. It can without too great harm to the well-being of its population renounce foreign trade and live in economic self-sufficiency. But for the obstacles which Czarism first put in the way of capitalist production, and for the later shortcomings of the Bolshevik system, the Russians even without foreign trade could have long enjoyed the highest standard of living in the world. In such a country the application of the bureaucratic system of production is not impossible, provided the management is in a position to use for economic calculation the prices fixed on the markets of foreign capitalist countries, and to apply the techniques developed by the enterprise of foreign capitalism. Under these circumstances socialism results not in complete chaos but only in extreme poverty. A few years ago in the Ukraine [Mises was writing in 1944—SCP], the most fertile land of Europe, many millions literally died of starvation" (Ludwig von Mises, *Omnipotent Government: The Rise of the Total State and Total War* [Spring Mills, PA: Libertarian Press, Inc., (1944), 1985], p. 56f.).

[4] Max Weber's controversial theory set forth in *The Protestant Ethic and the Spirit of Capitalism* (London: George, Allen and Unwin, 1930) will be dealt with in detail in Chapter Three and Appendix F.

in the West made cultural advancement possible—that is, the *Christian* world-view—declines, the *kind* of culture that previously characterised British society will also disappear. We are already in a process of transition from a Christian culture to a "post-Christian," i.e. neo-pagan, culture. The end result of this religious transformation of society will be the loss not only of economic power but also of all those ideals and principles that the nation has for so long taken for granted—e.g. justice, the rule of law, the right of private ownership, freedom of movement and, ultimately, freedom to practise a *Christian* way of life in its fulness.

This prognosis is not scaremongering on the part of those who look back nostalgically to a more Christian culture of previous centuries. It is a realistic assessment based on the facts of history. Socialism has been tried and has failed. This is borne out by the course of Soviet history. It may take longer for the West to arrive at the same end result, and the process may be dressed up in apparel more familiar to Western man, but the outcome will inevitably be the same in substance. Our society has already embarked upon this ruinous course. If we are to change the course of events and avert the ruin of our civilisation, and, by God's grace, experience a renewal rather than the demise of Western culture, it is vital that Christians should understand the issues and address them decisively from a Christian perspective. A Christian perspective on the economic issues facing the nation at the beginning of the twenty-first century will be vital for the renewal of Christian culture in Britain. Of course, economics is one issue among many, but it is an important issue and it must be addressed if we are to be delivered from the dark age that, without a revival of Christian civilisation in our land, looms large before us.

Before we can determine where we need to go, however, we need to understand where we are, where we have come from, and how we arrived at the present situation. In this respect the modern church faces a number of problems: first, there is among Christians generally an apathy to such matters. Many Christians are inclined to view economics as a "worldly" affair that is of no concern to those whose attentions, it is supposed, should be focused primarily on "heavenly" matters. For such the faith is no longer seen as a life- and culture-transforming way of life. But such sentiments have not characterised the Christian religion throughout its long history—at least not until the twentieth century. Biblical Christianity is diametrically opposed to the apathy and escapism that characterises the modern church. The Christian religion has turned the world upside down, or rather right side up—i.e. from depravity to righteousness—wherever and whenever it has been in the ascendant.

Second, among some Christian groups and churches—one is tempted to say "cults" since this term describes many such churches far more accurately[5]—the problem is much more serious than this, more pathological in nature. Pietism, which sees the Christian faith purely in personal terms, i.e. which sees Christianity as relevant only to one's private life and perhaps one's family—though even this is usually restricted considerably—and which regards the corporate or public aspect of the faith as confined purely to the church as an institution, has provided a theological rationale in the twentieth century for the apathy mentioned above. For those who embrace pietism such apathy is not merely an acceptable attitude to "worldly" matters, it is the *only* acceptable attitude in their view. Pietists are convinced, it would seem, that their pietistic perspective has been the norm throughout the long history of Christendom.

This is peculiar since all of Christian history points to the opposite conclusion. Throughout the two millennia of its history the Christian church has demonstrated that the Christian faith is a culture- and nation-transforming, indeed a world-transforming religion that addresses every aspect of human life and culture. This peculiar blindness to the facts of Christian history can be explained however. The church in the twentieth century has, by and large, abandoned the study and appreciation of Christian history. Yet the problem amounts to more than ignorance of Christian history.[6] Such ignorance is part of a much larger problem, namely the church's failure to understand its calling

---

[5] See Stephen C. Perks, "Christianity as a Cult," in *Christianity and Society*, Vol. IX, No. 4 (October 1999), pp. 2–5.

[6] By "Christian history" I do not mean *church* history, though the latter is encompassed by the former. The study of church history is a well-established and popular field in academic circles and beyond, but the study of the history of the West as a Christian civilisation is much less common among historians. The secular universities of Britain are, of course, busily promoting "revisionist" history, which from a religious perspective means history without reference to Christianity or in which Christianity is vilified as the cause of the individual's and society's gravest ills. Doubtless this is to be expected given the religious perspective of secular humanism, which underpins and controls academic life in modern Western society. But the church must not let it be forgotten that Christianity has been the single most important influence on the development of Western civilisation and that the modern revisionist fad of writing this influence out of our history can only end in a distortion of the truth and the misunderstanding of history.

in the world. Pietism rendered the church of the twentieth century impotent and irrelevant at a time when the Christian gospel in its fulness—that is to say the whole counsel or word of God, not simply the truncated message peddled by modern evangelicalism—needed to be heard desperately. The modern church's failure to articulate and proclaim the comprehensive claims of the Christian faith to a society gripped by a revival of paganism more virulent than it has been for over a millennium is itself a major cause of the decline of Western culture and, as part of that general decline, of Western economies also. A pietistic imitation of the Christian faith may have seemed attractive to many in the genteel culture of a largely Christianised Victorian England, but it is no match for the resurgent paganism that threatens to destroy Christendom at the beginning of the twenty-first century. For that the real thing is needed.

This pietism is pathological for another reason however. In spite of the aloofness that pietists try to create in their personal lives, the results of pietism are anything but unrelated to the world of everyday affairs. Pietists seek to be otherworldly to such an extent that they are not concerned with banal and unspiritual subjects such as economics—about which the Christian Scriptures have so much to say. They see no need to develop a Christian perspective on social issues because these are "worldly" whereas the faith, or so it is thought, is above the world and unrelated to such issues. But this attitude succeeds only in creating a vacuum. Even pietists must live in the real world and think about and act in terms of the everyday social, economic and political issues that face us all. Hence, without a well thought-out *Christian* perspective on these issues pietists unwittingly imbibe the worldly attitudes around them. Because they believe these issues are neutral from a religious perspective they do not stop to consider whether their views are Christian, whether or not they conform to biblical principles. They simply imbibe the views of the world around them unwittingly. In so doing they become perpetrators of the very worldliness they think and claim they have escaped by devotion to a purely personal or church-oriented faith. Thus it is that the church, by its apathy and pietism, has become an avenue by which British culture has been repaganised. Wherever the church leaves an intellectual vacuum—i.e. wherever it asserts that a given sphere of life is religiously neutral—some other ideology will be imbibed to fill that vacuum, by non-believers and believers alike. That ideology in the twentieth century was secular humanism, and it prepared the way for the repaganising of Western society. But the problem does not stop here.

Third, when the church is then challenged over its apathy it so often responds by merely regurgitating the latest secular humanistic sentiments in the dress of Christian language, thereby baptising, as it were, utterly unbiblical and un-Christian ideals. Thus, in the twentieth century the church, because it did not develop a biblical perspective on economic and social issues, ended up espousing socialist ideals and principles, insisting that these are Christian ideals and principles simply because good intentions have been imputed— though often incorrectly—to those who developed or popularised socialist ideology. But good intentions do not guarantee that a man will hold to *biblical* principles. Had such careless thinking been adopted with regard to the doctrine of the atonement the church would have abandoned a distinctively Christian (i.e. biblical) theory of the atonement long ago and adopted instead Unitarianism and universalism *en masse*. The Christian faith demands, however, as vigorous an application of biblical principles to social, economic and political issues as it does to theological issues such as the atonement. Only as this is done will the church be able to articulate a distinctively *Christian* voice on these issues as opposed to the old and worn out secular humanistic answers dressed up to look Christian.

The task before us, therefore, is to develop a biblical perspective on the issues that face society and thereby help to revive the nation's Christian heritage. The first step in this process is to pursue under-standing. With regard to political economy, we must understand how the economy works and how biblical principles apply to it. It is in order to facilitate that task that this book has been written. It is offered in the hope that it will help to give the church a clearer vision of where we are, how we got here, and what we should do if the economy is to conform to Christian—i.e. biblical—principles and ideals.

In conclusion, it should be mentioned that economic injustice perpetrated by the modern State is not the only kind of problem facing modern Western society. A sense of balance is therefore called for. Far more serious abuses of power are tolerated and supported by most modern Western States than those arising from government-control and government-regulation of the economy. Compared to the State-legalised and in many cases tax-funded murder of thousands of unborn human beings every year economic injustice pales into insignificance. The gravity of this obscene offence gives it a singular priority over mere economic matters in the reformation of society. However, economics is the subject under consideration here, not abortion. Nonetheless, the following two points are relevant to our discussion of economics: first, abortion is not totally without relevance to the economic growth and prosperity of the nation since a society that is declining in population or even just reproducing itself numerically has to allocate a greater proportion of its resources to care of the elderly and welfare generally than a comparable society with a growing population. Such welfare is unproductive in general terms and the greater the degree to which society has to channel its economic resources into it the less it has to invest in the creation of wealth, to capitalise itself and thus generate the kind of economic prosperity that would enable it to fund welfare more effectively. Second, we must not underestimate the significance of economic decline as an aspect of the judgement that God visits upon a society that tolerates practices such as abortion and refuses to acknowledge him as Lord, worshipping the creature rather than the Creator (Rom. 1:18–31).

CHAPTER ONE

ECONOMICS AND ECONOMIC DISCIPLINES

§1
Definition of Economics

ECONOMICS is the study of the management and productive use of scarce resources with alternative uses. The word *economics* is derived from the Greek word *oikonomia*, meaning *the management of a household, husbandry* or *thrift*. This word is itself formed from the combination of two other Greek words *oikos*, meaning *house*, and *nemo*, meaning *to distribute* or *to manage*. An *oikonomos* was the manager of a household or estate, a steward or administrator. Economics, therefore, deals with the stewardship of scarce resources.

§2
Various Kinds of Economic Study

Economists today generally distinguish between various kinds of economic study. There are text books dealing with subjects such as macroeconomics, microeconomics, development economics, econometrics, positive economics, normative economics. International trade, though often considered as part of macroeconomics, also tends to be treated in a somewhat specialist way as if it constituted a form of economic activity governed by principles quite different from those of domestic trade.

Macroeconomics is concerned with an overall view of the economy and therefore deals with economic activities in terms of large aggregates—e.g. total production, total employment, total investment, total consumption, savings and investment, the general level of prices and wages, inflation, economic growth and problems relating to international trade such as an unfavourable balance of trade. The purpose of macroeconomic theory, according to Seldon and Pennance, is "to study systematically the influences that determine the levels of national income and other aggregates and the level of employable resources."[1] Macroeconomic theory plays a large part in the formulation of government economic policy and tends to inform much of the thinking done by development economists devising models for investment and economic growth in underdeveloped countries.

Microeconomics, by contrast, studies the economic actions of individuals and particular groups of individuals, particular firms and businesses, the fluctuations in prices between various goods and services and the factors determining the allocation of resources to particular industries. Its purpose is to analyse and understand the minutiae of economic activity that generate the wealth and resources of the nation.

Development economics studies the economies of underdeveloped countries such as Third World nations, whose populations generally have been unable to raise themselves out of a state of subsistence living, semi-starvation and general underutilisation of available economic resources. Development economists analyse such economies and attempt to construct development models that will, usually with the help of international aid programmes, promote economic growth and social improvement. The purpose of this is to bring these backward nations into line with Western standards of living and welfare. In spite of its being considered an aspect of economics, development economics has far more to do with the international politics of aid, which properly has little relevance to economics as such and is more correctly an aspect of charity.

Econometrics, write Seldon and Pennance, is "the branch of economics in which economic theory, mathematics and statistics are fused in the analysis of numerical data. Econometrics presents economic theories in a form in which they can be tested statistically against observed events."[2] It relies, therefore, on the compilation and analysis of economic statistics. Econometrics plays a significant role in the testing of modern macroeconomic theory.

Positive economics purports to treat the subject as a science and attempts to discover and analyse the "facts" of economic phenomena, what *is*, in contrast to *normative economics* (e.g. welfare economics),

---

[1] Arthur Seldon and F. G. Pennance, *Everyman's Dictionary of Economics* (London: J. M. Dent and Sons Ltd, 1965) p. 266.

[2] *Ibid.*, p. 136.

which attempts to determine what *ought* to be and therefore deals with value judgements.

§3
Problems with the Definition of Some Economic Disciplines

These distinctions can be misleading since they really only represent the abstraction of particular aspects of economic phenomena from the complex reality of human action, and cannot be pushed too far without distorting one's understanding of the nature of economic activity. Such abstractions are valid and useful to the extent that they enable us to understand the relation between certain economic phenomena and thereby help to provide us with a better understanding of the subject as a whole. However, when this qualification is not borne in mind and the limitations of such abstractions are not given sufficient attention it is often assumed that these different areas of economic study have a quasi-autonomous character. It is then not infrequently claimed that the particular circumstances with which a field of study is concerned, e.g. Third World economies, necessitate the modification of fundamental principles of economic activity as these apply to the particular conditions under consideration. This can and often does lead to confusion and to the formulation by politicians of economic policy that cannot achieve its aim and that often produces in the event the very opposite of what it is intended to accomplish.

The confusion resulting from the abuse of these distinctions can readily be observed in the frequent disputes between left- and right-wing political parties in Britain over the outcome of government economic policy. The economic theoreticians of each party disagree not only about the practical outcome of each other's policies, but also about the economic realities on which their policies are based. Each side is committed to models constructed in terms of those aspects of economic life that they prioritise and wish to see reformed, and each side refuses to acknowledge that their economic policies are essentially based on abstract models operating in terms of quasi-autonomous aggregates that do not adequately represent the concrete factors prevailing in the real economy. In short, in their eagerness to promote the interests of those sectors of society from which they believe they derive their mandate politicians constantly fail to take account of the whole picture. When the economic policies of the party in government have run their course and economic reality catches up with politics, the result is economic depression, inflation, unemployment etc. The opposition party then gains power, usually on the ticket of solving all the problems created by the previous government's policies, and simply inverts the problem by stressing different but equally artificial answers based on a distortion of economic realities. The result is that the economy plunges headlong into another crisis. Consequently, the economic pendulum swings back and forth with ever more damaging results for those who have to live in the real world.

We shall now look a little more closely at some of the problems arising from the abuse of these artificial distinctions and definitions.

§4
Development Economics

Development economists often assume that the economies of many Third World societies are not able to sustain economic growth and social amelioration on the basis of the same economic principles that led to the rise of Western economies over the past four hundred years. Because of the conditions prevailing in these societies it is thought that their economies operate in terms of economic principles that are essentially different from those relevant to developed economies. Societies exhibiting these special economic conditions are deemed to require help from the First World, usually in the form of aid to governments to enable them to plan the growth of their economies. Yet after many years of special aid programmes on a massive scale these societies are still languishing in poverty, starvation and disease. India is a good example: between 1951 and 1959 India received foreign aid worth £580 million from the USA, £65 million from the UK, £65 million from Canada, and £72 million from Germany.[3] Yet from 1957 to 1959 there were acute and widespread food shortages.[4] In 1958–59 weather conditions were exceptionally good from the agricultural point of view, but there were still food riots.[5] Under British rule, however, India had been a net exporter of food.[6]

---

[3] P. T. Bauer, *Indian Economic Policy and Development* (London: George Allen and Unwin Ltd., 1961), p. 134.   [4] *Ibid.*, p. 67.   [5] *Ibid.*, p. 55.
[6] David Chilton, *Productive Christians in an Age of Guilt Manipulators* (Tyler, Texas:

On the other hand, similar societies that have adopted the same basic principles of economic organisation that led to the rise of Western economies have flourished and begun to challenge Western economies in many industries—e.g. Malaysia, Hong-Kong, the Philippines, Singapore, South Korea and Taiwan.[7] In fact, as P. T. Bauer has shown, the most that foreign aid can do for Third World nations in terms of development and growth of the economy is equivalent only to offsetting the costs of borrowing, since if development programmes are economically viable they will be funded readily by private enterprise and commercial loans from abroad.[8] At worst, however, aid can lead to the fossilisation of government economic policies that create disinvestment and thus cripple industry.[9] This is because by the very nature of the case aid tends to be offered to nations whose governments have already demonstrated their inability to safeguard the social conditions necessary for economic growth and social amelioration.

Institute for Christian Economics, Third Edition, 1985), p. 119.

[7] P. T. Bauer, *Reality and Rhetoric, Studies in the Economics of Development* (London: Weidenfeld and Nicolson, 1984), p. 20.

[8] P. T. Bauer, *Equality, The Third World and Economic Delusion* (London: Methuen, 1982), p., 101. Bauer writes: "Even though foreign aid can alleviate immediate shortages, it cannot appreciably promote the growth of the national income. It is more likely to retard this growth. Countries where government or business can use funds productively can borrow abroad. The maximum contribution of foreign aid to development in the sense of the growth of the national income cannot therefore exceed the avoided costs of borrowing. As a percentage of the national income of large Third World countries this maximum contribution is at best minute, a fraction of 1%, far too small to register in the statistics" (*ibid.*, p. 100f.). This argument remains entirely valid in spite of the fact that many Third World governments today owe massive debts to First World banks. Such debt is the result precisely of socialist planning by governments rather than the creation of a free market order in which private economic enterprise and initiative are allowed to flourish. Government economic planning is inevitably irrational from the economic point of view and thus invariably counter-productive. *Government* borrowing is never a suitable means of pursing economic growth and social amelioration and it was not such planning of economic activity on the part of governments that initially led to the economic growth and strength of the First World nations. The fact that Britain, under a Labour government in 1976, had to go cap in hand to the IMF demonstrates admirably the fact that such socialist policies, even when pursued by economically strong First World countries, inevitably lead to economic decline. It was *private* enterprise in a free market order based upon Christian principles of honesty, thrift and hard work in a society abiding by the rule of law with a limited civil government and the rationalisation of economic activity in accordance with the Christian ethic that led to the economic strength of the Western nations, not the economically irrational and unproductive policies dreamed up by government bureaucrats. See Appendix F, "Max Weber and the Protestant Doctrine of the Calling." [9] *Ibid.*, pp. 103–109.

There are, in particular, a number of serious problems arising from government to government aid programmes based on models that do not require the creation of the same economic conditions that led to economic prosperity in the developed world:

(a) Such aid primarily supports governments and the policies those governments choose to pursue, not the poor, who may not benefit at all from these policies.[10] P. T. Bauer points out that "much spending undertaken or directed by government and termed investment does not represent capital formation on any sensible interpretation, but is merely spending on various activities and projects deemed useful to the government and its agents. And aid brings about a host of repercussions which adversely affect the basic determinants of development and are likely far to outweigh any benefit from aid."[11] Usually countries receiving aid are poor precisely because the policies pursued by their governments create economic impoverishment. Aid given to such governments tends to increase governmental power and control over society and thus helps to prolong the very problem it is ostensibly aimed at eliminating by helping to reinforce the kinds of policies that created the problem in the first place.

Many Third World governments have persecuted some of the most productive groups in their societies.[12] Communist governments in Third World nations, for example, which are hostile to the idea of private capital accumulation because it is considered a "capitalist" way of life, tend to punish prudent economic activity, often very severely. Under the Mengistu Government in Ethiopia saving money from the sale of the proceeds of past harvests and investing it in future food production was called "capitalist accumulation" and made a "crime against the people." Earning a living by transporting food to districts where it was needed was considered "exploitation" and was punished by confiscation, imprisonment and even execution. Saving food from good harvests for droughts and bad seasons has also been punished with mass executions.[13]

---

[10] *Ibid.*, p. 111.   [11] *Ibid.*, p. 101.

[12] P. T. Bauer, *Reality and Rhetoric*, p. 50.

[13] This information is taken from a lecture given by Yonas Deressa, Director of the Ethiopian Refugee Education and Relief Organisation, at a special White House Briefing sponsored by the Ethics and Public Policy Center in the United Sates on February 1st. 1985. The lecture was reprinted as "The Politics of Famine" in *Biblical Economics Today* vol. III, no 3 (Tyler Texas: Institute for Christian Economics, 1985. See also Archbishop Abba Mathias, "Religious Repression in Ethiopia," Appendix 5 in David Chilton, *op. cit.*

Aid given to such governments does nothing to benefit the poor, who are denied the economic means necessary to improve their conditions by the government, and helps to promote the kinds of economic policy that have led to the decline of these economies in the first place. Aid in such cases actually helps to prolong the misery of such economically impoverished nations and helps to create the desperate economic conditions that are then deemed by development economists to necessitate further injections of aid.[14]

(*b*) Aid given to governments also fosters the adoption of *political* rather than economic means of social amelioration since it provides immediate resources for short-term social amelioration in the form of State subsidies, grants and welfare, but without requiring the fundamental reforms necessary to sustain economic growth in the long term. This leads to the increasing politicisation of life, which encourages people to divert their time, resources and energy away from productive economic activity towards securing favourable treatment from government—e.g. State subsidies, the granting of licenses and monopolies, imposition of tariffs on imports that compete with domestic industries, discriminatory tax concessions, all of which have detrimental effects on the economy. P. T. Bauer states the problem clearly:

Foreign aid has thus done much to politicize life in the Third World. And when social and economic life is extensively politicized, who has the power becomes supremely important, sometimes a matter of life and death —witness Burundi, Kampuchea, Ethiopia, Indonesia, Iraq, Nigeria, Pakistan, Tanzania, Uganda, Vietnam and Zaire among countries whose governments have received substantial Western aid. In such conditions, people at large,

---

[14] "The pattern of spending by aid-recipient governments is unrelated to help for the poor. This spending often aggravates the position of the poor, since recipient governments often spend heavily on politically inspired prestige projects made possible by external aid: airlines, inefficient industries, Western-type universities whose graduates cannot find jobs, and the creation of new capitals at vast cost (Brasilia, Islamabad, Dodoma in Tanzania and Lilongwe in Malawi). These often have to be subsidized by local taxes, including those on the poor. When demanding aid from the West, Third World governments emphasize the poverty of their people, whose condition is a major plank in aid advocacy. But the policies of most Third World governments are not designed to relieve poverty. The poor, particularly the rural poor who are the great majority, are politically ineffective and thus of little interest to the rulers. In fact in many, perhaps most, Third World countries, organized state relief of poverty does not accord with local mores, and no machinery exists for this purpose." (P. T. Bauer, *Equality, The Third World and Economic Delusion*, p. iii.)

especially those who are alert and ambitious, become much concerned with what happens in politics and in public administration, as decisions taken there come crucially to affect their livelihood and even threaten their physical destruction. People divert their resources and attention from productive economic activity into other areas, such as trying to forecast political developments, placating or bribing politicians and civil servants, operating or evading controls. They are induced or even forced into these activities in order either to protect themselves from the all-important decisions of the rulers or, where possible, to benefit from them. This direction of people's activities and resources must damage the economic performance and development of a society, since these depend crucially on the deployment of people's human, financial and physical resources.[15]

Thus, foreign aid given to Third World governments, because it provides much of the funding necessary to effect this politicisation of life, initiates, or at least helps to sustain, a cycle of events that is extremely damaging to the whole economy and hence to real economic growth and social amelioration in the long term for the majority of the population.

The effects of aid when misdirected in this way are also often detrimental to those minorities and groups that do not have the political muscle to secure favourable treatment by the government in office. Those with access to political power use that power to better their own conditions by granting favourable concessions, privileged status and accesss to government funds for themselves, for their own class, ethnic group or tribe and by penalising and disadvantaging other groups—e.g. by restricting opportunities for skilled work and reserving entrance into monopoly trades for members of the privileged groups. Those groups that are not able to control the policy and machinery of State, which are often the most economically productive groups in society, are disadvantaged and become second class citizens.[16] Foreign aid given to Third World governments, since it helps to provide the funding necessary for such policies to be pursued, is essentially irrational from an economic point of view and therefore detrimental to economic growth and social amelioration in the long term. For the same reason it helps to institutionalise prejudice and injustice.

Foreign aid, therefore, can, and often does, promote economic backwardness. Aid given to governments often finances policies that frustrate the efforts of many to improve their social conditions. It

---

[15] P. T. Bauer, *ibid.*, p. 104.   [16] *Ibid.*, p. 94.

also leads many to pursue political measures as a means of social amelioration when in the absence of such politicised aid they would be forced back upon *economic* measures to better their conditions, which would be more desirable and able to produce the required long-term results.

The political road to social amelioration is thus not only economically irrational, but from the human point of view cruel, since it cannot be sustained when the aid runs out and tends to *dis*courage the kind of real economic reform needed to create the conditions necessary for the development of a productive economy that would sustain long-term social amelioration. Furthermore, aid given to governments that pursue such policies tends to strengthen and consolidate their hold over society and free up other resources for irrelevant and unnecessary prestige and showpiece projects[17] and even for the machinery of oppression. A good example of this latter point was the Mengistu regime in Ethiopia, which, whilst most of the rural population was in the grip of severe starvation and receiving massive aid from the First World, spent £35,000,000 on a colour television system for its capital and millions more on a whisky gala. At the same time it conducted a civil war in twelve of the country's fourteen provinces.[18]

Disaster aid and private aid directed to those in need rather than to governments is less easily misdirected, yet even this is subject to much abuse. In spite of the world-wide publicity given to the Ethiopian disaster much of the private aid sent to Ethiopia was subject to both misappropriation and governmental interference and obstruction, and this abuse was widely reported in the media at the time.

(*c*) The effect of aid-financed political initiatives is thus government *control* of wealth through the manipulation of market conditions in accordance with government policy directives, rather than the *creation* of wealth as a result of provision of greater opportunities for real economic enterprise in a free market order. It is possible for Third World governments receiving aid from the First World to generate social amelioration in the short term—i.e. while the aid lasts—but such policies usually end in economic bankruptcy since

---

[17] *Ibid.*, p. 248f., cf. note 14 above.

[18] Yonas Deressa, "The Politics of Famine" (for the source see note 13 above). There are many other similar examples of Western aid going to oppressive regimes, including those of Idi Amin in Uganda and Pol Pot in Kampuchea. See P. T. Bauer, *Equality, The Third World and Economic Delusion*, p. 93f.

the conditions necessary for real economic growth through the development of a sound economy are not only not materially improved but actually weakened by aid programmes.[19]

The conditions prevailing in such countries necessitate in the long-term *not* aid programmes—disaster aid is a different matter however—but the creation of free markets and real economic opportunities for people to better their conditions through thrift and hard work without being penalised by the State for being productive. That is to say, backward Third World nations are not helped by the imposition of artificial aid programmes devised by development economists. Such programmes are based on theories that involve the fallacious abstraction of certain aspects of economic life from the reality of the concrete situations that exist in the Third World. Those aspects of economic life are then treated as if they were phenomena involving economic principles essentially different from those relevant in the developed world. Third World economies are therefore deemed to require the recognition and accommodation of special factors by the First World if they are to grow. Such programmes are generally linked with State regulation of the economy and thus discourage development of the kinds of real economic enterprise that would facilitate general economic growth and social amelioration.

The economic principles relevant to the developed world are equally relevant to the underdeveloped world and the social conditions necessary for the creation of wealth are the same in both kinds of society. Development economists who refuse to take cognisance of this fact and attempt to construct special economic models for underdeveloped Third World nations that require ever increasing amounts of aid from the First World in order to keep their economies afloat do not help to liberate the people of such countries from social and economic backwardness, which they rightly see as being debilitating and undesirable.[20] Government policy based on such models, rather than leading to economic growth, fosters the very backwardness it is designed to eliminate, as well as encouraging the dependence of Third World societies on First World aid.

[19] P. T. Bauer, *Equality, The Third World and Economic Delusion*, p. 105.

[20] A typical example of a left-wing economist calling for such aid—typical also of the superficial Christian attitude to such problems that has become one of the hallmarks of neo-evangelical social concern—is Allan Storkey. According to Storkey: "Europe should be prepared to be the larder of Africa" (*Transforming Economics* [London: SPCK, 1986], p. 173). Storkey spells out precisely what he means by this when he goes on to say that "aid should be the biggest growth industry and should

Development economists concentrate on the discrepancy between standards of living and general welfare in First and Third World societies, and the underdeveloped condition of Third World economies is generally thought to be related to essentially economic factors such as lack of cultivable land, natural resources and capital. This is quite evidently false however, since, as P. T. Bauer has written, "many millions of very poor people in the Third World today, as in the past, have ready access to cultivable land . . . Such groups as aborigines, pygmies and various African tribes are extreme cases of poverty amidst abundant land. Even in India, much land is officially classified as uncultivated but usable."[21] Bauer concludes that "The small size and low productivity of so many farms in the Third World primarily reflect want of ambition, energy and skill, and not want of land and capital."[22] Furthermore, he observes that "the notion of uncultivable land is misleading, since cultivability depends heavily upon the economic qualities of the people as well as on official policies affecting the use of land. Examples of the last point include price policies of governments, control of immigration and inflow of capital, and the terms on which state lands are made available."[23]

Other important factors relevant to the backwardness of many Third World societies are the kinds of religious belief, attitudes and traditional values espoused by the general population.[24] Most pagan religions and the traditional values associated with them—Hinduism and its concomitant caste system is a good example—institutionalise a way of life that makes economic progress and social amelioration for most of the population impossible, since such progress requires

be rivalling defence in the government accounts" (*ibid.*). Yet no attempt is made to put these statements into their proper context by considering the possible effects that government to government aid produces and whether it actually succeeds in stimulating economic prosperity for the recipient or just more dependence on foreign aid, thereby prolonging economic impoverishment and retarding movement towards the development of a viable economy. As usual there are the accompanying warnings and threats to Western nations if they refuse to cough up: "The time for this kind of giving and help is running out. As Third World countries become more bitter and helpless and the seeds of antagonism grow, each physical bit of help will be valued less. The selfish western strategies will be thrown back in the face of the West and the judgement will be more fierce" (*ibid.*). Aid or else! The fact is that the more aid such governments receive, and the more they are told they have a right to such aid from the West, the more dependent they become on it and the less likely they will be to develop the conditions necessary to foster real economic growth and prosperity.

[21] P. T. Bauer, *Reality and Rhetoric*, p. 8.   [22] *Ibid.*   [23] *Ibid.*
[24] P. T. Bauer, *Equality, The Third World and Economic Delusion*, p. 100.

the abandonment of many of these traditional beliefs, mores and practices and therefore tends to be rejected by the majority of the population on religious grounds. One's way of life and general standard of living are intimately linked with one's belief system. Many in such countries are willing to accept aid packages and programmes that do not essentially affect their way of life, but not the kind of change to their belief system and the traditional organisation of their society that would enable them to become self-sufficient. As a result one crisis follows another, and more aid is received, but with very little real change and hardly any effect in the long term.

The crucial factors affecting economic conditions in such countries are essentially *non*-economic, yet development economists tend to analyse underdeveloped and backward societies in terms of economic criteria. The attempt to analyse and address the discrepancy between economic conditions in First and Third World societies without taking account of the psychology, traditions and religious beliefs of the human actors upon which the economy depends is misguided to say the least. It is precisely the motivation, ambition and determination of those human actors, rather than the availability of natural resources and capital, that create economic growth and social amelioration. P. T. Bauer has cited as an example of this point Hong-Kong,[25] which lacks virtually all those economic factors deemed necessary by most development economists for economic growth, yet which, under British rule, prospered enormously and even challenged the economies of Western nations. In contrast China has vast areas of land and natural resources, yet the majority of its people live in abject poverty.

The economies of underdeveloped nations would be far better served by an analysis that recognises the same basic principles of economic activity that are relevant to the growth of developed economies, indeed that are relevant to the growth of all economies. Such an analysis would help to promote the formulation of policy geared to safeguarding those conditions, common to all societies, under which economic growth and social amelioration can thrive.[26]

[25] *Ibid.*, pp. 185-190.

[26] P. T. (Lord) Bauer, Emeritus Professor of Economics at the London School of Economics and Political Science, is Britain's leading development economist and his books should be read carefully by anyone wishing to obtain a thorough understanding of the subject. He has exposed the problems and fallacies current in much modern thinking in development economics. See the bibliography for a list of his books.

§5
Macroeconomics and Microeconomics

A similar kind of distortion of economic reality can occur when macroeconomic theory is divorced from consideration of the concrete everyday economic decisions and actions taken by people on the microeconomic level. For instance, we are told by Seldon and Pennance that "Macro-economics has its own rules because aggregate economic behaviour does not compare to the total of individual activities."[27] This statement shows a confused understanding of economic reality. It is to say that the whole is *not* the sum of its parts. The economy, however, is precisely the sum of all individual economic activities. Even taking account of the fact that the economic actions of individual people, firms and businesses are often influenced and regulated by government policy, aggregate economic behaviour must compare with the total of individual economic actions. Aggregate economic behaviour *is* the total of individual economic actions. Such an artificial dichotomy between macroeconomics and micro-economics is confused and misleading. Besides, it is an almost meaningless use of language to say that aggregate economic behaviour does not compare with the sum total of individual economic activities. The latter phrase is simply another way of defining aggregate economic behaviour.

Macroeconomic models developed on the basis of such a fallacy can only lead to economic delusion. When such models are adopted by governments as a rationale for the formulation of policy aimed at controlling the economy in terms of government plans for national aggregates they invariably lead to serious problems for many of the individuals, firms and industries that comprise the economy; and it is the latter that generate the wealth and resources for economic growth, not government policy, however much politicians would like us to believe otherwise. Such a confused understanding of economic reality lies at the root of many of the problems faced by the economies of both developed and underdeveloped nations today. To the extent that government economic policy is informed by such spurious macroeconomic notions it is simply out of touch with reality. The result is economic schizophrenia, and in the end ruin for the economy.

---

[27] Seldon and Pennance, *op. cit.*, p. 266.

The use of macroeconomic theory increased after the publication of John Maynard Keynes' *General Theory of Employment, Interest and Money* in 1936. Keynes in effect inverted the economically sound procedure of basing theory concerning the behaviour of economic aggregates on a thorough analysis and understanding of microeconomic factors. Instead he made microeconomics dependent on macroeconomic theory. Macroeconomics has gained importance with the rise of government regulation and control of the economy since ostensibly it is able to provide theoretical justification for such controls. However, government macroeconomic policy is usually achieved at the expense of the individuals, firms and businesses operating on the microeconomic level, who have to make a profit— or perhaps even just survive—while juggling the regulations, avoiding the pitfalls, and suffering the handicaps and penalties thrown in their way by politicians seeking to manipulate the economy for political ends and taking their advice from tenured academics and economic gurus sitting in ivory towers. When government macroeconomic theory and policy are seriously out of touch with the realities prevailing on the microeconomic level—as they usually are to varying degrees—the result is the business cycle, i.e. the constant swing between booms (periods of high inflation, easy credit and the growth of a debt based economy, imprudent investment, excessive and unsustainable business expansion and often wild speculation) and slumps (periods of recession, widespread business failures, bankruptcies, high levels of unemployment and the decline in standards of living generally).

The problem with this kind of macroeconomic theory is that it abstracts general concepts such as the level of prices and total employment from the concrete microeconomic realities upon which they rest and assumes that they are controllable by governments in such a way that the knock-on effects of such controls on the microeconomic level can be contained and channelled to the desired ends. But this fails to take account of the fact that aggregate economic activity is the result of millions of individuals making subjective evaluations of the economic choices before them in accordance with their own particular needs and desires. In order to control the aggregate economy successfully, therefore, the government would have to be able to understand the motives, priorities and intentions of the whole population and predict people's reactions when faced with a series of possible but as yet unrealised economic conditions.

There is, quite obviously, no way that such information can be made available to a central authority directing the economy; and even if it could, it would be impossible for finite human beings to make sense of it, so vast would be the task. In other words it would require omniscience.

Government control of the economy, therefore, seldom produces the desired results because government is to a large extent unable to control the knock-on effects of its policies on the microeconomic level, and this leads to an aggregate economic situation that does not correspond to that desired by government and so often forecast by macroeconomic theory. It is misleading, however, to say that the discrepancy between the effects produced by macroeconomic government policy on the microeconomic level and the forecasts of macroeconomic theory is because macroeconomics has its own rules. The reason for the discrepancies between macroeconomic theory and microeconomic reality is the fact that the former is quite simply out of touch with the realities of behaviour in the real economy—i.e. the economy generated by the millions of subjective decisions made by individual people, firms and businesses as they respond to new choices and economic conditions, many of which, because they are the result of government initiatives geared to *political* objectives, may lead to actions that are irrational from an economic point of view. Such actions are unforeseeable and therefore not susceptible of analysis by macroeconomic theory. In this situation the only course government can take that would lead to greater economic rationalisation and hence economic growth is one in which it increasingly withdraws from regulating the economy, thereby freeing it from the restraints and disincentives that control and regulation inevitably put in the way of individual economic activity.

Macroeconomic theory assumes that the economic principles and rules relevant to economic aggregates are different from those relevant to individual economic activity. When economic aggregates are subject to this kind of analysis the concept of the economy takes on a quasi-autonomous character and it is thought that this aggregate economy can then be controlled and manipulated successfully without creating confusion and conflict on the microeconomic level. But this is a false assumption since the macroeconomic situation, i.e. *total* employment, *total* investment, the *general* level of prices etc. is the result of the combination of all the individual employments, investments and prices determined by the factors analysed in microeconomics.

Donald A. Hay, in his book *Economics Today, A Christian Critique*, provides a typical example of the kinds of conclusion reached by economists working in terms of this false dichotomy between micro-economics and macroeconomics. In arguing against the monetarist contention that inflation of the money supply by the government effects a redistribution of wealth within the economy that is basically immoral Hay concludes that "it is *unexpected* inflation which can have redistributional effects. Fully anticipated inflation cannot."[28] But, claims Hay, since according to monetarist theory inflation is fully anticipated "monetary policy has no *real* effects on the economy."[29] Our concern here is not with Hay's argument against monetarist theory and whether its claim concerning the immorality of inflation is valid or not—though I believe it is valid—but with the fact that the author, a tutor in economics at Oxford University, considers that monetary policy, e.g. aggregate growth in the money supply, has no real effects on the economy. Hay assumes that if it is known that there will be inflation manufacturers and suppliers will simply put prices up accordingly. He writes: "In practice, if they tender for contracts, they will adjust the terms under which they are willing to supply."[30]

This shows a lack of understanding of how the economy works on the microeconomic level, particularly of how economic actors in the real world have to tender for contracts at *competitive* rates. Even if manufacturers could anticipate the effects of inflation correctly in the way that Hay assumes, which has not been proved, it by no means follows that they can adjust their costs accordingly. Many will be competing for contracts against the very groups that have been unfairly advantaged by the inflation through being in receipt of, for instance, government subsidies or cheap loans that enable them to tender at far more competitive prices than those not benefiting from the newly created money. This means that even if those firms not in receipt of government grants or cheap loans are aware of the effects of inflation they cannot compete *and* put up their prices, but can only compete by *not* putting their prices up, or by not putting them up in line with inflation. Perhaps it would be better if academics who are inclined to make such sweeping claims were to try earning a living under such conditions before they glibly brush aside the plight of many of the firms and businesses that have to compete against

---

[28] Donald A. Hay, *Economics Today, A Christian Critique* (Apollos, Inter-Varsity Press, 1989), p. 226.   [29] *Ibid.*, my emphasis.   [30] *Ibid.*, p. 225.

those who receive the newly created money.[31] Being able to anticipate inflation and being able to avoid its consequences are two very different things, a basic distinction one would have expected a lecturer in economics at Oxford University to have appreciated.

Such reasoning is naïve and economically unsound. Hay contends that evidence of the redistributive effects of inflation is generally unsubstantial.[32] He does, however, consider that those on welfare benefits and low income groups may be affected. Since he thinks that inflation does not affect the economy this implies that the spending power of such groups is irrelevant for the economy, which is far from being true. Even here, however, those considered to be affected by inflation are arbitrarily confined to a narrow income group. This assumption is quite false. On the contrary, inflation affects all individuals and groups that do not have the political muscle to secure the benefits of inflation, that it to say to ensure that *they* are the ones who receive the newly created money. Those who are members of groups that can bargain successfully for pay increases commensurate with inflation, e.g. labour and professional unions, are able to benefit at the expense of those who do not have the power to command increases in pay either personally or through the representation necessary to bargain with the government. This includes many of those self-employed people and small businesses that have to compete against industries and firms subsidised by inflation. The fact that these people may be quite aware of what inflation is doing to their incomes does not help in any way to compensate for the loss of purchasing power that they have to bear as a result of inflation. The knock-on effects of inflation affect a great many such people who are vital economic actors and upon whom the welfare of the economy depends every bit as much as those with bargaining power and political influence, and who have, as a proportion of the workforce, increased considerably since the early 1980s.[33]

---

[31] For more on this point see Chapter Four, pp. 108–111; 143f.

[32] Donald A. Hay, *op. cit.*, p. 226.

[33] The reasoning behind Hay's conclusion is that because people are aware of inflation it is not immoral. He writes: "This [i.e. that the redistributive effects of inflation constitute a form of theft—SCP] is a correct description of the outcome if there is an element of deception; that is, if those who hold government liabilities have no idea that paper money is being issued or that the consequences will be inflation. If they *are* aware of these matters, then no deception is involved" (*ibid.*, p. 225). This is tantamount to saying that robbery only occurs where there is deception. If a footpad stops me and relieves me of my possessions at gunpoint it is not robbery because I am aware of what is happening! Hay's contention that

By analysing economic phenomena in this way without taking care to stress the limitations of such an abstract approach economists create confusion and mislead politicians into thinking they can manipulate the macroeconomic factors for their own ends without throwing into confusion the factors involved on the microeconomic level, which are responsible for real economic behaviour and hence economic growth and decline. In other words it gives them leave to manipulate the economy as if overall economic performance can be determined from above by political policy. Such control from above affects the economy greatly but seldom for the good, since it rarely produces the anticipated results. The effect of policies based on this artificial distinction between macroeconomics and micro-economics and the construction of aggregate models that do not adequately relate to the concrete economic circumstances under which the economy works is that the economy runs into difficulties and becomes even more difficult to control by political fiat.

A graphic illustration of this last point was provided on the 16th of September 1992—"Black Wednesday" as it was subsequently called—when sterling plunged into a nose dive on the currency markets and all attempts by the Chancellor of the Exchequer, Norman Lamont, to stop its decline by the use of draconian measures failed miserably. The Bank of England announced a minimum lending rate of 12 per cent.[34] This had the desired effect of pushing up the

---

"they do not have to accept government contracts, nor do they have to hold government bonds" (*ibid.*) would surely stretch the credulity of the most ardent Keynesian. What this means is that if people don't like inflation they can opt out. But how can we opt out of a system upon which our livelihood, our survival, depends? This is sheer nonsense, a good example of the kind of thing we have come to expect from academics who live in sheltered environments away from the real effects that government policy has on the businesses, livelihoods and lives of those who create the wealth in society and thus upon whom the health of the economy depends.

[34] The minimum lending rate had officially been abolished in August 1981; that is to say the rate of interest at which the Bank of England would rediscount eligible paper or lend against its security to the discount market was no longer announced officially or made available to the public. A minimum lending rate had been invoked on two previous occasions after August 1981: on January 14th 1985 at a rate of 12 per cent, and on October 8th 1990 at a rate of 14 per cent. Since "Black Wednesday" it has been invoked another three times: on September 17th 1992, the day following "Black Wednesday," when it was reduced to 10 per cent in order to cancel the increase of the previous day, on November 13th 1992 at a rate of 7 per cent, and on January 26th 1993 at a rate of 6 per cent (source: *Financial Statistics*, January 1994, No. 381 [HMSO], p. 121). On the mechanism by which the minimum lending rate (repo rate since 1997) is used to influence interest rates generally see "The Modern Banking System" in Chapter Four.

commercial banks' base rates accordingly; it was also announced on the same day that interest rates would rise another 3 per cent on the following day.[35] These measures proved useless against the real economy, however, since the exchange value of sterling continued to fall below its permitted ratio within the ERM (European exchange-rate mechanism). The Chancellor came down to earth with a bump, eventually suspending sterling within the ERM and cancelling the interest rate increases on the following day. It was estimated that during the period in which sterling came under pressure on the currency markets until its suspension as a member of the ERM the Bank of England lost half its foreign currency reserves trying to push up the value of the rapidly devaluing British pound. This incident represented the complete failure of one of the main planks of the government's macroeconomic policy, namely membership of the ERM, which was in effect a trial mechanism for the creation of a pan-European super-currency under the de facto control of the Bundesbank.

Macroeconomic theory only has meaning and value when it is grounded in a thorough analysis of microeconomics, that is to say when it is based on a proper understanding of the subjective and decentralised nature of economic activity in the real world. Macro-economic models of the economy that fail to take account and operate in terms of microeconomic factors, when used as the basis for government policy, can be and have been extremely damaging for the economy as a whole, including the many individuals and the businesses they own or work for, which produce the wealth of the nation. To the extent that the distinction between macroeconomics and microeconomics has meaning and value it is to *clarify* analysis of economic phenomena. The abuse to which it has been subjected in recent decades, however, has miserably failed to meet this requirement.

The difference between macroeconomic and microeconomic theory is one of analysis only. Macroeconomics deals with precisely

---

[35] Just how draconian these measures were is illustrated by the response taken by the monetary authorities to a similar crisis thirty-five years earlier. In 1957 the Bank Rate was increased from 5 to 7 per cent in one step in order to check the outflow of gold and dollar reserves caused by a collapse of confidence in the exchange value of sterling, a measure the *Report of the Committee on the Working of the Monetary System* (the "Radcliffe Report"), published two years later, described as "an abnormally large rise to an abnormally high level" (*Report of the Committee on the Working of the Monetary System* [HMSO, 1959], para. 5, p. 2).

the same phenomena as does microeconomics, but simply looks at those phenomena from a different perspective. To abstract aspects of economic phenomena from the concrete situation that gives them meaning and to treat them as quasi-autonomous features of economic reality is to embark upon a course that can only end in confusion. Once politicians have got the idea that the political prospects of manipulating such phenomena are useful to their cause this confusion turns to delusion and ultimately economic catastrophe and decline of the economy. The slumps, recessions, depressions, inflation and unemployment experienced by Western nations in recent history are the result of such interference with the economy by politicians deluded as to the nature and extent of their powers and abilities. It seems that politicians today would do well to learn that no matter how convinced they are of their "mandate" from the electorate they can no more roll back the tide of economic reality in the modern world than Cnut could roll back the tide of the sea.

§6
International Trade

Similar problems occur when economists assume that the economic principles relevant to international trade are essentially different from those relevant to domestic trade. In fact international trade is no different economically from domestic trade: the problems associated with the former are *political* in origin. Yet the idea that international trade poses special problems for the economy and thus necessitates special consideration by politicians has persisted.

One of the most pertinacious manifestations of this mistaken notion is the almost ubiquitous obsession with the balance of trade among both politicians and economists. At times this obsession seems almost pathological in nature. If ever there was a political neurosis this is it. There is an almost feverish anxiety displayed by governments when the economy is running a so-called unfavourable balance of trade[36] and all efforts are directed to securing a favourable balance

[36] This terminology is derived from the mercantilists (protectionists) of the sixteenth and seventeenth centuries. The mercantilists looked to a strong central State to guarantee the expansion and protection of markets and commercial interests. They believed that a nation's wealth could only be preserved and increased by exporting goods and accumulating large stocks of gold and silver in return for them (precious metals were considered at that time to be the most desirable form of wealth), rather

of trade, often at the expense of many domestic industries that rely on imports for survival.

But from an *economic* point of view there is no such thing as a favourable or unfavourable balance of trade. Moreover, the term *balance of trade* is ill-defined and misleading. In the strict sense in which it is used in reference to trade in visibles, or even trade in visibles and invisibles but excluding those elements of the economy analysed in the capital account table of the balance of payments, it is of course true that a nation may have imported more than it has exported, i.e. that it may have imported more than it has exported of *certain kinds* of goods and services. But to call this an "unfavourable" balance of trade, or even a "deficit," is misleading since it implies an un-desirable state of affairs that governments deem within their mandate to rectify by means of economic intervention or even by direct political fiat. Such deficits will be balanced by credits in other sectors of the economy, e.g. foreign investment in the British economy, which is classed as a credit item in the capital account table of the balance of payments. The exclusion of the latter from the assessment of what

---

than by providing goods and services that satisfy peoples' wants. Like socialist ideology today, therefore, mercantilism was a doctrine based on mammonism, i.e. the idea that money and the gain of money, rather than work and the exchange of goods and services produced by work, is the source of wealth. The irony of this is that rather than leading to increased national wealth, which is what it was ostensibly designed to guarantee, mercantilism tended to hinder economic progress, since it impaired the operation of international markets and specialisation. For example, if a nation exports goods in return for gold and discourages the outflow of gold in exchange for imported goods (e.g. by imposing tariffs), the effect will be rising prices in the domestic economy, since more money (gold) is chasing the available supply of goods. In other words there will be domestic inflation created by the exporting of goods in return for gold and restrictions on imports paid for by gold. This will mean that exportable goods will be less attractive to those in other countries because of their higher prices, and therefore exports must decline also. The existence of larger stocks of gold in the domestic economy is in itself of no particular benefit. There may be as a result more money, but since prices will be higher this in itself is of no particular benefit. (As explained in Chapter Two, all that an increased stock of money means in itself—i.e. assuming that it does not represent a redistribution of wealth and thus that each person receives a share of the increased stock pro-portionate to his holdings of the previous stock—is that the same supply of wealth is represented by a larger supply of money.) This erroneous view of wealth (a form of mammonism), i.e. the desire to export goods continuously and import only gold or goods designed for re-export in exchange for gold, hindered the market for exports as well as imports. Like socialist governments today, mercantilists were concerned to protect the domestic economy, but, as will be explained, such protectionism is detrimental to the domestic economy and to the long-term economic interests of everyone in society.

is best for the British economy by government is a *political* decision. In terms of Britain's overall trading relationship with the rest of the world, however, foreign investment in British industry is important and it is misleading to assess the nation's foreign trade without taking this into account. Just as goods and services can be exported to foreign consumers, investment opportunities in British industry can be made available to foreign investors. Such investments are a vital part of British trade with the rest of the world.

A favourable or unfavourable balance of trade is thus entirely a *political* phenomenon, and the attempts of governments to remedy so-called unfavourable balances through the imposition of trading restrictions, tariffs and currency regulations are made not to maximise economic efficiency but to protect uncompetitive domestic industries and trading groups whose interests government is particularly sensitive to. In other words, the difficulties and problems normally associated with the balance of trade are problems relating to government manipulation of the economy for its own advantage and the advantage of those industries that employ large numbers of workers whose employment prospects are deemed to count in terms of votes at general elections.

From the economic point of view there cannot be a favourable or unfavourable balance of trade. But there can be a balance of trade that, due to its composition, is deemed unpropitious by politicians and government bureaucrats with certain misguided ideas about what *kinds* of industry are good for the domestic economy. For example, politicians generally seem to think that it is better for the economy to export the products of heavy and manufacturing industry (visibles) rather than those of the financial and service industries (invisibles). It is thought that the former create greater employment for the domestic economy and that if the government is to stay in office it has to develop policies that will benefit the employable population. This usually means that manufacturing industry and other visibles are favoured at the expense of the financial and service industries. However, this is an erroneous way of assessing the needs and well-being of the domestic economy. The assumption that the domestic economy will be in trouble, that there will be greater unemployment, if heavy and manufacturing industry decline, has not been proved. On the contrary, with the growth of the financial and service industries and the decline of manufacturing industry, along with increased exports of the former and less imports of the latter, the domestic economy can still flourish, other things being equal—e.g. provided there is no counteractive government intervention in the economy. Since specialisation and division of labour would be enabled to find its most natural, and therefore its most efficient, level under these conditions the result would be a *growth* in the creation of wealth in the domestic economy.

The popular conception that the financial and service industries tend to concentrate wealth into the hands of a few, whereas heavy and manufacturing industry disperse it more evenly throughout society is entirely false. This notion is based partly on a superficial assessment of the effects of the location of industries and partly on the propaganda put out by socialist political parties, industrial pressure groups and labour unions seeking political advantages for their own industries at the expense of others. In fact, the contrary is the case in some measure where industry involves unionised labour blocks, as much of British industry does, since large labour cartels benefit closed shop labour and penalise those who do not have access into the restricted areas of work. The result is greater unemployment for many for the sake of secure employment for the privileged. By contrast the financial and service industries, being less dominated by unionised labour, tend to be far less irrational economically, since they provide greater opportunities for self-employment and the creation of small decentralised businesses, more competition, which benefits the consumer, and access to employment by those denied work by union labour cartels.

Myths about heavy and manufacturing industry being necessary for a viable domestic economy have helped to produce an inefficient economy hampered by political interference. International trade and division of labour has been one of the casualties and the growth of the economy and progress generally have, as a result, been impeded considerably. Those manufacturing industries with large labour unions and the commensurate political muscle associated with them have been able to intimidate governments into rigging international trade in their favour to the disadvantage of the majority.

In the ethos created by such industries and groups, which through their propaganda help to mould and inform the opinions of the general public, the financial and service industries *seem* less essential to the overall conditions necessary for the growth of the economy. Therefore consideration of these industries features less in the formulation of government policy and informs the voting intentions of the population less than does that of manufacturing industry. The fact that domestic manufacturing industry may be vastly uncompetitive and economically irrational, and therefore that greater efficiency and thus growth of the economy could be achieved by importing such products, is a secondary matter to governments who always have an eye on the next election. In the political ethos of our age, with its idolatry of the crassest form of democracy, the first principle of government is to stay in power. No matter how much they may *talk* of progress, therefore, governments are usually willing to sacrifice progress for the sake of votes from employees of large domestic manufacturing industries and those unemployed people who have been led to believe that their only hope of employment is in government investment in heavy and manufacturing industry. The result of government policy informed by such views is that tariffs and import quotas are placed on products manufactured in foreign countries, and this damages not only foreign economies through restricting their sales outlets in those industries in which they excel, but also the domestic economy by benefitting industries that are uncompetitive and wasteful—that is to say it leads to a less efficient use of capital in the domestic economy than would otherwise be the case.

Any supposed unfavourable balance of trade is thus a *political* concept, an unfavourable balance of trade in a particular industry or group of industries deemed necessary for the domestic economy by the government and requiring special consideration if the government's prospects of re-election are to be prioritised. Policies aimed at remedying any such supposed unfavourable balance of trade are economically flawed: first, is it *possible* ultimately, in terms of Britain's *overall* trade with the rest of the world, to export more than we import? If so, why not export as much as possible and import nothing? The absurdity of the balance of trade fetish now becomes apparent. In fact we can only export if we also import. Importing and exporting is simply trading over a national boundary, which is a political not an economic phenomenon. Just as there is no point in selling goods and services in the domestic economy if we do not wish to purchase goods and services from others, so also there is no point in selling goods and services abroad if we do not wish to buy foreign goods and services.

When a British manufacturer wishes to export his goods, those abroad intending to purchase them have to obtain sterling to pay for the goods. This means that some of those holding sterling have to be prepared to exchange their sterling for foreign currency. They will only do this if they believe they can use foreign currency to purchase goods or services from abroad. If they are denied the right to spend their foreign currency in this way they will stop holding it and those wishing to purchase British goods will be unable to obtain sterling with which to trade, and therefore *exporting* must cease also. Ultimately, therefore, we cannot export more than we import— although we can import more of certain types of goods than the government and domestic manufacturers of those goods would like us to import. Trading is a two way thing, whether at home or abroad. Each party benefits, each party gains something, and the use of a common medium of exchange (money) or of several mediums (foreign currencies) to make trade easier and more rational does not alter this basic fact of economic life. To suggest that we should, or could, export more than we import is nonsense.[37] (As we shall see, the

---

[37] When the economy's exports and imports are assessed *at a particular date*, a deficit or "trade gap" in goods and services may appear due to sterling being held by foreigners. Likewise, there may be an excess of exports of goods and services over imports of the same or "trade surplus" due to foreign currency being held by British citizens. Under such conditions it is misleading to speak of an unfavourable balance of trade since the sale or purchase of currency must be classified as an item in the accounts. And, of course, sterling sold in exchange for foreign currency must ultimately find its way back into the UK economy either to be spent on goods and services or invested. An excess of imports over exports and vice versa, therefore, can ultimately be no more than an anomaly created by the accounting procedure of arbitrarily drawing a line across the books at a particular date. This is also true in the case of imports paid for by borrowing foreign currency. Such debt must ultimately be paid. But this is only possible if British goods and services are exported to foreign consumers, thereby providing British importers with the foreign currency necessary to repay their debts. If a nation writes off the trade debts that are owed to it by a foreign country, it simply gives away its products. This is the only way, ultimately, in which it is possible for a nation to export more than it imports. Often, however, the political obsession with a balance of trade deficit, and more generally with an overall deficit in the balance of payments on current account, is related to fear of foreign investment in the UK that will lead to increasing foreign ownership of UK assets. This is, however, a political problem, not an economic problem. Foreign investment in the UK is a credit item on the balance of payments capital account. Such investment creates employment, often where domestically owned industries, because they are inefficient or produce poor quality or expensively priced goods, have gone out of business when faced with competition. From the economic point of view such foreign investment is of great advantage to British residents, especially those who are unemployed as a result of socialist mismanagement of the economy. Foreign investment in the UK, like visible exports, creates industry and employment, and thus greater wealth, leading to increased standards of living for UK residents as well as for foreign investors, and is therefore to be welcomed as part of the function of a free market economy. In terms of Britain's overall trading relationship with

argument that exchange rates could be fixed at levels that would help to create such an excess of exports over imports is equally mistaken from the economic point of view.)

Second, does the British population really want to export more than it imports? The very existence of this so-called balance of trade problem demonstrates that the public does want to buy foreign goods. It is certain domestic industries and the governments that support those industries that do not wish consumers to buy from foreign companies the same kinds of goods that these domestic industries produce. Therefore the government limits the number and volume of goods allowed to be imported or imposes tariffs on them, which makes them less attractive to domestic consumers. This helps *selected* domestic industries by giving them an unfair advantage. This advantage is not only unfair to foreign companies but also to domestic consumers who wish to buy from foreign companies because they perceive that they will get better value for their money if they do so. The balance of trade problem is a problem only for politicians and domestic manufacturers who do not wish consumers to exercise their freedom to buy the goods they desire from manufacturers of their own choice. Government is lobbied by domestic industries that cannot compete with superior or more competitively priced products from abroad to enforce regulations that deny consumers the freedom to purchase foreign goods or induce them to purchase domestically manufactured goods by imposing tariffs and quotas (rationing) on imported goods. The so-called balance of trade problem is simply a euphemism for a protection racket—a form of economic tyranny.

Third, if British consumers wish to buy foreign goods and services they *must* also produce goods and services that foreign consumers will

---

the rest of the world, therefore, foreign investment in the UK performs the same function as exports, i.e. in exchange for the goods and services that Britain imports from abroad foreigners invest in the UK—e.g. the creation of a new Nissan car factory—thereby creating wealth and economic growth for Britain's domestic economy and prospects for the growth of exports produced in industries benefiting from such investment. Foreign investment in the UK economy is a form of export; what are being exported in this case are investment opportunities. A strict dichotomy between exports and foreign investment in the British economy, as this is implied in the tabulation of the balance of payments, is an artificial distinction, especially in relation to an assessment of British trade with the rest of the world (i.e. from the economic point of view), that is prone to misunderstanding. While this is not meant to call into question the way the balance of payments is tabulated, it does call into question the popular misconceptions that a faulty understanding of the figures analysed in the balance of payments often creates.

buy, otherwise there is no market and thus no import or export. The same holds for foreign consumers wishing to purchase British goods. A market is a two-way thing. How can we export goods to foreign countries without importing goods unless we are determined to give them away? And how can we export more goods than we import without selling them for less than their market price? To suggest that we should export more than we import is to suggest that we should give away at least part of our goods, that we should take less in return for them than they can command in the open market.

Of course, this is the absurdity of the government's subsidising of industries that it wishes to develop and expand, whether in international or domestic markets. When the government subsidises an industry it helps it to reduce its real costs thereby making its products more attractive to consumers. That is to say, the subsidy pays part of the costs for those wishing to purchase the product. When the government subsidises industries that would not survive without its help it is forcing British taxpayers to give away their wealth—i.e. it forces them to subsidise uncompetitive industries with funds raised through taxation in order to make inferior goods look attractive to consumers who would not otherwise consider buying them, whether in domestic or foreign markets.

The effect is the same when the government artificially manipulates the exchange rate between sterling and foreign currency or devalues the pound in relation to foreign currency in order to make British goods more attractive to foreign consumers. Particular industries or companies may benefit in the short term by increasing their sales abroad, but the overall effect is damaging since by devaluing the pound or manipulating exchange rates the government simply forces British people to give their money away—i.e. to take less in exchange for sterling than it could command in a free market. Giving British goods away or selling them at artificially low prices—i.e. selling them for less than they are worth in the open market—is the only way that we can export more than we import ultimately; but such activity should not be considered *trade* in the proper sense. And because it disturbs the price mechanism and gives false information to manufacturers and consumers alike, it is extremely detrimental to the economy. The argument for artificially lowering the costs of British goods to foreign consumers by manipulating exchange rates— i.e. devaluing sterling—in order to stimulate exports is thus nonsense economically. It is tantamount to saying that we should give away certain goods to foreign consumers, or at least pay for them partially ourselves, in order to stimulate sales and thus greater productivity in these industries.

Furthermore, when governments engage in such interventionist activities—e.g. exchange rate controls—those who import products are penalised since exchange rates are rigged against them. This is damaging not only for individuals who wish to purchase consumption goods from abroad, but also for domestic businesses that rely on imported capital goods, raw materials and semi-manufactured products. Businesses affected in this way are forced to respond to the new conditions facing them. On the one hand they could raise prices themselves. In this case the cost is passed on to the consumer. This may result in falling sales, depending on the nature of the product. If it is a non-essential or luxury item consumers may stop buying the product or reduce their purchases, thereby creating difficulties for the company, perhaps resulting in redundancies. Alternatively, they could absorb the extra costs themselves, thereby reducing the profitability of the business and slowing down development and expansion as well as movement towards more competitive prices, again with possible knock-on effects such as redundancies.

In the case of imported capital goods, i.e. goods consumed in the manufacture of other goods,—raw materials, semi-finished products, machinery etc.—that are used in the manufacture of goods destined for exportation this may lead to the anomalous situation in which the attempt to promote exports by controlling exchange rates artificially raises the costs of these goods, thereby making them less attractive to foreign consumers and possibly resulting in a fall in exports.[38] The effect for some exporters, therefore, may be at best useless and perhaps even harmful in the *short* term.

---

[38] This may not be offset by the decrease in prices for foreign consumers brought about by the devaluation or currency exchange-rate controls. To what extent it is will depend upon a variety of factors by no means all of which are accessible to analysis by the government or its financial advisers in the determination of exchange rate policy. It is impossible, in a market system based on the highly specialised division of labour, to predict exactly how such devaluations and currency exchange controls will affect the economy (see above §5, "Macroeconomics and Microeconomics"). The overall result is simply not calculable. In attempting to benefit one sector of the economy, therefore, the government unleashes a series of events the consequences of which it cannot foresee or control. The results of such political manipulation of the market will be detrimental to the economy as a *whole* as well as to those particular firms and businesses that have to bear the brunt of the rising costs of imported capital goods, since the rise in costs of imported production factors may lead either

"Buy British!" the consumer is told, as if this were the best course under all possible conditions and in all situations. Buying British goods is always deemed by these politicians to be beneficial for the British economy. Governments motivated by such ideology seek to develop policy aimed at inducing the public to buy certain goods from British rather than foreign manufacturers by penalising the purchase of those goods from abroad with high tariffs or by limiting the number of imports to a level that will not significantly affect the output of domestic manufacturers of such goods.

A good example of the kind of damage done by such policies is the effect on the economy of import tariffs. Tariffs on goods imported from abroad destroy competition, or rather make it impossible outside national boundaries (except on black markets for smuggled goods), and this distorts the price mechanism, resulting in an inefficient (i.e. less productive) allocation of scarce resources. Tariffs prevent economic rationalisation and thus hinder economic progress. Their rationale ostensibly is to protect domestic industries, but any supposed gains are purely short-term. Furthermore, they affect the privileged groups themselves in a limited way only since ultimately it is in no one's interests, including such privileged groups, —since where tariffs exist they are generally applied across a large range of products—to hinder the efficient functioning of the free market order. While the beneficial effects of tariffs are very limited even for those industries that are protected by them the disruption and damage they cause in the wider economy is extensive. They protect domestic manufacturers of goods that are of poorer quality or more expensive than imported goods of the same kind and penalise the manufacturers of better quality or more competitively priced goods in other countries. Such protection of domestic manufacturers is disadvantageous not only to the domestic consumer but ultimately to the privileged domestic manufacturer since an economy that is heavily protected by tariffs will be less competitive, less economically efficient, and hence less dynamic—that is to say there will be less economic growth and social amelioration generally and this will affect all in society, including those who are ostensibly protected by tariffs. No one wins in the end since the ultimate effect of applying tariffs is a backward economy.

---

to a rise in the prices of the consumer goods and services these firms provide, whether for domestic or foreign markets, or perhaps even to redundancies and bankruptcy, with all the knock-on effects that this creates.

A pertinent example of the consequences of such measures is the price of food in Britain since its entry into the EEC. Food prices in Britain today are far more expensive than they need be since the sale of much cheaper food is penalised by heavy tariffs if it is imported from non-European Union countries.

When tariffs are combined with the subsidising of exports the problems are only exacerbated. The domestic consumer again loses out. Not only is he denied the right to buy cheaper or better products from abroad. As a taxpayer he also has to help pay the costs of domestically manufactured products bought by foreign consumers. Since the tariff and subsidy systems are inextricably linked, the one inevitably leading to the other as nations in turn retaliate against subsidies with tariffs, consumers and taxpayers are further abused with every new round in the development of an ever escalating trade war.

Such policies are unnecessary if British goods really are superior to imports. But they are economically irrational if British goods are inferior to imported goods. They are therefore detrimental to domestic consumers, who do not get maximum value for their money, harmful to foreign manufacturers, who are penalised for producing competitively priced or superior goods, and harmful to the domestic economy, which is stimulated into producing goods that are uncompetitive in real terms or of inferior quality. Furthermore, the manufacture of uncompetitively priced or inferior quality goods does not constitute the best use of the scarce resources available to the economy. In a free market economy without tariffs and subsidies such capital will be used to generate productivity in industries where British firms excel and this in turn will lead to greater exports. Thus, while the tariff and subsidy system often produces the very opposite of its intended purpose, the abandonment of this system will, in the long run, create the very conditions it is *ostensibly* designed to foster, and on a much more sustainable basis.

Buying British goods ultimately only helps the British economy when the goods bought are the best value for money. Where this is not the case buying foreign goods is ultimately of more benefit to the British economy since it helps to rationalise the economy in terms of sound economic principles. It also helps to rationalise the international division and specialisation of labour, thereby helping to maximise world productivity and world economic amelioration, which in turn, of course, is of benefit to the British economy also. Buying British when British goods are inferior gives the wrong information to British industry concerning what it is best at producing. As a result the economy does not function at its most efficient level, a situation that is detrimental to all concerned, since it leads manufacturers to believe that their products are better than in fact they are, and this encourages second-rate practices and the waste of scarce resources. When tariffs, import restrictions and embargoes are used to support an inefficient and uncompetitive domestic industry both the domestic and foreign economies suffer immeasurably.

For politicians the real problem of a so-called unfavourable balance of trade is that people on the microeconomic level, that is to say actors in the real economy, do not produce the aggregate or macroeconomic results required by government policy. People do not trade in the goods and services or with the particular manufacturers or groups of manufacturers that the government would like them to trade with. Government therefore restricts their freedom to trade by introducing economic disincentives for trade in certain imported goods. If this economically irrational and unproductive procedure is to change, and greater international division and specialisation of labour, leading to greater wealth creation, is to be attained, there must be a change in perception by the population and politicians alike of what, in terms of both domestic and international trade, is of real *economic* benefit to the economy.[39]

Short-sighted concentration by governments on economic policies aimed at maximising output in traditional domestic industries and protecting them against foreign competitors can also be detrimental for the nation on a political level. It tends to foster a fortress-nation mentality and overlooks even the political advantages that the international division of labour and economic interdependence create, namely, political security on the international level and friendship between nations generally. Matters of national security and defence may justify, in *some* circumstances, the subordination of certain kinds of economic interdependence and free trade between nations to rational *political* rather than economic objectives, but instances of this

[39] It is to the credit of the Thatcher Government that while it was in office in the 1980s there was a significant shift in the popular understanding of the conditions necessary for the creation of wealth in the domestic economy, and this was a stimulus to the economy as a whole: popular opinion concerning economic matters was changed for the better in many ways and some traditional economic myths were expunged from the popular consciousness. Unfortunately the same kind of understanding with regard to international trade was not evident and the "Buy British!" nonsense was still promoted vigorously.

are far less common than is often supposed. More often than not arguments for protecting certain industries for the sake of national security and defence are thinly disguised attempts by uncompetitive firms and industries to create monopolies within national borders by restricting the consumer's freedom to purchase goods and services from abroad. Again, to the extent that such arguments succeed they only serve to subsidise second-rate or uncompetitively priced goods, thereby encouraging inefficiency and the wasteful use and management of the scarce economic resources available to the economy. In other words they slow down economic progress by granting privileged status to uncompetitive industries.

The fortress-nation mentality leads to a less developed and stable world economy and to less trade-based interdependence between nations. Hostile relations and even war are far more likely when nations are economically isolated or engaged in trade wars in this way. International trade, on the other hand, encourages stronger links between nations and therefore greater peace and co-operation, resulting in less likelihood of war, less need for the financing of massive war machines—which are usually irrational from an economic point of view—and thus greater prosperity for all.

A pertinent example of this last point was the breakdown of relations between Britain and Argentina and the Falklands War in 1982. Prior to Britain's entry into the European Economic Community trade between Argentina and Britain in beef products was considerable. After entry into the EEC, however, a tariff of 70 pence was imposed on each pound of meat products imported from Argentina.[40] Within two years meat imports from Argentina were cut in half and continued to decrease from then on.[41] Then in 1982 came the Argentinian invasion of the Falklands. The cost to the British taxpayer of liberating these islands ran into many millions, and it costs millions each year to protect the Falklands from further threat. Richard Body put his finger on the point when he wrote: "So long as the British consumer is denied the supply of cheap beef from Argentina, which means so long as we subscribe to the CAP [the Common Agricultural Policy of the EEC—SCP], and so long as the British taxpayer has to pay these massive sums of money to ward off the Argentinians, we are entitled to ask one or two questions. Would Argentina, while so dependent upon her export trade with

[40] Richard Body, *Farming in the Clouds* (London: Temple Smith, 1984), p. 78.
[41] *Ibid.*

us for her prosperity, have deliberately cut off that trade? What could she have gained by acquiring those bleak islands when she could have lost so much? Common sense seems to suggest that the British people would have remained blissfully unaware of the Falklands if the economic alliance with Argentina had not been severed by us in 1973."[42]

Before Britain entered the EEC cheap Argentinian beef was available to the British household and the trade with Argentina was good. When Britain entered the EEC, however, import tariffs were imposed on Argentinian beef in order to keep prices in line with EEC beef products, which were more expensive. As a result the cost of beef rose sharply and beef became a luxury for many average households. On top of having to pay vastly inflated prices for beef, the British taxpayer now has to pay for the defence of the Falklands. Had the British trade with Argentina been allowed to continue operating on rational economic principles of free trade, rather than being hampered by politicians seeking to bolster the EEC's Common Agricultural Policy, which is irrational from an economic point of view, the Falklands War would most likely not have been fought. Millions of British taxpayers would be better off through not having to pay exorbitant prices for beef and substantial tax sums to defend the Falkland Islands against a former trading partner,—to say nothing of the lives that would have been saved and the unnecessary destruction that would have been avoided.

International free trade based on rational economic principles is a bulwark against the kinds of conflicts the world over that the Falklands War was an example of. This is in stark contrast to the creation of political power blocks aimed at establishing economically self-sufficient States and federations of States, which tends to aggravate hostility and mistrust between nations and as a consequence has a negative effect on world peace. International free trade, on the other hand, helps to promote and safeguard world peace and world and national economic stability.

According to B. V. Marshall "International trade involves the exchange of goods and services across national frontiers, and it is on this account that special characteristics are involved, which cause it to differ from trade within national boundaries."[43] The special

---

[42] *Ibid.*

[43] B. V. Marshall, *Comprehensive Economics* (London and New York: Longman, Second Edition, 1975), Part One, p. 385.

characteristics and problems of international trade are not economic in nature but entirely political. To treat them as *economic* problems, or even to deal with them under the discipline of economics without making clear that these are *political* problems that are economically irrational in nature, is misleading. It gives the impression that there are *economic* problems associated with international trade that necessitate government management in this area. In fact all the distinctive characteristics of international trade as compared with domestic trade are *political* in nature, and most of the problems involved in trading with foreign countries are created by government interference and mismanagement. Quite simply put, a national boundary is not an *economic* phenomenon, it is a *political* phenomenon, and awareness of the difference is essential if we are to have a proper understanding of economic reality. The *economic* principles relevant to international trade are no different from those relevant to domestic trade.

§7
Economics as a Science

The growth of the exact sciences over the past two hundred years, and the attendant status that these disciplines have achieved in both the academic and non-academic world, has fostered among many of the practitioners of the social sciences the desire to mimic the methods of exact science. To a large extent this may have been motivated by the desires of sociologists to obtain the same kind of respect and social adulation that is heaped upon scientists in modern Western society. Whether this is so or not the social sciences generally are still not taken seriously as sciences by the vast majority of people. The exceptions to this are psychiatry, which has been able to hitch a ride on the back of medicine, and certain branches of economics that attempt to deal with their subject matter in a precise mathematical fashion.

The value of presenting economic principles and theories in terms of mathematical formulas, however, has been considerably overestimated. It is generally thought that mathematics, the purest of the sciences, is able to provide mankind with certainty, a prize that man has always shown himself most eager to obtain and for which he has been prepared to expend the greatest efforts. This has been and continues to be a potent manifestation of fallen man's basic idolatry of the created order. Having denied the God of Scripture, the Creator of all things and thus man's ultimate certainty—i.e. the light without which nothing else can be understood and therefore whose existence must be presupposed in all human thought if it is to be meaningful and according to truth—man seeks in the created order some other ultimate certainty or principle upon which to base his life. Science, that is to say the exact sciences, particularly mathematics, has in our time provided mankind with this idol.[44] Modern man's faith in mathematics as the source of ultimate certainty is very much in evidence in Western culture and the idea that if something can be proved mathematically it must of necessity be true is a common notion. In the popular mind-set of our day even an argument purporting to prove or disprove the existence of God *mathematically* carries far more weight than any other form of argumentation. Mathematics deals with certainties, or so it is generally thought. The practitioners of the exact sciences have become the priests of our technocratic society. Therefore, if an academic discipline is to find the unquestioning acceptance among the general public that its practitioners wish it to achieve, and of course the attendant social status for themselves as the guardians of the knowledge it represents, it must be considered among the exact sciences, and this is accomplished by adopting the methods of the exact sciences.

The problem with this is that the methods of the exact sciences are inappropriate to the social sciences, since what is studied in a discipline such as economics is not constant relationships between physical properties, but the subjective decisions and choices of millions of individuals reacting to the conditions facing them in diverse and unpredictable ways. It is not possible to quantify and measure such phenomena in the way that it is possible, for instance, to quantify and measure the properties of a gas. The factors in the equation of each individual choice made by consumers in the market-place are different in each individual case, being based not only on the unique antecedent outward conditions affecting and future pos-

---

[44] A good example of this is Bertrand Russell, who wrote: "I came to philosophy through mathematics, or rather through the wish to find some reason to believe in the truth of mathematics. From early youth, I had an ardent desire to believe that there can be such a thing as knowledge, combined with a great difficulty in accepting much that passes as knowledge. It seemed clear that the best chance of finding indubitable truth would be in pure mathematics . . ." (B. R. Russell, "Logical Atomism" in A. J. Ayer, ed., *Logical Positivism* [The Free Press of Glencoe, 1959], p. 31).

sibilities open to the individuals involved, but also upon the subjective psychological conditions peculiar to each individual. Such phenomena, either individually or in the aggregate, are not susceptible of rational mathematical analysis. Theories regarding the outcome of changes occurring in the economy, which is simply the total of all these individual subjective choices, cannot be tested or predicted in the way that, say, the strength of an iron girder can be tested and its performance when placed under a given amount of stress predicted. Mises writes:

Technology can tell us how thick a steel plate must be in order not to be pierced by a bullet fired at a distance of 300 yards from a Winchester rifle. It can thus answer the question why a man who took shelter behind a steel plate of a known thickness was hurt or not hurt by a shot fired. History is at a loss to explain with the same assurance why there was a rise in the price of milk of 10 per cent or why President Roosevelt defeated Governor Dewey in the election of 1944 or why France was from 1870 to 1940 under a republican constitution. Such problems do not allow any treatment other than that of understanding.[45]

In other words history is not an exact science and can never be turned into an exact science by the amassing of statistical data relating to historical events. The attempt to turn economics into an exact science by the use of economic statistics is equally unsatisfactory. Yet increasingly economists have sought to present the discipline in terms of the methodology of the exact sciences. The use of mathematical language, therefore, has become a prominent feature of modern economics.

This is not to say that the use of all mathematical formulae in economic theory is necessarily illegitimate, but it is to warn against placing too much confidence in the use and value of such methods. In fact, the most that mathematics can achieve in economic theory is to provide the discipline with a kind of shorthand, an algebraic method of stating economic theory. Nonetheless, the use of such a shorthand, though not illegitimate *per se*, is not essentially part of the process of economic reasoning and can only have meaning for those who have learned the notation involved. That is to say it can of itself make no contribution to our understanding of economic phenomena. The value of the use of mathematics in economic theory is limited to that of condensing logical theory into algebraic representations.

[45] Ludwig von Mises, *Human Action: A Treatise on Economics* (Chicago: Contemporary Books, Inc., Third Revised Edition, 1966), p. 56f.

In spite of this the use of mathematics in economic theory has increased, and the attempt to gain scientific status for the discipline has continued. Econometrics, for example, is an attempt to turn what is essentially a social—and thus far from exact—science into an exact science. The dictum "science is measurement" has led the proponents of econometrics to conclude that if economics can be turned into a *quantitative* discipline through the analysis of statistics, its theories can be tested like the theories of any other exact science. Models can then be constructed that can forecast future economic conditions. The problem with this is that economics is not an exact science and statistical data relating to economic phenomena, like statistical data relating to other fields of historical study, are open to a bewildering variety of interpretations and explanations. "As there are in the field of social affairs no constant relations between magnitudes," writes Ludwig von Mises, "no measurement is possible and economics can never become quantitative."[46] Models based on statistical data operate in terms of the assumptions programmed into them by their creators or programmers, and it is these assumptions that govern a model's interpretation of the statistics available to it. Any forecasts based on such models would be intrinsically no more reliable than the forecasts based on non-statistical models using the same criteria. In the field of economics the most that mathematics can do is to state *past* economic phenomena in terms of mathematical formulae. Thus, as Mises has written:

If a statistician determines that a rise of 10 per cent in the supply of potatoes in Atlantis at a definite time was followed by a fall of 8 per cent in the price, he does not establish anything about what happened or may happen with a change in the supply of potatoes in another country or at another time. He has not "measured" the "elasticity of demand" of potatoes. He has established a unique and individual historical fact. No intelligent man can doubt that the behavior of men with regard to potatoes and every other commodity is variable. Different individuals value the same things in a different way, and valuations change with the same individuals with changing conditions.[47]

It is not possible, therefore, for econometrics to provide us with the kind of information—viz. constant relations between economic phenomena—necessary to construct models of the economy that will forecast accurately the economic conditions resulting from, say, changes

[46] Ludwig von Mises, *The Theory of Money and Credit* (Indianapolis: Liberty Fund, 1981), p. 460.   [47] Ludwig von Mises, *Human Action*, p. 55f.

in government monetary or fiscal policy. The value of econometrics has thus been greatly overestimated, and the hope that it will provide economists with the statistical data necessary to treat economics as an exact science is misguided and futile.

Not surprisingly the growth of econometrics—which has been considerable since 1930 when the Econometrics Society was formed—and the concept of economics as an exact science, has tended to foster the belief that growth of the economy can be effectively planned and controlled by government policy based on the forecasts of econometric models. As with all ostensible justifications of government control of the economy the results fail to come up to expectations and further tinkering with the economy is deemed necessary. This results in greater discrepancy between expectations and reality, which in turn leads to further regulation. This goes on until total control turns into mismanagement and total failure to control, with the consequent decline of the economy under a morass of regulations, obstructions and disincentives to the creation of wealth.

§8
Economics and Political Economy

All the distinctions between the various economic disciplines discussed above to some extent misrepresent the basic principles of economic reality upon which the economy works. Under these classifications much that is essentially *non*-economic is brought to bear upon the consideration of economic principles. The result is a complex group of interrelated sub-disciplines that are difficult to understand and relate to each other at many points—what we should, perhaps, in common parlance call a mess. Even graduates with higher degrees in economics often find it difficult to make sense of the economic theories they have devoted so much time to studying. This problem is much in evidence in the media; its coverage of politics and its examination of the proposed economic policies put forward by the various political parties as the basis upon which they make their promises to the electorate demonstrate very well the lack of unanimity among politicians and economists alike regarding the effects of government policy on the economy.

Many of these problems boil down to confusing the effects of political manipulation of the economy with economics proper.

Development economics, macroeconomics and international trade are meaningless distinctions once the disruptive effects of political interference are stripped away. Yet the point is seldom made. It is as though politics were somehow inescapably tied up with economics; and although this is in practice the case today in the highly politicised and bureaucratically manipulated economies of the Western world, and perhaps has been throughout much of history, it is certainly not valid to infer from such *historical* facts that political considerations are necessarily relevant to economics proper.

The failure to maintain a clear distinction between economic and political principles when dealing with economies operating under the controlling influence of political strategies and goals that are essentially irrational from the economic point of view has led to much confusion and misunderstanding. Perhaps it would be far better to abandon the distinctions between the types of economic disciplines discussed above altogether, therefore, and concentrate on the basic distinction between economics proper, i.e. the study of the use and management of scarce resources with alternative uses, and political economy,[48] that is to say the study of how economies are affected by the constraints imposed upon them by the organisation of society under particular political regimes. This distinction would help to keep the essentially economic from the essentially non-economic factors more clearly in view. It would also help us to see the remedies for many of the problems facing both First and Third World societies, and different income groups within those societies, more clearly in terms of rational economic principles, or at least to understand why such problems are unresolvable in the context of prevailing political conditions. The study of both economics and politics would be considerably more rational under such a procedure.

[48] Although formerly the term *political economy* was used to mean different things by different writers, including pure economics, in the nineteenth century it meant generally what is today understood by the term *economics*. This term has now almost entirely fallen into disuse. Its adoption here to distinguish the study of politicised economies from the study of economics proper is not intended to correspond to any particular previous usage of the term. (Cf. Joseph A. Schumpeter, *History of Economic Analysis* [London: Allen and Unwin, (1954) 1982], p. 21f.)

CHAPTER TWO

SOME BASIC CONCEPTS
AND DEFINITIONS

§1

Economic Value

IF something is to have economic value it must be relatively scarce and in demand. An economic good is a scarce resource for which people are prepared to exchange other scarce resources in order to obtain. If a good is in abundant supply it is worth nothing economically—it is free. This is so even if it is vital to life, e.g. air. Of course, it might be argued that in some places air is to some extent an economic good since people do pay for it; they pay to live away from pollution in a clean, healthy environment where property is more expensive than in polluted areas. But in this case they do so because clean air is no longer available in such abundant supply in polluted areas. It has become scarcer and therefore it can be bought for a price. People will pay higher prices for houses that are situated in areas where there is a cleaner atmosphere than those situated in polluted industrial areas—other things being equal.

In saying that some things are worth nothing *economically* we are not making a statement about these things in ultimate terms; we are not making an ontological statement about their worth. That is to say, we are not assessing the value of their being or existence. Sea water, for instance, is valuable ontologically speaking. It is vital to our very existence. Without it life as we know it would cease. It is thus of inestimable value from an ontological point of view. In other words it is *objectively* valuable. But it is not normally of *economic* value. It cannot normally be exchanged for other goods in the market because it is not scarce. We must therefore distinguish between *ontological* or *objective* value, and *economic* value. Economic value is based on one's evaluation of a good's worth in a specific situation and for a specific end, viz. exchange for other goods in a market. Economic value is a *subjective* phenomenon, i.e. it depends on an individual's estimation of a good's worth in exchange for other goods. It arises out of one's personal assessment of a good's ability to satisfy or lead to the satisfaction of a want for which one is prepared to exchange other scarce goods. Hence, one must ask the question: Is it worth my while to part with a piece of gold for a bucket of sea water? Both are ontologically valuable, both are made by God and are "good." But sea water is not normally of any *economic* value.

§2
Markets

In a market economy people exchange economic goods to their mutual advantage. Each party to the exchange values what he receives from the other more than what he exchanges it for. Both come off the better. If a man exchanges a pig for a cow, it is because he values the cow more than the pig, and vice versa. In such a case the exchange value of a pig equals that of a cow, though from the point of view of the parties involved each gets something he values more. This demonstrates how economic value is a subjective phenomenon. The effect of everyone exchanging goods in a market, however, is to establish exchange rates, i.e. market prices. Thus, a market is "a group of buyers and sellers who are in sufficiently close contact for the transactions between any pair of them to affect the terms on which the others buy or sell."[1]

In the free market suppliers compete with suppliers and buyers compete with buyers. Suppliers do not compete with buyers. Theoretically, as this process of competition and exchange takes place prices stabilise at a level where supply is equal to demand and the whole supply of a good is purchased by those wishing to acquire it at that price. Economists call this the equilibrium price. Although in most markets the existence of equilibrium is a hypothetical situation that will never be attained perfectly there is a tendency towards equilibrium in the free market, other things being equal.

The free market works to the mutual advantage of all. It is a mechanism for *harmonising* interests. Although it is true that there is a *conflict* of interests between suppliers and consumers—because suppliers naturally want the highest price they can get for their goods

[1] Arthur Seldon and F. G. Pennance, *Everyman's Dictionary of Economics* (London: J. M. Dent and Sons Ltd, 1965), p. 271.

and consumers wish to acquire the goods at the lowest price possible—the market works to mitigate this conflict of interests. Competition for custom between suppliers reduces prices, which is to the
advantage of the consumer, while the constant bidding of consumers
against each other for goods raises prices, which is to the advantage
of the supplier. The market order thus reduces the conflict of interests
between suppliers and consumers to the benefit of all. The concept
of the market as a mechanism for harmonising economic interests,
therefore, is not predicated on the idea that there is a natural harmony
of interests between suppliers and consumers. There is not. Rather
there is a natural conflict of interests, which the market mitigates
so that each party benefits from the exchange. Both parties are forced
to offer their goods at a rate of exchange that is to their mutual
advantage. Far from creating opportunities for exploitation, therefore,
as it is often thought, the free market order reduces exploitation by
allowing competition to temper the interests of suppliers and consumers.

It might be objected that the free market only works to harmonise
interests between the supplier who gets the sale and the consumer
who buys goods from him, but that it creates a *dis*harmony of interests
between suppliers, who compete against each other for customers,
and also between consumers, who bid against each other for the
available supply of goods. This has led some to view the free market
economy generally in a critical light and to assert that free markets
are detrimental to the poorer classes in society, the rich being able
to obtain all their needs via the market while the poor are left without
enough economic power to bid against the rich. It is therefore claimed
that the market does not harmonise the interests of all but only the
interests of those suppliers who can dominate the market, forcing
their weaker competitors out of business, and the wealthier members
of society who can bid up prices. In other words, the free market
order provides adequately for the wealthy but creates a system in
which the poor cannot escape their poverty.

This analysis is faulty, however: first, it fails to take account of
the fact that all consumers are also suppliers in some market, whether
for labour or goods, and all suppliers are consumers in some market.
Thus, a market situation that is to the mutual advantage of supplier
and consumer is advantageous to all. It is in reality a mechanism
for harmonising the conflicting interests of all. Since all produce and
sell something and all buy and consume what others produce, all

benefit ultimately. Second, the more demand there is for a good—
i.e. the more consumers bid against each other for the available supply
of a good—the more entrepreneurs will be induced to find new ways
of meeting that demand. The existence of mass demand—i.e. of an
increase of consumers bidding against each other for goods—creates
the necessary conditions for mass production, which leads to a greater
supply of goods being made available at prices that more people can
afford. A free market order is therefore to the advantage of all
consumers *as* consumers and all suppliers *as* suppliers. Furthermore,
the same conditions of mass demand provide more opportunities for
new suppliers to enter the market, thereby creating more opportunities for employment, and this in turn leads to lower prices since
a greater supply of goods is made available on the market.

In a free market economy, therefore, production and distribution
occur together. It is the failure to understand that production and
distribution in a free market economy are complex interdependent
processes taking place between all people at all times, and hence that
the free market order is advantageous to all, that has led to an
economic analysis based on the idea that free markets are disadvantageous to all but the few who are able to exploit the rest of society
economically. In this analysis production and distribution are artificially abstracted from each other and from the reality of the conditions that prevail in the market economy. It is then assumed that
production can be organised more efficiently and "fairly"—i.e. in a
way that can be of benefit to the poor as well as the wealthy—if
it is separated from distribution. This is a fallacy however. The false
abstraction of these economic factors from the reality of the situation
that prevails in a productive market economy distorts one's understanding of how wealth is created. At the bottom of socialist economic
theory this kind of thinking is at work. When an economic system
is organised around this fallacy the result is the decline of productivity
and decapitalisation, and ultimately the failure of economic activity
based on the division of labour. Before this latter occurs, however,
the system is abandoned and a de facto market economy takes its
place, even where this is formally illegal. A good example of this
last point was the Soviet Union, where black markets were common,
and even encouraged by some governments. Even formal allegiance
to such a system has now been abandoned by some of the former
Soviet nations. The free market economy, because it harmonises the
interests of suppliers and consumers and creates more opportunities

for employment, maximises productivity and, consequently, works to the mutual advantage of all concerned. The only real alternative ultimately is subsistence living, a condition that is only too real for many in advanced socialist, communist and ex-Soviet States.

§3
Money

In the market economy people acquire goods and services by exchanging them for other goods and services. This can be done in two ways: (a) through barter, in which the actual goods to be sold are calculated in value against the goods to be bought. This is a clumsy and time and effort consuming process. It makes for a slow and less efficient market. (b) A common medium of exchange can be used. This is the commodity that is considered the most marketable good, i.e. that is acceptable to the greatest number of people in exchange for the greatest and most varied number of goods. If a sheep fits this description the medium of exchange will be a sheep. The use of a common medium of exchange facilitates economic activity by providing a widely accepted means of payment and a reliable means of economic calculation. It rationalises economic activity in other words. A community's common medium of exchange is its form of money. Simply put, money is the most marketable good.[2]

Historically, certain goods became established more than others as common media of exchange because they have certain qualities that facilitate their use as such. There are four essential qualities that a good needs if it is to function effectively as money: it must be (a) scarce in comparison with other goods, (b) easily portable, (c) easily divisible, and (d) durable, not easily perishable. A good that possesses these four qualities is more likely to be used as a common medium of exchange. The two substances that have been most widely used as money throughout history excel in these qualities: gold and silver. In the last 150 years or so gold has been established as the most suitable and most widely used of these two. Silver has been demonetised.

One more thing needs to be said about the qualities of money. Money is essentially an *economic* good not a political good. Gold is

[2] Ludwig von Mises, *Human Action, A Treatise on Economics* (Chicago: Contemporary Books, Inc., Third Revised Edition, 1966), p. 401. See also note 7 on p. 152 below.

not an internationally accepted form of money because it is politically enforced. Indeed many politicians would like to be rid of it as a form of money. Gold is a universally accepted standard because of its *economic* value. Although it may seem that this is no longer true and that the value of modern currency is determined politically in relation to other politically manipulated currencies, it still remains true that *economically* gold is the de facto standard. The current situation in which the value of currency is artificially manipulated by the authorities to meet their political exigencies is a transitory phenomenon. When political money fails—and it always does fail eventually—gold will most likely be re-established as the de facto standard for monetary transactions.[3]

Because of its marketability, commodity money (e.g. gold and silver) became a standard for measuring the value of goods generally. Once this happened money took on a value that related to its function as a medium of exchange; that is to say it became valuable for its use as a medium of exchange as well as for its use as a commodity. But it must be remembered that the value imputed to money as a medium of exchange was not established independently of a particular medium's historic value as a good. If money has no value as a good its basis as a medium of exchange has gone since its value as a medium of exchange rests on the fact that it is the most marketable good. Thus, modern fiat money is not in the historical sense money. It was referred to originally as *fiduciary media*, i.e. claims to money accepted merely on trust. Banknotes were originally promises to pay a certain amount of gold or silver, IOUs for money, not money in their own right. The *fiduciary issue* was the excess of notes issued by the Bank of England over and above its reserves. It functioned as

---

[3] I am not arguing that gold should be legal tender. A gold standard that makes gold a legally enforceable medium of exchange is, in a sense, as arbitrary as a fiat paper standard. My point is simply that gold, because it excels as a common medium of exchange, will establish itself as the de facto standard when it is allowed to function as a medium of exchange and not subjected to political manipulation and restrictions on its use as such. Modern British governments have normally penalised the use of gold as a medium of exchange either by suspending domestic trading—as happened with the Defence (Finance) Regulations under the Emergency Powers (Defence) Act of 1939 and Exchange Control Act of 1947—or by subjecting it to sales tax, as happened between 1975 and January 2000 with the imposition of VAT on gold. This enables the government to debase fiat currency without the risk, or at least with a significantly reduced risk, of flight into hard money, which would vitiate the government's ability to control the money supply effectively for its own purposes. See Chapter Five pp. 157–172.

money only because people believed it to be redeemable for gold. Similarly, coin that today functions as a medium of exchange but is of little value itself—materially worth less than its face value— is called "token money" and not considered legal tender over a certain amount. (This latter fact is inconsistent from a political point of view, but it is a tacit acknowledgement that political fiat money is not money in the *economic* sense.)

Unfortunately, money and its creation has been transformed considerably in modern Western societies as a result of State control of the monetary systems and all Western economies now operate on fiat standards. Fiat money is so called because it is created out of paper by State decree. It has no value other than as State-enforced legal tender. Thus, we use the term *hard money* to mean what used to be called money, e.g. gold and silver coins. The term *money* today means fiat money, money that exists because it is printed on paper (or coined in base metals) by the government or its agents. But modern fiat money is essentially a fraud and will last only as long as governments can cajole people, or coerce them through legal tender laws, into using it. (*Hard currency* is a term used to mean a currency that is undervalued in international exchange, its hardness being due to its trading strength over other currencies. It should not be confused with *hard money* as used here, which means metal or specie.)

§4
Profit

Profit is the difference between the selling price of a good and the cost of producing it. If it costs £5.00 to produce a particular good, taking into account all the production factors—e.g. raw materials, production processes, capital depreciation (the cost of replacing the capital or part thereof consumed in its production), labour and management (salaries), marketing, transportation and implicit opportunity cost[4]—and the good sells at £8.00, the profit is £3.00.

---

[4] The term *profit* as used in every-day language by most non-economists is an accountant's term. Economists usually define profit in terms of *opportunity cost*. This is the minimum return necessary to keep capital in a particular use. If the owners can make a better return on their capital by investing it in an alternative business they will usually do so, other things being equal. This opportunity cost is known

If the cost of production rises above the price that people are prepared to pay for a good it becomes uneconomic to produce. Since no profit can be made, no excess of income over expenditure, there can be no surplus that could then be put to further productive use. No matter how much labour, care and effort were to go into its production, its economic value would be less than the production costs involved in manufacturing it. To manufacture such a good would be an unproductive use of capital. Its production under such circumstances would not constitute the creation of wealth, and would contribute instead to decapitalisation. In other words it would be a waste of scarce resources that are required for the production of other, more useful goods.

It is thus profit, the production of a surplus of income over expenditure, that leads ultimately to capital accumulation and the creation of wealth. Without profit there can be no growth economically and hence no increase in standards of living. If we want our standard of living to get better we must increase our wealth, and this is only possible if we make a profit. Without profit society would enter a period of decapitalisation, i.e. consumption of the wealth that society has already accumulated (saved) and that is needed to fund further production (economic growth). Hence there would be a lowering of the standard of living and eventually shortages and poverty, as there was in the USSR. Ultimately we should reach the archetypal profitless mode of existence: subsistence living.

Profit is therefore vital to economic growth and social betterment. If we want better health care, better housing, a better environment, better amenities, a better standard of living generally, we must make a profit. These things can only be produced by the creation of wealth, and without profit this is impossible. Profit is vital to our economy and to our lives. The only alternative to an economy based on profit is subsistence living. Those who think profit is evil or incompatible with the Christian virtues should consider the plight of the poor populations of India, Africa, South America and other Third World countries, especially those that have had least contact with Western societies, and observe what subsistence living is all about. That is the alternative.

---

as *normal profit. Supernormal profit* (sometimes called *pure profit, economic profit* or just *profit*) is any return over and above normal profit. Normal profit is equal to the return that the owners of capital could have earned had they invested in the next best alternative enterprise.

The choice before us in terms of the economic organisation of society is a simple one: productivity and profit, or stagnation and subsistence living, with all that that implies, e.g. poor health care, disease, bad housing, insufficient resources to cope with even the slightest emergencies—basically a hand to mouth existence. Without profit there would be no way of helping others since one's means would be sufficient only for oneself and one's immediate family. If Christians want to be in a position to help others, to provide charity— and we must assume that they do since this is a command of Christ— they must make a profit. Even charity, therefore, which is a biblical requirement, necessitates an economy based on profit.

§5
The Price Mechanism and Economic Calculation

Prices perform an essential function in the economy. Without prices economic calculation becomes impossible. The price mechanism provides three essential pieces of information: (*a*) how much it costs to produce a good or supply a service, (*b*) how much people are prepared to pay for it, and thus (*c*) whether the manufacture of a good or supply of a service is a productive use of capital. In other words the price mechanism tells us whether the manufacture of a good constitutes the creation of wealth or the waste of scarce resources.

This principle holds good for all production in all societies, in- cluding communist and socialist State-controlled economies. Socialist and communist economies are wasteful and less productive economies because they have corrupted the price mechanism, which provides manufacturers and service providers with information about how much goods and services are worth—i.e. how much people are prepared to pay for them—and therefore whether it is worth manu- facturing and supplying such goods and services. Without the price mechanism it is not possible to engage in rational economic calcu- lation, and therefore it is not possible to maximise productivity. The result of the destruction or corruption of the price mechanism is that society engages in uneconomic and unproductive enterprises that lead to the decapitalisation of society through the waste of scarce resources needed for the creation of wealth. Instead of the creation of wealth and prosperity through economic rationalisation society enters a period of economic stagnation and increasing poverty—witness the former Soviet nations, which are now abandoning their previous socialist economic strategies and attempting to promote a market economy. Yet at the same time they are seeking help from the West by asking for favoured trading terms, an anomaly few seem to recognise.

This analysis of profit and the price mechanism and their role in the economy is based on an assessment of the *economic* value of goods and services offered for sale in the market. It does not presuppose that economic value is the only kind of value that people appreciate or impute to goods. One may wish to use one's wealth to create a picture that, due to its poor quality, is of no economic value whatsoever. One may derive great pleasure from doing this, and from admiring the fruits of one's efforts. The picture may be of great personal value to its creator. Similarly, an object may have little economic value yet have great sentimental value. These kinds of value are just as valid as economic value, and no criticism or deprecation of such is here intended. But they are not relevant to an understanding of economics. We must distinguish between *economic* value, on the basis of which wealth is created, and other kinds of value that are not based on economic considerations.

§6

Supply and Demand

As we have seen, people compete against each other to obtain scarce goods that are in demand. The scarcer a good is the higher its price will be; the less scarce it is the lower its price will be. If a good is in short supply those who wish to purchase it will bid against each other for it. The more plentiful a good is the less people will bid against each other for it and the more *suppliers* will compete against each other by reducing prices in order to obtain sales.

Supply and demand for a good are thus regulated by the price mechanism. When the price mechanism is allowed to function properly—e.g. without government or State interference—it will tend to establish an equilibrium between supply and demand; that is to say at a given price the whole supply of a certain good will be purchased by those who wish to acquire it. When the supply rises above demand prices will fall, since suppliers will compete with each other by offering lower prices, thereby attracting more customers and increasing demand. There will thus be a tendency for equilibrium between supply and demand to be re-established at a lower price. When supply falls below demand prices will rise, since consumers will bid against each other for goods is short supply, thereby limiting the number of people who are prepared to pay the higher price. There will be a tendency for equilibrium between supply and demand to be re-established once again at a higher price.

If the price of a good in short supply is kept artificially low—by State regulation for example—the result will be a shortage, since the supply will be exhausted before all those wanting to purchase the good at that price are able to obtain it: e.g. meat in Soviet Russia. This may lead to economic stagnation due to the undervaluing and thus wasteful use of scarce resources needed for use in more essential or more productive industries. If the price is kept artificially high—by cartels and trade agreements, State-imposed tariffs, union imposed minimum wage agreements in closed shop industries etc.—the result will be a glut, since only a limited number of people wanting to purchase the good will be able to afford it: e.g diamonds, EEC food mountains, unemployed labour etc., again leading to economic stagnation through the waste and underutilisation of scarce resources needed for the creation of wealth.

§7
Capital

Suppose someone were shipwrecked and washed ashore on a desert island with no possessions or provisions. The task of merely surviving for such a person would be immensely difficult. His first priority would be to obtain food and shelter, a simple enough task for anyone living under normal conditions in a developed society. But on a desert island with nothing except perhaps the clothes in which he stood this simple task would be a major hurdle to overcome. He would have to start from scratch. In other words he would have no capital with which to work.

His first job would be to obtain the material provisions that are vital for life: food and water. But even catching a fish or hunting an animal for food under such conditions would present immense problems. Suppose our castaway wished to eat some fish. First he has to catch it, a considerably difficult task without a fishing rod or net of some kind. Perhaps most of his day would be taken up with trying to catch a fish for his first meal, and his success would most likely be very limited. But suppose he does catch a fish. He then has to prepare it for eating. A knife and a few matches would make his task much easier, since he would be able to cut and gut the fish and cook it. With a resource such as a knife he would also be able much more easily to make a fishing rod or netting device. Without a knife or any other such tool he would be forced into a very primitive form of life, almost as basic as that of the animals, having to eat raw food caught with his bare hands. Of course he would still have his most important resource, far more important than any material possessions, namely his human initiative and creativeness. It is these human qualities that enable man to excel above the animals and to use the material resources at his disposal so effectively. These qualities are part of the image of God in man, which sets him apart from every other creature. Nonetheless, without capital, resources such as tools or materials from which he can make tools, his task would be very difficult and his standard of living would be that of abject poverty. Even Robinson Crusoe lived a life of considerable ease compared with our castaway, since he had a vast amount of capital, in the form of provisions from the ship, with which to work.

Let us assume, however, that our castaway has been able to make some kind of water retainer or bucket for storing rain water for drinking and a fishing rod. His life is now immeasurably easier since he can store water and food at least for a few days, thereby freeing up time to create and develop other tools and collect further resources. He has now accumulated capital in the form of a fishing rod and a bucket, resources that will enable him to work more efficiently and productively thereby helping him to progress towards a better stand-ard of living. He may be able to spend time planting seeds for crops and herding any tamable animals together such as goats for milking and sheep for wool and food. Each time he obtains some other useful tool or resource that increases the efficiency and productivity of his work he capitalises himself—i.e. his stock of capital increases. Each new project he undertakes relies on the availability and productive use of the equipment and resources he has previously accumulated in order for it to succeed. These physical resources constitute capital, and the process of accumulating them is capitalisation. It is this process of capitalisation that makes civilisation possible on the physical level. Of course, as we have seen, this process can only take place where there is the initiative and creativeness to utilise the available physical resources (the animal kingdom is not characterised by capital accumulation in the way that human society is generally). Capital is thus the result of the creative combination of two more basic factors: raw materials and labour.

Suppose now that a second castaway is washed up on the island without possessions or provisions. He is immediately able to benefit from the capitalised form of living that the first castaway has developed. Through co-operation and the division of labour both are able to accomplish more than they could on their own. The second castaway offers to work by catching fish with the first castaway's fishing rod in return for supplying him with some of the fish he catches. This frees up more time for the first castaway to develop other skills and projects. Being able to use the fishing rod means that the second castaway does not have to spend all his time looking for food and can therefore accumulate other resources and develop tools and skills not presently available to the first castaway. The two can trade, each benefiting from the other's accumulation of capital and thereby increasing their ability to develop other tools and accumulate further resources that can then be traded. As this goes on their standard of living becomes more developed and their means of procuring the necessities, and even perhaps in time some of the luxuries, of life becomes increasingly capital intensive. Eventually they develop a standard of living that is vastly superior to that endured by the original castaway when he was first washed ashore. This higher standard of living is only made possible through the accumulation and productive use of capital—material resources such as raw materials, tools and semi-manufactured goods—to facilitate further production, leading to a greater stock of material resources, a higher standard of living and the possibility of further capitalisation and progress. This process of capitalisation is also greatly enhanced by the division and specialisation of labour.

The existence of capital and the process of capitalisation is a basic fact of human life. Civilisation is impossible without it; men would simply die unless they were prepared to capitalise themselves to some degree. Productive work is essential to human life—and this is true psychologically no less than physically. The idea of an idyllic society where men have all their needs and desires provided for them without the necessity of work and where play is all that occupies their time is a denial of the role assigned to mankind in the created order by God; it has never existed—it was not a feature of man's life in the Garden of Eden prior to his fall into sin—and, moreover, never will.[5]

Societies that rely on only a minimal amount of capitalisation are backward cultures characterised by subsistence living. If society is to have a high standard of living it must pursue the process of capitalisation. In this sense all societies are capitalist to some degree, even socialist and Marxist societies, since they rely on the use of capital to further economic and social development. The term capital*ism*, however, has been used to describe an economy based on the *private* ownership of capital or the means of production—though this does also involve a certain philosophy of life or world-view based on the virtues of honesty, thrift and hard work in a free society abiding by the rule of law and with a limited civil government. As I argue elsewhere in this book, such an organisation of economic, social and political life is far more able to benefit society materially and socially. Socialist and communist societies where capital is owned by the State in the name of the people have a tendency to *de*capitalisation rather than capitalisation since the human factors necessary to generate economic progress are distrusted, discouraged and even outlawed, and the mechanisms essential for the smooth transmission of the information necessary to make capitalisation possible are obstructed and impaired by State decrees and manipulation of the economy.

Capital is thus the stock of material resources at the disposal of an individual or society that is used to produce goods and satisfy

---

[5] I am convinced that one of the major causes of death in our culture is retirement. Men were created to work, and to work for the glory of their Creator. Where this is denied the meaning of life is lost. In this life, where the effects of man's sin are mitigated to some extent, many work without dedicating themselves and their callings to God, and still to some degree they find meaning to life. This is an aspect of common grace. Without such common grace non-believers would find all work devoid of meaning and purpose, since it is only in God that man can find true meaning to life. By *work* here I am not necessarily referring to work of a financially remunerative kind. It is also my conviction that in the Resurrection men will not only work hard for the glory of God but find the true meaning of life in serving God by such work. Man is created in God's image and the God of Scripture is the God of *creation*. The fact that man is a creative being made in God's image means that he must work and that he must find the meaning to life in work as a means of serving God. Jesus said "My Father worketh hitherto, and I work" (Jn 5:17). As long as man bears God's image he will work. Work is not the result of the Fall or the curse. (According to Gen. 3:17 it is the *toil* or pain of work that man suffers because of the Fall. Adam was given work to do before the Fall. Only after the Fall did work become painful and associated with drudgery).

wants. Economists distinguish between various technical uses of the term capital however. Basically capital can be divided into two kinds: fixed capital, and working or circulating capital. Fixed capital consists of resources whose form does not change essentially through use, such as factories, buildings, machinery and equipment used in the manufacture of goods. Working or circulating capital consists of goods that are in the process of being manufactured, e.g. stocks of raw materials, semi-finished goods and finished goods stocked by manufacturers, wholesalers and retailers. A third category, specific capital, refers to goods and resources that can only be used for the purpose for which they were originally designed.

The development of a highly capitalised economy and enjoyment of the high standard of living associated with it, such as exists in modern Western societies, requires a high level of saving, i.e. postponement of the enjoyment of the profits of one's labour, and the investment of these profits in capital. It is such investment that facilitates greater productivity, which in turn leads to higher standards of living. A highly capitalised economy is characterised, therefore, by *investment*, whereas a highly uncapitalised or decapitalised economy is characterised by the immediate *consumption* of profits. Obviously, total postponement of the enjoyment of the fruits of one's labour is not possible since a certain amount of consumption is necessary for life to continue. Likewise, no society totally consumes the products of its labour immediately. But the extent to which saving and investment are prioritised over immediate consumption will determine the level of capitalisation and hence the level of economic progress and general standards of living enjoyed by a society.

It is the process of saving that provides the resources necessary for investment in capital. In a society with a highly developed monetary system savings will be accumulated and measured in the economy's medium of exchange. Money can be lent out at interest to those wishing to obtain funds to purchase capital. Consequently, the availability of capital in a highly developed society is linked to the financial sectors of the economy. This has led to various investment and money related uses of the term capital. *Long-term capital* is a term used to denote money invested in securities and bonds, i.e. interest-bearing financial claims, and in shares in companies. These are long- and medium-dated investments. The market for such investments is called the *capital market*, and consists of institutions such as the joint-stock and merchant banks, issuing houses, the Stock

Exchange, building societies and insurance companies. The capital market is the market for long- and medium-term loans. *Short-term capital* denotes money invested in short-dated bills of exchange, Treasury Bills and repos. The market for these investments is called the *money market*. The institutions comprising the money market are the settlement banks and other financial institutions, such as building societies and securities firms that deal in short-dated bills of exchange and repos, the discount market, accepting houses and bullion and foreign exchange markets. The money market, therefore, is the market for short-term loans.

§8
Interest [6]

The possession of a good today is of more value than the possession of that same good at a later date, other things being equal—e.g. provided demand remains constant. Given the choice of owning a scarce resource today and owning that same resource in a year's time one would choose to receive it today, since it can either be consumed to gratify one's immediate wants or put to productive use in order to create the wealth that will gratify one's wants. It is therefore more valuable now than at a future date. The ratio between the value one places on the gratification of a want today and the value one places on the gratification of that same want at a future date constitutes *originary interest*.[7] Time is thus an important factor in economic calculation. In a sense time is an economic good since it is a scarce resource for mankind. This preference for the possession of a good now rather than at a future date is called *time preference*. The time factor is essential to a proper understanding of interest. Just as the possession of a good is more valuable now than in the future, so also the possession of a sum of money is more valuable now than in the future, and the difference between its value now and at some future date constitutes interest. One's time preference determines the *rate* of interest one is willing to pay for the use of that sum now rather than later.

---

[6] This section deals with interest as an *economic* phenomenon and does not seek to address questions concerning the morality of lending money at interest. For the biblical teaching on interest and consideration of the ethics of charging interest see Appendix B. [7] Ludwig von Mises, *op. cit.*, p. 526ff.

If an individual sets a high premium on the future, if he is concerned about providing and planning for his future rather than consuming his resources in order to gratify his immediate wants, he will demand less interest for deferring the gratification of his wants than the one who sets a high priority on the immediate gratification of his wants. Why? Because it takes less to induce him to wait for the enjoyment of his resources. He does not set such a high premium on the gratification of his wants *now*. He values the interest that can be gained at a future date from loaning out his funds more than the immediate gratification of his wants. He is not so consumption oriented and is prepared, therefore, to forgo the use of his funds on the gratification of his immediate wants in order to gain an advantage in the future. He is also less likely to borrow at high interest rates in order to gratify his immediate wants. This helps to reduce the rate of interest, stimulate entrepreneurial activity and facilitate the creation of wealth.

It is exactly the reverse for the one who values the immediate gratification of his wants more than the advantage to be gained by forgoing present consumption and lending his funds out at interest. He is not so concerned about building for the future; he wants his cake now. It will take a higher rate of interest, therefore, to induce him to forgo the consumption of his resources now. He will also be prepared to pay a higher rate of interest for loans in order to gratify his immediate wants, which will help to push up the cost of borrowing. This then has a knock-on effect in industry. Since the cost of borrowing is high, productivity and the creation of wealth will be less advanced.

Obviously, these are pure types and no human being or society completely embodies the one or the other. All need to engage in immediate consumption to some extent and all need to rationalise consumption in order to plan for the future to some extent. But one's time preference, the premium one sets on present consumption as against the growth of one's capital over time in the form of interest, determines the degree to which resources can be released for productive use and the further creation of wealth. Societies in which there is a consensus that sets a high priority on the future—i.e. societies that are production oriented rather than consumption oriented—will be wealthier societies. There will be more funds available at lower interest rates and this will facilitate greater capitalisation and productivity and hence economic growth and social amelioration.

It has been claimed that this is exactly what happened after the Reformation, especially in the Netherlands, but also generally among the Protestant nations.[8] The Protestant faith produced a future-oriented world-view. The subjection of men's lives and minds to the Christian religion brought about a change in outlook that led to a significant reduction in interest rates. This facilitated greater trade and commerce and led to economic growth. Belief in the legitimacy of biblical concepts such as the cultural mandate, the command to have dominion over the earth, the legitimacy of wealth and capital accumulation—all of which, as we shall see in the following chapter, are to be found in the Protestant, and particularly the Puritan world-view—led to a transformation of the way men perceived their calling in this life and thus how they lived in the world. The Christian faith began to affect the everyday life of society. The result was a gradual transformation of society from feudalism to *capitalism*.[9] The Christian faith, therefore, realigns men's priorities and gives them a perspective on life, a world-view, that enables them to use the world and its resources properly and productively according to God's law, thereby facilitating the creation of wealth, without which it would not be possible—and indeed has not been possible historically—to provide better health care to those in need, better conditions and standards of living, which are essential for the eradication of disease, better education, better food production, better transportation, communication etc. All this has occurred in the context of a *Christian* culture to a degree that has been historically unique. This is because the eradication of poverty and suffering is both a promise and a duty for Christian nations (Dt. 15:4, Lk. 4:18–19), and the pursuit of economic growth and social amelioration by legitimate means both encouraged and blessed by our merciful God (Ps. 35:27).

[8] G. North, "Time as it Refers to Interest Rates" (Finstown, Orkney: Christian Reformed Tapes), no. GN 101.4.

[9] But see how this term is defined and the process of transformation explained in historical context in Chapter Three.

§9
Inflation

Inflation is an increase in the money supply.[10] By *money supply* I mean the quantity of money *in circulation*. Deflation is a decrease in the money supply. Inflation is not a rise in prices, nor is deflation a fall in prices, though significant fluctuations in the supply of money usually do lead to fluctuations in prices generally. It is essential to have a proper grasp of the true nature of inflation if one is to understand the behaviour of modern Western economies. Control of the money supply in modern Western nations is in the hands of the political authorities and it is used as a means of manipulating the economy in accordance with government policy. A government's performance in handling the economy is deemed to be the most important factor in its appeal to the electorate. If the "feel good factor" is not sufficiently felt by the population the government's prospects of re-election are usually considered poor. Even fundamental issues of justice are considered secondary to this issue in the modern hedonistic societies of the West.

Inflation leads to a rise in the aggregate level of prices, other things being equal. This is because the value of money, like that of any other commodity, is subject to supply and demand. This is what happens: if the money supply is increased while productivity remains stable, a situation develops in which there is more money chasing the same supply of goods. Prices rise therefore until all the available money is used to purchase all the available goods. The reverse happens in deflation. If the money supply is reduced there is less money chasing the same supply of goods. Prices fall until all the available goods are sold for all the available money. When the money supply is increased, therefore, whether by printing fiat money

---

[10] Inflation can be defined in three ways: (*a*) as an increase in prices, (*b*) as an increase in the supply of money over aggregate demand for money, and (*c*) simply as an increase in the supply of money. Although it is common today (*a*) describes a symptom of the phenomenon, not the phenomenon itself, and is therefore misleading; (*b*) is also misleading in that an increase in aggregate demand for money may camouflage an expansion of the money supply. It is a definition that obscures rather than elucidates the real problem and for this reason is inadequate. On the other hand (*c*) is a simple and accurate definition that elucidates the real cause of the phenomena that (*a*) and (*b*) seek to describe. I shall use this definition of inflation throughout this book.

or creating bank money, or by an increased inflow of gold for use as currency in hard money economies, wealth is not thereby created. Inflation merely leads to a situation in which the same amount of wealth is represented by a greater supply of money. The value of the monetary unit falls therefore.

It is true of course that if everyone were to receive a share of the newly created money equal to the percentage of the total supply that he previously held the inflation would not affect his relative wealth—although it by no means follows in such a case that the exchange value of money would decrease in direct proportion to the increase in the money supply. Practically, however, it would be impossible to maintain such proportionality in an inflationary economy. Inflation has an inherently redistributive effect on the economy. Since inflation creates a situation in which the total wealth in the economy is represented by a greater supply of money, those who receive the newly created money benefit at the expense of the rest of society. *They* receive wealth in the form of purchasing power that they previously did not have. Those who do not receive any of the new money have to stand a reduction in the purchasing power of the money they hold and consequently a decrease in real wealth. The effect of inflation therefore is to *redistribute* the wealth that was represented by the previous stock of money.

This effect is usually much more severe when inflation is caused by the fraudulent creation of money by the political authorities rather than by processes such as the mining of precious metals for use as currency in hard money economies. However, unlike inflation caused by increases in the supply of specie in hard money economies, the inflationary effects of which are usually minimal, the manipulation of the volume and value of money by the political authorities, no matter how well-meaning and fair the government may *claim* its monetary policies are, is a form of theft and forbidden by the Eighth Commandment. Why such government-controlled inflation should be considered immoral will be discussed in detail in Chapter Four.

Inflation *per se* is not immoral therefore. Whether inflation is morally acceptable in terms of Christian ethics will depend on how the inflation is created. The mining of gold and silver for use as currency in hard money economies, for example, is not morally repugnant to the Christian faith. Inflation produced by such proc-esses, no matter how unwelcome its effects on the economy might be considered by some, cannot be classed as fraud and therefore immoral. On the whole, however, such inflation tends not to have unwelcome effects in hard money economies. One can buy today with an ounce of gold roughly what one could buy with an ounce of gold two hundred years ago. Although the price of gold fluctuates considerably over the short term it has been remarkably stable over the long term. The effects of inflation caused by the mining of precious metals for use as currency in hard money economies, therefore, would tend towards the creation of long-term price stability, whereas without such inflation there would be a slow reduction in the aggregate level of prices over the long term—other things being equal. However, this is largely a hypothetical scenario since historically European rulers have constantly debased their coinage over the long term, which has of course resulted in a continual rise in the aggregate level of prices throughout much of our history.

Government-generated inflation based on the issue of fiat currency, and inflation caused by debasement of the coinage and fractional reserve banking practices are an entirely different matter however. Such inflation is immoral since it is fraudulent in principle. It also has much more serious and damaging effects on the economy since where rulers resort to such practices they usually do so with little moderation. By contrast, increases in the supply of precious metals for use as currency have usually been relatively moderate.[11] Debasement of currency, issue of fiat money and fractional reserve banking have provided a potentially limitless source of revenue for our rulers, few of whom have shown themselves ready to resist the temptation to exploit such immoral practices. It is these fraudulent practices—i.e. debasement of currency, issue of fiat money, and fractional reserve banking—perpetrated by governments and government-licensed institutions that constitute the engine of inflation in modern Western society, and to which attention will be drawn in this book as being fundamentally immoral and therefore necessitating political and economic reform if our economic way of life is to conform to the ethical principles of the Christian religion.

This explanation of the effect of inflation on prices is usually referred to as the *Quantity Theory of Money*. However, we must distinguish between a strict mechanical Quantity Theory of Money and a general Quantity Theory of Money. The strict theory assumes that,

[11] There are some notable exceptions to this where a greatly increased inflow of specie has led to significant increases in the aggregate level of prices—e.g. the influx of silver into Europe from the New World during the reign of Elizabeth I.

other things being equal, any variation in the quantity of money will lead to an inversely proportionate variation in the exchange value of the monetary unit. In other words it assumes that there is a strict proportional relation between the supply of money and the level of prices. If the supply of money is doubled, therefore, it is assumed that prices will double. But this is not necessarily so. There are a number of arguments that can and have been raised against this theory,[12] some of which are based on misconceptions of the theory itself coupled with an inadequate understanding of the economic realities on which it rests. Nevertheless, there are legitimate criticisms of the theory, usually to be found among those who have defined and developed the theory more correctly.[13]

The basic problem with this strict formulation of the theory is that it fails to take account of the fact that economics deals primarily not with mathematical models that operate according to fixed laws, but with individuals who make *subjective* evaluations of their economic situation and the goods and services they wish to exchange in the market. All kinds of considerations affect one's assessment of the value of a good, including the exchange value of money. Higher prices may and often do affect one's economic priorities. The fact that an individual has received an increase in income commensurate with the level of inflation (increase in money supply) does not mean that he will be prepared to pay a proportionately higher price for a particular good that he has been accustomed to buy. Inflation affects more than the relation between the supply of money and the level of prices; it affects the *demand* for goods also, and this leads to a change in buying patterns. It may also affect an individual's time preference. For example, the prospect of a sustained period of inflation that would wipe out a person's savings might induce him to stop saving and start consuming his capital, or even begin borrowing in order to gain some advantage from inflation. If this were to happen on a significant scale the demand for certain goods—goods and assets that will keep their value over the long term—would increase while the demand for others—e.g. investments and financial services linked to saving— would decrease. Furthermore, if enough people stop saving and start

---

[12] See J. Harvey, *Modern Economics* (Macmillan, 1969), Chapter 27, for a typical text book critique of the theory.

[13] See for instance Ludwig von Mises, *The Theory of Money and Credit* (London: Jonathan Cape, 1934 trans. by H. E. Batson), Part Two, Chapter II, "The determinants of the Objective Exchange-Value, or Purchasing Price, of Money."

spending their savings in order to avoid the devaluation of savings that inflation produces, or even start borrowing more in order to take advantage of an inflationary boom, prices generally may rise faster than inflation (i.e. expansion of the money supply). Economists call this phenomenon an increase in the velocity of circulation of money.[14]

Inflation affects a great many variables within the economy that fluctuate according to individual subjective assessments of priorities in changed economic conditions. The price of all goods will not rise proportionately therefore. Some may not rise at all, and others may rise far in excess of the level of inflation. For example, while the growth in the money supply (M4) for the year ending April 1988 was 16.9 per cent (this is the official Bank of England figure) the price of housing in London, and then later throughout the country, rose far in excess of this. At the same time the prices of many other goods (notably those that the government includes in the retail price index) did not rise nearly as much.

Even if everyone were to receive a share of the newly created money commensurate with the percentage of the total supply that he previously held, the fact that his income had risen proportionately with inflation, and therefore that his relative wealth had been unaffected, does not mean that the exchange value of money would fall in exact proportion to the level of inflation. The increase in the money supply would still most likely lead to a significant change in the conditions of demand. This would affect buying habits and there would, consequently, be a disproportionate rise in the prices of individual goods. In other words there would not be a *uniform* rise in prices, and the new state of equilibrium would embrace far more than a *general* rise in prices. The overall configuration of market conditions would be different. This new situation would certainly be reflected in the prices of goods and services offered for sale in the market. But it would be impossible to predict precisely how and to what extent the price level would be affected. That would demand an exhaustive knowledge of each individual's physical resources as well as his economic priorities, how they changed over time and in relation to inflation, and what new considerations would determine his future economic priorities, since all these factors are the source of changed buying patterns. In other words it would require exhaus-

[14] See Hans F. Sennholz, *Age of Inflation*, Belmont, Massachusetts: Libertarian Press, Inc., 1979), p. 65f.

tive knowledge of both the distribution of wealth throughout the economy and the state of mind of every individual in the economy and how his state of mind affected the use of his wealth. It is not even possible for men to understand their own minds much of the time, and when asked for a reason people often do not know themselves why they have acted in a certain way. How then could a central authority determine to what extent inflation would affect prices according to a crude and simplistic mathematical model?

However, in criticising this strict formulation of the Quantity Theory we must not throw the baby out with the bath water. As a general theory explaining an inescapable fact of life it holds good. Although there is no fixed ratio between the money supply and price levels, increases in the supply of money generally lead to increases in the aggregate level of prices (other things being equal), not because there is any mechanical relation between the two, but because individuals compete against each other in the market to obtain economic goods, and any increase in their purchasing power will lead them to bid up the price of goods offered for sale. How much they will be prepared to bid up the prices of individual goods, however, will depend not merely on their increased purchasing power, but also on the extent to which this increased purchasing power has affected the balance between other subjective economic considerations. Inflation therefore leads to an overall alteration in market conditions that is reflected in, among other things, the price of goods and services offered for sale. Assuming that all the money circulating in the economy will be used to purchase all the available goods, an increase in the money supply will lead to an aggregate increase in the level of prices, other things being equal. But not all goods will rise proportionately. Some prices may rise more than others, some may not rise at all, and some prices may even fall.

To summarise, we can illustrate this general theory by the following examples: (*a*) In a growing economy with a stable money supply prices will steadily fall, other things being equal, since money is needed to finance the production and purchase of new products and services and this must necessarily come from the existing stock. Since the same supply of money is chasing a greater supply of goods and services prices generally must fall. (*b*) In a growing economy with a level of inflation that is proportionate to the increase in productivity, prices generally will remain stable, other things being equal. The supply of money is increased in line with the demand for money.

In this situation wealth is being redistributed to those who receive the new money irrespective of the fact that prices are stable. This is what monetarists aim for. But what is theoretically desirable is not always practically attainable, as the Thatcher government discovered in the 1980s. It is extremely difficult to create this kind of situation because of the factors mentioned above regarding the subjective and unpredictable nature of economic activity. (c) In a growing economy with a level of inflation in excess of increased productivity prices will rise generally, other things being equal. Since the supply of money has increased over demand for money prices will rise until a new equilibrium has been established. Obviously this also constitutes the redistribution of wealth to those who receive the new money.[15]

This explanation of the general Quantity Theory of Money is necessarily simplistic. Its simplicity, however, does not undermine its validity.

§10

Economic and Legal Ownership

The free market economy, or capitalism, is based on the private ownership of the means of production. It is of the utmost importance, however, that we make a distinction between the concepts of *economic* ownership and *legal* ownership. Economic ownership consists of the ability to *use* and *control* an economic good, whether a consumption good or a production good. Legal ownership consists of the *title* to

---

[15] This model assumes a constant velocity of circulation of money. If the velocity of circulation of money increases significantly faster than general productivity prices will be affected, i.e. prices generally will either rise or not fall to the extent that they would have done otherwise. But as G. North has pointed out "Changes in the 'velocity of money'—the number of exchanges within a given time period— are also slow, unless the public expects some drastic change, like a devaluation of the monetary unit by the political authorities. These changes can be predicted within calculable limits; in short, the economic impact of such changes can be discounted. They are relatively fixed in magnitude in comparison to the flexibility provided by a government printing press or a central bank's brand new IBM computer" (*An Introduction to Christian Economics* [The Craig Press, 1973], p. 98). This model also assumes that the money supply is defined as money *in circulation*. Obviously, the withdrawal of money from circulation—for example an increase in savings that do not re-enter the economy via bank borrowing during a period of general slump, when businesses and consumers may try to avoid borrowing money at any rate— will tend to counteract the effects of increases in the money supply on the part of the monetary authorities.

a good, which should, but does not always, guarantee the right to use and control that good.

Capitalism is based on the private ownership, both legal *and* economic, of the means of production. Under a capitalist system of economic organisation those who own property legally have the right to dispose of their property as they think fit. If an individual has legal ownership of property, but the State, or the Mafia or anyone else, makes it impossible for him to use that property as he sees fit, by means of coercion, by taxing particular uses of the property in order to discourage certain kinds of economic activity, or by any other means, he does not have economic ownership of the property. He owns it in name only. The State or whoever controls *how* he uses it has economic ownership. For example, if I have a legally owned plant for producing certain goods, but the State instructs me to use this plant in a particular way—e.g. to pay a certain wage, to employ a certain kind of person, to sell products at a certain price etc.—in other words if it controls my use or part of my use of the plant, it usurps my power to dispose of my property as I see fit. It has effectively appropriated economic ownership of my plant. I do not own it in the capitalist sense: it is no longer *private* ownership of the means of production. Obviously, if it is nationalised I own it neither economically nor legally. Capitalism, however, maintains the right of private ownership, both legal *and* economic, of the means of production. A society that does not maintain this right of private economic ownership as well as legal ownership cannot properly be described as capitalist.

Marxism and all other forms of communism maintain the right of State ownership of the means of production, both legally and economically. Under fascism the individual has the right of legal ownership, but not economic ownership. Economic ownership in a fascist system is under the control of the State. Fascism is thus in no sense a capitalist phenomenon. It is vitally important that this point should be understood if one is to have a proper grasp of the nature of the modern State-planned economy. By leaving legal ownership in the hands of private citizens, while acquiring economic ownership for itself, a fascist State gives the impression to those outside that it is an economic order based on private ownership of the means of production—i.e. that it is capitalist. But this is not so. F. A. Hayek's book *The Road to Serfdom*, published in 1944, was written in order to expose this fallacy. Unfortunately, the common misunderstanding of the true nature of fascism has persisted. It needs to be stressed therefore that fascism is a form of socialism. Indeed, Hitler's version of fascism was called National Socialism and was the policy of the German National Socialist Labour Party. It must be understood therefore that the term "right-wing," which is today used to mean "fascist" and "capitalist" to some extent, entirely fails to convey the true nature of the capitalist mode of production and the kind of society it presupposes and helps to maintain. Capitalism is *not* a right-wing phenomenon, since it refers to the organisation of the means of production under a system that has nothing in common with fascism. Fascism is a form of socialism.

CHAPTER THREE

THE CREATION OF WEALTH

§1

The Division of Labour and Free Trade

DIVISION of labour is a fact of life, a result of the way that God has created the world. The principle of the division of labour is thoroughly biblical. It is a creation fact, a manifestation of the symbiotic nature of the whole creation. Mankind was created male and female. The division of labour is fundamental to the nature of human life. Man cannot escape the necessity of the division of labour if he is to fulfil his calling as God's image bearer and vicegerent on earth. Adam required "an help meet for him" in his creation mandate. The human race was not complete without the creation of woman (Gen. 2:18–24). Division of labour is present in and basic to the whole creation.[1] We shall be dealing with one aspect of it however, namely the division of labour in the field of economics and the creation of wealth.

The creation of wealth through economic rationalisation is only possible on the basis of the division of labour. If everyone were to provide for his own needs by himself without utilising the work and skills of others in mutual cooperation, civilisation could not advance very far. Everyone would spend his time feeding and clothing himself, and perhaps his family—though of course the very existence of the family constitutes a basic and vital division of labour—and such pro-

---

[1] The presence of the division of labour in the created order is a reflection of the divine being himself, since God is one, yet a trinity. All persons in the Trinity are equally God, "the same in substance, equal in power and glory," yet distinct persons with a particular relation to each other. This can be seen especially in the economic Trinity—i.e. God as he relates to his creation—since here the division of labour is manifested in God's creating and sustaining the universe, and especially in the salvation of his people. Stated in a somewhat crude form this can be expressed with regard to the salvation of God's elect in the following way: the Father initiates his eternal plan to bring glory to God's name by choosing a people to be redeemed in Christ before the foundation of the world, the Son accomplished their salvation in history, and the Spirit applies this salvation to God's elect personally.

visions would exist only on the most basic level: subsistence living. If someone were particularly good at something, some form of manufacturing process such as building houses for instance, he would not have sufficient time to develop his skills because of the need to secure other provisions in areas where he has less skill. Providing for his basic existence would absorb most of his time. Without someone to provide for his food and clothing and generally take care of his other needs he would not have the time and energy to develop his particular architectural skills.

But if A is good at building houses, and B is good at farming, their skills can be harmonised to achieve greater efficiency and therefore greater productivity in both industries. The former, A, spends more time building houses and as a result of concentrating his time and efforts on this form of industry increases the productivity of his skill rather than spending time on other things, which he does not do as well and which other people can do more skilfully. The latter, B, likewise increases his productivity by concentrating his skills on the farming industry. Even if A is better and building houses *and* farming than B it is still advantageous for A to specialise in that industry in which he has the greater specialisation and productivity, let us say construction, leaving B to concentrate on what A does less well (farming), since under these conditions total productivity will be maximised.[2] Division of labour leads to more productivity and a higher standard of living, since more skilled labour can be given to each specialist occupation. The result is the creation of wealth.

The most efficient means of creating wealth, that which facilitates the greatest and most productive division and specialisation of labour, is *free trade*, i.e. the rational capitalistic organisation of free labour, to use Max Weber's words.[3] Slavery, for example, is an inherently less rational form of economic enterprise than trade based on free labour.[4] Free trade harmonises and promotes the interests of all. It

---

[2] Economists call this the law of *comparative cost* or *comparative advantage*. This principle was first clearly set forth by David Ricardo (see *The Principles of Political Economy and Taxation*, Chapter VII, "On Foreign Trade." See also Ludwig von Mises, *Human Action: A Treatise on Economics* [Chicago: Contemporary Books, Inc., Third Revised Edition, 1966], p. 159ff.).

[3] See the discussion at note 7 below.

[4] Max Weber lists the following eight reasons explaining this fact: (*a*) the amount of capital needed for investment in human resources is greater under slavery; (*b*) capital risk has been much greater under slavery and more irrational due to slave labour being exposed to many non-economic influences, particularly political influence; (*c*) slave markets and prices are unreliable and this impedes rational economic

is important to grasp this fact: free trade is about promoting and advancing our own interests by promoting and advancing the interests of others, with whom we trade for goods and services. Division of labour and free trade work to harmonise the interests of everyone.

§2
Moral and Legal Predictability in the Market Order

The creation of wealth, therefore, depends on the division of labour and men's willingness to trade to their mutual advantage. When such trade takes place between a small number of people, barter trading may suffice. But as society becomes increasingly complex a common medium of exchange and various other institutions are needed in order to facilitate the development of an efficient and stable economy. Greater economic rationalisation leads to economic growth and rising standards of living. Economic institutions become more complex and economic actors and procedures become more interdependent. In turn the rising standard of living helps to stimulate the development of civilisation generally.

The development of such a free market society, however, requires a high degree of *moral* and *legal* predictability. It is only worth trading

---

calculation; (*d*) recruitment problems relating to political factors; (*e*) the high cost of maintaining the families of slaves; (*f*) where, because of the cost of maintaining the slaves' family members slaves have been separated from their families this has exacerbated recruitment problems; (*g*) the use of tools and apparatus requires a high level of responsibility and involvement of the operators' self interest, and this is typically lacking where slave labour is used, thus impeding economic rationalisation due to technical advances; and (*h*), most importantly, the impossibility of selection and dismissal of slaves in accordance with the economic conditions and personal ability, which can only be discovered when slaves are put to work on a job. On the other hand, where free labour is used capital risk and investment in human resources are diminished; the cost of reproduction and rearing families falls on the worker, not his employer; because of the latter the risk of dismissal is an important incentive for employees to maximise productivity; and it is possible to select the labour force according to ability and economic conditions (Max Weber, *Economy and Society: An Outline of Interpretive Sociology* [Berkeley: University of California Press (1968), 1978], Vol. I, p. 162f.). In other words, *free* trade, the capitalistic organisation of free labour, is economically more rational than the organisation of labour under other conditions, and this includes not only chattel slavery of the kind that was practised in antiquity and in the American colonies, but also the more subtle forms of slavery implicit in communistic and highly socialistic societies. The reasons for abolishing slavery, in *all* its various forms, therefore, are not only moral, but economic as well.

with others if the parties involved can trust each other, not fearing that they will be swindled. At least there must be a degree of confidence that if they are swindled there is sufficient legal backup to make sure that the offender is caught and made to pay restitution. The correct functioning of all human relations requires a moral and legal foundation. Without this moral and legal foundation economic activity based on the division of labour in a free society becomes useless. Robbery and cheating are then the only means of economic amelioration. As we shall see, it is significant that this kind of society has only developed to an advanced stage within a specifically Christian cultural setting.

What I have been describing so far is capitalism, i.e. private individuals using their skills and resources in order to exchange the fruit of their labour with others to their mutual advantage. This kind of trade is based on the desire for profit, quite obviously. But it is not based on the desire for profit at *any* expense or by *any* means. Capitalism, that is to say, assumes that business will be done honestly and that each party will be trustworthy in their dealings with each other. In other words it assumes moral and legal predictability. It assumes that honest contracts can be made between free individuals and that infringements of such contracts can be dealt with by the legal authorities. Capitalism, therefore, is private ownership of the means of production and distribution in a free society where economic activity takes place on the basis of a moral code enforceable by the magistrate or civil government.

§3
Economic Rationalisation

This means that the raw desire for profit at all costs and by any means is *not* what characterises capitalism. What characterises capitalism is *economic rationalisation*, i.e. the *subordination* of the profit motive to a particular means of acquisition based on the mutual advancement of all parties involved and the *growth* of that means of social amelioration through the virtues of honesty, thrift and hard work. This is precisely what Max Weber argued in his famous essay *The Protestant Ethic and the Spirit of Capitalism*. The raw desire for profit has existed in all societies and in all ages, and Weber used the term "capitalistic adventurer" of those who sought profits by means of economic activities that were "predominantly of an irrational and speculative character."[5] The activities of these capitalistic adventurers were often "directed to acquisition by force, above all the acquisition of booty, whether directly in war or in the form of continuous fiscal booty by exploitation of subjects."[6] But such practices do not constitute the distinctive form of capitalism that has characterised modern Western economic activity, and it is this Western form of economic activity that is usually denoted by the term capitalism. The kinds of acquisition described by Weber under the term "capitalistic adventurer" can be and were achieved by means of piracy and military domination, not economic rationalisation. Indeed, this kind of capitalism can be observed in the policies of even modern Marxist and socialist States,—e.g Germany under Hitler, the USSR, and a host of other Soviet satellites and Third World regimes—which repudiated Western capitalism as described by Weber.

However, capitalism as I am using the term, i.e. Western capitalism from the mid- seventeenth century to the mid-twentieth century (less consistently since the end of the Second World War), has been the product of a desire for profit subjected to a particular means of acquisition based on a distinctive ethic. According to Weber this distinctive means was the "rational capitalistic organization of (for-

[5] Max Weber, *The Protestant Ethic and the Spirit of Capitalism* (London: Unwin Paperbacks, 1985 [1930]), p. 20. See also Appendix F, "Max Weber and the Protestant Doctrine of the Calling."

[6] *Ibid.* A good example of such capitalistic adventurers was the group of conquistadores organised under the leadership of Hernando Cortés, who conquered Mexico in the early sixteenth century (for a good modern account see Hugh Thomas, *The Conquest of Mexico* [London: Hutchinson, 1993]). Walter Ralegh and Francis Drake were good examples of the capitalistic adventurer in sixteenth-century England. Renaissance Italy provided many similar examples of this phenomenon. Of the highly developed Renaissance Italian, Jacob Burckhardt wrote: "The force of his imagination explains, for example, the fact that he was the first gambler on a large scale in modern times. Images of future wealth and enjoyment rose in such lifelike colors before his eyes, that he was ready to hazard everything to reach them. The Mohammedan nations would doubtless have preceded him in this respect, had not the Koran from the beginning set up the prohibition against gambling as a chief safeguard of Islamic morals, and directed the imagination of its followers to the search after buried treasure. In Italy the passion for play reached an intensity that often threatened or shattered the existence of the gambler. At the end of the fourteenth century Florence had already had its Casanova, a certain Buonaccorso Pitti who, in the course of his incessant journeys as merchant, political agent, diplomat, and professional gambler, won and lost sums so enormous that only princes like the Dukes of Brabant, Bavaria, and Savoy could play with him." (Jacob Burckhardt, *The Civilisation of the Renaissance in Italy* [New York: The New American Library of World Literature, Inc., 1961], p. 306.)

mally) free labour"[7]—in other words economic activity based on the division of labour in a free society that guarantees a high degree of moral and legal predictability.[8] Only in the West has this been present in any significant degree: "only suggestions of it are found elsewhere"[9] says Weber. And the ethic on which this kind of capitalism was based was the Protestant (i.e. biblical) ethic of honesty, thrift and hard work. But this distinctive ethic and means of economic betterment was set in the context of the Protestant understanding of the calling.[10] According to Weber, "that side of English Puritanism which was derived from Calvinism gives the most consistent religious basis for the idea of the calling . . ."[11] Accordingly, the Protestant concept of the calling will be examined and analysed here in reference to the thought and teaching of English Puritanism.

The essence of the Puritan concept of the calling was the belief that man has a duty to serve and glorify God in whatever walk of life and whatever situation he is placed, since according to the Protestant doctrine of predestination nothing happens by chance or

[7] Weber, *The Protestant Ethic and the Spirit of Capitalism*, p. 21.

[8] Weber also stressed the necessity of moral and legal predictability: "modern rational capitalism has need, not only of the technical means of production, but of a calculable legal system and of administration in terms of formal rules. Without it adventurous and speculative trading capitalism and all sorts of politically determined capitalisms are possible, but no rational enterprise under individual initiative, with fixed capital and certainty of calculations. Such a legal system and such administration have been available for economic activity in a comparative state of legal and formalistic perfection only in the Occident. We must hence inquire where that law came from" (*ibid.*, p. 25). As Weber goes on to demonstrate, this law came from the Protestant religion, especially from the Puritans. That is to say it came from a people who viewed the creation as the work of a rational and law-giving God, and who thus saw the whole of life, including economic life, in terms of a divinely instituted covenant between God and his people. Such a view of life necessarily produces a social order based on ethical and legal stability and facilitates rational economic activity.   [9] *Ibid.*, p. 21.

[10] According to Weber the word *calling* "is known only to the languages influenced by the Protestant translations of the Bible" (*General Economic History* [New Brunswick: Transaction Books], p. 367). See Appendix F, "Max Weber and the Protestant Doctrine of the Calling."

[11] *The Protestant Ethic and the Spirit of Capitalism*, p. 155. Weber's definition of Puritanism was a very broad one however. He says: "When we use the expression it is always in the sense which it took on in the popular speech of the seventeenth century, to mean the ascetically inclined religious movements in Holland and England without distinction of Church organization or dogma, thus including Independents, Congregationalists, Baptists, Mennonites, and Quakers" (*ibid.* p. 217). This definition is considerably wider than that usually given to the term by either theologians or church historians. For a more precise definition see Stephen C. Perks, *A Defence of the Christian State* (Taunton: Kuyper Foundation, 1998), p. 10, n5.

mistake and God is the ultimate author of all the circumstances in which man finds himself. The Puritan saw God's hand in all situations and sought to glorify God in all situations, and this meant in the workplace and in business and commerce just as much as in church and in private devotional life. According to Weber, for the Puritan "the only way of living acceptably to God was not to surpass worldly morality in monastic asceticism, but solely through the fulfilment of the obligations imposed upon the individual by his position in the world. That was his calling."[12] In other words man is called to labour diligently to the best of his ability in all circumstances for the glory of God. The effect of this conception of the calling on society was the rationalisation of economic life in accordance with the ethical principles of revealed religion (biblical Christianity). This Puritan concept of the calling was a fundamental element historically in the rise of modern capitalism as defined above.

The distinctive feature of Western capitalism is, therefore, *economic rationalisation*, i.e. the subjection of the desire for profit to rational economic principles based on honesty, thrift and hard work in a social order based on moral and legal predictability safeguarded by the magistrate. The development of this kind of capitalism took place significantly, though not perfectly, only in one period of history, viz the post-Reformation period of Western Europe, particularly northern Europe—i.e. Protestant Europe—and the United States of America, which consisted of former European colonies sharing a common Protestant heritage. This period lasted roughly up until the outbreak of World War Two. All forms of capitalism in other parts of the world today that share this distinctive form of economic rationalisation are based on the developments that took place in Protestant Europe and North America during this period—i.e. they are imitations of Western economies. An essential ingredient for the development of this kind of capitalism, though not the only one, was, as Weber has shown, the Puritan understanding of the calling and the "worldly asceticism" that accompanied it. Weber argued that the Puritan morality or "worldly asceticism," as he termed it, and the Puritan view of one's calling in life were important elements historically in the development and expansion of Western capitalism. The Puritan concept of the calling was essential to the world-view that produced the kind of morality that made the development of modern Western capitalism possible.

[12] *The Protestant Ethic and the Spirit of Capitalism*, p. 80.

§4
Puritanism and Capitalism

This thesis of Weber's has not gone unchallenged. Indeed, debunking Weber has become rather popular among some left-wing sociologists and economists. This being the case, it will be instructive to look a little closer into this connection and illustrate the Weber thesis from an actual Puritan document that typified, probably more than any other, Puritan thought and practice: the Westminster Confession of Faith and Catechisms.

Capitalism, as it has been defined above, can be seen quite clearly in Puritan thought—not as systematically developed and stated as I am presenting it here, but it is there nonetheless. For the Puritans, again citing Weber, "The campaign against the temptations of the flesh and the dependence on external things, was . . . not a struggle against the rational acquisition, but against the irrational use of wealth."[13] As we shall see, it is precisely the irrational use (i.e. consumption) of wealth, rather than the rational acquisition of wealth, that characterises socialism. Consequently, in the long term, socialism leads to the decapitalisation of society and to reduced standards of living. This is in stark contrast to capitalism, which leads to capitalisation generally and to economic growth and social amelioration for the whole of society. Weber goes on to say:

On the side of the production of private wealth, asceticism condemned both dishonesty and impulsive avarice. What was condemned as covetousness, Mammonism, etc., was the pursuit of riches for their own sake. For wealth in itself was a temptation. But here asceticism was the power "which ever seeks the good but ever creates the evil"; what was evil in its sense was possession and its temptations. For, in conformity with the Old Testament and in analogy to the ethical valuation of good works, asceticism looked upon the pursuit of wealth as an end in itself as highly reprehensible; but the attainment of it as a fruit of labour in a calling was a sign of God's blessing. And even more important: the religious valuation of restless, continuous, systematic work in a worldly calling, as the highest means to asceticism, and at the same time the surest and most evident proof of rebirth and genuine faith, must have been the most powerful conceivable lever for the expansion of that attitude toward life which we have here called the spirit of capitalism.[14]

[13] *Ibid.*, p. 171.   [14] *Ibid.*, p. 172.

The picture Weber paints of the Puritan is a very austere one, and doubtless there was an austerity to the Puritan ethic. However, many have considerably overemphasised this austerity, at least as a general characteristic of Puritanism. The result has been a caricature of Puritanism that does not do justice to all the facts.[15] Nevertheless, Weber's thesis is essentially correct and is now often referred to—and as often misunderstood and misconstrued—as the "Protestant work ethic." This work ethic was a vital ingredient for the success of modern Western-style economies.

The positive attitude of the Puritans towards the acquisition of wealth by lawful means can be seen quite clearly in the Puritan teaching on the Eighth Commandment. According to the Westmin-

---

[15] It is worth remembering that it was John Owen, considered by many to be the epitome of seventeenth-century Puritanism, who, while Vice-Chancellor of Oxford, was criticised for not dressing soberly enough, scorning formality and undervaluing his office "by going in quirpo like a young scholar, with powdered hair, snakebone bandstrings, lawn bands, a large set of ribbons pointed, and Spanish leather boots with large lawn tops, and his hat mostly cocked" (Peter Toon, *God's Statesman: The Life and Work of John Owen* [Exeter: The Paternoster Press, 1971], p. 73. Toon cites as his source Anthony Wood, *Athenae Oxonienses*, IV, col. 98). Also of interest in regard to this caricature of Puritanism is the following point made by Weber, which suggests a quite different motive for the antagonism shown towards Puritanism than the one usually encountered: "Calvinism opposed organic social organization in the fiscal-monopolistic form which it assumed in Anglicanism under the Stuarts, especially in the conceptions of Laud, this alliance of Church and State with the monopolists on the basis of the Christian-social ethical foundation. Its leaders were universally among the most passionate opponents of this type of politically privileged commercial, putting-out, and colonial capitalism. Over against it they placed the individualistic motives of rational legal acquisition by virtue of one's own ability and initiative. And, while the politically privileged monopoly industries in England all disappeared in short order, this attitude played a large and decisive part in the development of the industries which grew up in spite of and against the authority of the State. The Puritans (Prynne, Parker) repudiated all connection with the large-scale capitalistic courtiers and projectors [i.e. 'capitalistic adventurers'—SCP] as an ethically suspicious class. On the other hand, they took pride in their own superior middle-class business morality, which formed the true reason for the persecutions to which they were subjected on the part of those circles. Defoe proposed to win the battle against dissent by boycotting bank credit and withdrawing deposits. The difference of the two types of capitalistic attitude went to a very large extent hand in hand with religious differences. The opponents of the Nonconformists, even in the eighteenth century, again and again ridiculed them for personifying the spirit of shopkeepers, and for having ruined the ideals of old England. Here also lay the difference of the Puritan economic ethic from the Jewish; and contemporaries (Prynne) knew well that the former and not the latter was the bourgeois capitalistic ethic" (*The Protestant Ethic and the Spirit of Capitalism*, p. 179f.). For a good assessment of Puritan beliefs, attitudes and culture generally see Leyland Ryken, *Worldly Saints: The Puritans as They Really Were* (Grand Rapids, Michigan: Zondervan, [1986] 1990).

ster Shorter Catechism, "The eighth commandment *requireth* the lawful procuring and furthering the wealth and outward estate of *ourselves* and others" (Q. 74 *A.*). The Larger Catechism expands on this, and in what it says we can see many of the elements of economic life that have been mentioned above:

Q. 141. *What are the duties required in the eighth commandment?*
A. The duties required in the eighth commandment are, truth, faithfulness, and justice in contracts and commerce between man and man; rendering to every one his due; restitution of goods unlawfully detained from the right owners thereof; giving and lending freely, according to our abilities, and the necessities of others; moderation of our judgements, wills, and affections concerning worldly goods; a provident care and study to get, keep, use, and dispose these things which are necessary and convenient for the sustentation [support] of our nature, and suitable to our condition; a lawful calling, and diligence in it; frugality; avoiding unnecessary law-suits, and suretiship, or other like engagements; and an endeavour, by all just and lawful means, to procure, preserve, and further the wealth and outward estate of others, as well as our own.

The Catechism is essentially capitalistic in its understanding of the economic function of man's life. It promotes private ownership of property, including the means of production, and economic rationalisation based on the Christian virtues of honesty, thrift and hard work in a morally upright social order protected by the magistrate. Here the getting and keeping of wealth is encouraged as long as it is rationalised according to the moral teaching of the Christian faith. This means that wealth is not simply to be acquired for its own sake or purely out of a desire to consume it in the satisfaction of one's own desires and lusts—that is rather a feature of socialism, as we shall see. To seek wealth for its own sake or merely for oneself is wrong because the whole of life, including one's economic life, should be lived for the glory of God. What the Catechism advocates is the use of lawful means of economic acquisition and good economic management to further one's own interests and the interests of others in a life of service to *God* in a particular calling. In such an order we can help each other to preserve and better our own economic conditions and that of our neighbour. And this is precisely what the capitalist mode of production is all about, namely, promoting our own interests by promoting the interests of others. For the Puritans there was nothing inconsistent with the getting and keeping of wealth and serving God according to his will. Acquiring wealth lawfully is a means of serving God according to his will. Man can give thanks to God for his wealth and enjoy it knowing that it comes to him as God's blessing. It is the fruit of a life dedicated to God's glory and service in a particular calling, which is of benefit not only to oneself but also to one's neighbour with whom one trades. This is the biblical position, and we are told quite clearly in the Bible that the Lord delights in the prosperity of his people (Ps. 35:27).

Weber saw the Puritan element in the capitalist mentality. He saw that the Puritan asceticism—the willingness to be thrifty and hard working, to forgo present consumption in order to provide for the future and leave an inheritance, to subject the use of one's wealth to rational economic principles—created a surplus of capital, which could then be put to productive use and thereby facilitate the general economic amelioration of society. The Puritan did not profligately spend whatever he earned but ploughed as much as he could back into his business. As a result capital was created and put to productive use that would not otherwise have been available. This process is the very essence of capitalistic activity and it led to greater productivity and the creation of wealth and prosperity. It advanced the possibilities and specialisation of labour and brought about a sustained period of economic growth. But this would not have happened without the kind of mentality that characterised the Puritan outlook. The Puritan outlook was future oriented; it took seriously the biblical injunction to leave an inheritance to one's grandchildren (Pr. 13:22). It was this Puritan work ethic, combined with the process of economic rationalisation, that led to the capital accumulation and immense economic productivity and creation of wealth in the period of the Industrial Revolution in England.

The effect of this Puritan mentality on the English economy can be seen quite clearly in the turbulent history of the seventeenth century. Up until the mid-seventeenth century in England most industries were controlled by guilds, which restricted output and regulated quality. Under the Stuarts before the Civil Wars there was also a wide variety of monopolies, granted by the crown, which controlled the supply of materials. With the exception of the most basic necessities of life almost every area of industry operated under government licence at some time or other during this period.[16] Those who belonged to guilds or had access to a monopoly trade were able

[16] Christopher Hill, *The Century of Revolution* (Edinburgh: Thomas Nelson and Sons Ltd., 1961), pp. 28–37.

to benefit from a restricted and protected means of livelihood, which was essentially irrational from an economic point of view, and therefore less efficient. This situation restricted the development of free trade and slowed down economic amelioration considerably. "In so far as Stuart governments had anything which could be described as an economic policy, it was to support the monopoly London export companies against interlopers, to slow down industrial development and control it through the guilds and monopolies, to suppress middlemen."[17] Thus, "During the general slump of the early twenties 'England was left saddled with a rigid, oligopolistic, high-cost economy, ill-fitted to cope with a competitor [the Dutch] who throve on low costs, adaptability and up-to-dateness.'"[18] With the rise to power of the Puritans all this changed. The industrial monopolies were abolished by the Long Parliament and under Cromwell the power of the guilds was largely broken. Freedom of trade and entrance into former guild occupations increased considerably. Christopher Hill described the economic achievements of the Commonwealth period in the following terms:

Employers and *entrepreneurs* were freed from government regulation and control in various ways. Attempts to supervise quality of manufacture and to fix prices were abandoned; industrial monopolies were abolished. Greater freedom was established in relations between employers and workmen. The government stopped trying to regulate wage rates, to compel employers to keep their employees at work in time of slump. Taxation became regular, if heavy, and (except under Army rule) it was controlled by representatives of the taxpayers. Henceforth employers were limited in expanding or contracting their business solely by economic considerations. "The relation between masters and servants," wrote Clarendon nostalgically, was "dissolved by the Parliament, that their army might be increased by the prentices against their masters' consent." The Act of 1563, insisting on a seven-year period of apprenticeship, was not enforced. The common law, so favourable to absolute property rights, triumphed over the prerogative courts.[19]

These measures were part of an extensive rationalisation of economic life that greatly facilitated productivity and led to the *creation* of wealth, rather than the *control* of wealth, which was what essentially characterised Stuart economic policy. Cromwell also successfully crushed the socialistic movements that began to appear at this time, the

[17] *Ibid.*, p. 29.
[18] *Ibid.*, p. 37. The quotation is from J. D. Gould, "The Trade Depression of the Early 1620s," in *Economic History Review* (second ser.), 7, p. 87.   [19] *Ibid.*, p. 146.

Diggers, which was a proto-communistic movement, and the Levellers, which was not really a communistic group so much as a moderate democratic group.[20] The Commonwealth represented in a very real sense therefore the beginning of both the Industrial Revolution—which is usually dated from about the middle of the eighteenth century when technical improvements in industry began to appear much more rapidly—and the British Empire, which would not have been possible without the wealth generated by the Industrial Revolution.

§5
Investment and Capitalisation

Let us now pursue the mechanics of the capitalist mode of production a little further. Suppose someone were living at the beginning of the Industrial Revolution and practising a traditional craft or trade as a means of livelihood—making cloth for instance. After his needs are taken care of he has some excess income left over. Over a period of years he is able to save this excess income, perhaps even lend it out at interest, until he has accumulated a substantial sum of money. He can now consume this wealth directly by purchasing a very expensive luxury item that he has always admired and desired and that is hand made and therefore produced in very small quantities.

Alternatively, he can forgo the use of this luxury item and use the money to buy a power loom,[21] which is able to produce more cloth at a cheaper price than his old handloom. He then sells the cloth he has made and makes a little more profit. He ploughs this profit back into his business (i.e. he uses it to purchase more capital equipment) and each month his output increases, and of course his profits increase also. As a result of the use of the power loom productivity increases, and as more cloth becomes available on the market prices fall. The cost of clothing then falls. The product becomes available to more people at a price they can more easily afford, which further stimulates productivity and increases profits.

---

[20] The democratic credentials of the Levellers have, however, been exaggerated and misconstrued by modern politicians and political historians. For a good assessment of Leveller aims see Christopher Hill, *op. cit.*, p. 129ff. See also Stephen C. Perks, *op. cit.*, p. 98ff.

[21] The power loom was invented by Edmund Cartwright in 1785.

This process then has knock-on effects in other industries also, since the increase in discretionary income for the general public generated by greater productivity and cheaper prices in one industry will be spent on a wide variety of goods and services, thereby increasing demand in other industries (creating *new* jobs also). The increased profits generated by this process can then be invested in capital and technical development, leading to innovation and greater productivity, mass production and lower prices generally. By using his wealth productively (i.e. by investing it in capital), rather than consuming it immediately, our cloth maker has created wealth not only for himself but also for those with whom he trades by helping to provide a greater supply of goods at a cheaper price. As this process is undertaken throughout other industries other goods, including those that were formerly luxury items—perhaps the one that the cloth maker had previously forgone the consumption of in order to buy the power loom—come within the reach of the majority of the population and standards of living increase generally. Everyone benefits from this mode of production therefore. This process of investment and capitalisation leading to greater productivity, lower prices and the general rise of standards of living fulfils the Westminster Catechism's understanding of economic life, which requires "the lawful procuring and furthering the wealth and outward estate of ourselves and others." Capitalism leads to the creation of wealth and the general economic amelioration of everyone in society.

This process is the essence of the capitalist mode of production. This is necessarily a rather simple explanation of the process, and it must take place on a large scale to have any significant effect on the economy. But it is essentially what happened in the Industrial Revolution. It could not have happened, however, without the change in attitudes and practices brought about by the Puritans in the seventeenth century, and without the private ownership of the means of production in a market economy based on moral and legal predictability. It required honesty, thrift, hard work, moral and legal predictability and a future-oriented view of life. In short, it required a Christian (biblical) world-view.

§6
Socialism and the Decapitalisation of Society

We have seen that thrift and economic rationalisation led to the greater accumulation and productive use of capital in northern Europe after the Reformation. But we now live in an age that is characterised more by the *consumption* of wealth than by capital accumulation. The age of capitalism has been replaced by the age of consumerism. Of course, the availability of a much greater and varied supply of goods to satisfy consumer demands is testimony to the success of capitalism as a form of economic organisation of society. This in itself is a good thing. But this is not the only feature of modern Western economies. The problem is what we might call the characteristic spirit of the modern age. In the sphere of economics this characteristic spirit, which is *political* in nature, has supplanted the ideals upon which Western capitalism was based. Our society today is slowly but surely moving towards a form of political organisation in which the economy is dominated and controlled by political rather than rational economic criteria. This political system, if it is allowed to function unfettered according to its characteristic spirit—i.e. centralised political control of human activity (what used to be called slavery)—will lead ultimately to the consumption of the vast capital base that has been built up in previous centuries. Why?

Just as capital accumulation, economic rationalisation and the productive use of wealth are distinctive features of Western capitalism, the irrational use of wealth and the wasteful consumption of capital are distinctive features of socialism; and the twentieth century was the century of socialism. It is the rise of the socialist world-view and government management of the economy according to socialist principles that has, over the past fifty years or so, led to the present state of economic irrationality in the British economy. Although the Thatcher government of the 1980s was considerably less socialist than the left-wing and centre parties in Britain, it needs to be recognised that it was still essentially a socialist government. Of course it must be acknowledged that the implementation of the Thatcher government's policies did lead to some significant reforms and to some extent helped to move economic thinking away from socialist ideals; and doubtless any government must go slowly in seeking to reform the economy. But the true nature of Conservatism is not capitalistic necessarily, even if the Thatcher government did try in some measure to move towards capitalism. The effect of the twelve years of the Thatcher government was that the nation moved towards the grand socialist debacle more slowly than it would have done under the policies of either the Liberal Democrat or Labour parties. But move towards that debacle it surely did, and with a relentless illogicality that confuses and dismays, as can be seen from the current state of the nation's involvement with the grandest and most wasteful policy of economic irrationality in the history of the modern world next to Communism: the European Union. Unless this trend is reversed the kind of steady economic growth and social amelioration that we have come to expect and take for granted in the West will become a thing of the past. We must now consider the irrationalities of socialist economics.

The rest of this chapter will deal with the problems of economic calculation and capital consumption under socialist management of the economy and the characteristic spirit of socialism as compared with capitalism. The following chapter will deal with the central banking system, which is at the heart of the socialist economic machine.

(a) *Economic calculation under socialism.*[22] Under socialism, with its reliance on government-controlled and government-financed industries, subsidies, production quotas, import tariffs, wage and price controls, tax penalties and handouts to favoured groups, regulation of economic activity generally, and with all these factors a good deal of legal unpredictability, it becomes impossible to calculate rationally to the degree necessary to maintain the use of capital at its maximum productivity. Since socialism, by means of these policies, ruins the price mechanism, or at least significantly hinders its proper functioning, time, money and scarce resources get sidetracked into unproductive or less productive uses. The waste resulting from this situation is over and above the amount of taxpayer's money that is squandered by left-wing governments and councils. The result is, at best, a fall in the rate of economic growth, or stagnation, and in extreme socialist countries even a reverse, a decline in productivity and standards of living, i.e. decapitalisation. Socialism has reversed the trend towards economic rationalisation that Weber described in his essay.[23]

---

[22] See "The Price Mechanism and Economic Calculation" in Chapter Three.
[23] The problem of economic calculation in a socialist society has been dealt with in Ludwig von Mises, *Human Action, A Treatise on Economics* (Chicago: Contemporary

The motivation behind this mentality is twofold: first, there is the desire to cushion people from the realities of life in the real world, life in the world as God has created it and providentially governs it. It is an attempt to enable people to run away from their responsibilities into the arms of the benevolent State. Socialists want an easy ride on easy terms, social security and a living provided on a plate by the paternalistic State. Second, socialists are often motivated ideologically by envy of others. They see others who are more wealthy, who have a better standard of living, and they cannot bear it. They are gripped with envy. They therefore support those who promote policies aimed at appeasing their envy, at taking from the rich to give to the "poor," so-called. They want what they do not have. They therefore insist that the State take steps to provide them with it and with the general standard of living they desire, or at least, failing this, make sure that no one else is allowed to have such a standard of living. The capital base of the nation, which took centuries to build up, has been plundered in order to pay for this envy-driven redistribution of wealth within society. This has been accomplished through legalised theft on a grand scale by the State—income tax, sales tax (VAT), tariffs, control and expropriation of private property, inheritance tax, capital gains tax, company tax, graduated income tax, and fraud on a grand scale by means of government-generated inflation controlled through the central banking system. All this has been done in the name of "social justice." In reality, however, this amounts to little more than the politics of envy.[24]

(*b*) *Capital consumption*. The onslaught of socialism in this way, however, has also changed the way that those who have capital use it. Socialism has made the capitalist mode of living increasingly difficult. It confiscates and taxes away all it can of the profits that private individuals and companies make. By doing this it takes away the motivation to use one's wealth productively. Socialism flies flat in the face of the biblical principle that the legitimate fruit of one's labour is to be enjoyed and used with thankfulness. It denies the biblical dictum that "the hand of the diligent maketh rich" (Pr. 10:4 cf. Ps. 35:27). According to socialist theory individual prosperity is

---

Books, Inc., [1949] 1966), pp. 698–715; *idem, Socialism* (Indianapolis: Liberty Classics, [1936] 1981), pp. 67–107; and comprehensively in T. J. B. Hoff, *Economic Calculation in the Socialist Society* (Indianapolis: Liberty Press, [1949] 1981).

[24] Helmut Schoeck, *Envy, A Theory of Social Behaviour* (London: Secker and Warburg, 1969).

the result of oppression and expropriation. Socialism therefore works to confiscate wealth from those who have it and to redistribute it.

The effect of this is to create an immense disincentive to accumulate capital—in other words to *save*—or to pass on an inheritance to one's children. Rather than saving and freeing capital for productive use people consume their wealth while they have it. Socialism creates a disinclination to save and promotes a mentality of immediate consumption. Since individual thrift and hard work are heavily penalised people stop being thrifty and hard working. This was a well-known fact of life in Soviet Russia and the communist States. Under socialism all that saving does is to satisfy someone else's immediate wants, so people satisfy their own wants. And who can blame them?

When this kind of mentality is imbibed by a community the result is the decapitalisation of society. This consumption mentality, the short-sighted materialistic desire to consume one's wealth now rather than put it to productive use, is all part and parcel of the socialist system. Materialism, in the sense that the term is used today—i.e. ever increasing greed for more consumption goods that one cannot afford unless one squanders one's resources wastefully—is a feature of socialism not capitalism. Socialism leads to irrational economic policies aimed at appeasing a population that has swallowed a social ethics based on envy. As a consequence it retards capitalisation and eventually leads to decline, economic stagnation and even decapitalisation. The ultimate result of socialism therefore is not the redistribution of wealth, but the redistribution of *poverty*.

§7
The Spirit of Capitalism and the Spirit of Socialism

The "spirit of capitalism," so clearly analysed by Max Weber, and the spirit of socialism are diametrically opposed to each other and involve, indeed require, not only radically different forms of economic organisation but also incompatible political systems. The history of the Western economies from the Reformation to the mid-twentieth century and the history of Soviet Russia and any number of other Soviet satellites and Third World communistic regimes bears out this lesson with such clarity that only the blind ideologue who refuses to accept the facts of history can fail to recognise it. The former leads to economic rationalisation and social amelioration across the whole of society; the latter leads to decapitalisation on a national scale and the consequent pauperisation of all but the few who are able to seize the reins of despotic political power.

However, the diverse economic, political and social trends and ideologies observed in the history of Western and communist societies have a deeper religious cause than most historians, economists and political commentators are prone to admit of today. Few, especially among economists, have followed the lead given by Max Weber in this respect. The kind of economic order that we have been used to and that has flourished in the nations of the West for the past three and a half centuries is intimately bound up with the predominance of the Christian—and particularly the Protestant—world-view in these nations. It was a Christian cultural matrix that gave birth to the modern world, with its scientific and economic achievements, its high view of progress and the insistence on the necessity and value of man's bettering his conditions in life. With the waning of Christian influence in the Western nations there will be not only a decline in the value placed upon human life, but also a demise of the whole value system and culture that was a necessary precondition for the economic transformation of Northern Europe after the Reformation.

Perhaps *technological* progress will continue—although even this is by no means certain. But to what *ends* it will be directed and *who* will benefit from it will be determined by the kind of moral, or a-moral, values that inform the culture in which such technological improvements occur. In a culture that has a pagan view of life and a pagan view of justice and mercy it is doubtful whether the term progress will have the same content that it has had for a predominantly Christian culture; indeed, it is doubtful whether the term could be correctly used in a non-Christian culture since the very concept of progress as it is used today is intimately bound up with the Christian understanding of life and history.[25]

An indication of the use and value of technological progress in such a society can be ascertained by assessing the results of the purely technological progress, divorced from a Christian moral foundation, that have accrued to those former Soviet Union nations that have availed themselves of the benefits of the technological developments achieved in the West. On the whole the effects of technological

[25] See Stanley L. Jaki, *Science and Creation: From eternal cycles to an oscillating universe* (Edinburgh: Scottish Academic Press, 1986).

progress in these countries, rather than filtering through to the average man and thereby raising his standard and quality of life, as they did in the Christian West, were used merely to help strengthen a totalitarian regime that oppressed its people and denied to them virtually all the benefits that technological progress has brought to the peoples of the West. The few whose quality of life did change for the better were those who played the system, joined the party and climbed their way up by means of political influence. Their better standard of living was not the result of progress in the Western sense therefore. Rather, it was the result of exploitation of political power and privilege. Such exploitation has existed in all societies, even in those that for most people were the poorest and the least amenable to progress in the Western sense. This latter form of exploitative economic and social amelioration is of a piece with the kind of enterprise undertaken by Weber's "capitalistic adventurer" and is in sharp contrast to the "rational capitalistic organization of (formally) free labour" that has characterised Western economies. It is ironic that capitalistic Western economies should be considered exploitative by so many when the greatest and most severe forms of economic and political exploitation have arisen in those societies that have self-consciously and deliberately rejected the capitalistic (i.e. Christian) form of economic organisation of society.

Yet it is faulty logic for the newly de-communised ex-Soviet nations to think that a mere freeing up of markets will produce the kind of economic transformation that is presently desired and anticipated as the fruit of such reforms by the leadership of those nations. Such transformations do not occur in a religious and moral vacuum, much less in an environment whose social and political ethos is strongly antagonistic towards the religious attitudes necessary for such a transformation, as is that of modern Russia. The kind of economic progress desired by the Russian people today—i.e. a Western life-style—was only achieved in the West because the Reformation trans-formed society's world-view in the sixteenth and seventeenth centu-ries. And this is because there must needs be, along with the mere technology of progress, an acceptance of the morality of work, honesty, thrift, a commitment to building for future generations,— and thus a view of the meaning of life that goes beyond the indi-vidual's own self-interest and finds its purpose in the creative act of God—and, particularly relevant in a society heavily influenced by socialist ideology, a denial and rejection of the sin of envy, if society is to achieve economic growth and prosperity on the scale that the West has experienced it. Such were the virtues that, for example in England, where the Christian understanding of the meaning of life and work was able to flourish, made Western economic prosperity possible. The economic factors were necessary also, of course; but without these fundamental religious and moral foundations it is doubtful that the outcome would have been the same.

As Weber pointed out in his essay *The Protestant Ethic and the Spirit of Capitalism*, the basic elements of the capitalist mode of production were already in existence before the Reformation.[26] But not until after the Reformation, when the Protestant ethic and doctrine of the calling had transformed the everyday lives of ordinary people, did the *spirit* of capitalism begin to transform the economic landscape of northern Europe. The dramatic growth of the Western economies in the two centuries following the Reformation was totally without historical precedent. It has been estimated that total economic output during this period doubled.[27] In the eighteenth century this rate of growth increased considerably, with the more advanced economies such as Britain growing by a full percentage point each year.[28] By comparison, between A.D. 500 and 1500 the economies of Western Europe grew on average only by one tenth of a percentage point per year.[29] The rates of growth experienced by Western economies in the twentieth century have been exponential. Paul Ormerod states that "the Western economies grew as much in percentage terms between 1950 and 1970 as they did between 500 and 1500. And given the much higher base at the start of the 1950s, the absolute increase in the volume of goods and services produced was enormously greater."[30]

This kind of growth was not a feature of Soviet Russia. According to G. North, "Naum Jasny, in his book, *Soviet Industrialization 1928–1952* (1961), reveals how Stalin used growth figures as propaganda devices, setting goals for the five-year plans (themselves propaganda devices more than planning tools) so high that no economic system could have produced the anticipated results. It was growth for the sake of growth. The actual per capita output of consumer goods did not significantly increase until the mid-1950's; only in 1952 did wage

---

[26] Weber, *The Protestant Ethic and the Spirit of Capitalism*, p. 91. See also Appendix F, "Max Weber and the Protestant Doctrine of the Calling."

[27] Angus Maddison, *Phases of Capitalist Development* (Oxford University Press, 1982), cited in Paul Ormerod, *The Death of Economics* (London: Faber and Faber, 1994), p. 10.   [28] *Ibid.*   [29] *Ibid.*   [30] Ormerod, *op. cit.*, p. 10.

rates reach the level that Czarist Russia had attained in 1913."[31] The Soviet economy, dominated by political control and lacking freedom of any kind (except perhaps on the black markets) was incapable of producing the kind of economic growth and social amelioration that has characterised the economies of Protestant Europe. The two systems of economic organisation are radically different in spirit and produce an enormous disparity in general standards of living. Unfortunately, under the aegis of the European Union the economies of Western Europe are now moving closer to the spirit that characterised the socialist economies of the Soviet Union. And this is happening at the very time when socialism has been proved incapable not only of delivering economic growth of the magnitude experienced under capitalism in the West but of even *maintaining* general standards of living much *lower* than those of contemporary Western nations.

Only a return to the Christian spirit of capitalism—i.e. the subordination of the acquisitive impulse (the profit motive) to rational economic principles based on the Christian ethic—will save the nations of the West from the irrational economics of socialist ideology and the inevitable economic decline that is the lot of nations that are seduced by the Siren-songs of a fairer society and greater wealth for all that socialism offers.

[31] G. North, *An Introduction to Christian Economics* (The Craig Press, 1973), p. 81.

CHAPTER FOUR

THE BANKING SYSTEM

§1
Definition and Relevance of the Banking System

THE best definition of the modern banking system I have seen was that given by R. S. Sayers: "Banks are institutions whose debts— usually referred to as 'bank deposits'—are commonly accepted in final settlement of other people's debts."[1] This is a precise definition of the modern banking system as far as it goes. However, in order to understand the banking system and how it affects the economy we need to understand the mechanism by which the banks' debts come to be accepted in final settlement of other people's debts. Further- more, the relevance of this subject is far wider than the practice of banking itself. Given the importance of the role that the banks play in the modern economy it is essential to a proper understanding of how the economy works as a whole that one has a proper grasp of the basic principles upon which the modern banking system operates. In order to gain an understanding of this we need to go back to the birth of modern banking in the seventeenth century. Before doing so, however, it will be instructive to look briefly at the biblical teaching on just weights and measures in order to gain a proper moral perspective on the issue of currency debasement, which is at the heart of the modern banking system.

§2
Biblical Teaching on the use of Just Weights and Measures

In the eighth century B.C., towards the end of the reign of King Uzziah of Judah, the prophet Isaiah rebuked the people of Jerusalem sharply for their crimes, corrupt morals, fraudulent business practices

---

[1] R. S. Sayers, *Modern Banking* (Oxford: The Clarendon Press, 1967, Seventh Edition), p. 1.

and neglect of the poor and needy. This is what Isaiah said of Jerusalem:

How is the faithful city become an harlot! it was full of judgement [i.e. justice—SCP]; righteousness lodged in it; but now murderers. Thy silver is become dross, thy wine mixed with water: Thy princes are rebellious, and companions of thieves: every one loveth gifts, and followeth after rewards: they judge not the fatherless, neither doth the cause of the widow come unto them. (Is. 1:21–23)

At the time coins were not in use as a form of money. However, silver was used as money and when something was bought for silver the purchaser would weigh out the silver in front of the vendor (cf. Gen. 23:16; Jer. 32:9). In this way small bars or ingots of silver would be used as a medium of exchange. When Isaiah says "Thy silver is become dross" he is referring to a process whereby base metals, e.g. tin, were mixed with the silver, thereby decreasing the silver content of the metal while at the same time increasing the total number of ingots that could be produced.[2] When this was done the appearance of the ingot would be that of silver, even though a percentage of it was tin, which is a less valuable metal than silver. This debased ingot could then be passed off as pure silver in exchange for goods and services. By mixing tin with his silver in this way the debaser could increase his money supply and buy goods and services cheaper than he could were he to pay for them with pure silver. The one receiving the money would most likely not be able to tell the difference between pure silver ingots and debased ingots containing tin.

The Bible is very strict about the use of fair weights and measures. Here are some of the laws covering weights and measures:

Ye shall do no unrighteousness in judgement, in meteyard, in weight or in measure. Just balances, just weights, a just ephah, and a just hin, shall ye have: I am the Lord your God, which brought you out of the land of Egypt. Therefore shall ye observe all my statutes, and all my judgements, and do them: I am the Lord. (Lev. 19:35–37)

Thou shalt not have in thy bag divers weights, a great and a small. Thou shalt not have in thine house divers measures, a great and a small. But

---

[2] Gary North, *An Introduction to Christian Economics* (The Craig Press, 1976), p. 4ff. The rabbis, however, understood this verse to refer to the taking of interest (see Exodus Rabbah, XXXI, 4).

thou shalt have a perfect and just weight, a perfect and just measure shalt thou have: that thy days may be lengthened in the land which the Lord thy God giveth thee. For all that do such things, and all that do unrighteously, are an abomination unto the Lord thy God. (Dt. 25:13–16)

These laws forbid fraud. When tin is mixed with silver and then made into ingots of a particular weight the silver content is less than it appears to be. The weight of silver contained in a given bar is less than the total weight of the bar. To use these debased ingots as a medium of exchange under the pretence that they are pure silver is fraud and a direct breach of God's law. Such practices are unacceptable to God: "a false balance is an abomination to the Lord" (Pr. 11:1).

What Isaiah condemns in chapter 1:21–23, therefore, is precisely the same phenomenon as the debasement of coinage. Such fraud is immoral and forbidden by God's law whether it is practised by individuals or by governments.

§3
Inflation and the Debasement of Currency

We are led to believe today that inflation is a general and sustained rise in the level of prices. This is not so, although inflation usually leads to rising prices. Inflation is *an increase in the money supply*. An increase in the money supply in turn causes prices generally to rise, other things being equal. When inflation is caused by the debasement of monetary metal or by counterfeiting of any kind it is a direct transgression of God's law, as stated in the Eighth Commandment and further expounded in Lev. 19:35–37 and Dt. 25:13–16. These laws clearly require the use of fair weights and measures and forbid all forms of deceit in economic and monetary affairs.

We have a long history of inflation caused by the debasement of currency. At the end of the thirteenth century, for example, the weight of the English silver penny was 22 grains troy. By the beginning of the seventeenth century it had fallen to 7¾, a reduction in weight of nearly 65 per cent.[3] For a government with sufficient power to

[3] H. O. Meredith, *Economic History of England* (London: Sir Isaac Pitman and Sons Ltd., 1936), p. 162. On the history of English coinage generally see C. R. Josset, *Money in Britain, A History of the Coins and Notes of the British Isles* (Newton Abbot: David and Charles, 1971). Anglo-Saxon coinage, in contrast to English coinage in the second

enforce its will debasement of coinage has always been an easy and favourite method of meeting unforeseen financial liabilities. In the reign of Henry VIII, for instance, the weight of the penny was reduced by one sixth from 12 to 10 grains.[4] Henry VIII also debased the gold coinage, reducing the weight of the sovereign from 240 to 192 grains and its fineness from 23.75 to 20 carat gold.[5] There was, consequently, throughout Henry's reign, and particularly in the two decades following his debasement of the coinage (the 1540s and 1550s) a sustained and widespread increase in the cost of living. Between the succession of Henry VIII in 1509 and 1558, when Elizabeth came to the throne, prices of foodstuffs generally had nearly quadrupled.[6] From the point of view of the modern phenomenon of inflation, however, the crucial step came in the seventeenth century with the development of fractional reserve banking by the goldsmiths.

§4
The Origin of Fractional Reserve Banking

The history of modern banking goes back to the reign of king Charles I in the period just before the outbreak of the first Civil War. Normally the merchants kept their gold in the Tower of London. In 1640 Charles I was short of money. He closed the mint and seized £200,000 of merchants' bullion in the Tower, agreeing to return it only when he had extracted a forced loan of £40,000 from its owners on the security of the customs.[7] Naturally, confidence in the Tower

---

millennium, was remarkably pure. Æthelred and Cnut, for example, passed laws requiring the improvement of the coinage and the correction of all unjust weights and measures (VI Æthelred 32, II Cnut 8 and 9). The rationale for this legislation came from a stated concern that God's law (i.e. biblical law: Lev. 19:35–37, Dt. 25:13–16) be adhered to in these matters. See Stephen C. Perks, *Christianity and Law: An Enquiry into the Influence of Christianity on the Development of English Common Law* (Whitby: Avant Books, 1993), pp. 25–30.

[4] Meredith, *op. cit.*, p. 170.

[5] James Mackay, *A History of Modern English Coinage: Henry VII to Elizabeth II* (Longman), p. 14f.

[6] Sir John Clapham, *A Concise Economic History of Britain from the Earliest Times to 1750* (Cambridge University Press, 1966 [1949]), p. 187. The coinage was restored early in Elizabeth's reign but prices continued to rise sharply thereafter due to the influx of silver into Europe from the New World (*ibid.*).

[7] George Chandler, *Four Centuries of Banking as illustrated by the Bankers, Customers and Staff associated with the constituent banks of Martins Bank Limited* (London: B. T. Batsford Ltd, 1964), Vol. 1, p. 62. This was a consignment of gold destined for Dunkirk

as a place of safe deposit was destroyed by this and the merchants and moneyed men looked elsewhere for a safe place to store their money. This business fell to the goldsmiths, whose strong-rooms offered relative safety from such political outrages.

As bankers the goldsmiths developed a number of important techniques for transferring money and creating credit within the economy.[8] The first of these was the banknote.[9] When someone deposited his money with a goldsmith for safe keeping he was issued with a receipt for the said amount. It soon became apparent that it was much easier to pay for goods and services by handing over these receipts than by withdrawing gold or silver from the goldsmith's strong-room, which would then be redeposited with another or even the same goldsmith. Consequently, these receipts, or "running cash notes" as they were called, began to circulate as money. They were essentially claims to a given amount of money deposited with a certain goldsmith bearing a promise to pay the bearer on demand the sums specified on them. As the use of these running cash notes increased they were issued in standard units such as £5 and £10. These notes were the forerunners of the modern banknote.

A second development in banking practice came when it was realised that payments could be made without the use of banknotes either. A letter instructing the goldsmith to pay out a certain amount of gold or silver from one's own stock to a third party was all that was needed. If the one to whom the payment was to be made already had a deposit with the same goldsmith as the one making the payment, or was prepared to make a deposit with the same goldsmith, the money could be transferred by simply debiting one account and crediting the other. This kind of transaction was the forerunner of the modern cheque. These early cheques were in circulation in the

---

(Meredith, *op. cit.*, p. 221. Meredith puts the value of the bullion seized by Charles at £130,000).

[8] See E. L. Hebden Taylor, *Economics, Money and Banking* (Nutley, New Jersey: The Craig Press, 1978), p. 72ff. This book is an excellent general introduction to Christian economics. For a more detailed account of the emergence of the goldsmith bankers see J. Milnes Holden, *The History of Negotiable Instruments in English Law* (London: The Athlone Press, 1955), p 70ff., 204ff. See also Sir John Clapham, *The Bank of England, A History* [Cambridge University Press, 1944], Vol. I, p. 20ff.

[9] Negotiable instruments had a long history prior to this development and their use can be traced back to the Arab traders of the eighth century A.D. But it was during the period under consideration here—i.e. the second half of the seventeenth century—that they first began to function as the prototype of the modern banknote. See J. Milnes Holden, *op. cit.*

latter half of the seventeenth century, but they really came into more extensive use after an Act of 1708 limited the issue of banknotes by banks other than the Bank of England.[10]

The third and most important development came when the goldsmiths began the practice of fractional reserve banking. In any other walk of life this kind of practice would be known by another name, but it is a peculiar fact of economic life that men will not acknowledge the phenomenon of fractional reserve banking for what it really is: *fraud*.

Only a certain proportion of the gold and silver deposited with the goldsmiths was, at any one time, being withdrawn and used in circulation as cash. The rest was simply sitting in their vaults gathering dust, although it was represented by the goldsmiths' notes, which functioned in the economy in the same way that the gold would have done had it been in circulation—the notes simply replaced the gold. The goldsmiths soon realised that once their reputation as bankers had been established and there was considerable public confidence in their notes they could loan out, at interest, this stock of gold not normally in circulation. This meant that they could offer interest on money deposited with them for safe-keeping and thereby attract more customers, enabling them to expand their business. George Chandler commented on this aspect of the goldsmiths' business:

> After the Civil War the practice increased of encouraging people to deposit money with the goldsmiths by allowing them interest. This was a great step forward in modern banking and was practised by Backwell. Country gentlemen began to deposit their rents with him and servants their masters' money, which had been placed in their custody for safe-keeping. Pepys refers in his diary to his delight when he first received interest on the money he had deposited.[11]

However, once the goldsmith had taken this step the total amount of claims for gold against him was greater than his ability to meet

[10] J. Milnes Holden, *op. cit.*, p. 93f., 212ff. This Act made it illegal for any corporation (other than the Bank of England) or a partnership of more than six members to issue notes payable on demand. It's effects were eventually overturned outside London by the Country Bankers Act 1826, which permitted banks outside a 65 mile radius of London to issue banknotes. Eighteen years later the Bank Charter Act, 1844 again placed restrictions on the issue of banknotes by private banks, thereby ensuring that the issue of banknotes would ultimately be concentrated in the Bank of England.

[11] Chandler, *op. cit.*, p. 69. This practice probably began during the Civil Wars; see J. Milnes Holden, *op. cit.*, p. 70ff.

those claims. In other words he was insolvent. This was hardly the "great step forward in modern banking" that Chandler claims for it. In fact this practice was the root cause of the unstable economic conditions that blight the economy to this day.

Suppose, for example, that a goldsmith has £1,000 of gold deposited with him for safe keeping. He observes that only a small proportion of this gold is withdrawn for use in circulation. As some customers withdraw gold others are depositing it and he needs no more than £100 at any one time in order to maintain an adequate cash reserve. He therefore loans out the remaining £900 of gold in his vaults. The important point to grasp here is that although this gold was not previously in circulation as gold coin it was nonetheless represented by running cash notes or receipts to the value of £900, which functioned in the economy in the same way that the gold would have functioned had it been in circulation. The goldsmith has now loaned out the £900 of gold previously kept in his vaults, which was represented by these notes. He now has claims against him for £1,000 of gold in the form of notes—promises to pay the bearer on demand—but only £100 of gold reserved to meet these claims. From his original stock of £1,000 of gold he has therefore created an extra £900 in the form of running cash notes (i.e. banknotes). As long as public confidence remains high and his customers have no reason to suspect what he is doing they will probably not all claim their gold at the same time.

But the goldsmith's ability to create money does not stop here. Once he observes that less than say 10 per cent of the gold deposited with him is being withdrawn for use in circulation at any one time he can make loans using his own notes rather than the £900 of actual gold stored in his vaults. If, as in the example above, he starts with £1,000 of gold he can issue *extra* notes for up to £9,000. The £1,000 of gold in his vaults then functions in the same way that the £100 of gold not loaned out in the first example functioned, i.e. it becomes merely a cash reserve. Again, as long as there is public confidence in his trustworthiness and in his ability to meet his liabilities he is safe. But in fact he is not able to meet his liabilities. He has issued multiple notes that are circulating in the economy as claims against the same amount of gold. In fact he has claims against him for £10,000 of gold but has only £1,000 of gold reserved to meet those claims.

This kind of banking is called *fractional reserve banking*. The amount of gold reserved for meeting the goldsmith's liabilities represents only a fraction of the total claims for gold against him in the form of notes. The goldsmith is able to meet only a fraction of his liabilities therefore. He has created notes containing a promise to pay the bearer on demand a certain sum of gold or silver. But he is unable to honour that promise. He has up to nine times more liabilities than he is able to meet.

§5
Problems with the Fractional Reserve System

There are a number of important criticisms to be levelled against the fractional reserve system. In the first place, this kind of banking practice is quite obviously fraudulent because up to ninety per cent of the goldsmith's notes are bogus claims. If everyone holding these notes were to claim their gold at the same time the goldsmith, unable to meet the demand, would be declared bankrupt. The goldsmith is therefore making an immoral profit by loaning out other people's money, or else using it as a basis for creating a vast amount of IOUs in the form of banknotes that cannot be honoured, without their permission and without informing them of the considerable risks involved. When confidence in the goldsmith fails the holders of these banknotes will attempt to claim their gold. But not everyone will succeed in doing so before the goldsmith is declared insolvent, and hence a large number of people will be defrauded of what rightfully belongs to them. The action of everyone trying to claim their gold at once is called a *run on the bank*. The first recorded incident of such a run on a bank occurred in 1667 following the defeat of the English fleet by a Dutch squadron in the Medway and the bombardment of Sheerness.[12]

The immoral profits made in the form of interest by this kind of banking cannot be construed as a legitimate reward for the taking of risks involved with lending money. This is not to say that lending money at interest is wrong *per se*. The fact that people value present economic goods more than they do the same goods at a future date makes interest inescapable. Lending money at interest is a legitimate practice since the Bible allows men to charge interest, though not

---

[12] Chandler, *op. cit.*, p. 73; Hebden Taylor, *op. cit.*, p. 77. The incident was recorded by Samuel Pepys in his diary.

in all circumstances. The point to note about the fractional reserve banking system is that the goldsmith in effect loans out money that he does not have; he creates the money that he lends at interest by issuing unbacked banknotes that function in the economy just like money. These banknotes, once they have entered the economy, represents wealth that neither the goldsmith nor the one who borrows them from him has the right to dispose of. The goldsmith makes his profit out of a fraud.

Looked at from another point of view the goldsmith has monetised his debts, since each note he issues is an IOU, a claim against him for a certain amount of gold that he is obligated to pay the bearer on demand. By issuing unbacked notes he has contracted debts, consisting of claims against him for gold that he does not have, which function in the economy as money.

Second, this kind of banking practice violates an important biblical principle, namely that one should not contract multiple debts against the same security:

If thou lend money to any of my people that is poor by thee, thou shalt not be to him as an usurer, neither shalt thou lay upon him usury. If thou at all take thy neighbour's raiment to pledge, thou shalt deliver it unto him by that the sun goeth down: For that is his covering only, it is his raiment for his skin: wherein shall he sleep? and it shall come to pass, when he crieth unto me, that I will hear; for I am gracious. (Ex. 22:25–27)

Compassion demanded that when a poor man borrowed anything against the security of his only coat and the coat was then deposited in the custody of the creditor, it had to be returned to him at night since he had nothing else to sleep in.[13] But upon rising the coat was to be handed over again to the creditor as security for the loan.[14]

---

[13] Dt. 24:17 stipulates however that a cloak is not to be taken as a pledge from a widow: "You shall not pervert the justice due to an alien or the fatherless, nor take a widow's garment as a pledge."

[14] The kind of security contemplated in Ex. 22:25–27 is very different from the kind of security required for modern commercial loans however. The difference is that in Ex. 22:25–27 the poor man's security is inalienable, and the loan remains throughout a mercy loan. Even upon default the poor man's cloak could not be permanently appropriated by the creditor to compensate him for his loss. Furthermore, the Jubilee laws meant that after a maximum of six years the debt would be cancelled altogether. By contrast a non-charitable loan is not subject to the laws governing poor loans and the security taken is such as would ensure that the creditor would be reimbursed in case of default, i.e. the security consists of assets that can be sold in order to make repayment to the creditor if need be. The security offered

As a result the debtor could not use the coat as security for a second loan. This practice of lodging the security for a loan with the creditor meant that it was not possible to acquire multiple debts against the same security. This limited a poor man's ability to acquire debt. G. North comments on this law:

> The collateral ("surety") in this case is a benefit to the creditor only indirectly. Its real function is to limit the indebtedness of the borrower. The man who needs a loan is permitted to indebt himself and his family only up to the value of his collateral. His immediate property determines the extent of the mortgage on his future. While his collateral is in the possession of one creditor, it cannot simultaneously be used as collateral for additional loans from other creditors. The benefit to the creditor is indirect: his possession of the collateral during the day guarantees him that the debtor is not in debt beyond his probable capacity to repay. The size of the loan (and therefore the extent of the debtor's enslavement) is limited by the debtor's general economic capacities. He is forbidden to indebt himself too far.[15]

In principle Exodus 22:25–27 forbids multiple indebtedness and therefore the kind of fraud involved in the fractional reserve banking system. When a goldsmith issues claims in the form of notes or creates demand deposits that can be drawn upon by cheque he creates debts, claims against him for gold. If the gold stored in his vaults covers only a fraction of these liabilities he is multiply indebted and unable to honour fully his promise to pay out on demand the gold deposited by his creditors should they all exercise their right to redeem their notes or withdraw their deposits at the same time. Fractional reserve banking is therefore in principle a transgression of the law governing debt in Scripture.

Third, this kind of banking is also a debasement of currency and inherently inflationary. The goldsmith has increased the amount of

---

in a charitable loan of the kind discussed here, therefore, has a very different purpose from that required by a non-charitable loan, namely, to limit the indebtedness of the borrower. The purpose of security offered on a non-charitable loan is to ensure that the creditor can be compensated if the borrower defaults. This difference between the nature of the security required distinguishes a charitable loan from a non-charitable loan. Security offered on a charitable loan would be such that to be without the use of it would put the borrower at risk of his health or life—i.e. it is property that cannot be distrained without transgressing a more fundamental law, viz. "thou shalt not kill." Likewise Dt. 24:6, "No man shall take the nether or upper millstone to pledge: for he taketh a man's life to pledge." See also Appendix B, "A Christian View of Interest" note 31, p. 261f.

[15] G. North, *op. cit.*, p. 9f.

money in circulation. Though a large percentage of his banknotes are not backed by gold they still function in the economy as money because the unsuspecting public believes them to be redeemable for gold and therefore people are willing to use them as a medium of exchange.

As these unbacked banknotes filter through into the economy the value of money falls—other things being equal. This is because the value of money, like that of any other good, is subject to supply and demand. Goods that are scarce are more valuable than those that are available in more abundant supply. When the supply of money is increased its value per unit falls because it is then less scarce. By issuing unbacked notes the goldsmith has increased the amount of money in circulation, but he has not increased the amount of *wealth* within the economy; he has simply brought about a situation in which the same amount of wealth is represented by a greater supply of money. But the goldsmith has increased the purchasing power, and thus the *wealth* of those who borrow from him by issuing them with unbacked notes. This increase in wealth for those who borrow and spend into circulation the newly created money is offset by a decrease in the wealth of the rest of the money-holding population. Those who do not borrow the unbacked notes still have the same amount of money, but once the inflation has run its course in the economy, with the consequent effect this has on the aggregate level of prices, their money is worth less in terms of the goods it will buy (purchasing power). The goldsmith, by inflating the money supply, does not create more wealth; what he does is to *redistribute* it to those who borrow his newly created banknotes.

This is quite unjust; it is in reality a form of theft. The goldsmith has not broken into anyone's house and stolen their goods, but he has, nonetheless, defrauded others by debasing the currency. This is what happens: inflation of the money supply leads to an aggregate rise in the level of prices (other things being equal), though there is a time lag during which the effects of the inflation slowly filter through into the economy. Initially the demand for certain goods increases whilst the supply remains unchanged. Prices rise, therefore, until supply once again meets demand.[16] Those who are forced to

---

[16] Were the prices of these goods to be kept artificially low instead of being allowed to find their market level the result would be a shortage. This is what happens when governments impose price controls. The combination of shortages and price controls then leads to black markets.

pay higher prices for these goods then raise the price of the goods and services they sell in order to maintain their income in real terms. This process is eventually repeated throughout the whole economy. But not everyone is able to do this, at least not to a level that would make up for the loss of purchasing power caused by the debasement. This is because inflation effects a redistribution of wealth within society to those who initially have access to the new money and away from those who do not. The effect of an aggregate rise in the level of prices will be to price some consumers out of the market for certain goods. For example, in an inflationary economy those on fixed wages will have to pay higher prices for the essentials of life. This will affect their discretionary income and therefore their overall standard of living. They will have to cut back on the amount of money they spend on non-essential goods in order to allocate funds to essentials, the prices of which, as a result of inflation, have risen, even though their own incomes have not risen accordingly. Thus, service providers and manufacturers and retailers of some goods may not be able to raise prices in line with inflation and stay in business. On the other hand, those initially having access to the new money benefit by having increased purchasing power; they will be able to afford higher prices. Not everyone is affected by inflation in the same way. Some service providers and manufacturers will benefit from this, i.e. they will experience a boom. Inflation effects an overall reconfiguration of market conditions. Although there is a rise in the aggregate level of prices, it is not an *even* rise; not all prices rise together or to the same extent, and some may not rise at all.

Other things being equal—e.g. no price controls—there is, therefore, a general rise in prices after an increase in the money supply. This is because the supply of goods and services remains the same while the supply of money has risen. Assuming all the money circulating within the economy will be used to purchase all the available goods and services, prices generally must rise until equilibrium between supply and demand are re-established. In other words, goods and services eventually find a new price level at which all the money circulating within the economy is used up. The important thing to remember is that not everyone gets the use of the new money simultaneously. The fractional reserve banking system produces, therefore, a permanent redistribution of wealth to those who are prepared to borrow the new money.

Those who borrow the new money are able to purchase goods

and services that previously they could not afford. It might be objected that no permanent redistribution of wealth has accrued to those who borrow the new money, since they will still have to pay off their debt eventually. But this is not entirely true because the money with which they will pay off their debt is debased money; it is worth less when they pay off their debt than when they borrowed it. Although the wealth redistributed to them is not *equivalent* to what they borrowed, a *permanent* redistribution of wealth has, nonetheless, taken place. Inflation, therefore, favours those who are able and willing to borrow at the expense of those who are not able or willing to do so. Those who are prepared to gamble their future earnings on the rate of inflation, i.e. on the future devaluation of the currency, benefit at the expense of the prudent and thrifty, whose savings are plundered by inflation.

Fourth, this situation is complicated by the fact that it is impossible to determine precisely to what extent the inflation has disturbed the economy. No accurate predictions or assessments can be made about inflation because the resulting situation affects the decisions that people make about their economic life. There is no way of collecting or assessing the information needed in order to make accurate statements about how and to what extent inflation affects the way people make economic decisions. Our inability to assess the effects of inflation in this way makes any attempts to redress the injustice caused by inflation for everyone affected by it virtually impossible.

Fifth, the influx of new money creates an artificial situation within the economy. The spending power generated by the new money affects industries in a way in which they would not otherwise have been affected. The situation resulting from this kind of artificial stimulation of the economy does not constitute the best use of the scarce resources available to society. This is because the price mechanism, which provides the information necessary for the efficient allocation of scarce resources, is corrupted—i.e. the information it provides to the economy (e.g. the cost of goods and services) is incorrect in real terms (goods and services initially appear to be cheaper than in fact they are) and this information only gets corrected (adjusted to take account of inflation) after a redistribution of wealth has been effected within the economy. In times of sustained expansion of the money supply the price mechanism cannot be relied upon as a trustworthy guide to the value of goods and services—and there is no other mechanism known to man that is able to provide this kind of information. There is, therefore, an uneconomic or inefficient allocation of resources within the economy. People and businesses live beyond their means (though without realising it) while the economy is booming and consequently have to economise drastically when recession hits.

This situation is *artificial* and the corresponding allocation of resources *inefficient* because the spending power generated by the extra money does not represent an increase in real wealth. But it does give the *impression* of greater wealth. Those who borrow the new money are able to spend it on goods and services that they would not otherwise have been able to afford. As the new money filters through into the economy people begin to think they are wealthier than they are. They have more money, but they fail to realise that they are no better off, perhaps even worse off in real terms, because the depreciation of the monetary unit has led to a rise in the cost of living. This initiates a process of decapitalisation within society, which, if not checked, will eventually have dire consequences. By the time people begin to realise what is happening the damage has been done. Scarce resources needed for use in industries that are vital to the health of the economy generally have been misused to provide a standard of living that is beyond the means available to society. This standard of living, therefore, must eventually come to an abrupt end. The result is that in times of severe economic crisis there is often an excess of unessential or luxury goods while at the same time there is a critical shortage of essential goods. Inflation, therefore, leads to a misallocation of scarce resources and capital, which inevitably results in economic depression. A depression is simply a period of time during which the economy readjusts to a situation in which there are less resources and capital available to society. There is therefore a general lowering of standards of living during such times. This reduction in the availability of scarce resources and capital is the result of their misuse or misallocation during the period of inflation.

The monetary authorities can for a time avoid recession by continuing to inflate the money supply. But the rate of inflation increases exponentially with every new injection of money into the economy. A slump is postponed for a time but eventually the consequences become more serious and destructive to the economy. In severe inflation such as that experienced by the Weimar Republic early in the twentieth century the economy eventually experiences a crack-up boom, i.e. demonetisation of the currency and the development of a barter economy. Wherever this kind of banking practice is allowed to continue society will not be able to escape the continuous cycle of booms and slumps (i.e. the business cycle), which characterised so much of twentieth-century economic life.

These criticisms are equally applicable to the modern banking system. They have been explained in terms of the practices of the goldsmiths because this provides a much simpler model with which to work.

§6

The Modern Banking System

The modern banking system, though more complicated, is not essentially different in principle from that practised by the goldsmiths. The most important difference lies in the role that the Bank of England and the Treasury play in the economy. The Bank of England was established as a joint-stock company in 1694 by Act of Parliament. The purpose of the Bank from the beginning was to finance government borrowing and manage government debt. The government's need for money in this instance was occasioned by war with France. The whole of the Bank's original capital of £1,200,000 was to be loaned to the government at a yearly return of £100,000—i.e. 8 per cent on the loan per annum plus a £4,000 per annum management fee. In return for the loan the subscribers were granted a charter authorising them to act as a joint-stock company with limited liability under the name of "The Governor and Company of the Bank of England." The Bank was permitted to issue "sealed bills" to the value of its original capital,[17] to receive deposits, deal in bullion and commercial bills and make secured loans. Over and above the issue of sealed bills, however, the Bank issued cashier's notes. These

---

[17] Sealed bills, which bore the seal of the Bank of England, a Britannia sitting on a bank of money, were the only bills mentioned in the Bank's charter. They were made out to a named person, not to the bearer, and are to be distinguished from the running cash notes (or cashiers' notes), which were made out to the bearer. They usually bore interest at 2*d.* per £100 per day. The £1,200,000 originally subscribed was paid into the Exchequer mostly in the form of these sealed bills before the full capital had been raised from the subscribers. Indeed, of the 60 per cent of the capital that had been raised (i.e. £720,000) by the date the Bank paid the full £1,200,000 into the Treasury some of this existed only in the form of subscribers' bonds, which were "reckoned as cash." (Sir John Clapham, *The Bank of England, A History*, Vol. I, p. 20ff.).

cashier's notes were the equivalent of the goldsmiths running cash notes and the forerunner of the modern Bank of England note. The decision to have running cash notes printed with blanks for names, amounts and the cashier's signature was taken on July 31st, 1694, only a few days after the Bank began trading.[18] This led to complaints by some of the Bank's critics, who claimed that the Bank "was limited by Act of Parliament not to give out Bills under the Common Seal for above £1,200,000; and if they did every Proprietor was to be obliged . . . to make it good, so that they give out Bank Bills with interest for but £1,200,000. But they give the Cashier's notes [observe the term he uses] for all sums (*ad infinitum*) which neither charge the Fund nor the Proprietors, which seems to be a Credit beyond the intention of the Act . . . and never practised before by any Corporation, and almost a Fraud on the Subject."[19]

In 1946 the Bank of England was nationalised and its capital was acquired by the State. As the nation's central bank the Bank of England has a number of functions and responsibilities: (*a*) in the first place it is the government's bank. In this capacity it traditionally acted as financier to the government by floating government debt on the capital and money markets, i.e. by issuing government securities and Treasury Bills, and generally by managing government debt. Since 1997 the Bank's role as manager of the government's debt has been transferred to the Treasury (see *open market operations* below). The Bank also keeps the central government accounts (the Consolidated Fund or Exchequer and the National Loans Fund) and those of various government departments and acts as an advisory body to the government on economic matters. (*b*) The Bank of England acts as banker to the settlement banks. Any debt owed by one bank to another at the end of the day is settled by an adjustment to the respective banks' balances with the Bank of England. (*c*) The Bank of England is responsible for the issue of banknotes, over which it has a monopoly in England and Wales.[20] Before 1914 Bank of

---

[18] Clapham, *The Bank of England, A History*, Vol. I, p. 22. "The bearer notes took two forms—a promise to pay A.B. or bearer the whole amount of a deposit, or some irregular sum; and a promise to pay a round sum, against a larger deposit, in connection with the discount business, or possibly as a loan . . . But the note to A.B. or bearer for a round sum, a multiple of £5 or £10, usually £10, very soon prevailed because of its obvious convenience in circulation" (*ibid.*, p. 21f.).

[19] From a broadsheet entitled *The Mint and the Exchequer united*, cited in Clapham, *The Bank of England, A History*, Vol. I, p. 22.

[20] Apart from a limited "authorised circulation" all issues of Scottish banknotes must be backed by holdings of Bank of England notes.

England notes, except for the fiduciary issue of £14 million, were backed by gold and redeemable on demand. Today however the Bank of England note issue is merely a fiat standard enforced by government authority as legal tender.[21] (*d*) The Bank of England is responsible for the general management of the monetary system of the United Kingdom in accordance with government policy. (*e*) The Bank also manages the gold reserves and the Exchange Equalisation Account. The Exchange Equalisation Account is a fund set up to enable the government to manage the value of sterling in relation to other currencies by influencing exchange rates between sterling and foreign currency in accordance with government policy. For example, if those holding large amounts of sterling began selling it the effect would be to depress the value of sterling against other currencies. If the government wished to counterbalance the effects of this the Bank of England would intervene in the currency markets by buying sterling. If sterling exchange rates are stronger than the government would like them to be the Bank will sell sterling, thereby lowering the exchange rates. In other words the Bank seeks to influence exchange rates by manipulating supply and demand for sterling. This mechanism is not always successful however, as the Chancellor of the Exchequer discovered on September 16th, 1992— "Black Wednesday." The Bank of England lost over half its foreign currency reserves trying to maintain the value of the British pound on the foreign currency markets, but sterling still continued to fall in value against the Deutschmark. Eventually sterling was suspended in the ERM, the very move the government had pledged itself not to take. The Bank also operates the central government's daily foreign currency banking transactions through the Exchange Equalisation Account. (*f*) The Bank has a number of international responsibilities in the modern world, e.g. it participates in the work of the International Monetary Fund and International Bank for Reconstruction and Development (World Bank), both of which are agencies of the United Nations. In addition it provides services to the central banks of non-sterling countries.

It is the Bank of England, acting in accordance with government policy and in tandem with government offices and departments, such as the Treasury's Debt Management Office, that ultimately controls the supply of money in the economy. The settlement banks are linked to this central banking system and together they form one national

---

[21] Between 1914 and 1928 government Treasury notes were also in circulation.

banking system operating on the fractional reserve principle described above. There have been a number of developments and refinements to the system though.

Although the Country Bankers Act, 1826 had permitted banks outside London to issue banknotes the Bank Charter Act, 1844 again restricted the right of note issue of private banks, ensuring that the issue of notes would ultimately be concentrated in the hands of the Bank of England. This Act also limited the amount of fiduciary media that the Bank of England was permitted to issue. The fiduciary issue is the excess of banknotes issued over the amount of gold reserved to back them—in other words it is a euphemism for fraud. The 1844 Act fixed the Bank of England's fiduciary issue at £14 million and required that this be backed only by government securities. That is to say, £14 million of the Bank of England's debt was to be backed only by £14 million of government debt. But the framers of this legislation failed to realise that a cheque is precisely the same phenomenon as a banknote, and no formal limitations were placed on the use of cheques to create money beyond the principle of leaving enough reserves to cover emergencies. Hence, the banking system has developed more systematically on the chequing and credit side. It may seem much more complex today, but the system is essentially the same as that practised by the goldsmiths, except for the fact that it is controlled by the government through the Bank of England and the Treasury.

We no longer use gold and silver coins in Britain as a medium of exchange and the money in circulation is not backed by gold or silver. This makes it much easier for the banks to inflate the money supply. Furthermore, the ease with which government can adopt inflationary policies compared with the days when gold and silver coins were in circulation makes the temptation to do so much stronger; and few governments have resisted that temptation. Because the mechanisms that have been developed for artificially inflating the money supply are so complicated the immorality of inflating the money supply in this way is far less apparent.

The government can control the creation of money by the banking system for its own advantage and for the advantage of those groups in society to which the new money is made available. The result of inflating the money supply to finance government policies and government-favoured groups is the debasement of the monetary unit. Such government-controlled and government-licensed inflation is a form of theft. Yet control of the money supply is essential to socialist governments—and here under the term "socialist" we must include modern Conservative governments also. Without it they would be unable to finance the implementation of socialist ideology. With it they can promote and control the redistribution of wealth within society as a means of implementing Party ideology.

Modern British governments, both Labour and Conservative, have discouraged the use of gold as money and between 1939 and 1979 even the holding of gold as a form of money was illegal. VAT was charged on the purchase of gold bullion and coin between 1975 and January 2000, and, with the exception of British denominated coin, capital gains tax is payable on its sale. This is because gold is an *economic* money. But politicians want *political* money that they can create and control. The government is able to achieve this in two ways: first, through the creation of *fiat money*, i.e. money created by government authority alone. This consists of the token coin and banknotes that we usually refer to as cash. This currency is no longer backed by gold or silver. The Bank of England note is a fiat standard, i.e. printed money regulated by the Treasury, enforced as legal tender by government authority and backed only by government debt (government bonds and Treasury bills). Secondly, through the Bank of England the government is able to control the creation of *bank money* by the banks. This is money that exists in the form of bank deposits subject to withdrawal by cheque but not backed by cash. This kind of money exists *only* as numbers in bank accounts. Because it is transferred by cheque it is never redeemed for cash (i.e. currency). Banks receiving cheques drawn on other banks put them through the *clearing system*, in which cheques drawn on the various banks are offset against each other. Any money owed by one bank to another at the end of the day is settled by an adjustment to the respective banks' balances at the Bank of England. No cash changes hands. Consequently, there is far greater scope for the banks to create money and fraudulently redistribute wealth within society with this kind of banking system.[22] The government uses this banking system to

---

[22] It might be argued that consumers could put the system into check by demanding redemption. This would precipitate a run on the banks, which in theory would stop the system dead. However, the government would be unlikely to let this happen. Were depositors to start demanding redemption the government would probably declare a "bank holiday," which is what happened in the United States a number of years ago when the banks found themselves in difficulties. As a last resort the government could simply print the money and thereby facilitate nominal

monetise its debt, the effect of which is to inflate the money supply. In fact the creation of government debt is one of the principal causes of expansion of the money supply.

Since 1997 a number of changes have been introduced in the way the government delegates management of the monetary and banking system. Some activities that were previously functions of the Bank of England have been transferred to other government agencies (these changes will be explained below). The system as a whole works as a government-controlled monopoly; i.e. it is a government-licensed and government-regulated banking system. Although the banks are not owned or run by the government they are subject to government control and regulation. With the exception of building societies, which are subject to supervision and control by the Building Societies Commission, and the foreign banks of other EU member States, which are subject to their own countries' authorisation practices, no-one is permitted to accept deposits from the public in the UK as part of a deposit taking business (i.e. banking business) without authorisation from the Financial Services Authority (FSA), which is responsible for prudential supervision of the banks. Thus, although the banking system in the UK is not owned by the government it is regulated by the government and subject to the controls exercised by the Bank of England and the FSA in accordance with government policy.

In this system bank money has the same relation to a bank's reserve assets that the goldsmith's notes had to the gold stored in his vaults. Thus, the means that the government uses to control the creation of bank money function by regulating the ratio between the banks' reserve assets and the volume of bank money in circulation. There are five chief means available to the government that it can use to control the money supply. These are:

(a) The *minimum reserve asset ratio* or *liquidity ratio*. Prior to 1997 the Bank of England could require the banks to maintain a certain ratio between their eligible reserve assets (or liquid assets) and their bank deposits (bank money). Eligible reserve assets included cash

---

redemption. A run on the system would not ultimately change the situation therefore. The government would not allow the banks to go under. After the "bank holiday," or whatever expedients were used to obviate the crisis, the system would be essentially the same as before and the currency would continue to depreciate. What is needed is a far-reaching reform of the whole banking system that would make it illegal for banks and governments to practise fractional reserve banking in the first place.

reserves and balances with the Bank of England, Treasury Bills, money at call with the London money market, commercial and local authority bills eligible for re-discount at the Bank of England, company tax reserve certificates and government securities with less than a year to maturity. By altering the reserve asset ratio the Bank of England could control the amount of bank money in circulation. If it increased the ratio the banks were forced to reduce the amount of loans they could advance to their customers, thereby reducing the volume of bank money in circulation. By decreasing the ratio it empowered the banks to increase advances to their customers, thereby increasing the volume of bank money in circulation. When these bank loans are spent in the economy and then redeposited in the banks they add to the banks' reserve assets, thereby enabling the banks to advance more loans to their customers and expand the volume of bank money in circulation further.

The government can also facilitate inflation of the money supply by increasing the reserves held by the banks without reducing the minimum reserve asset ratio. For example, if the government decides to increase significantly the amount of money it borrows by issuing Treasury Bills (short-dated government IOUs that are sold and circulate prior to maturity at a discount) there will be an expansion of the money supply to the extent that the bills are bought by the banking sector. This is because Treasury bills are considered very liquid and form an important part of the banks' reserve assets. An increase in the purchase of these bills by the banks will increase the banks' reserve assets, since although the banks will have to reduce their balances at the Bank of England in order to pay for them initially, this money, once it is spent into circulation by the government, will be re-deposited in the banks, thereby restoring the banks' balances with the Bank of England once more. The banks' balances at the Bank of England will ultimately remain unchanged therefore, but they will have a larger holding of Treasury bills and thus more reserve assets on the basis of which they can expand the money supply by advancing loans (bank money) to their customers. (Provided the sale of Treasury bills does not represent an increase in government debt, but simply the renewal of existing debt as it matures, their purchase by the banks will not affect the overall reserve asset ratio of the banks, and thus there will be no expansion of the money supply).

The sale of Treasury bills to the general public and non-banking

Figure 1

MULTIPLE CREDIT EXPANSION BY THE BANKS
(CREATION OF BANK MONEY)

*Assuming a reserve asset ratio of 10 per cent and
an initial new loan of £100 bank money created
by bank A when its reserve assets are increased*

Bank	£s Deposit	£s Reserve	£s Loaned out
A			100.00
B	100.00	10.00	90.00
C	90.00	9.00	81.00
D	81.00	8.10	72.90
E	72.90	7.29	65.61
F	65.61	6.56	59.05
G	59.05	5.91	53.14
H	53.14	5.31	47.83
I	47.83	4.78	43.05
J	43.05	4.31	38.74
K	38.74	3.87	34.87

Total deposits	Total reserves	Total loans advanced
651.32	65.13	586.19

This process can continue until a further £900 of bank money has been created on the basis of the original £100 deposited in bank B.

If, as a result of changes in the banks' minimum reserve asset ratio or increases in their reserve assets, £10 million of new deposits are created, this process will expand the money supply by a further £90 million.

firms, the "non-bank private sector," will not affect the money supply in the same way that their sale to the banking sector would. When Treasury bills are sold to the non-bank private sector they will be paid for by cheques drawn on the bank accounts of those who purchase them. This will reduce the banks' balances with the Bank of England. Once the government spends into circulation the proceeds of the sale of these bills, however, the money will be deposited in the bank accounts of the recipients and the banks' balances with the Bank of England will be restored to their previous level. There will be no change ultimately in the cash reserves held by the banks. An increase in the purchase of Treasury bills by the non-bank private sector, therefore, will have a neutral effect on the money supply to the extent that it represents an increase in government debt that is not taken up by the banking sector, since the non-bank private sector cannot use Treasury bills as a basis for making multiple loans to the public, thereby expanding the money supply. (An increase in the purchase of Treasury bills by the non-bank private sector would be deflationary to the extent that it was accompanied by a decrease in purchases by the banking sector while the overall volume of bills remained constant.)

The effect of decreasing the minimum reserve asset ratio or of increasing the banks' reserve assets is to set in motion a process of multiple credit expansion, i.e. creation of bank money. This process works in the following way. Assume there is a reserve asset or liquidity ratio of 10 per cent. As a result of an increase in its reserve assets bank A makes a new loan of £100 to Mr Smith, who spends it on goods bought from Mr Jones. Mr Jones then deposits the £100 in his account at bank B. Bank B retains 10 per cent of this deposit (£10) as a reserve and lends out the remaining £90 to Mr Brown. Mr Brown buys £90 of goods from Mr Green. Mr Green then deposits the £90 in his bank account at bank C. Bank C retains 10 per cent of this deposit (£9) as a reserve and loans out the remaining £81. This process continues until the original deposit of £100 loaned out by bank A has become a 10 per cent reserve in the banking system on the basis of which a further £900 of bank money has been created (see fig. 1).

Long- and medium-dated government securities (bonds) are not considered liquid until they are near maturity and therefore sale of these securities to the public by the government is neither deflationary nor inflationary. Money is withdrawn from the banks to pay for them, thereby reducing the banks' balances with the Bank of England. This money is then credited to the government's accounts. Once it enters the economy again via government spending it is deposited in the recipients' accounts with the banks thereby increasing the latter's balances with the Bank of England. There is no change ultimately in total reserves held by the banks therefore. The effect of such sales on the money supply is neutral. Purchase of government bonds from the market by the Bank of England, however, is inflationary (see *open market operations* below).

Prior to 1971 the banks had to maintain a 28 per cent liquid asset ratio, of which 8 per cent was cash—i.e. coin, notes and balances with the Bank of England. In 1971 this was dropped and the banks were required instead to maintain a ratio of 12½ per cent of eligible reserve assets to eligible liabilities. (Eligible liabilities were total sterling deposits held by the non-bank sector less time deposits with a maturity in excess of two years and 40 per cent of items in transmission— i.e. funds being transferred from one customer to another.) In fact, however, these two types of reserve requirement were broadly the same. The main differences after 1971 were that cash in bank tills was no longer considered an eligible reserve asset and government securities with less than a year to maturity, which were not previously regarded as liquid assets, were now considered eligible reserve assets.

Since 1981, when statutory reserve requirements were abolished by the Thatcher Government, the banks' reserve asset ratio has not been fixed by the government. Between 1981 and 1997 the banks' liquidity position was supervised on an individual basis by the Bank of England ("prudential control") and government concentrated on interest rates as a major means of controlling the aggregate level of prices, although the Thatcher Government continued to set targets for growth of the money supply until 1985. In 1997 the new Labour Government transferred prudential control of bank liquidity from the Bank of England to the Financial Services Authority and gave the Bank of England "operational" freedom to set the rate of interest independently of government. The government, however, sets an "inflation target" (i.e. a *price* inflation target), which the Bank must achieve by controlling interest rates. Although formal responsibility for setting interest rates on a monthly basis has been transferred to the Bank of England, therefore, the Bank is still tied to government policy. In practice the Bank's independence in setting the rate of interest, though hailed by the Labour Government as a great leap forward, means very little. The difference between the system now in operation and the system in operation prior to 1997 is that the Financial Services Authority supervises the liquidity of the banks on an individual basis and the government attempts to control price inflation (i.e. rising prices) by setting the "inflation target," which the Bank of England is expected to meet by controlling interest rates.

(*b*) The *bank rate* (before October 1972) or *minimum lending rate* (between October 1972 and March 1997) or *repo rate* (after March 1997). In order to explain how the modern interest rate system works it will be helpful to explain how the system operated prior to 1997. The old *bank rate* or *minimum lending rate* was the rate of interest at which the Bank of England provided cash to the discount market by rediscounting first-class commercial bills, Treasury Bills and British government stocks with five years or less to maturity, or by lending against their security. Prior to 1997 the discount market was a group of firms, most of which were authorised banks and all of which were members of the London Discount Market Association, that traded in such short-dated bills and had a direct dealing relationship with the Bank of England. The minimum lending rate was made effective through *open market operations*. Since interest rates generally were kept in line with the minimum lending rate any increase in the latter would lead to a fall in borrowing from the banks and a decrease in the volume of bank money in circulation. The minimum lending rate was always a penal rate of interest ($\frac{1}{2}$ per cent above the average discount rate for Treasury Bills rounded up to the nearest $\frac{1}{4}$ per cent). Although the Bank of England could not legally require the banks to change their base rates in line with the MLR it could induce them to do so since if the banks failed to follow the lead given by the Bank of England they would be penalised economically.

The minimum lending rate was *formally* abolished in 1981. Nevertheless, the Bank of England's policy towards the discount market, though more flexible, did not essentially change. The rate at which it would rediscount bills or lend against their security to the discount market was no longer officially announced or made available to the public. But the mechanism worked essentially in the same way. Thus, although officially there was no minimum lending rate there was a de facto penal rate of interest at which the Bank of England would act as "lender of last resort" to the discount market. Since August 1981, however, when the minimum lending rate ceased to be continuously posted, it has been invoked on six separate occasions: once in 1985, once in 1990, three times in 1992, and once in 1993. Abolition of the minimum lending rate simply meant, therefore, that the Bank of England usually preferred to act as "lender of last resort" by rediscounting bills rather than by lending money to the discount houses and that the rate at which it would rediscount bills, or lend against their security, was not continuously posted or made available to the public.

By 1997 the number of discount houses had declined considerably and in March 1997 the Bank of England declared itself ready to enter into a direct dealing relationship with a much wider range of financial institutions than previously represented by the discount houses—e.g. banks, building societies and securities firms—provided certain supervisory and functional criteria are met. Firms that have a direct dealing relationship with the Bank of England through the discount market are now called "counterparties" by the Bank.[23] Since 1997 the Bank has also expanded the range of instruments with which it will work in the money market. The Bank now deals in "repos." Repo is short for "sale and repurchase agreement." A repo is an agreement by one party "to sell bonds or other financial instruments to another party, with an agreement to repurchase equivalent securities in future, under a formal legal agreement."[24] The range of instruments in which the Bank will now deal includes repos in British government debt in sterling and foreign currency, eligible bank bills, eligible local government bills and Euro-debt. The *repo rate* (the interest rate on repos) is broadly equivalent to the old minimum lending rate. The repo rate is set monthly by the Monetary Policy Committee.

(c) *Open market operations.* This is the sale or purchase of Treasury Bills and government securities on the open market and operations in the repo market by the Bank of England. Open market operations

[23] The Bank of England requires counterparties in its money market operations to meet four functional criteria, but the main criterion is that counterparties must be able to maintain an active presence in the money market. The Bank has stated that "This means that counterparties will be expected to be trading in the gilt repo and/or bill markets on a reasonably continuous basis, with a range of unrelated counterparties, on a scale that would enable them to contribute in a material way to distributing around the system the liquidity provided by the Bank in its rounds of operations with its counterparties. A counterparty whose operations are limited to managing its own liquidity requirements may not fulfil this criterion" (*Reform of the Bank of England's operations in the sterling money markets: A paper by the Bank of England* [Bank of England, February, 1997], p. 8af.

[24] "The First Year of the Gilt Repo Market," *Bank of England Quarterly Bulletin,* May 1997, Vol. 37, No. 2, p. 1.

will be explained here first in terms of the system that operated prior to 1997. A number of changes have been introduced since 1997. These changes will be explained below as part of an ongoing evolution of the system operating prior to 1997.

Before 1997, when the Bank of England increased the sale of long- and medium-dated government securities money would be withdrawn from the banks to pay for them. This had the effect of reducing the banks' balances with the Bank of England. If this caused the banks' balances at the Bank of England to fall below what was considered to be a safe level the banks would be forced to call in loans to the discount houses, which obtained short-term loans from the banks in order to finance their business ("money at call" with the discount houses was the main reserve that banks drew upon when they were short of cash because it was the most liquid form of money market loan and could be withdrawn at a few hours' notice; banks were required by the Bank of England to keep deposits with the discount houses of at least 2½ per cent of their eligible liabilities). The discount houses, unable to get funds from the banks, then had to apply to the Bank of England as "lender of last resort," either to rediscount bills or borrow money against their security at the *minimum lending rate* (under these conditions the discount houses were said to be "in the Bank"). If the minimum lending rate had gone up the discount houses were forced to increase the rate of discount on bills (i.e. reduce the price at which they tender for bills). This increase in the rate of interest on bills was then passed on to the banks in two ways: (1) if the banks were unable to replenish their balances at the Bank of England sufficiently by calling in loans to the discount houses they would sell commercial bills and Treasury bills back to the discount houses in order to obtain funds, but at a reduced price, making the sale less profitable—in other words the discount houses would get a higher rate of interest on the bills. Having to pay higher rates of interest to the discount market in this way induced the banks to raise their own interest rates to those who borrow from them. (2) If the banks were able to replenish their balances with the Bank of England by calling in loans to the discount houses the new higher rate of interest on commercial and Treasury bills still had the effect of driving up interest rates generally since the banks bought these bills near to maturity from the discount houses because of their liquidity. Interest rates generally rose therefore to compete with the rate of interest on bills. The effect of increasing the minimum lending rate, therefore, was to drive up short-term interest rates generally, thereby reducing the demand for loans and contracting the money supply.

Open market selling by the Bank of England in the bond market (i.e. sale of medium- and long-dated securities) was thus used to support or make effective an increase in the minimum lending rate. Moreover, whether the banks rebuilt their balances at the Bank of England by calling in money loaned to the discount houses or by selling bills back to the discount houses, or by a combination of both, there would still be an overall contraction in their reserves, since money at call with the London discount market and Treasury and commercial bills are classed as eligible reserve assets. If the banks were already operating at the limit of their eligible reserve asset ratio they would be forced to reduce advances to their customers thereby contracting the volume of bank money in circulation.

Open market buying in the bond market by the Bank of England has the reverse effect: when the Bank buys securities the money it pays for them enters the economy and is deposited in the bank accounts of the recipients, thereby expanding the reserves held by the banks. This increase in reserves allows the banks to advance loans to their customers and increase the supply of bank money in circulation until the ratio between eligible reserve assets and bank money once again falls to the minimum permitted by the monetary authorities. A process of multiple credit expansion will take place (see fig. 1).

An increase in the sale of Treasury bills to the banking sector by the Bank of England in open market operations will not affect the money supply directly since when the banks buy the bills one form of reserve asset (cash balances at the Bank of England) is substituted for another (Treasury bills). It will, however, lead to a rise in the rate of interest on Treasury bills since the increased supply of bills will depress their market price (i.e. the lower price paid for the bills means that holders of the bills will receive a higher rate of return when the bills mature). A rise in the rate of interest on Treasury bills will cause short-term interest rates generally to rise in order to compete with the rate on Treasury bills. Open market selling by the Bank of England in the bill market, therefore, was also used to support a rise in the MLR. Increasing the rate of interest will have an indirect affect on the money supply by reducing the demand for borrowing.

The sale and purchase of Treasury bills and government securities on the open market by the Bank of England is really a kind of fine-tuning that the Bank uses in its ongoing everyday work of managing the government's debt and controlling interest rates on behalf of the government. The real significance of open market operations for the expansion or contraction of the money supply must be seen therefore in the greater context of overall monetary policy (cf. *minimum lending rate* above and *funding* below). When a new issue of government bonds was made only a proportion of the issue was sold immediately to the public. The remainder of the issue was taken up by the Issue Department of the Bank of England, which sold them gradually over the following months. This continuous release of government bonds via the Stock Market was referred to as the "tap." Treasury bills are issued partly by tender and partly on "tap." The tap bills were taken up by government departments with money in hand, including the Issue Department of the Bank of England and the Exchange Equalisation Account, and by certain overseas monetary authorities. Issues of Treasury bills sold to the public are by weekly tender. Any bills not bought by the public were bought by the discount houses. The Bank of England could always ensure that the discount houses had enough cash to purchase the Treasury bills allotted to them in the weekly tender by lending to the discount houses or rediscounting bills. This was how the Bank acted as lender of last resort. This mechanism ensured that the government could always borrow as much as it needed from the market. By lending to the discount market or rediscounting bills the Bank of England was lending indirectly to the government by creating the cash to enable the market to fund the Exchequer through the purchase of Treasury bills. By lending to the Exchequer indirectly through the market in this way the Bank of England is able to control short-term interest rates; e.g. by deliberately selling enough bills to keep the discount market short of cash the Bank could enforce the MLR.[25]

[25] "When the Bank of England provides the cash (either by open market operations in the money market or by lending against bills or short bonds at the Discount Office . . .) to enable the discount houses to take up Treasury Bills allotted to them in the tender, the Bank is in effect lending to the Exchequer. By lending cash to the market (which then lends it back to the Exchequer) rather than lending it direct to the Exchequer, the Bank of England makes sure that its control of the money market is not weakened, since it can in effect dictate the terms (as to interest and date of repayment) on which the cash is lent to the market. Either way the Bank of England creates the cash to finance the Exchequer. From the point of view of the Exchequer the difference is that under the present system its increased indebtedness is to the banking system, not to the Bank of England; from the point of view of the market the difference is that the assets which they [*sic*] hold as a

As explained above, since 1997 a number of changes have been introduced into this system. There are no longer any specialist discount houses and the Bank of England has a direct dealing relationship with a much wider range of firms. Since 1997 it has also conducted a significant proportion of its business in gilt repos. The Bank now uses both bills and gilt repos in its money market operations. The Bank's combined bill and repo business provides control over liquidity in the money market; i.e. the Bank provides cash to the money market or keeps cash short, depending on the policy being pursued, by repoing gilts and rediscounting eligible bills in open market operations. In the second quarter of 1999 55 per cent of the Bank's business was in gilt repos and 31 per cent in bills. Essentially, the system works in the same way as it did prior to 1997 but has evolved in terms of the money instruments that the Bank is prepared to use and in terms of the range of counterparties with which it is prepared to deal in order to achieve its aims.[26]

Another change introduced in 1997 was the transfer of the Bank of England's role as the government's agent for debt management, cash management and oversight of the gilt market to the Treasury. In April 1998 the Debt Management Office was set up as an executive agency of the Treasury and took over management of the government's debt. Prior to this, sale of government bonds (medium- and long-dated securities) was managed by the Bank of England. This aspect of the Bank's work has now been transferred to the Treasury's Debt Management Office. Government stock is now sold by the DMO at scheduled auctions or on "tap" to DMO-recognised stock market traders known as GEMMs (gilt-edged market makers), who then sell it on to brokers and clients. As part of the same framework for change introduced in 1997 the government also stated its intention to transfer responsibility for cash management from the Bank of England to the Treasury. When this takes place the DMO will take over the Bank of England's responsibility for issuing Treasury bills. However, the original timetable for this transfer of responsibility to the DMO was not met and the new timetable scheduled the change as taking place gradually in the first quarter of 2000. Although the

---

result of the present operations are not cash (deposits at the Bank of England) but Treasury Bills" (*Report of the Committee on the Working of the Monetary System* [HMSO, 1959], para. 121, p. 40).

[26] *Reform of the Bank of England's operations in the sterling money markets: A paper by the Bank of England*, p. 4a.

first issue of Treasury bills managed by the DMO took place on the 14th January 2000, the completion of the transfer of responsibility to the DMO is, at the time of writing, now scheduled for the second quarter of 2000.

(*d*) *Funding*. Open market operations are an important part of the every-day work of the monetary authorities in our modern government-controlled economy. It is in the context of overall government economic policy, however, that they become significant as a mechanism for implementing government control of the economy. As we have seen, this mechanism was used to support the minimum lending rate. It can also be seen at work when the Bank of England engages in *funding*. Funding operations are undertaken in order to reduce the amount of reserve assets available to the banks, thereby forcing them to reduce the volume of bank money in circulation. This is done by converting the government's short-term debt into long-term debt. The selling of more long- and medium-dated bonds coupled with a reduction in the sale of Treasury Bills, which are short-dated and thus very liquid, has the effect over a sustained period of withdrawing Treasury Bills from circulation and replacing them with bonds that are less liquid. Since Treasury Bills form a significant part of the banks' eligible reserve assets this operation over a period of time reduces the banks' reserves. In order to keep their liquidity at a level that is considered safe, therefore, they are forced to reduce the amount of loans they make, thereby contracting the volume of bank money in circulation. The conversion of the government's long- and medium-term debt into short-term debt, or unfunding,—i.e. the sale of more Treasury bills and purchase of government securities— has the reverse effect: more reserve assets are made available to the banks. This enables the banks to increase deposits (i.e. advance more loans) and expand the volume of bank money in circulation,—in other words it enables them to inflate the money supply.

(*e*) *Special deposits*. Since 1958 the Bank of England has had the right to require the banks to hold special deposits with it equal to a given amount of their total deposits. These special deposits, which were first used in 1960, earned interest at the Treasury Bill rate but they could not be withdrawn and were thus completely illiquid. By requiring these special deposits the Bank of England effectively freezes part of the banks' reserves. This forces the banks to cut back on loans to their customers, thereby contracting the money supply. When special deposits are released or unfrozen the effect is reversed: the banks' reserves are effectively increased and this enables them to advance more loans to their customers, expanding the money supply in the process.

These are the various means of controlling the money supply available to the government. Not all of these mechanisms are in use at the same time. As explained above, since 1981 the banks' reserve asset ratios have not been fixed by the government. The liquidity position of the banks is now supervised by the FSA on an individual basis ("prudential control"). The government no longer seeks to control growth of the money supply directly. Instead it seeks to control the *effects* of monetary inflation, i.e. rising prices, by setting an inflation target (i.e. a *price* inflation target), which the Bank of England is responsible for meeting through its control of interest rates. This has an indirect affect on the money supply. By controlling the cost of borrowing (i.e interest rates) the Bank of England affects the *demand* for money and therefore the amount of bank money that is ultimately created by the banks by advancing loans to their customers. This means, however, that the potential for expansion of the money supply by the banks is far greater now than it has ever been.

Of course the government cannot demand that banks increase advances to their customers, nor can government insist that people make use of the credit facilities offered by the banks. Growth of the volume of bank money must be initiated by individuals and companies who wish to borrow from the banks. The volume of money in circulation, like all other economic goods, is determined by demand as well as supply. However, the government can create the conditions that will make such borrowing attractive to individuals and companies; it can facilitate the creation of bank money by permitting the banks to satisfy the demand for more borrowing, and since the banks make their profits by lending they will and do under such circumstances seek to induce the public to borrow from them as much as possible. The consequences of the government's relaxation of monetary controls, therefore, will usually, if not inevitably, lead to expansion of the money supply. Furthermore, the government can also initiate the process of monetary expansion itself by its own borrowing and spending policies.

It is sometimes claimed by economists that in the modern economy the government and the Bank of England do not and cannot control growth of the money supply, which is said to be endogenous; i.e. it is argued that the size of the money supply is determined by the demand for money, not by the monetary authorities (the money supply is said to be exogenous if it is fixed by the monetary authorities). However, growth of the money supply can be described as endogenous in the UK today because restrictions on the banks' ability to create bank money are much less stringent now than they have ever been before. The monetary authorities no longer set money growth targets and concentrate instead on interest rates as a means of controlling the aggregate level of prices. The only direct control over bank lending now is prudential control, which restricts the banks' ability to expand the money supply by creating bank money much less rigorously than the previous statutory reserve ratios did. Under the present system, the argument that the government cannot control growth of the money supply because the money supply is endogenous is tantamount to saying that the government cannot control growth of the money supply because it does not attempt to control growth of the money supply.[27] Instead it attempts to control rising prices, i.e. it sets a price inflation target that the Bank of England has to meet by controlling interest rates, which affect the money supply indirectly by influencing the demand for money.

The modern banking system is thus far more complex than that practised by the goldsmiths, but it is essentially based on the same principle: the fraudulent creation of money (monetisation of debt). Despite the disclaimers issued by Prime Ministers, Chancellors of the Exchequer and any number of other government spokesmen, it is the government, through its banking and monetary policies, that is ultimately responsible for the expansion of the money supply—i.e. inflation—in modern Britain. The significance of the changes initiated in 1997 to the way the banking system works is not very great in terms of the overall effect on the government's management of the

---

[27] My argument here relates to the current system in the UK and is not meant to imply that government has a moral responsibility to control the supply of money. As will be argued in Chapter Five, in a Christian economic system the money supply would indeed be endogenous; the government would not have responsibility for controlling growth of the money supply, nor would it be expected to control the aggregate level of prices by manipulating interest rates as a means of influencing the demand for money. Under a Christian system the government would be a ministry of public justice with the responsibility of ensuring that honesty and fairness prevail in the economy, including the way the banking system works. Growth of the money supply in the current system, however, is caused mainly by practices that are not honest or fair. Irrespective of whether the present government policy of controlling demand for money works (i.e. achieves its stated aims), it is the argument of this book that such a policy is not legitimate morally. Control of the

economy. The new framework introduced in 1997 by the Labour Government means that some of the tasks formerly undertaken by the Bank of England on behalf of the government have been transferred to the Treasury. Although the Bank of England has "operational" independence from the government in setting interest rates, it is still constrained by its responsibility to meet the government's price inflation target. The banking system has been modernised but not essentially changed in principle. It remains a government-licensed and government-controlled monopoly.

§7
How the Government Benefits

A chief beneficiary of this banking system is the government itself, since it is able to use the system to help it fund its policies and extend its influence and control over the economy. Those to whom the government allocates the wealth it is able to expropriate from the nation via the banking system also benefit, although who these are will vary depending on which party is in power. Under traditional socialist governments direct government subsidies have been used to benefit privileged groups and industries, usually unionised and manufacturing industry. This in turn helps to keep non-unionised labour and small private firms under control by making it difficult for them to compete on fair terms with nationalised industries and government-sponsored and government-subsidised firms. The growth of nationalised and unionised industry is the result. Conservative governments tend to favour private enterprise since they generally discourage the creation of government-subsidised industries—at least relatively in comparison with traditional socialist governments. Under Conservative governments therefore the growing money supply tends to be tapped more by those who are prepared to finance business by borrowing at artificially low rates of interest from the commercial banking system. This tends to encourage expansion of private en-

---

money supply is not a legitimate function of the government or of its quasi-independent agent, the Bank of England. Nor is it a legitimate function of the government to license certain institutions (banks) to inflate the money supply by means of fractional reserve banking practices. Government should instead concentrate its attentions on policing the banking system according to strict ethical principles so that the fraudulent creation of money is proscribed and prosecuted.

terprise. In either case[28] the creation of a boom leads ultimately to recession.

Government bureaucracy, of course, is also a prime beneficiary of this system since the continual expansion of government control over society means the continual expansion of government departments and the creation of new departments. This vast growth of government administration—i.e. government control over our lives and society—is not cheap. The expanding civil service has become a major "industry" in our society—to use an inappropriate term, since it is not industrious, i.e. productive, in the economic sense of the term—consuming a vast amount of the resources generated by the productive sectors of the economy. Total government expenditure in 1993 accounted for over 43 per cent of the GNP. Government has been able to grow to this enormous size in a relatively free society because it has been able to expropriate the wealth of the nation. Although the greater part of the funds expropriated from the nation by the government is raised by taxation, and increasingly by *indirect* taxation, taxation alone, because of its unpopularity, is not able to provide the modern State with all the resources it requires without risking the government's rejection at a general election. The mechanism that the government uses to fund the shortfall between what it raises in taxes and what it wishes to spend works through its monopolistic control of the fractional reserve banking system. Furthermore, as will be explained below, economic booms generated by inflation of the money supply contribute to the government's ability to raise revenue by means of taxation. The government itself benefits directly from this system in four ways:

(*a*) By inflating the money supply the government is able to open up a cheap source of credit with which to fund its ever growing spending requirements. As we have seen, in 1971 the banks' liquid asset ratio was reduced from 28 per cent to a 12½ per cent reserve asset ratio. In the following decade there was severe inflation, the

---

[28] These are pure types and all governments today generate booms in varying degrees both through direct subsidies and through permitting the commercial banking system to expand the money supply—and of course booms invariably lead to recession. The general character of such booms will vary, however, depending on which method is used as the primary stimulus to the economy. Under traditional Labour governments booms have tended to stimulate heavy manufacturing and nationalised industry, while the boom of the 1980s under the Conservatives led to the expansion of a private enterprise economy, especially in the service and financial industries.

Figure 2

CENTRAL GOVERNMENT BORROWING REQUIREMENT 1970–1981			
Year	£million	Year	£million
1970–1	13	1976–7	5,944
1971–2	515	1977–8	4,431
1972–3	1,981	1978–9	8,084
1973–4	2,164	1979–80	8,227
1974–5	5,087	1980–81	12,956
1975–6	8,803		

Source: *Financial Statistics* (HMSO), No. 140, December 1973, p. 18; No. 188, December 1977, p. 28; No. 248, December 1982, p. 29.

cost of living more than tripled, and the government's borrowing requirement grew exponentially. Growth of the money supply reached a peak in 1973 (M3 grew by 27 per cent and M4 by 22.3 per cent in that year) and the rise in the cost of living reached a peak in 1975 (the Retail Price Index showed an increase of 24.2 per cent). Between 1970 and 1981 the CGBR (Central Government Borrowing Requirement) increased from £13 million to £12,956 million, an increase of nearly 100,000 (one hundred thousand) per cent (the figures for the decade are given in fig. 2). Even when monetary inflation and rising prices are taken into account[29] this is still a prodigious increase in government debt.

During the Thatcher government's period of office an attempt was made to put a stop to this economically disastrous method of raising government revenue. By the late 1980s there was a central government financial surplus and the government was able to repay some of its debt.[30] As can be seen from fig. 3, this prudent policy

[29] The money supply (M3) grew by 79.7 per cent over the same period and the Retail Price Index figures show an increase in the cost of living of 303.6 per cent. The money stock (M3) rose from £18,175,000,000 in 1970 to £89,628,000,000 in 1981. The RPI showed an increase from 73.1 in 1970 to 295 in 1981 using January 1997 as a base (Forrest Capie and Alan Webber, *A Monetary History of the United Kingdom 1870–1982* [George Allen and Unwin, 1985], Vol. I).

[30] The overall public-sector surplus (the public-sector debt repayment or PSDR) for 1988–9 was over £14 billion. However, over £7 billion of this was accounted for by privatisation proceeds. Although this policy of reducing the deficit was entirely laudable in itself, it must also be remembered that the benefits accruing from it were offset by the fact that it was achieved to some extent as a result of increased

Figure 3

CENTRAL GOVERNMENT BORROWING REQUIREMENT 1988–1993			
Year	£million	Year	£million
1988–9	−7,119	1991–2	12,899
1989–90	−5,630	1992–3	36,301
1990–91	−2,459		

Source: *Financial Statistics* (London: HMSO), No. 381, January 1994, p. 13.

was abandoned in the early 1990s. The total government deficit (PSBR) for 1993 was an enormous £46 billion.

Obviously, the government needs to borrow this money as cheaply as possible, and it is able to create the right conditions for such massive borrowing by expanding the money supply, thereby reducing the real rate of interest (i.e. the nominal rate of interest minus the rise in the cost of living—*price* inflation). In fact the government is able to expand the money supply and reduce the rate of interest at the same time *by* borrowing on this enormous scale. Government

---

tax revenues raised in an inflationary boom period. In a booming economy tax revenues increase due to increased economic activity, but this economic activity does not represent an increase in real wealth to the extent that it is fuelled by inflation. Any increased tax revenues accruing to the government's coffers as a result of such inflation-generated booms represent a tax on capital therefore. Such increased tax revenues are a windfall for the government accruing not from the creation of wealth but from the redistribution of wealth—see point (c) on p. 137ff. In 1987 the government ran a public-sector surplus (a PSDR of £3.4 billion) for the first time since 1971. The Chancellor stated that "Some two-thirds of this substantial undershoot of the PSBR I set at the time of last year's Budget is the result of the increased tax revenues that have flowed from a buoyant economy; while the remaining one-third is due to lower than expected public expenditure, again the outcome of a buoyant economy: less in benefits for the unemployed, higher receipts from council house sales and improved trading performance by the nationalized industries." (Cited in John Sloman, *Economics* [Harvester Wheatsheaf, 1991], p. 634). The buoyant state of the economy, however, was by no means due entirely to prudent government policy (i.e. lower tax rates and reduced government expenditure) since the money supply figures (see "The Money Supply and the Retail Price Index" below) show that inflation also played a substantial part in generating the economic activity that led to increased tax revenues during this period. The price paid for the proportion of the PSDR between 1987 and 1990 generated by inflation was a long and very difficult recession in the early 1990s, greatly exacerbated by the Major administration's £46 billion deficit in 1993 and the massive tax rises subsequently implemented to deal with it. Such recessions are a consequence of inflationary booms.

borrowing, therefore, is itself a contributing cause of the trade cycle today.

But there is a cost to the government's obtaining cheap loans in this way. During the 1970s government benefited from the lower real costs of borrowing created by inflation. In the 1980s, however, the markets responded by building an inflation premium into the real cost of long-term borrowing that was in excess of the actual rise in the cost of living (price inflation). As a result real interest rates rose sharply. The inflationary period of cheap borrowing led ultimately to an increase in the real cost of long-term borrowing.[31]

(b) The government benefits from this process of inflation in another important way. In an inflationary economy the debtor benefits at the expense of the creditor because the money with which he eventually pays off his debt is debased money, worth less in real terms, i.e. in terms of purchasing power, than when it was borrowed. Interest does not normally compensate creditors for this loss of purchasing power since, as already mentioned, during times of inflation (i.e. in the early period of the trade cycle) real interest rates are usually reduced to artificially low levels. Hence, by inflating the money supply the government not only opens up a cheap source of credit but also ensures that it is able to pay off its debts with debased money. This means that the government's creditors are in effect plundered of their capital. In the case of creditors holding government bonds that never mature this situation is much worse. War Loan securities are a good example of this. These were issued in 1917 at 5 per cent and converted in 1932 to 3.5 per cent.[32] As a result of inflation and higher interest rates since World War Two holders of these bonds lost out significantly between 1948 and 1981. Inflation

[31] Marvin Goodfriend, "Discussion" in Charles Goodhart, "Monetary policy and debt management in the United Kingdom: some historical viewpoints" in K. Alec Chrystal, *Government debt structure and monetary conditions* (Bank of England, 1999), p. 100. Goodfriend's comments relate to the USA, but the same process occurred in the UK. Real interest rates rose from minus 9.8 per cent in 1975 at the peak of the inflationary '70s (the nominal rate—average on 20 year bonds—was 14.4 per cent, growth of M4 was running at 12.4 per cent, the RPI grew by 24.2 per cent and the PSBR was £10,161,000,000) to 6.5 per cent in 1986 (the nominal rate was 9.9 per cent, M4 grew by 15.4 per cent, the RPI grew by 3.4 per cent and the PSBR was £2,497,000,000). In 1969 the nominal rate of interest was 9.1 per cent and the real rate of interest was 3.7 per cent (M4 grew by 5.1 per cent, the RPI grew by 5.4 per cent and there was a public-sector surplus of £534,000,000) (source: Sloman, *op. cit.*, p. 758).

[32] B. V. Marshall, *Comprehensive Economics* (London: Longman, Second Edition, 1975), Part One, p. 617.

wiped out the value of the yield on the bonds for investors who held on to them and higher interest rates (relative to pre-War rates) reduced their market value so that investors who sold their stock had to bear capital losses.[33] During this period the government in effect plundered, in one way or another, the resources of those who invested in these War bonds.

(c) Another way in which the government benefits from this banking system is its ability to increase tax receipts in a booming economy created by inflation. Some economists claim that although the share of the gross domestic product (GDP) spent by the government has grown over the past century there has been a fall in the value of the government's debt relative to the size of the economy over the same period. With the exception of some heavy periods of borrowing (e.g. the inflationary 1970s) the growth of government, therefore, has been financed mainly by taxation. Government spending, therefore, has nothing to do with the government's control of the monetary system as long as it is covered by tax receipts, asset sales and borrowing. In short, because the growth of government over the past century has been financed mainly by taxation it has very little, if anything, to do with the monetary system.

However, this argument fails to take account of the fact that a significant proportion of the taxes raised over this period has been generated by inflationary booms. For example, between 1950 and 1975 the value of the British pound declined by 78 per cent and the cost of living increased by 345 per cent.[34] Even during the anti-inflationary Thatcher decade the money supply nearly doubled.[35] The increased tax revenues received by government in an inflationary economy are closely linked with such growth of the money supply. How?

The effect of inflating the money supply is to create a boom, a period of artificial prosperity, i.e. a period in which people *think* that they have more wealth than in fact they do have. This illusion is created by the expansion of the money supply and the consequent easy availability of credit in the economy. People act as though they have more wealth when in fact they only have more money, money that is constantly depreciating in value and therefore increasingly

[33] *Ibid.*

[34] F. A. Hayek, *Denationalisation of Money* (London: Institute of Economic Affairs, Hobart Paper 70, Special [1976], Third Edition 1990), p. 136.

[35] The money supply (M4) increased from £15,953 million in 1981 to £29,438 million in 1991, a growth of just over 84.5 per cent (source: *Annual Abstract of Statistics, 1993* [London: HMSO], p. 292).

represents less wealth (remember that an increase in the money supply creates a situation in which the same total amount of wealth within the economy is represented by a greater supply of money but in which wealth is being redistributed to those who initially have access to the newly created money). The artificial and misleading stimulation of the economy created by inflation of the money supply leads to increased business activity, greater spending etc. and for a while the economy looks buoyant. This increased economic activity within the economy leads to increased tax receipts for the government—even though income tax rates may be falling, as was the case in the late 1980s when increased tax revenues generated by a booming economy contributed to a public-sector debt repayment (PSDR).[36] Government-licensed and government-generated inflation of the money supply, therefore, not only brings in funds to the government via borrowing; it leads to greater revenues from taxation.

This situation is extremely deceptive however. The extra tax revenue accruing to the government during such a boom is not the result of the creation of wealth but rather of greater capital consumption—i.e. it is a tax on the consumption of resources generated by the redistribution of wealth, not a tax on the creation of wealth. The government is effecting a redistribution of wealth within the economy by inflating the money supply, or by permitting the banks to inflate the money supply, and raising extra taxes from the process, which it can then further use to redistribute the wealth of the nation. But wealth is not being created. The greater profits made in this kind of booming economy are not the results of genuine growth but rather of an artificially created *illusion* of growth. Greater profits are being made because people are unwittingly consuming their capital, not because the economy is experiencing genuine growth. This is why booms are followed by recessions: the economy has to adjust to a situation in which there is less capital available within the economy, and therefore less wealth, and hence standards of living generally must go down. Any tax based on this illusion of greater wealth is really a tax not on increase but on capital.

It is the failure to see this link between the illusion of greater wealth, capital consumption, wealth redistribution and increased tax receipts generated by a booming economy that has led some economists to argue that because the growth of government over the past century has been financed mainly by taxation it has very little, if

---

[36] See note 30 above.

anything, to do with the monetary system. The increased tax revenues received by government in an inflationary economy are linked with the inflationary process itself and therefore with the government's control of the monetary system. Such tax receipts constitute a form of expropriation of the nation's wealth by means of monetary debasement.

(*d*) The government further benefits from this system because it is able to use the system to exert a controlling influence over the economy, and government control over the economy has contributed significantly to government control over society generally. As a result of its exploitation of the monetary and fiscal systems government has become the chief economic actor in the economy—what other industry can spend 43 per cent of the GNP?—and is thus able to influence and control the economy in accordance with its own policies. Taken together, the monetary and fiscal systems provide the State with enormous power over society. Government not only raises funds cheaply, pays off its debts with depreciated money and taxes the wealth of the nation; it also becomes a major influence in our lives and acquires considerable control over society generally through the spending power that it can exert on the economy. The effects of such government influence on the economy are extremely damaging.

For example, large sectors of the economy become dependent on the government, and the more dependent the economy is on government the more government is able to influence the economy for its own purposes. These purposes may be politically rational—e.g. the creation of an enormous military machine by the Soviet Union or the creation of government sponsored and subsidised jobs on a massive scale by socialist governments in Western countries—but economically they are extremely debilitating, as was evident in Soviet Russia by the shortage of basic food stuffs. Such problems are endemic in government-controlled economies to a greater or lesser degree. The effects of government influence on the British economy are not as extreme or severe as the effects of government interference in the economies of the Soviet countries were, since the British government's control of the economy is not nearly as total as was the State's control over the economies of the Soviet nations. But there are effects, with the result that the economy is sluggish and inefficient and British standards of living are lower than they otherwise would be. Examples of this effect can be seen in Britain in the nationalised Health Service,

Figure 4

Total Government Expenditure
as a Proportion of the Gross National Product 1982–93
(rounded up or down to the nearest percentage point)

1982	1983	1984	1985	1986	1987
46%	45%	45%	44%	42%	40%

1988	1989	1990	1991	1992	1993
37%	37%	39%	40%	42%	43%

Source: *United Kingdom National Accounts* (HMSO, 1993 and 1994).

which lags behind privately funded systems in societies with enterprise economies that are more developed than the British economy, and in the State education system, which also lags behind the private systems both in Britain and in other countries with more fully developed enterprise economies.

Government today has massive spending power at its disposal, which it is able to use to influence the economy and thereby exercise greater control over society—and such influence and control is always achieved at the expense of individual freedom. We have already seen that total government expenditure in 1993 accounted for over 43 per cent of the GNP (see fig. 4). If the proportion of the GNP spent by the government continues to grow at the rate that it grew in the twentieth century the kinds of economic catastrophe experienced in Soviet Russia will become more commonplace in British society—and, doubtless, with the forming of the European Union in Europe generally.

The provision of government funded services that are free or virtually free at the point of delivery effectively prices private competitors out of the market, destroys consumer choice—at least for the average person—and creates uncompetitive and second-rate monopoly industries that are seldom good value for the money spent on them and serve the interests of those employed in them rather than the general public, which ultimately pays for them. Such government influence in the economy cripples private enterprise and holds down general standards of living. The power that the government exerts on the economy in this way affects all of us either directly or indirectly and plays an important part in determining our general standard of living and the level of prosperity and economic freedom we enjoy.

Government manipulation of the economy through government-created and government-licensed expansion of the money supply is a means of taxing the nation's capital, of expropriating the private wealth of the nation, by borrowing at artificially cheap rates of interest and repaying government debt with devalued money, and by creating an *illusion* of wealth and prosperity on the basis of which government can then increase its tax receipts. These methods of raising government revenue are fundamentally unjust and contribute significantly to the growth of government control over our lives and society. Government manipulation of the economy in this way is quite simply immoral. It is a form of theft and forbidden by the law of God.

§8
The Money Supply and the Retail Price Index

The Retail Price Index is not a reliable indication of the rise in the aggregate level of prices. It is an index of price increases for certain goods. What goods are included in the Retail Price Index is a political decision. The government tries to keep certain goods out of it because they give a more realistic indication of what the government is doing to the money supply. Thus, the prices of houses are kept out, and the Thatcher government was keen to have the interest payments on mortgages taken out also. This was because the increase in house prices during the late 1980s gave a more realistic indication of the inflation figures—i.e. expansion of the money supply. But house prices should feature in the British Retail Price Index, even if they do not feature in the price indices of other countries, since Britain is—or at least was during the Thatcher government's term of office—a big house buying nation compared with most European countries, and surely a country's Retail Price Index should be geared to the buying priorities and patterns of its own people, not the irrelevant patterns of people in other countries. The Thatcher government's argument for keeping house prices out of the Retail Price Index because other countries do not include them was preposterous.

Much of the inflation that occurred under the Thatcher government's second and third terms was camouflaged by two factors: first, the general growth of economic activity generated during Thatcher's premiership, and secondly, the proportion of overall inflation—i.e. increase of the money supply—that was absorbed by the housing market, which, as we have seen, was not properly represented in the Retail Price Index.

The Retail Price Index is thus misleading as an indicator of the real effects of inflation. Indeed it often serves to camouflage the real inflation figures,—i.e. expansion of the money supply—which give a true indication of how the government is debasing the currency or permitting other government-licensed institutions (banks) to debase the currency. For example, the money supply figures for April 1990 are as follows: M4 rose over this month alone by £1.865 billion (6 per cent seasonally adjusted, 4 per cent not seasonally adjusted). The twelve-month growth rate of the money supply (M4) at the beginning of 1990 was 18 per cent. This is the official Bank of England figure.[37] During this period not all prices rose by 18 per cent. Some did not rise that much. Others rose more than 18 per cent. While the growth in the Retail Price Index reached a high point of just under 11 per cent in 1990 the real inflation figure—i.e. growth of the money supply (M4)—was running at 18 per cent, and it had been running at around that figure, or slightly higher, for several years (14.1 per cent in 1987, 16.9 per cent in 1988 and 18.1 per cent in 1989).[38] Increases in house prices during this period were far higher than the official inflation (i.e. price inflation) figures suggested by the Retail Price Index. There was also during this period a redistribution of the nation's wealth, which the Retail Price Index is unable to reflect; nor are there other indices that can reflect such redistributive effects of inflation. Such redistribution of the nation's wealth, i.e. redistribution of wealth resulting from government-licensed and government-managed debasement of the money supply, is an abuse of the government's authority and power and a transgression of the Eighth Command-

---

[37] *Bank of England Inflation Report*, February 1993, p. 29, reprinted from the *Bank of England Quarterly Bulletin*, February, 1993.

[38] The twelve-month M4 growth rate of 18 per cent reached in 1990, as a result of the boom generated by the government following the "Black Monday" Stock Exchange collapse, fell to 6 per cent at the beginning of 1992. As the recession began to bite companies and businesses could no longer afford to expand by means of borrowing, as they had been doing throughout the previous boom, since interest rates had risen considerably.

ment, which it is the State's duty to uphold and enforce according to the Christian Scriptures.

§9
The Consequences of Monetary Inflation for Society

As we have seen, when there is an increase in the money supply the value of each unit of money falls, other things being equal. This is because there is more money chasing the same supply of goods. Prices rise as the purchasing power of each unit of money decreases.

This is what happens: those with the new money spend it into circulation. They are able to purchase goods and services at today's prices with the new money. As the new money enters the economy the market responds to the new situation of a larger money supply and prices rise. Those who do not have the use of the new money then have to pay higher prices for the goods and services they require, though their income has not risen accordingly. Those with the new money benefit at the expense of those who are least able to afford it. Since the value of the monetary unit, its purchasing power, depreciates against the rising price level, those who suffer are people on fixed incomes who do not have the political muscle to secure an increase in income commensurate with the rising price level. This includes people who are not in government-favoured trades and professions or members of powerful trade unions, which can bargain with government and make sure their members are among the privileged number who receive some of the newly created money. It also includes people like pensioners who receive fixed incomes. Those who are unable to defend themselves against government-generated inflation are invariably the ones who have to bear the brunt of it.

The problem does not stop with the debasement of currency and rising prices however. Inflation often leads to a debasement in the quality of goods and services offered for sale also. In an inflationary economy businesses that do not receive some of the newly created money find it increasingly difficult to compete in the face of rising prices. They are faced with two alternatives: raise prices themselves or cut the quality of goods and services offered for sale. If prices are raised sales will probably drop because those who buy their goods will also be feeling the effects of higher prices—unless, of course, they are part of the group favoured with the newly created money. This may lead to firms going out of business because they are unable to compete at higher prices with firms that are subsidised with the new money.[39] In order to keep costs of production down and compete with government-favoured groups—viz. government-subsidised industries and companies—and those who have access to the new money, manufacturers may decide to cut corners or use materials of an inferior quality. As a result the quality of goods and services goes down. This is the kind of thing that happens in an inflationary economy. Debasement of the money supply often leads to the debasement of the quality of goods and services offered for sale also. Ultimately no one gains from this kind of monetary inflation since the inevitable consequence of sustained debasement of the currency is the squandering of the scarce resources available to the economy and hence eventually recession and a general lowering of standards of living.

Conclusion

The adverse consequences of government-licensed and government-generated inflation of the money supply on the scale that the nation experienced it in the twentieth century are serious and extremely debilitating for the economy. The damage inflicted upon the economy by the constant swing between booms and slumps has become much more acute with each cycle, and the economy's ability to recover from recession has been increasingly weakened. This was very evident in the recession that began in the late 1980s/early '90s. Few politicians and economists anticipated the recession would be so long and so deep, and in spite of the continual optimistic talking-up of the economy and the numerous pronouncements made by government officials and ministers, chief among them the Chancellor of the Exchequer, that the recession had "theoretically" ended—an utterly preposterous statement by anyone's standards when the economy was clearly still in recession—the economy still continued to languish, unemployment continued to rise and businesses continued to go bank-

---

[39] It makes no difference whether this subsidy is a direct government grant, or whether it is made available indirectly through the commercial banking system; the effect is the same. As we have seen, traditional socialist governments tend to favour the former whereas Conservative governments generally favour the latter.

rupt at an alarming rate. Doubtless many of these businesses could never have hoped to last long into the recession, being no more than the ephemeral symptoms of a false climate of economic prosperity generated by the previous boom. Still, the effects of such bankruptcies are extremely damaging for those involved.

Sooner or later, given the continuance of the monetary system that has created the business cycle, the economy will enter a recession from which it cannot recover. We shall then find ourselves in the midst of a full-blown depression, possibly even accompanied by social anarchy, which history teaches has usually been followed by authoritarian rule of the most oppressive kind. Such prospects are by no means absurd or unimaginable, as a brief look back at the history of the twentieth century will show, and they are much exacerbated by our membership of the European Union. It is vital, therefore, that the prevailing state of affairs be ameliorated. In order to accomplish this a thoroughgoing reform of the economic mechanisms that have created the present malady is necessary. It is to an outline of such reform that we shall now turn.

CHAPTER FIVE

ECONOMIC REFORM

The Political Economy of a Christian Society

REFORM of the economy in terms of a Christian theory of political economy requires the recognition of three essential principles relating to economic behaviour. These three principles constitute the foundation of a Christian economic order. Without this foundation a Christian political economy is not possible. Before looking at these principles of economic life it is important to remember that we are dealing here with the *economic* organisation of society. A society is far more than an economic phenomenon, however. What is said here, therefore, should not be understood on its own as a paradigm for social reform or regeneration. Rather, it is *one* element of a Christian paradigm for social reform. To define mankind or society merely in terms of the economic aspect of life would be a reductionist and therefore ultimately an idolatrous view of human life. Nevertheless, as part of an overall Christian social theory the economic aspect of life is important and must be addressed. What follows is not meant to be a complete social theory by any means. It offers a Christian perspective on the *economic* organisation of society.

The three principal foundations of a Christian theory of political economy are: (1) recognition of the moral nature of economic behaviour and therefore of the necessity that such behaviour conform to the ethical precepts of the Christian faith as revealed in the canon of Scripture; (2) acceptance of personal responsibility as the context of economic life; and (3) private ownership of economic power. The last two principles are the consequence of the consistent application of the first. It may be assumed that all who seek to develop a specifically and consistently Christian theory of political economy will accept this first principle. It may also be assumed that the second of these principles will be accepted by economists who are committed to a specifically Christian approach to their subject. About the third principle, private ownership of economic power, there has been much disagreement between Christians, including Christian economists, and especially between those for whom socialism functions as a primary aspect of their religious world-view and those for whom it does not.

This chapter will attempt to show why the consistent application of biblical ethics to economic behaviour must lead to private ownership of economic power and what political reforms are necessary if the British economy is to conform to a Christian theory of political economy. Taking these three principles in reverse order we shall now look at their implications for the economic organisation of society.

(a) *Private ownership of economic power*

The Bible condemns the accumulation of economic power by the State (Dt. 17:17). Instead of economic power being concentrated in the hands of the State, the Bible teaches that economic power should be vested primarily in the family and the individual, and the State is required to protect the private ownership of economic power by its enforcement of the Eighth Commandment: "Thou shalt not steal." The State is permitted to collect taxes only for the specific purpose of enabling it to pursue its God-ordained function as a ministry of public justice, i.e. for the purpose of funding the administration of the State (Rom. 13:1–7).[1] It is this principle of private ownership of economic power that constitutes the basic *economic* framework of a Christian theory of political economy.

This restriction on the State's authority to concentrate economic power into its own hands and the stress on its duty to protect and preserve the economic power of the individual and the family has far-reaching consequences for the economic organisation of society. Private ownership of economic power requires private ownership of the means of *production, distribution* and *exchange* of economic goods and services. Private ownership of the means of production necessitates the privatisation or eradication of nationalised industries and the cessation of government economic controls over these and other industries. Private ownership of the means of distribution requires that there be no minimum wage laws or wage and price controls, rationing, government subsidies, government-imposed restrictive practices, import and export quotas and controls, tariffs, and State-

---

[1] For a more detailed statement of this doctrine see Stephen C. Perks, *A Defence of the Christian State* (Taunton: Kuyper Foundation, 1998), Appendix A and *passim*.

controlled or State-enforced wealth redistribution programmes. It also means there should be no State-controlled or State-assisted welfare and education programmes or services. Private ownership of the means of exchange requires the abolition of State-owned mints and State-enforced fiat money. It also means there should be no State-enforced controls on currency exchange rates or restrictions on the exchange of specie into foreign currency and vice versa, no State controls on the volume and value of the money in circulation, and that free coinage and banking practices should be permitted, i.e. there should be no State-imposed licence requirements and controls on entry into the economic enterprise of banking and minting coin other than those required by the administration of public justice, e.g. fair weights and measures.

(b) Personal responsibility

What has been described above would be called today a free enterprise or free market economy; i.e. a society in which there is freedom from government direction and control in the economic decisions that people make. A Christian economic order, however, requires more than the mere application of the mechanisms and technology of free enterprise. The Christian theory of political economy does not presuppose that mere freedom from State control and access to free market economic technology, e.g. the availability of technological improvements in industry, of highly developed financial institutions and methods of payments, greater economic rationalisation etc., can, on their own, produce economic growth and the general social amelioration that economic growth makes possible. Nor does it suppose that a policy of *laissez-faire* on its own will produce a Christian economic order. The Christian theory of political economy recognises that the most important economic resource is human initiative. Where this is lacking or is socially prohibited in some way,[2] economic growth and general social amelioration will be

---

[2] The disincentive to use one's initiative in economic activity can be either legal, e.g. punitive taxation rates, or cultural, i.e. by means of social disapprobation. Punitive taxation rates are endemic in socialist States to varying degrees, and in some former Soviet States only the black markets were able to provide sufficient opportunity for rational economic activity to stop the country from falling into abject poverty. For an example of cultural suppression of economic initiative see the comments on the Lovedu in Helmut Schoeck, *Envy, A Theory of Social Behaviour* (London: Secker and Warburg, 1969), pp. 39–41.

limited. Economic growth, therefore, requires a social order in which the Christian virtues of honesty, hard work and thrift are accepted and prized, and in which personal initiative and effort are rewarded without social disapprobation being shown to those who succeed. This requires a society in which envy is not accepted as a legitimate response to the success of others, or at least a society in which envy is not institutionalised as virtue by politicians who are eager to appease the envy of voters by promising punitive social controls over the wealth and freedom of those who succeed in business.

Of course, this means also, and inevitably, a social order in which personal failure is shouldered by the individual and not imputed to other individuals, groups or society as a whole. That is to say, the Christian theory of political economy requires a social order in which both the freedom and the responsibility of the individual, as well as the necessity of honesty, hard work and thrift, are recognised as essential to a sound economy and, moreover, in which these ideals are prized *above* the mere acquisition of material things.

Private ownership of the means of production and distribution is widely recognised as an essential feature of capitalism ("private ownership of the means of production" has been a classic definition of capitalism *vis-à-vis* socialism). But a *Christian*—i.e. a biblically informed—theory of the economic organisation of society requires more than this. It requires private ownership of the means of *exchange* as well as private ownership of the means of production and distribution. The reasons for this will be explained below.

(c) The ethical foundations of a Christian political economy

The epistemological and ethical foundations of a Christian theory of political economy should be explicitly articulated and provide the intellectual, moral and economic framework within which the Christian economist seeks to understand his subject. It is in the context of these epistemological and ethical guiding principles that the Christian economist must seek to develop norms for economic behaviour. This intellectual, moral and economic framework is a *theonomic* framework. That is to say, it is a framework that seeks to explicate the precepts of God's law as they apply to economic behaviour in the modern world and thus provide ethical criteria for assessing different types of economic behaviour and economic policy. Christ said "If ye love me, keep my commandments" (Jn 14:15) and the apostle Paul taught us that "Love worketh no ill to his neighbour: therefore love is the fulfilling [i.e. the keeping] of the law" (Rom. 13:10). The Christian economist seeks to show us how we can love God and our neighbour in the way we behave economically and what kinds of economic activity are proscribed by God's law. It is this explicitly biblical epistemological and ethical perspective, along with the biblical concept of private ownership of economic power and the Christian ethic of personal responsibility, that constitutes a distinctively Christian theory of political economy.

This theonomic framework accounts for the Christian view of the role of the State. In the Christian perspective the State's authority over the individual and society is limited.[3] But this limitation is of a specific nature. It is not libertarian in nature. The State is there to protect and preserve the moral environment in which the individual, the family, church and society generally can function obediently in response to God's revealed will for and calling upon mankind. Without the preservation of moral and legal order sin would reign unchecked in society and rational economic activity would become impossible.[4] The State thus has a vitally important, God-ordained role to play in society, without which it is not possible for a free market economy to function properly. As a ministry of public justice it creates the social order necessary to enable the free market to flourish. By establishing justice it enables the law-abiding citizen to go about his business with confidence in the legal and moral predictability of the market order, lack of which would render rational economic behaviour according to the fixed moral standards of the Christian religion impossible. But its role is *political*, not economic in nature. When the State does engage in management of the economy it disrupts this moral order; i.e. it confuses politics with

---

[3] See Stephen C. Perks, *op. cit.*, pp. 141–179.

[4] Cf. Gen. 6:1–8; 9:6–10. It would seem that prior to the Flood there was no State or magistrate and personal vengeance was expected as the consequence of acts of injustice (cf. Gen. 4:14–15, 23–24). By contrast, the covenant with Noah requires the death sentence for murder to be carried out by man himself (9:6); i.e. man is for the first time required to act as a magistrate, a minister or avenger of God's wrath upon the one who does evil (Rom. 13:4). The implication is that without a human agency to restrain certain kinds of evil human society in the state of sin cannot last long before there is a total breakdown of morality, indeed a total breakdown of social order. The State, as a God-ordained institution charged with preserving law and order according to the principles of equity set down in God's law, plays a vital role in restraining the kind of evil that makes social co-operation, including economic co-operation, impossible.

economics and becomes a disruptive influence on the very order it is charged by God with preserving. The State is not given authority by God's word to manage the economy or redistribute the wealth it produces. The family is stressed as the primary economic institution in the Bible. God has granted economic power to the family and to the individual, not to the State, and this delegation of economic power to the individual and the family is protected by the Eighth Commandment. The State is authorised to levy taxes specifically for the purpose of funding the administration of public justice, which is the State's only legitimate function under God's law (Rom. 13:1–7). It is not authorised to act as an agency for redistributing wealth within society. The Eighth Commandment forbids all compulsory wealth redistribution programmes of any kind.

The State, therefore, is limited by God's law in the amount of taxes it may collect and the purposes for which it may levy taxes. Its functions and jurisdiction are limited. It exists to preserve maximum freedom under God's law for the individual, the family, church and society at large. Only as the State preserves this freedom under God's law will society be able to develop an enterprise economy that can sustain the long-term economic growth that will lead to the kind of general social amelioration for all in society that the West has come to expect and take for granted. The role of the State is thus essential in a Christian economic order. But its role is *juridical* not economic. It exists to preserve legal and moral predictability and accountability within society as a whole, and within the economy as an essential part of society, so that society can flourish.

The Christian theory of political economy sets forth, therefore, a form of economic organisation based on private ownership of the means of production, distribution and exchange and the Christian virtues of honesty, hard work, thrift and personal responsibility in the context of a free society abiding by the rule of law[5] with a limited civil government appointed to administer public justice according to the general principles of equity laid down in God's law.

If our economy is to conform to a Christian model of economic organisation, therefore, a far-reaching programme of economic and political reform must be implemented. It is to such a programme

[5] On the Christian doctrine of the rule of law see Stephen C. Perks, "Christianity and the Rule of Law" in *The Salisbury Review*, Vol. 18, No. 2 (Winter, 1999), pp. 4–9. See also, *idem, Christianity and Law: A Enquiry into the Influence of Christianity on the Development of English Common Law* (Avant Books, 1993).

of reform that we shall now turn. It must be recognised, however, that economic reform on its own cannot create a Christian economy, much less a Christian society. Unless people are prepared and willing to behave in a Christian, i.e. a biblically-informed, way when they engage in economic activity no amount of political reform will produce a Christian economic order. Reform of social structures on its own cannot redeem society from sinful behaviour. Nevertheless, social structures form the context of all human activity, including economic activity, and if such activity is to conform to Christian ideals these social structures must also conform to Christian ideals. The rest of this chapter will be occupied with delineating the kind of structural reforms that are necessary if our society is to conform to the Christian theory of political economy.

§2
Abolition of Legal Tender Laws

As we have already seen,[6] money can be defined simply as *the most marketable good*.[7] Men should be free to trade in whatever medium of exchange they choose, whether gold, silver or Stilton cheeses. The function of the State in this area, as a ministry of public justice, is to police weights and measures and to enforce legally binding contracts between individuals who have freely entered into those contracts. This is the limit of the State's God-ordained role in economic affairs (Rom. 13:1–6). Thus, if two parties freely choose to enter into a legally binding contract for the supply of certain goods in exchange for a given amount payable in a nominated medium—e.g. gold or silver—the function of the civil government is to enforce that contract should either party default or commit fraud by supplying something other than that specified in the contract, whether faulty goods or payment in a debased medium of exchange. Banknotes promising

---

[6] See above p. 54ff.

[7] Ludwig von Mises, *The Theory of Money and Credit* (London: Jonathan Cape, 1934, trans. by H. E. Batson), pp. 30–34. In *Human Action* Mises writes: "Money is a medium of exchange. It is the most marketable good which people acquire because they want to offer it in later acts of interpersonal exchange. Money is the thing which serves as the generally accepted and commonly used medium of exchange. This is its only function. All other functions which people ascribe to money are merely particular aspects of its primary and sole function, that of a medium of exchange" (*Human Action, A Treatise on Economics* [Chicago: Contemporary Books, Inc., third revised edition, 1966], p. 401).

to pay the bearer on demand a given sum must be fully redeemable in the specified medium. If the bank fails to redeem its notes or tries to suspend payment the State should step in and force the bank to meet its obligations. If the bank is unable to do so it must be declared bankrupt, the receiver called in, and possibly its shareholders required to reimburse their creditors and make restitution to those holding the bank's notes.[8] Equally, the coining of money that is debased, i.e. worth less than its face value in terms of weight and fineness, must be punished and restitution made to those holding such currency.

Commercial contracts freely entered into specifying settlement of account in gold, silver or even cornflakes would be equally valid from a legal point of view. It is not the function of the civil government to establish and maintain a common currency of the realm, whether based on gold, silver or any other standard, and pass laws making that currency legally binding upon creditors in settlement of debt. Its obligation in monetary affairs is simply to police weights and measures, punish fraud and ensure that legally binding contracts are fulfilled faithfully according to the terms of agreement on both sides. If a party agrees to pay a given sum of gold or silver in exchange for goods or services he is legally obligated to honour that agreement in the nominated medium of exchange. If he wishes to settle his account in a currency other than that stipulated in the agreement and the vendor refuses to receive payment in the medium offered the State must ensure that the original terms of the contract are honoured. The State does not have the moral authority to pass legislation that standardises a particular medium of exchange as currency of the realm, obliging all creditors within its jurisdiction to accept that medium in the settlement of debt. For the State to create and maintain such legal tender[9] and enforce its use on society is an abuse of its God-given authority and power and an attack on the individual's freedom under God's law.

[8] See the discussion of limited liability law in Appendix A. See also note 44 below.

[9] In Great Britain legal tender is defined as currency that cannot legally be refused in the settlement of debt. This means that a vendor is not legally obliged to accept payment in legal tender *except* as settlement of a debt. It is this exception that defines legal tender. However, it effectively gives legal tender the force of a universally accepted medium of exchange in the UK in all everyday economic transactions no matter how devalued it may have become. In England and Wales Bank of England notes and pound coins are legal tender up to any amount, token "silver" coin, which actually contains no silver at all, and bronze coin is legal tender up to a limited amount. In Northern Ireland and Scotland only pound coins have legal tender status for unlimited amounts.

In a society basing its monetary transactions on just weights and measures and legally binding contracts and where the government's role in the economy is limited in the way described above there might theoretically be multiple currencies or mediums of exchange in use. In practice a single medium, as the most marketable good, which historically has been gold, would probably establish itself as the main currency or standard of payments. That is to say, people would tend to demand a certain medium in exchange for goods and services since as the most marketable good the use of that medium of exchange would maximise their options and give them a more competitive position in the market. Less marketable mediums of exchange would therefore tend to be demonetised. This is a process of economic rationalisation that develops over time and in fact accounts for the emergence of gold as a de facto international medium of exchange and the general demonetisation of other mediums of exchange.

Given the economic conditions described above, therefore, gold would most likely become the common medium of exchange and payments would be settled either in gold coin, cheques drawn on gold accounts or by means of gold instruments—i.e. claims to gold— and promissory notes redeemable in gold on demand (banknotes etc., but see the discussion below on p. 178ff.). Other mediums in circulation such as silver and less valuable metals for lower denominations, such as copper, would be valued against gold, but no legally binding fixed exchange ratios would exist. Thus, the situation that existed in Britain prior to 1914 when the face value of silver coin was greater than the value of its metal content, and between 1914 and 1920 when silver coin was undervalued and worth more than its face value,[10] would be avoided. There would in other words be

[10] The reason for the rise in value of silver after 1914 was the increased demand for it as a medium of exchange in the Orient. H. O. Meredith comments: "Before 1914, for instance, the rouble note had been used in trade between China and Siberia; it had, in great measure, won the confidence of Chinese traders, mainly through its stability in purchasing power. When this note depreciated in value owing to the excessive war-time issue, there came a quickening desire for 'hard' money. The paper representation no longer commanded trust; for it had repeatedly failed to bring the anticipated amount of real goods. But for this affecting of their pockets, the millions of China might have looked upon the European conflict as an inexplicable freak of the distant barbarians. As it was, the loss of confidence in the discredited paper brought about a change in their economic life. It enhanced the world demand for silver. Its price rose to such a point that the Mint, if it had wished to issue new silver coins, would have lost heavily in the process" (*Economic History of England* [London: Sir Isaac Pitman and Sons, Ltd, 1936], p. 402). In early 1920 the silver coinage in Britain was debased to 50 parts silver and 50 parts alloy and thus the

floating exchange rates between different mediums, and silver and bronze coin would effectively function as currency only up to a certain amount, beyond which it would tend to be demonetised due to the greater value and efficiency of gold as a medium of exchange. Gold would probably function as the de facto standard.[11]

This does not mean that gold should be made a legally binding standard of payments enforceable by legal tender laws, the establishment of government mints and a central bank to regulate and control the issue of money in terms of an official gold standard. The only monetary standard enforceable by the State should be that of *honesty*. Parties to economic transactions would be required by law to honour the terms and conditions of contracts and agreements freely entered into and governments would be obligated to enforce such contracts and agreements by bringing to justice those who failed to fulfil the terms and conditions of their contracts. As regards every day cash transactions, the agreement to exchange goods and services for a given amount in a particular medium of exchange would constitute a contract and should either party subsequently be found to have renegued on his contractual obligations, by supplying goods and services other than those agreed upon or by paying for them with debased money, he would be liable to prosecution. Banknotes offered in exchange that banks subsequently failed to redeem would, however, be considered a breach of contract on the part of the bank that issued them not the holder; likewise, debased coin passed on to the unsuspecting public would be considered fraud on the part of the agency that minted it.

Only by limiting the government's role in monetary affairs to the task of enforcing legally binding contracts and policing weights and measures shall we be able to regain our economic freedom, since governments pass legal tender laws in order to enable the State to control the creation, volume and value of the money in the economy. Governments demand such powers ultimately in order that they might be able to expropriate the nation's wealth for their own purposes,

---

value of the silver coinage again fell below its face value. Not long after this, however, the price of silver fell again.

[11] Even if this were not the case and various different currencies competed alongside each other as media of exchange (e.g. gold and silver) this would be an entirely acceptable situation and much to be preferred, for economic as well as ethical reasons, over government monopoly of the issue of money. On the case for currency competition see F. A. Hayek, *Denationalisation of Money* (London: Institute of Economic Affairs, [1976] 1990; Hobart Paper [Special] 70).

e.g. in order to redistribute the nation's wealth. Such government-created and government-controlled legal tender, whether it is based on a gold standard or a fiat paper standard, involves the curtailing of the individual's freedom and usually the plundering of his economic resources by the State. This is theft by government decree and thus economic tyranny.

Abolition of legal tender laws would hamstring the State's ability to control the money supply by rendering its debased paper notes ineffective as the only medium of exchange legally binding in the settlement of debt. Eventually, as this and the other reforms discussed in this chapter were put into practice, this currency would become worthless[12] and its continued creation would be rendered illegal since its issue would not be considered a legitimate function of the State. Parties to an economic exchange would be free to stipulate the currency of their choice, which would be legally binding even in the settlement of debt. The government would be forced increasingly to finance its own borrowing by raising taxes and it would be required to make payments in the medium of exchange agreed upon by the parties involved in any contract it entered into. This would force the government onto an honesty standard like everyone else. If the government contracted for services or bought goods under an agreement that required payment in gold, it would be legally bound to honour its contractual obligations. Since governments should not be immune from the law any failure on the part of the government to make payment in the medium of exchange agreed upon in a government contract would render it liable to prosecution and bankrupt governments would be forced to resign from office and make restitution to their creditors. Governments should not be treated as limited liability corporations.

---

[12] The principle known as Gresham's Law, namely that bad money drives good money out of circulation, only operates where the former exists as a legally enforceable means of payment; e.g. where it has legal tender status or is subject to fixed exchange rates. Gresham's Law should be stated in the following way therefore: Overvalued money drives undervalued money out of circulation where there is a fixed exchange ratio between the two. Where this is not the case Gresham's Law will not operate. For example, where legal tender and fixed exchange rates are abolished either Gresham's Law will be reversed, i.e. good money (e.g. hard money) will drive bad money (e.g. unredeemable paper currency) out of circulation, or, where a previously overvalued currency is not entirely worthless, it will be devalued against a previously undervalued currency.

§3
Abolition of Government-Imposed Restrictions on the use of Precious Metals as Currency

As we have seen, gold, because it excels above all other metals in the qualities necessary for a medium of exchange to function effectively, became the de facto monetary standard historically throughout the world. What is said here is equally applicable to all other forms of money, e.g. silver and bronze, but since gold is the historically accepted form of specie used as a monetary standard throughout the world the principles involved will be discussed in relation to gold.

In order for gold to function efficiently as a medium of exchange it must be allowed to function without political obstructions being placed upon its use as such. If the abolition of legal tender laws is to be effective, therefore, by allowing individuals to write legally binding contracts and generally trade in the medium of exchange of their choice, all regulations and laws penalising or obstructing the use of hard money must be removed. There have been two methods used to control the use of gold as a medium of exchange by our governments in recent times: (*a*) laws making the use of gold as money illegal, and (*b*) the imposition of sales tax and capital gains tax on gold. The former simply makes all trade using gold as a medium of exchange a criminal act. This is a rather Draconian measure and those governments wishing to present themselves as more enlightened and enamoured of a free market philosophy would, no doubt, choose the latter, which makes the use of gold as money much more expensive than government fiat currency; that is to say it makes its use as a medium of exchange unprofitable or at least less profitable than fiat currency and therefore uneconomic. Obviously, just as we should not expect to pay sales tax when exchanging token cupro-nickel coins for notes at the bank, neither should we have to pay it when exchanging fiat currency for gold. Yet this was precisely what happened prior to January 2000 if one used gold as a medium of exchange, since both gold bullion and coin were subject to VAT, and with the exception of British denominated coin the sale of gold is still subject to capital gains tax. Both these means of controlling the use of gold as money have been used by our governments since the Second World War. We shall now look at these blunt instruments of economic tyranny in more depth.

(a) Laws making the use of gold as money illegal

If the government is to control the economy for its own purposes it must of necessity have a means of controlling the creation, volume and value of the nation's currency. Without control of the nation's currency the government's power to control and manipulate the economy is severely handicapped. The freedom to trade, to use the medium of exchange of one's choice, to hold one's wealth in a form that the State has no control over, limits the power of the State over society. Economic freedom is thus a great bulwark against tyranny. If the government is to have the power to pursue its own policies without being hindered and limited by the electorate it must deprive people of their economic freedom and vest all power and authority over the money supply in itself and its agents. Taxation, no matter how heavy it may be, cannot accomplish this on its own since it still leaves the taxpayer with a degree of economic freedom and thus with a real, if limited, sphere of economic life that the State is not able to control. Once the authorities have obtained control of the currency, however, by denying people the right to trade in the medium of exchange of their choice, it matters not how much toleration the government may show in times of peace or prosperity by permitting people to trade in various mediums other than government currency. The government still has the power of control should it deem there to be an emergency serious enough to warrant the exercise of its monopoly over the money supply. Privileges, even great privileges, can be granted by those who have the authority and power to rescind such privileges. No matter how much free rope is given to people under normal conditions, the government can pull in the slack when it wishes to do so. This was the story of Britain's economic and political history in the twentieth century.

For example, in time of war the State needs to build up and maintain a war machine that will be able to defeat the enemy. The cost of doing this is immense, especially in times of mass warfare such as the First and Second World War. The State must amass the resources needed for this from the nation, which in theory it represents. The simple and honest way of doing this is through taxation. However, it seems that governments have always been prone to supplement taxation with deficit financing, i.e. borrowing. It was in order to facilitate such deficit financing on the part of the government that the Bank of England was created and for which it has existed to this very day. When faced with the necessity of pursuing hard fiscal policies, however, government lays itself open to the disapprobation and censure of the electorate. In order to obtain its ends without the risk of popular resentment or of losing office at the next general election, or possibly even revolt,[13] governments resort to the use of the less obvious and open methods—though much more damaging to the economy—of monetary policy, i.e. manipulation of the money supply.

But how can government do this effectively and efficiently, especially in times of high government expenditure such as our own, if people are able to redeem their currency in gold and therefore able to maintain their economic independence of the State? Such independence, i.e. economic freedom, necessarily limits the power of government. Suppose, then, that the government needs revenues, to finance a war, for example, or the creation of a State welfare agency, but fears it will not be able to obtain it through taxation without making itself unacceptable to the electorate and therefore without running the risk of losing office at the next general election. It cannot inflate the money supply by issuing fiduciary media *and* allow redemption in gold without facing a massive run on its reserves. And if it does not offer redemption people will not accept its notes. Thus, redemption in gold must be suspended. Indeed, as we shall see, all buying and selling of gold or even the holding of wealth in the form of gold or foreign currency that can be redeemed in gold must be made illegal and individuals required to surrender their stocks of gold coin and bullion to the government's coffers. The government is then able to inflate the money supply and monopolise the currency, and the population must accept payments in the form of devalued fiat notes issued by the central bank.

By suspending the use of gold as money and replacing it with fiat paper money, the government is able to expropriate the nation's wealth without running the risk of creating the same kind of hostile reaction that direct fiscal policy would most likely create, particularly

[13] This was of course the experience of the Thatcher government during its ill-fated third term of office when popular resentment of hard fiscal policy, e.g. reduction in government spending and in particular imposition of the poll tax, led to riots on the streets during demonstrations by those formerly not used to paying for the services they constantly demand from government. Although it was not Thatcher's line on fiscal policy that led to her political demise, but rather her opposition to a European super-State, it was significant that the Major government, upon taking office, succumbed to the demands of the rioting mobs by abolishing the poll tax and replacing it with a less equitable property tax.

among the wealth producing and property holding classes, who usually have to bear the heaviest tax burden of any taxable group. British society traditionally had a strong ethic of individual liberty informed by Christian values and a Christian view of responsible citizenship. In such a milieu one might expect dishonesty on the part of government in the management of the nation's monetary system to provoke a public outcry. But it seems Christian ideals have long since ceased to have any place in our greedy and envy-ridden socialist society. Nonetheless, for government to raise revenues through the monopolising and debasement of currency rather than by means of honest fiscal policy is deceitful and constitutes a form of theft on the part of the very institution whose purpose and duty it is to uphold justice, protect the innocent and punish wrongdoing. It is economic tyranny. The individual's rights and freedoms are outlawed and his livelihood becomes dependent on a State-managed economy. His economic prosperity, his opportunities for work, perhaps even his right to work, become inseparably tied to government economic and social policy. Economically he is no longer free; he has become enslaved to the State. Most people, of course, are unaware of what is happening; they are promised security and prosperity by an all-powerful State, and they begin to see their freedom as a mean thing alongside this. Once they are hooked on such propaganda this whole totalitarian ideology becomes reinforced throughout society and institutionalised. The result is that government power and control over people's lives is enhanced and reaches levels not previously countenanced or perhaps even thought possible. The population, by and large, since it is unaware of the danger that such absolute power brings, is apathetic about what is happening and fails to recognise the need for reform of government. People see only the promises that governments make—promises that are impossible to keep, though few politicians will admit it. Indeed the very failure of government promises is used in propaganda as an argument for the extension of governmental power and the creation of more State controls and regulations; and motivated only by self-interest the masses swallow this ideology without scrutinising its contents. The nation's ability to reassert its freedom is vitiated and it is unable to respond effectively to tyranny on the part of the government.

Far greater power accrues to governments that are prepared to pursue such methods than that accruing to governments determined to finance their policies by means of direct fiscal measures. A government that has to raise vast amounts through taxation is subject to the willingness of the people to accept its dictates and must always carry the people with it, otherwise revolt is possible. This restraint is absent to a large extent for a government that is prepared to finance its policies by means of monetary expansion, since it always has at its disposal the whole wealth of the nation and need not go to the people to raise funding for its policies by means of taxation.

The modern State has effectively taken control of the nation's wealth by taking control of the volume and value of the currency in circulation, which it is able to debase for its own ends whenever it deems it necessary to do so. In 1939 the government of Great Britain was able to raise the funds necessary to finance its total war machine by means of powers that extended to legislation requiring the British people to surrender all gold coin, bullion and foreign currency in their possession to the Treasury.[14] By means of the same legislation the government was also able to take control of securities payable in foreign currencies.

On the 24th of August 1939 the Emergency Powers (Defence) Act, 1939 was passed. This enabled the government to make Defence Regulations in accordance with the purposes set forth in the Act. On the following day The Defence (Finance) Regulations were made. These regulations stated that

4.—(1) Every person in whose case the following conditions are fulfilled, that is to say—

    (a) that he is, or has, at any time since the third day of September, nineteen hundred and thirty-nine, been, in the United Kingdom, or, being a corporation, he is, or has, at any time since the third day of September, nineteen hundred and thirty-nine, been, resident in the United Kingdom, and

    (b) that he is entitled to sell, or to procure for sale of, any gold, shall offer that gold, or cause it to be offered, for sale to the Treasury, or to a person designated by the Treasury for the purposes of this Regulation, at such a price as may be determined by or on behalf of the treasury:

Provided that the preceding provisions of this paragraph shall not impose upon any person an obligation to offer any gold for sale, or to cause any

---

[14] There was also an interesting change in the way the size of the fiduciary issue was determined at the beginning of World War Two: "At the outbreak of war in 1939 the whole of the gold held by the Bank's Issue Department, apart from a token amount, was transferred to the Exchange Equalization Account and the fiduciary issue was consequently increased to £580m. [from £300 million—SCP]. The 1939

gold to be offered for sale, if and so long as he is, in respect of that gold, exempted from this Regulation by the Treasury or by a person so designated.

(1A) Where a person has become bound under paragraph (1) of this Regulation to offer, or cause to be offered, any gold for sale, and has not done so, the Treasury may direct that that gold shall vest in the Treasury, and it shall vest in the Treasury accordingly free from any mortgage, pledge or charge, and the Treasury may deal with it as they think fit, but the Treasury shall pay to the person who would but for the direction be entitled to possession of the gold such price in respect thereof as may be determined by or on behalf of the Treasury.[15]

These regulations similarly required all residents and corporations of the United Kingdom to sell their foreign currency to the Treasury or its designated agents at a price determined by the Treasury, and to assign all rights to credit and bank balances payable in foreign currency to the Treasury or its designated agents, again with the Treasury determining the sum payable as consideration for the assignment of the rights to itself.[16] Securities payable in certain foreign currencies were also covered by these regulations and had to be registered with the Bank of England, the Treasury having power to vest in themselves and pay for them in sterling.[17]

In other words, all residents of the United Kingdom holding gold in the form of coin[18] or bullion were required to sell it to the Treasury or its agents at a price to be determined by the Treasury or its agents. Monetary transactions in gold were outlawed by this legislation and

---

Currency and Bank Notes Act introduced an entirely new principle for the regulation of the note issue. It provided that the size of the note issue should always be equal to the market value of gold and assets held by the Issue Department. Under the 1844 Act, notes could only be issued against additional gold, valued at the fixed statutory price of £3 17s 10½d an ounce. The automatic safeguard against inflation provided by the gold standard had been abandoned in 1931, and the remaining safeguard of parliamentary approval was on the face of it abandoned by the 1939 Act. Since a market rise in the value of gold reflects a depreciation of sterling, against not only gold but any other currency linked to gold, this Act logically turned the basic principle of the 1844 Act upside down. At the end of the war, the fiduciary issue reached £1,350m." (Forrest Capie and Alan Webber, *A Monetary History of the United Kingdom, 1870–1982* [London: George Allen and Unwin, 1985], Vol. I, p. 212)

[15] The Defence (Finance) Regulations, 1939, (*made under the Emergency Powers (Defence) Acts, 1939 and 1940, printed as amended up to the 14th October, 1942*) together with A classified list of Orders made under the Defence (Finance) Regulations, 1939, and in force on the 14th October, 1942 (London: H.M.S.O., Fifth Edition—14th October, 1942), p. 19f.   [16] *Ibid.*, Reg. 5.

[17] *Ibid.*, Reg. 1. See F. C. Howard, *Butterworths Annotated Legislation Service, Statutes Supplement No. 43. Exchange and Borrowing Control* (London: Butterworth and Co. (Publishers) Ltd 1948), p. 3.

[18] Genuine collectors' pieces were exempted from this order.

even the holding of gold, except with the permission of the Treasury, was forbidden. All residents of the UK were required to surrender all wealth in the form of gold coin or bullion to the Treasury in order to enable the government to fund the war effort. They were also denied the freedom to trade in any currency that kept its value against the debased fiat money issued by the Bank of England,[19] since they also had to surrender foreign currency.

The Act under which these regulations came into force was related to the war effort, being the Emergency Powers (Defence) Act, 1939. After the end of World War Two, however, the government, wishing to maintain this policy of outlawing the use of gold as money by the British people, could hardly maintain it under emergency powers taken in a state of war. The 1939 regulations were therefore superseded by the Exchange Control Act, 1947. This enabled the government to continue its monopolistic control of the gold supply in time of peace. Section 1 of the Act prohibited anyone in or resident in the United Kingdom from purchasing, borrowing, selling or lending either in or outside the United Kingdom any gold[20] or foreign currency from or to anyone other than an authorised dealer, and required anyone who did purchase or borrow gold or foreign currency from an authorised dealer to comply with such conditions regarding its use as the Treasury may impose upon it. Section 2(1) immediately then required everyone in or resident in the United Kingdom holding gold and who was not an authorised dealer to sell his gold or foreign currency to an authorised dealer, unless he had obtained consent to retain it from the Treasury. As in the 1939 regulations the 1947 Act also covered securities.

[19] In February of the same year the Currency and Bank Notes Act, 1939 had increased the Bank of England's fiduciary issue from £260 million to £300 million Under the Defence (Finance) Regulations, 1939, the requirement for parliamentary sanction of any increase in the fiduciary issue was suspended; as a consequence the fiduciary issue was increased at the outbreak of war to £580 million—cf. note 14 above (see also J. Milnes Holden, *The History of Negotiable Instruments in English Law* [London: The Athlone Press, 1955], p. 280f.). By 1946 the fiduciary issue had reached the figure of £1,450 millions. From 1844 to 1928 it had been fixed by the Bank Charter Act at £14 millions. Under the Currency and Bank Notes Act, 1914 the nation's stock of money was augmented by the issue of £1 and 10s Treasury Notes— i.e. fiat money issued by the Treasury. Although the Bank Charter Act of 1844 was suspended the Bank of England's fiduciary issue was not increased, but the issue of the Treasury notes had the same effect. The Currency and Bank Notes Act, 1928 placed the whole of the note issue under the Bank of England and increased the fiduciary issue to £260 millions. The Treasury notes were then called in.

[20] I.e. gold coin or bullion, but not scrap gold or gold articles.

Certain exemptions from the general provisions of the Act were allowed. For example, as under The Defence (Finance) Regulations, 1939, genuine collector's pieces were not required to be surrendered under the 1947 legislation. Specifically, under the Exchange Control (Collectors' Pieces Exemption) Order, 1947, which came into force on the same day as the Exchange Control Act, 1947, collectors were permitted to hold and deal in gold coin minted in or before 1816 and any gold coin minted later than that date provided its numismatic value was greater than that of its gold content were it to be offered for sale to an authorised dealer.[21] Other exemptions were granted where the holder had "obtained the consent of the Treasury to his retention and use of any gold or specified currency, and has stated in an application for the consent that he requires it for a particular purpose,"[22] but when that purpose lapsed the gold had to be surrendered. Furthermore, the Act states that "Where a person has become bound under this section to offer or cause to be offered any gold or specified currency for sale to an authorised dealer, he shall not be deemed to comply with that obligation by any offer made or caused to be made by him, if the offer is an offer to sell at a price exceeding that authorised by the Treasury, or without payment of any usual and proper charges of the authorised dealer, or otherwise on any unusual terms."[23] In other words, not only was he required to surrender his gold, unless it was held with the permission of the Treasury and for a specifically nominated purpose agreed with the Treasury; he had to sell it at a price determined by the Treasury, even if he could sell it for more than the Treasury price.

The purpose of the Act was to prohibit the use of gold as money or trading in gold as a means of livelihood by the people of Great Britain. The government reserved to itself alone the right to use gold as money. By denying people the right to trade in hard money and foreign currency[24] and forcing its own fiat standard upon the economy, the government greatly enhanced its power and influence over society. It had, through its monopoly of an inflationary mechanism for creating money, a means of plundering the wealth of the nation to fund its own policies and the extension of its authority over the lives of British people. F. C. Howard commented on this Act:

---

[21] Exchange Control (Collectors' Pieces Exemption) Order 1947 (1947 No. 2040).
[22] Exchange Control Act, 1947, Section 2 (2).   [23] Section 2 (4).
[24] At this time the United States was on the gold standard and the US dollar was redeemable in gold.

... almost every substantive sub-section in the Act contains words such as "except with the permission of the Treasury." This permission may be given generally by the Treasury or by notices to Banks, brokers, registrars and others which are published generally or issued to such persons from time to time or by the approval of forms by answer to a special application made in a particular case.

In addition in cases where a particular section applies it may be unnecessary to seek permission in consequence of an order made under section 31, *post*, exempting certain persons or transactions altogether from the effects of a particular section.

When considered in the light of these limitations, although the Act appears to prohibit the most every day and inoffensive transactions by persons all over the world, it will be found generally that the control is not greatly altered from that which prevailed under Defence (Finance) Regulations and in some respects it is rather lighter.[25]

That the Draconian measures implemented in time of war under emergency regulations should be enacted as permanent legislation after the cessation of hostilities, notwithstanding that the controls established may be eased from time to time under certain circumstances—and, after all, they may just as easily be enforced again— is a sobering example of the growth of government control over people's lives and of the acceptance of the ideology of State regulation of society (totalitarianism) over the past fifty years. The purpose of the Act was clearly to ensure that the authorities had control over the wealth and resources of the nation and that no transfer of such to parties outside the United Kingdom or outside the jurisdiction of the government of the United Kingdom took place without their prior approval and permission. Without this kind of power and influence over the economy and over the lives and actions of those normally resident in Britain the grand plans of the socialist régime that inherited the power of government after the end of World War Two would have been impossible to implement.

In 1966 the Exchange Control (Collectors' Pieces Exemption) Order, 1947 was replaced by the Exchange Control (Gold Coins Exemption) Order (1966, No. 438). This allowed dealing in gold coins minted in or before 1837 and the holding of up to four gold coins minted after 1837 provided they were in the holder's possession on or before 26th April 1966. Other than this the Order stipulated that any resident of the United Kingdom needed permission to "(1) HOLD any gold coin minted after 1837, and (2) BUY (or borrow) or SELL

---

[25] F. C. Howard, *op. cit.*, p. 13f.

(or lend) ANY gold coin minted after 1837 unless he is selling to an Authorised Dealer in Gold or a Trader in Coin (as defined in Statutory Instrument No. 2042 of 1949) or to a coin dealer specifically authorised by the Bank of England."[26] This order was revoked in 1971 by the Exchange Control (Gold Coins Exemption) Order 1971 (1971 No. 516), which enabled all gold coin to be freely bought, sold and held. The holding of gold coin after this date was not subject to restrictions but permission was required for certain purchases and sales between 1975 and 1979. These regulations related to coins obtained by collectors. As far as bullion was concerned, residents of the United Kingdom, except for authorised dealers, were not allowed to hold bullion. In 1979 the exchange control restrictions were fully suspended and the 1947 Act itself was repealed in 1987.

During the period 1939 to 1979 the use of gold as money was prohibited to the British people. This was Britain's greatest and most sustained period of socialist experimentation. With the election of the Thatcher government in 1979 this socialist experimentation began a brief decline. During the 1980s some significant changes were implemented that took the nation away from socialist regulation of the economy and moved it towards a more productive free-market system. Unfortunately the radical reform programme initiated by Thatcher was first weakened and eventually abandoned by the subsequent Conservative government. Under John Major the Conservatives failed to build on the gains achieved in the 1980s and the Major government's pro-European Union stance, followed by an even more pro-European Labour government elected in 1997, means that a move back towards socialism is now under way, only this time the régime will be directed by a grand Euro-bureaucracy administered from Brussels.

(b) The imposition of sales tax and capital gains tax on gold

With the suspension of the Exchange Control restrictions in 1979 and the repeal of the 1947 Exchange Control Act in 1987, government control of the use of gold as money was not at an end however, even if dealing in gold was legitimised. In 1975 VAT had been imposed on the purchase of gold. Although after 1979 people were allowed to trade in gold, to buy and sell gold, and to hold savings

[26] The Exchange Control (Gold Coins Exemption) Order 1966, *Aide Memoire for Coin Collectors* (published by the Bank of England 27th April 1966).

in the form of gold coin and bullion, the incentive to do so was greatly vitiated by sales tax,[27] which effectively made the cost of using gold as a medium of exchange prohibitive economically. The imposition of VAT on gold coin and bullion, therefore, meant that the use of hard money that was free from political manipulation continued to be restricted. The individual was still denied a medium of exchange that was impervious to government policy aimed at redistributing the nation's wealth. This continued until January 2000, when VAT ceased to be payable on gold coin and bullion in the European Union.

Whichever party is elected to govern the nation at a general election its first principle of government will be to retain power. It will use the means at its disposal to develop policies geared to enhancing its power and its chances of remaining in power. This inevitably involves control of the money supply, the purpose of which is to bolster government policy, which will be aimed at redistributing wealth to those sectors of the electorate from which the government derives the majority of its support. Traditional socialist governments tend to favour trade unions by means of direct subsidies and grants to nationalised and union-controlled industries, while Conservative governments tend to favour private sector business, facilitating the expansion of credit through the mechanism of the banking system.[28] Without a currency that is responsive to government manipulation it is far more difficult, perhaps impossible in the modern world, to do this.

Modern Conservative propaganda has promoted the ideology of freedom, free markets, consumer choice and limited government, but

---

[27] The exception to this was the Black Box, a group of firms dealing in gold that form the London Bullion Market Association (LBMA). These firms were allowed to trade in gold without having to pay VAT. Under this system a limited form of VAT-free investment in gold was permitted to British residents in that investors could buy, hold and sell gold through a member of the LBMA without having to pay VAT. But the gold had to remain in the possession of an LBMA member firm. If it was sold or transferred to a non-member or taken physical possession of by the investor VAT became payable. This system permitted a limited type of VAT-free investment in gold, therefore, but not the use of gold as a medium of exchange.

[28] These are pure types, of course, and governments vary in the degree to which they conform to these types. The Labour government elected in May 1997 did not seem to fit the pure type of a socialist government at all, and indeed was keen to be perceived as having embraced many elements of the Conservativism that had dominated the 1980s. It was widely held that only by adopting such an approach and by rejecting some traditional socialist shibboleths (e.g. Clause Four) could the Labour Party ever modernise itself enough to become electable again. The Conservatives complained that Labour has stolen their clothes, while some disgruntled

the reality is that even for Conservative governments the ability to apply strict controls on the nation's currency is considered an essential tool of government if it is to rule effectively. Inasmuch as this is accepted as political reality by Conservatives their claim to the ideology of freedom, consumer choice, free markets and limited government is disingenuous. While it is true that today the Conservatives—in the nineteenth century it would have been the Liberals— can point to the fact that they have promoted this ideology more than any other political party, it is not true that they have made freedom of trade and consumer choice a *principle* of individual freedom, and this was particularly shown to be the case by their denial of the individual's freedom in the choice of a medium of exchange. Conservative commitment to political control of the nation's currency was testimony to the fact that much of the free trade propaganda was rhetoric. As long as VAT was charged on gold transactions it was impossible for gold to function as a common medium of exchange. Although those who would use it as such were not legally forbidden to do so they were penalised *economically* in such a way that the development of a viable hard money system was rendered impossible.

The abolition of sales tax on gold is necessary for two reasons: first, there is an important sense in which sales tax—and this applies to other forms of indirect taxation—is a dishonest means of obtaining revenue. People tend to impute the value of the sales tax to the good being purchased. This is simply because of the waste of effort involved in constantly assessing costs in terms of the value of the good plus sales tax paid to the government for the privilege of buying it. It is a purely analytical calculation that is, at least for the average household or living budget, pointless. The two sides of the equation will still have to be combined and the total cost will be what is assessed in terms of rational budgeting and affordability of the good under consideration. The tendency is to treat sales tax as part of the cost of the good, which from the point of view of the consumer it is. Where vendors simply advertise a sales tax-inclusive price for goods, as is the case in Britain for many goods, the sales tax is more easily hidden, being disguised as part of the real cost of the goods, which

---

traditional socialists nick-named Tony Blair "Tory" Blair. This adoption of Conservative principles and ideals was perceived by others, however, as cosmetic—more a question of public image, motivated by the desire for power at any cost, than genuine conviction.

in fact are cheaper than the tax-inclusive selling price. Although there is no official or formal deception involved, and everyone knows that part of the costs they pay for goods and services is tax, the human tendency is to think and calculate in such a way that this fact is obscured. It is precisely this psychological tendency to see the total price paid as the cost of the good or service rather than as cost plus tax that attracts politicians to sales tax. The fact that everyone knows what is happening if they stop to think about it is irrelevant and does not render sales tax inefficient as a political tactic for obtaining revenues. Politicians prefer sales tax because they know that most of the time people will not stop to think about it, at least in most everyday transactions. Sales tax, in spite of the public's knowledge of how it works, is a dishonest tax used by politicians to hide the true rate of taxation and hence the real costs of government policy. Sales tax is also immoral because it is *indiscriminate*, i.e. payable regardless of whether one has an income, a net increase in wealth. Those who make a net loss or live off their savings have to pay just the same as those who make a net profit. This disregards the principle that tax should be paid on the *increase* (see below, §6 *Tax Reform*). Direct taxation, i.e. income tax, is thus a more honest and, from the citizens point of view—though not from the government's—a more rational form of taxation.

For the same reason that sales tax is immoral on all goods to which it is applied it is immoral when applied to a medium of exchange such as gold. But there is a second and much more important reason why sales tax should not be charged on mediums of exchange. The effect of charging sales tax on money is to *double* the sales tax payable for anyone purchasing goods with that form of money. For example, prior to January 2000, if one wished to purchase goods to the value of £100, the VAT at the current rate in Britain (17.5 per cent) amounted to £17.50. If one used a medium of exchange such as gold, sale of which by the banks itself attracted VAT at the standard rate, one had to pay £17.50 extra for the £100 of gold obtained from the bank in order to purchase the goods. This made the total VAT paid on the transaction £35 (£17.50 paid on the goods themselves and £17.50 paid on the gold obtained from the bank). The total sales tax was thus 35 per cent on the value of the goods. Obviously, under such conditions of taxation the use of gold as a medium of exchange is made impossible for economic reasons. Gold is rendered ineffective as a medium of exchange by

VAT and society is obliged to use the government's privileged fiat currency for its economic transactions.

The application of sales tax to money is a form of economic tyranny in which freedom of choice, if exercised in a certain way, is so heavily penalised economically that people are induced to act in the way that government desires—i.e. they are forced, for economic rather than legal reasons, to use only the fiat currency issued by the Bank of England, which the authorities are able to expand and contract as they see fit in conformity with government policy directives. The Bank of England is simply an instrument of government control over the economy with a monopoly over the issue of currency that the private sector is not able to break.

Capital gains tax, where applicable, affects the use of gold as a medium of exchange in the same way and should therefore be abolished for the same reasons. This tax is levied where a person's capital gains in any one year exceeds a certain amount (£6,800 in 1998–99). At present capital gains tax is payable on receipts from the sale of gold that is not legal tender in the United Kingdom. Of course, this tax is based on the measurement of a person's capital gains in terms of a depreciating fiat currency and thus it is a higher rate in real terms than the nominal rate. The very term capital *gains* is misleading here since in an inflationary economy a purely nominal gain may be made on the sale of gold—i.e. a gain calculated in terms of a depreciating currency—when in fact there has been no real gain from its sale, that is to say no increase in purchasing power. It is simply the exchange of one form of money into another. Historically gold tends to keep its value over the long term (though it fluctuates considerably in the short term). One can buy today with an ounce of gold roughly what one could buy with an ounce of gold two hundred years ago. But the fiat paper Bank of England note is devaluing all the time. This means that although gold retains its purchasing power over the long term, that purchasing power is represented by increasing quantities of Bank of England notes (political fiat money). Any gain from the sale of gold therefore may be quite fictitious. Yet government receives capital gains tax from the sale of gold. Such a tax, however, may not be a tax on a person's capital *gain* at all but simply a tax on wealth itself—i.e. a tax on savings in the form of gold. Capital gains tax on gold is therefore effectively another form of sales tax and subject to the criticisms set forth above.

One of the aims of a government committed to establishing a just economic order would be the removal of all forms of indirect taxation such as sales tax, since government should raise its revenues in an honest way by means of direct taxation, which is easily assessable from the taxpayer's point of view and which clearly indicates the real costs of government. Only through direct taxes is the taxpayer easily able to determine what the government is costing him. Direct taxation is therefore the only honest means of raising government revenue. All other means of obtaining revenue for the State, such as monetisation of debt (inflation) and repayment of debt with debased currency, sales tax etc. are ways of disguising the real level of taxation and therefore the real costs of government.

If we are to create a free and a just society we must move towards a free economic order based on Christian principles of economic behaviour as an essential element of such a society. Nevertheless, reform of the economy must proceed in a piecemeal fashion, and for the reason stated above the removal of sales tax from gold and all other forms of money is a necessary first step in tax reform. This process of reform must lead to the removal of all forms of sales tax on all goods. If, however, we are to create an economic order that is free from a fiat currency that the government is able to control for its own advantage, the existence of a hard money system of payments that is free from political manipulation is a necessary first step. It is important that sales tax should be abolished on gold and all other mediums of exchange in the early stages of reform since restoration of justice in monetary affairs is essential for building a sound economic order and thus for building a sound economic future.

That VAT is no longer payable on gold coin and bullion in the European Union is a welcome step forward, but it is not enough in itself. It does not signal that the monetary authorities wish to reform the monetary system on the lines set out above. Legal tender laws remain and the euro is an attempt to create a European-wide political super-currency. Neither does it mean that for the moment at least we are free to use gold coin as money without being economically penalised completely since capital gains tax is still payable on the sale of non-British denominated gold coin and bullion.

Acceptance of the principle that mediums of exchange should not be subject to sales tax, along with abolition of legal tender laws, is essential for the creation of a sound monetary system that is free from political manipulation. Since there would be no penalty involved in using gold as a medium of exchange under such a monetary system contracts could be written stipulating payment in gold denominations and payment made in accordance with such contracts in coin or gold instruments. This would help to force banks to observe strict liquidity practices in relation to any new issues of banknotes, since those holding their notes would be entitled to full redemption. From the economic point of view it would also ameliorate the whole banking system before a strict legal requirement of 100 per cent reserves for banks was enacted. By approaching reform of the economy in this piecemeal fashion the economy can be prepared for change gradually by the earlier, less radical reforms—abolition of legal tender laws and abolition of sales tax on gold—before the more radical measures relating to banking reform, to be discussed below, are implemented. By the time a legal requirement for 100 per cent bank reserves is enforced the banks should already have largely adjusted their practices in line with the reality of an economy where people are free to arrange legally binding contracts for payment in hard money such as gold or gold instruments.

The constant reference to gold here should not be misunderstood. It is not being argued that gold should be legal tender, except where contracts stipulate gold and those contracts are legal—in which case gold does not become legal tender in the accepted sense but simply part of a legally binding contractual obligation. There may be other forms of money such as silver. The likelihood, however, is that cheques and banknotes and other means of transferring money would be linked to gold, which would most likely function as a de facto standard, once political money had lost its monopoly powers and legal tender status. In effect there would be no legal tender, simply binding contracts and accepted money instruments that are fully redeemable in the denominations specified.

§4
Reform of the Banking System

Reform of the banking system is fundamental to any thoroughgoing reform of the economy that aims at eliminating fraud and establishing justice and fair practices in financial affairs. The banking system is at the heart of the British economic system, and the Bank of England is at the heart of the banking system. If reform fails to penetrate to the foundations of current banking philosophy and practice it will fail in every respect ultimately since economic reforms that do not address the central role that the banking system plays in the economy will be superficial and cosmetic. Any good intentions and actual reforms implemented in other areas of the economy will ultimately be undermined if the fraudulent practices upon which the central banking system works are not exposed and brought to an end. It is vital for the long-term economic stability of the nation that the economy should have a sound and just monetary system and this can only be achieved by bringing the nexus of institutions that presently comprises the banking system into conformity with the principles of honest commerce that are demanded in all other areas of business.

There are three necessary steps in the process of reforming the modern banking system: (*a*) abolition of the central bank, (*b*) reform of commercial banking practices, and (*c*) regulation and policing of the banking system. In order to minimise as much as possible any shock to the economy that these reforms might create it would be necessary to put into effect the reforms discussed above first and allow them to begin acting upon the economy. A time table for reform could then be issued so that banks are prepared for the following reforms in time to start putting their houses in order and to enable them to prepare for further change. By the time the following banking reforms become legally binding individual banks should already be operating on sound hard money principles.

(*a*) *Abolition of the central bank*

Although the Bank of England performs many complex functions in the economy its basic rationale is to fund government debt and control the monetary system upon which the British economy works in accordance with government policy. It does this by monetising government debt and regulating the money supply through its function as banker to the commercial banks. The development of the Bank of England as a privileged institution with a special relationship with the government, on whose behalf it performs services and functions that guarantee that the government will never become bankrupt, and its eventual nationalisation in 1946, has resulted in the institutionalisation of the fractional reserve banking system in such a way that the British economy is now held captive by inherently unstable banking practices based on the creation and manipulation of political fiat money. Consequently, as has become only too painfully obvious over recent decades, the economy is precariously balanced on the edge of an economic precipice and the slightest blow to its fragile foundations can cause severe problems and panics. As this banking system has developed and become more deeply entrenched in the nation's economic and financial institutions the business cycle—which is erroneously named and should perhaps be called the banking cycle[29]—has become more obtrusive and detrimental to the health of the whole economy, increasingly difficult to control, and its disastrous effects impossible to avoid or even limit by government policy, which usually only exacerbates the situation by applying as salve for the economy's ills more of the poison that originally caused the malady. Further tinkering with the system benefits no one in the long term and can only benefit certain privileged groups at the expense of the rest of society in the short term. If the economy is to be delivered from these problems it is necessary to reform the whole system and place the economy on a sound monetary foundation. Tinkering with the symptoms will achieve nothing. The problem must be dealt with at the root cause. In order to achieve this it will be necessary to abolish the central bank as a first step to reform of the whole banking system.

The main functions of the Bank of England can be stated briefly: (1) the Bank has traditionally funded the government deficit, i.e. the shortfall between total revenues and government expenditure. As we have already seen this was done by floating government debt on the capital and money markets as government stock, securities and Treasury Bills. As was explained in Chapter Four, the function of

[29] "Business cycle" is a term used to describe the oscillation between periods of easy credit, inflation, business expansion and increased perception of prosperity (booms) and periods of escalating interest rates, deflation, business failure, recession and even severe depression (slumps), which are common in Western economies. It is clear, however, that this phenomenon takes its name from the description of its effects or symptoms, not from its cause. The periods of cheap credit and business expansion, and thus the impression of prosperity,—which are in fact periods of decapitalisation and waste or irrational use of scarce resources—are a product of the growth in the money supply. The periods of recession are the result of the economy's readjustment to conditions in which there are less resources and capital available to maintain economic growth; hence the decline of investment and standards of living. Since this cycle is caused by the expansion of the money supply, generated by the fractional reserve banking system, it would be more appropriate to give the phenomenon a more accurate description based on its cause rather than its effects, such as, perhaps, the "banking cycle."

the Bank as manager of the government's debt has been transferred to the Treasury's Debt Management Office. Reform of the way government debt is managed will therefore need to take in the DMO as well as the Bank of England. Over and above this the Bank acts generally as banker to the government. (2) It issues banknotes and generally manages the nation's monetary system in accordance with government policy. (3) The Bank of England acts as banker to the commercial banks. (4) It controls the gold and foreign currency reserves. (5) It also controls foreign exchange rates and domestic interest rates. Although these aspects of the Bank's work have been separated out for analytical purposes, in practice they comprise one complex system that controls the whole economy. The Bank of England and DMO together act as the anchor to the whole economic system.

As we have already seen, reform of the economy according to just principles of economic activity as taught in the Bible requires at least the following changes to the system: (1) government should raise revenue by means of direct taxation so that it can be easily seen how much the government is costing and so that governments cannot make policies based on promises they are unable to fund honestly; (2) withdrawal of government from interfering in the economy generally, and hence (3) the abandonment of government wealth redistribution programmes; (4) abolition of government control of the money supply; and (5) just principles of banking, and therefore proscription of fractional reserve banking practices. Once these reforms are put into effect the rationale for a central bank that acts as a special agent for the government in controlling the economy generally and the money supply in particular, as well as the rationale for a central bank to act as banker to the commercial banks and to the government, disappears entirely. Such reforms would empty the Bank of England's role of any meaning as a national or quasi-governmental institution (whether nationalised or privately owned) with a distinctive function in the economy and a special status—i.e. the central bank. It would rightfully place the Bank in the same position as that of any other bank, subject to the same laws, constraints and limitations in the interests of fair and just commercial practices that the rest of the business world has to abide by.

In short, the implementation of these reforms would render the distinctive functions of the central bank illegal, thereby necessitating its abolition. Under such reforms a central bank would have no useful or positive role in the economy. The Bank of England, therefore, must be reduced to the status of a private business with the same responsibilities and obligations that are incumbent upon any other joint-stock bank.[30] Any claim to be a national bank by such a reformed Bank of England would be purely cosmetic, not legal or economic in nature. Subsequent issues of notes would be required to state the amount and fineness of gold or silver represented by the notes. These notes would have to be fully redeemable in the denominations specified. The Bank of England would have no monopoly of note issue as exists today and the issue of fiduciary media would be forbidden by law to the Bank of England, as would its issue by any other bank.

(b) Reform of the banking system

Reform of the present banking system in accordance with biblical principles of just weights and measures requires that the banks be forced to adopt honest business practices. This means that fraud in the form of fractional reserve banking must be made subject to criminal proceedings. As long as banks are able to pursue fractional reserve banking practices legally the economy will suffer the consequences and damaging effects of the business cycle, i.e. periodic recessions and depressions leading to rising unemployment and the general decline in standards of living. It is imperative, therefore, that banking reform should not end with abolition of the central bank but that it should be pursued vigorously throughout the whole of the banking system. Banks must be denied the legal right to issue fiduciary media—i.e. to issue banknotes payable on demand to the

---

[30] The current debate as to whether the Bank of England should be an independent institution is irrelevant to the point at issue here. For most of its history the Bank was a private institution and this made no difference to its status as a central bank with all the privileges that such status affords. Merely privatising the Bank will achieve very little—though private it certainly should be. The Bank's status as the central bank of the United Kingdom must also be abrogated and the Bank reduced to the same status as any other bank, regardless of whether its customers include the British government. It must be subject to the same laws requiring honesty and fair play in economic matters that all other business enterprises have to abide by. Its position as banker to the British government, should the government retain its services, would bring no special privileges or licences, nor would it give the Bank any greater authority and control over the economy than that exercised by other private bank. Such reform is of an order entirely different from the current discussion regarding what is clearly only a nominal independence from government control.

bearer in excess of the deposits reserved to redeem those notes. If a bank issues a note promising to pay the bearer on demand a certain sum in gold coin it must always have in reserve enough gold to meet that and all other such claims. The same holds for any other form of claim for which the bank is liable—e.g. cheques. All forms of banking fraud must be proscribed. These reforms must be embodied in statute law; all issues over and above the reserves held by a bank should be punished by the civil authorities and appropriate restitution enforced.

The effects of such reforms would be to split banking into two separate kinds of business: (1) demand deposit banking, and (2) investments and loans banking.[31] In the first of these the bank offers a place of safe deposit. In other words it acts as a security guard for other peoples' money, for which it charges a fee (bank charges). In the second it acts as a middleman, somewhat in the same way that a broker acts, between the one who wishes to invest his savings and the one who wishes to borrow to finance a business enterprise etc. In this kind of business the bank makes its profits from the difference between the interest charged to the one who borrows from the bank and the interest paid to the depositor who places his funds at the disposal of the bank for purposes of investment. We shall now examine these two sides of legitimate banking business in turn.

(1) *Demand deposit banking.* A demand deposit is a sum of money deposited with a bank that can be drawn upon by means of personal written instruction to the bank (cheques) or bank notes (promises to pay the bearer on demand—in other words IOUs) without advance notice having to be given to the bank. As we have seen, reform of the banking system necessitates the proscription of fractional reserve practices as fraud. It would be illegal, therefore, for a bank to lend out deposits that can be drawn upon instantly in the form of cheques or banknotes, which function in the economy in the same way that the deposits they represent would function were they in circulation. Likewise, it would be illegal for banks to use such deposits as a reserve for unbacked notes (fiduciary media). Under such conditions it would not be possible for the bank to make a profit on the demand deposit side of its business except by making a charge for its services. Such charges would be fees for the safe-keeping of deposits, whether these deposits are gold bullion, coin, foreign currency or any other kind of money or goods. Obviously, in such a system the payment of

---

[31] Gary North, *Honest Money* (Tyler, Texas: Dominion Press, 1986), p. 108ff.

interest on such deposits, which has become more common recently on certain kinds of personal current account, would disappear also.

With current accounts that can be drawn upon by cheque the payment of charges would be quite simple and pose no problems whatsoever. Charges would be payable, as they are now on trading accounts and some personal accounts. Provided that charges on current accounts are brought in along with the abandonment of fractional reserve banking this system would be of great benefit to those who use current accounts. Under the fractional reserve system, in which banks can profit from current accounts without making charges, indeed even while paying out small amounts of interest on them, the advantages to be gained from not having to pay banking charges or from receiving small amounts of interest on current accounts are greatly outweighed by the disadvantages arising from the constant depreciation of the value of the monetary unit—i.e. loss of purchasing power—that continuous expansion of the money supply creates. The fractional reserve system enables the banks to make their profits by means of expanding the money supply and redistributing wealth from their creditors to their debtors, taking for themselves a percentage in the form of interest on the loans they advance to their debtors. Under a reformed banking system in which this is forbidden the deposit side of banking becomes a *safe-deposit service*, which is arguably the antithesis of current banking practices. The depositor's interests are served far better with this kind of deposit since the value of his deposit is maintained. Under such conditions the total purchasing power of a sum of money kept in a demand deposit account over a given period of time, even allowing for deductions in the form of bank charges, would be greater than that of the same deposit plus interest kept in an interest-bearing account over the same period under the present fractional reserve system, since the fractional reserve system is inherently inflationary and leads to the constant devaluation of currency.

The use of banknotes under this reformed banking system, however, would pose certain problems. A banknote is essentially a receipt for a deposit made with a bank entitling the holder to the sum deposited on demand. Economically there is no difference between a banknote and a cheque. The deposits represented by the banknotes would have to be stored and always available should holders of the banknotes wish to redeem them. Only under such conditions would a bank issuing notes be solvent and therefore able to meet its liabilities in the event of a run on the bank. However, since a banknote is an entitlement to a deposit, the banker, if he is to profit from issuing banknotes that are fully backed by reserves, must charge for the service of storing the deposits they represent. Those initially making deposits for which they received banknotes to the value of the amount deposited would have to make a payment for the storage service, just as those holding current accounts would pay charges.

This system would probably mean that banknotes would become dated instruments with a limited period for redemption at their nominal value. If notes circulated beyond the date of redemption at face value the bank would only redeem them at a discount that would take account of the storage service provided after the date of maturity. This discount would increase with time. Theoretically, if left long enough the discount for storage charges would increase until it equalled the nominal value of the note and the bank would be entitled to take the whole deposit in payment for the storage service it has provided, at which point the note would become worthless as a claim on the deposit it originally represented.

Although it is probable that such banknotes would exist, it is unlikely that they would have the same role in the economy that banknotes currently have. Banknotes might well disappear as a means of payment in everyday monetary transactions. This may seem somewhat odd and some may find it hard to imagine not having the use of banknotes, but a little reflection will show that such a change in monetary practices would not be insurmountable nor indeed difficult to accommodate. In the first place, it should be remembered that banknotes are not essential to rational economic activity nor to the monetary requirements of the economy. As Ludwig von Mises observed: "Banknotes are not indispensable. All the economic achievements of capitalism would have been accomplished if they had never existed. Besides, deposit currency can do all the things banknotes do."[32]

Second, any objection to such reforms based on arguments relating to the convenience of using banknotes is easily resolved. As Mises has argued, to the extent that banknotes are considered more convenient than coins the public would be prepared and willing to pay a premium for their use,[33] making the issue of banknotes in exchange for deposits a chargeable service as described above. Indeed,

[32] Ludwig von Mises, *Human Action*, p. 447.   [33] *Ibid.*, p. 446.

Mises states that "in the earlier days banknotes issued by banks of unquestionable solvency stood at a slight premium as against metallic currency."[34] He goes on to observe that "travellers' checks are rather popular although the bank issuing them charges a commission for their issuance."[35] Moreover, any objection based on the convenience and ease of use of banknotes "does not provide a justification for the policies urging the public to resort to the use of banknotes. Governments did not foster the use of banknotes in order to avoid inconvenience to ladies shopping. Their idea was to lower the rate of interest and to open a source of cheap credit to their treasuries. In their eyes the increase in the quantity of fiduciary media was a means of promoting welfare."[36] The disastrous effects of the provision of this fraudulent cheap credit to governments and the concomitant credit expansion policies of the banks is far more detrimental to the public than the inconvenience of not having the free use of banknotes. To argue that fractional reserve banking should be tolerated in order that banks might issue notes that are convenient to use without charging for their services is to strain at a gnat and swallow a camel.

Third, computerised information technology has already made the use of credit and charge cards very popular, and banknotes have correspondingly ceased to play as important a role in the economy as they formerly did. With the growth of such devices and the introduction of other systems of payment such as the Switch method of accessing current accounts—again made possible by the development of computerised information technology—the use of banknotes has naturally become less frequent in any case. It is not so difficult after all, then, to imagine an economy with no or at least very few banknotes in circulation as a means of making everyday payments. Those formerly used to making payments in banknotes, if they did not wish to pay a premium for their use to cover bank charges, would soon adjust to new conditions and methods of payment. Since the current trend is to move away from the use of banknotes and towards "plastic money"—e.g. credit cards, banker's cards, Switch type facilities—the introduction of 100 per cent backed demand deposit banking would simply help to establish and encourage the development of a natural process that has already taken place to a considerable extent.

The introduction of these reforms into the economy would provide a just and morally acceptable foundation for the growing

[34] *Ibid.*, p. 446f.   [35] *Ibid.*, p. 447.   [36] *Ibid.*

"plastic money" industry, which it presently lacks, being inextricably linked to a banking system that operates on the fractional reserve principle. Under present conditions the development of computerised information technology in application to the banking and credit systems will open up far more opportunities for manipulation and control of the economy by privileged institutions—i.e. governments and banks. These institutions are able to expand and contract the money supply in accordance with their own interests to the disadvantage of the population generally while being legally immune from prosecution. With the reform of banking practices in accordance with Christian principles of fair weights and measures (Lev. 19:35–37, Dt. 25:13–16) and the application of that principle to all economic transactions the creation, deposit and transfer of money would be brought under a strict legal code of justice, with no privileged status for banks and governments and opportunity for free entry into the banking business. That is to say, the banking system would be subject to the rule of law without respect of persons. Under such conditions the application of computerised information technology to monetary affairs and the use of "plastic money" would be free to develop as far as is practicable yet remain firmly based on sound moral and monetary principles, and opportunity for legalised fraud would be denied to those using such technology in the banking and credit industries.

(2) *Investments and loans banking.* The second kind of banking practised by the commercial banks under the system of reforms set forth above would be investments and loans business. This would be based on *time deposit* banking; that is, deposits would be subject to withdrawal only after the elapse of a specific period of time for which the deposit is made. Once deposited the funds would be loaned out by the bank for a specific period of time, the final date for repayment falling due on the date of maturity of the original deposit. Only when the funds are returned to the bank in the form of repaid loans would the depositor be able to withdraw his deposit. Such deposits could not be subject to withdrawal on demand; they would be time deposits, but unlike demand deposits they would bear interest. The bank would make its profit from the difference between the interest charged to its debtors (borrowers) and that paid to its creditors (depositors).

This kind of banking is investments and loans business. It is important that we understand, therefore, that depositors would be *investors,* and that just as all other investments carry risks, so also there would be a certain degree of risk associated with investment in a time deposit. This risk would be that the bank's debtors (borrowers) may default on repayment of the loan on the agreed date, leading either to later payment or even cancellation of the debt. In such cases depositors (investors) could lose the interest or part of the interest on their deposit, or even the whole or part of their investment. For instance, bankrupt businesses severely in debt to the bank may make it impossible for the bank to bear the whole loss associated with that particular loan, and therefore the bank may have to pass on the loss to depositors either in the form of lower interest rates, loss of interest altogether, or even loss of part or the whole of the deposit.

Although this is true theoretically, in practice the degree of risk associated with investments and loans banking would be considerably reduced over that associated with direct investment in companies and business projects since loans would be pooled in order to spread risks (see below) and the bank would be expected to bear the greater part of the loss. In practice any bank that continually made bad loans and then passed its losses on to its creditors would get a bad reputation and soon go out of business. This means that investments in the form of bank time deposits would be relatively safe, but the profits (interest) made on such deposits would be lower than the profits made from direct investments,—those who take the greater risks receive the greater rewards, just as they are also subject to the possibility of greater losses.

If no such risk is acceptable in any degree to the depositor he would have to deposit his funds in a demand deposit account without interest and pay banking charges. These funds would not be loaned out under any conditions and would always be on call in the form of cheques or banknotes entitling the bearer to redemption on demand. The bank would not be permitted legally to use such funds for loan purposes and any such practice would be considered fraudulent.

On the investment and loans side of its business the bank would have to arrange its business carefully so that loans fell due for repayment in time for it to meet its own liabilities and contractual obligations to its creditors (depositors). In practice the bank would pool all deposits of the same date and duration. This would rationalise the bank's investments and loans business and also spread the risks of specific loans made by the bank over a greater number of investors (depositors). If the bank's debtors (borrowers) were to default on repayment investors might have to wait for repayment, in which case the bank could offer a higher rate of interest for the period of extended credit. The bank would in turn require higher rates of interest from the defaulting debtors, assuming that bankruptcies were not involved, during the period of extended credit.

Strictly speaking, under this kind of investments and loans business the bank is acting on behalf of its depositors (investors) in a capacity quite different from that of a broker. Although in one sense the bank would be acting as a middle man through which its depositors' funds are invested, it is incorrect to speak of this service as that of a broker. The profit made by the bank strictly speaking is not a brokerage, since the depositor (investor) and the borrower have neither a contractual (legal) relationship with each other nor financial (economic) responsibilities towards each other. Both deal directly with the bank itself. Thus, a depositor invests in the *bank*, not the one to whom the bank lends his funds, and the debtor borrows from the *bank*, not the depositor. The concept of broker works as an analogy for describing the way that investments and loans banking works, but does not adequately define the nature of this kind of business. It is investment and loans banking, strictly speaking, not broking.

With investments and loans banking, theoretically, a depositor who found himself in necessity and in need of the money he had invested in a time deposit would have to wait until his deposit reached maturity before he could withdraw his funds. In practice, however, there would in a free market economy be various means of circumventing this situation. Upon depositing his money in an investment and loans account the depositor would receive a certificate or note indicating the sum deposited, the date of maturity and the interest payable. According to G. North, a depositor who found himself in need of the money he had deposited would have to borrow from the bank and offer this certificate as security.[37] Although this is a possible means of overcoming the problem it is not the only alternative. These time deposit certificates themselves could be traded at a discount prior to their date of maturity just as interest-bearing bonds are traded today. Such certificates might even have a limited function as a medium of exchange or a form of "near" money. The important point is that the deposit represented by a certificate does not become the basis for the creation of multiple certificates, receipts, or promises

[37] Gary North, *Honest Money*, p. 108.

entitling the holders to the same deposit. In other words the funds deposited are represented by one claim against them, the certificate of deposit, and the funds represented by that certificate remain a constant factor in the economy. Of course, the bank itself may agree to buy the certificate or trade it on behalf of the depositor, as is common today with stocks and shares.

Banks may offer a whole range of other financial services to their customers, such as currency exchange, mortgages, financial advice, insurance, investment consultancy etc. just as many do today. A bank would be particularly well suited to provide such services to its customers. But these are not essentially *banking* services, although they are closely allied to banking services. Banks might also, under a banking system organised on Christian principles, provide services for minting of coin or issue its own denominations of coin (see below).

(c) Regulation and policing of the banking system

In a banking system operating under the reforms outlined above any reduction of a bank's reserves through the loaning out of funds accumulated in demand deposits or the issuing of multiple claims on the same deposit (fiduciary media) would be strictly illegal and punishable as fraud. The *opportunity* to practise such fraud would remain, however, and we must assume that in a fallen world there will be those who will exploit that opportunity. This brings us to the question of the regulation and policing of banks and the punishment of banking fraud.

As with public and limited companies of other kinds today, banks would be expected to keep strict records and accounts, have regular audits carried out and make the results of these available for public inspection. Any irregularities involving banking fraud that are discovered would render the bank subject to prosecution. However, the criterion for prosecuting a bank under a 100 per cent reserve law should not be failure to meet actual liabilities when called upon to do so, which would, for instance, be discovered by a run on the bank. Rather, the criterion should be whether the bank is, or *has been*, at *any* time insolvent due to the unauthorised loaning of funds in demand deposits or the issue of fiduciary media, regardless of whether the bank has in fact failed to honour its liabilities on any particular occasion. That a bank, having been through such a period of insolvency without being detected, is subsequently able to meet its liabilities and redeem all claims against it, should be no guarantee against prosecution for having reduced its reserves and issued fiduciary media during the period of insolvency, should this later come to light. The fact that the bank was eventually able to meet its liabilities does not alter the fact that a fraud has been committed, with the consequent unauthorised redistribution of wealth from the bank's creditors to its debtors and to its own shareholders. To establish as the criterion for prosecution the actual failure of the bank to redeem its liabilities when called upon to do so, rather than its having abandoned at any time the 100 per cent reserve requirement established in law, would be essentially to prosecute the bank not for fraud, but for the failure to get away with fraud. It is for this reason, therefore, that the banks must keep meticulous records and accounts, hold regular audits, and make them available for public inspection. Failure to do this would automatically cast suspicion on the bank in question.

This point is important since amongst the proponents of free banking there are those who would not require 100 per cent reserves by law, but would leave regulation of the banking system entirely to the free market, that is to say to the banks' ability to manage their affairs so that they can meet their liabilities when required to do so by their creditors. Under such a system banks would be free to pursue fractional reserve practices provided they did not become so insolvent that they could not withstand a run on their reserves, and prosecution would follow only when a bank failed to honour its notes. It is argued that such a system would result in more responsible banking practices than exist currently under a central banking system since individual banks, fearing for their reputation and wishing to avoid a run on their reserves, would exercise greater caution in the issue of fiduciary media. Regulation would be assured by the bank's desire to remain in business by avoiding the situation in which it could not meet its liabilities. Any bank that was even suspected of not being able to honour its notes, would be considered untrustworthy by the public and hence would most likely go out of business.

This is of course entirely true, as far as it goes, but it does not get to the heart of the problem. It is essentially an argument for a system that aims at *less* fraud, not the *elimination* of fraud, at least as a *legitimate* practice. A good analysis of the arguments in favour of this kind of system is provided in V. C. Smith, *The Rationale of*

Central Banking and the Free Banking Alternative.[38] As can be seen from the title of the book, the context of V. C. Smith's analysis is the relative merits of such a free banking system as against the demerits of a central banking system. The argument set forth for free banking is essentially a libertarian, pragmatic argument, not a *moral* argument. While there would be in a Christian theory of banking significant areas of agreement with V. C. Smith's arguments for free banking, and especially with her critique of the inefficiency of a central banking system, the amoral philosophy underpinning her analysis and the libertarian conclusions she draws about how banking should be practised would be unacceptable.

It is important to note also that it is the very lack of a moral foundation for the free banking argument as V. C. Smith presents it, and indeed in the whole libertarian argument for free banking, that ultimately is the Achilles heel of a banking system as conceived by the free banking school. Granted, its merits make it far superior to a central banking system. But its demerit is still that it accepts as legitimate in principle, and therefore would permit, the fraudulent creation of money through fractional reserve banking practices and hence the inflationary redistribution of wealth from a bank's creditors to its shareholders and debtors. Opposition to this practice in *principle*, and thus in all its possible manifestations, can only be mounted from a *moral* perspective, and it is the denial of the moral dimension that vitiates the libertarian argument and leads to its failure to proscribe, or even to provide a rationale for proscribing, in principle rather than merely in excess, the creation of fiduciary media. This will become apparent if we look at some of the libertarian arguments for free banking as conceived by V. C. Smith and Ludwig von Mises.

Smith defines free banking in the following way:

"Free banking" denotes a *régime* where note-issuing banks are allowed to set up in the same way as any other type of business enterprise, so long as they comply with the general company law. The requirement for their establishment is not special conditions authorised from a Government authority, but the ability to raise sufficient capital, and public confidence, to gain acceptance for their notes and ensure the profitability of the undertaking. Under such a system all banks would not only be allowed the same rights, but would also be subjected to the same responsibilities as other business enterprises. If they failed to meet their obligations they would be

---

[38] Vera C. Smith, *The Rationale of Central Banking and the Free Banking Alternative* (Indianapolis: Liberty Fund, [1936] 1990).

declared bankrupt and put into liquidation, and their assets used to meet the claims of their creditors, in which case the shareholders would lose the whole or part of their capital, and the penalty for failure would be paid, at least for the most part, by those responsible for the policy of the bank. Notes issued under this system would be "promises to pay," and such obligations must be met on demand in the generally accepted medium which we will assume to be gold. No bank would have the right to call on the government or any other institution for special help in time of need. No bank would be able to give its notes forced currency by declaring them to be legal tender for all payments, and it is unlikely that the public would accept inconvertible notes of any such bank except at a discount varying with the prospect of their again becoming convertible. A general abandonment of the gold standard is inconceivable under these conditions, and with strict interpretation of the bankruptcy laws any bank suspending payments would at once be put into the hands of a receiver.[39]

Free banking as conceived here by V. C. Smith leaves the door open to the creation of fiduciary media, i.e. claims for money on demand (banknotes) issued in excess of the stock of specie reserved to meet those claims. Smith goes on to rehearse the arguments in favour of this kind of free banking system, a system in which fiduciary media is issued in *moderation* rather than in *excess*:

The free banking party laid particular stress on another check which they contended worked automatically through the reciprocal claims of the banks upon each other's reserves. Any bank will continually be receiving payments from customers either in payment of loans or in the form of cash being paid in on deposit. In a system where all banks are competitors for business, one bank will not be prepared to pay out over its own counter the notes of rival banks, but will return them to their issuers through the clearing process. It is therefore to be supposed that if one bank expands out of step with the rest, the clearing balances will go against it and its rivals will draw on its gold reserves to the extent of its adverse balance. This mechanism would work at a much earlier stage than the external drain of gold and would cause the reserves to feel the effects of expansion almost immediately. It is unlikely that all banks will decide in concert to decrease their reserve ratios, and the bigger the conservative group which is not desirous of so doing, the stronger will be the check of these on the expansion of the other group. A bank which contemplates an expansion has got to take into account not only the direct effect on its reserve ratio, which comes about in the first instance when it increases its issue against the same absolute total reserve as before, but also the indirect effect occasioned by the withdrawal of cash to other banks. The size of the addition it can afford to make to its loans on the basis of a given drop in its reserve ratio will be correspondingly

[39] *Ibid.*, p. 169f.

reduced, and its action will react partly to the benefit of the other banks who secure an accretion to their reserves. While admitting that circumstances may occur in which the majority of the banks are willing to allow some reduction in their reserve ratios, it is unlikely that they will ever risk fluctuations of dimensions anything like as great as those which are viewed with comparative equanimity by the central bank.[40]

The argument here is essentially for a banking system that is likely to have less serious effects on the money supply. The severity of the business cycle would be considerably reduced under such a system. But fractional reserve banking is still accepted as a legitimate practice in *moderation*. It is only *excessive* expansion that this kind of free banking mechanism seeks to eradicate, and only when a bank fails to redeem its notes will the receiver be called in.

Ludwig von Mises also argued for this kind of free banking system: "Free banking is the only method available for the prevention of the dangers inherent in credit expansion. It would, it is true, not hinder a slow credit expansion, kept within very narrow limits, on the part of cautious banks which provide the public with all information required about their financial status. But under free banking it would have been impossible for credit expansion with all its inevitable consequences to have developed into a regular—one is tempted to say normal—feature of the economic system. Only free banking would have rendered the market economy secure against crises and depressions."[41] One would not wish to argue with Mises' contention that "only free banking would render the market economy secure against crises and depressions"—i.e. runs on banks and the business cycle—in the context of a comparison of free banking with a State- or central bank-controlled banking system. But *this* particular kind of free banking system, in which there is still the possibility of banks legally creating fiduciary media or expanding credit in the form of bank money, will not protect the economy fully; it simply reduces the extent of the problem. A free banking system is certainly necessary for a sound economic order; but on its own it is not enough. The economy must be underpinned by a legal order that proscribes banking fraud (e.g. fractional reserve banking) *in principle*, and therefore even the "slow credit expansion, kept within very narrow limits, on the part of cautious banks" that Mises' system would permit.

Mises is led to accept this possibility of "slow credit expansion, kept within very narrow limits, on the part of cautious banks" because

---

[40] *Ibid.*, p. 178f.   [41] Ludwig von Mises, *Human Action*, p. 443.

he opposes the legal requirement of 100 per cent reserves. His reason for this is that a legal requirement of 100 per cent reserves by the State establishes a dangerous precedent for State regulation of banking practices that could, in exceptional circumstances, be used to sanction the lowering of the reserve requirement by the State. If the State can require 100 per cent reserves by law, a precedent is set for the State's interference with banking practice and it can, when it suits its purposes to do so, lower this legal requirement to 80 per cent, then to 60 per cent and so on, thereby opening the door to excessive credit expansion with banks being legally protected by the State. Mises writes:

If banks are preserved as privileged establishments subject to special legislative provisions, the tool remains that governments can use for fiscal purposes. Then every restriction imposed upon the issuance of fiduciary media depends upon the government's and the parliament's good intentions. They may limit the issuance for periods which are called normal. The restriction will be withdrawn whenever the government deems that an emergency justifies resorting to extraordinary measures. If an administration and the party backing it want to increase expenditure without jeopardizing their popularity through the imposition of higher taxes, they will always be ready to call their impasse an emergency. Recourse to the printing press and to the obsequiousness of bank managers willing to oblige the authorities regulating their conduct of affairs is the foremost means of governments eager to spend money for purposes for which the taxpayers are not ready to pay higher taxes.[42]

One can readily appreciate Mises' fears. He has drawn attention to a danger inherent in attributing too much power to the State. However, it is here that the libertarian argument goes astray. There is a legitimate role for the State, and it is not to be established in terms of pragmatism but in terms of morality. The State is a ministry of public justice. It is precisely to issues such as fraud that the State has respect. Mises' conclusion that the State cannot be trusted is not valid if the role of the State is restricted to that of a ministry of public justice and the requirement of 100 per cent reserves based on a moral argument, namely the necessity of proscribing fraud, a transgression of the Eighth Commandment, which is always and under any conditions an injustice and a legitimate area for State intervention. But it is precisely the moral dimension that Mises drains out of his analysis. Hence, we are left with the alternatives of either

[42] *Ibid.*

the totalitarian State exercising power without moral authority or the banks, equally without moral authority, practising fraud in moderation. Mises chooses the latter, as I should if I had only those options. But these are not the only options available. The State has a legitimate role to play as a ministry of public justice, as a terror to those who practise evil (Rom. 13:3–4). Its rationale is the moral argument for bringing to justice and punishing those who commit evil, not a pragmatic argument based on considerations of what is the greatest good for the greatest number, which in this case—i.e. free banking as conceived by V. C. Smith and Mises—involves the justification of a little evil (moderate credit expansion) committed by a few (the banks).

We must conclude, therefore, that a 100 per cent reserve should be established as a legal requirement by the State and that all known infringements should be punished by the courts.[43] Once a bank has created demand claims over and above its reserves (i.e. once it issues fiduciary media) it is insolvent, though the public may be unaware of this. Irrespective of whether the bank subsequently restores its reserve ratio to 100 per cent and is able to meet its liabilities, the period of insolvency constitutes an inflationary fraud in which wealth is redistributed from the bank's creditors to its shareholders and debtors. Banks that are known to have pursued such inflationary policies, regardless of whether the fraud is discovered during the period of insolvency or afterwards, should be prosecuted and required to make restitution according to biblical principles of compensation.[44]

[43] It is rather disappointing to see Gary North, working from a self-consciously Christian perspective, agreeing with Mises that the State should not require 100 per cent reserves by law. North is aware of the inconsistency of his position—he says as much himself—yet still follows Mises. See Gary North, *An Introduction to Christian Economics* (The Craig Press, 1973, pp. 41–43). This is an otherwise excellent work and highly recommended reading for those interested in economics from a Christian perspective.

[44] In such cases it would be necessary to determine (*a*) to whom restitution should be made, (*b*) the degree of compensation payable, and (*c*) by whom it should be made, i.e. whether the executive staff under whose management the fraud was committed would be held entirely responsible or whether the bank's shareholders would be required to contribute to the compensation (on the position of shareholders see also Appendix A "Reform of Limited Liability Law"). These are not simple matters to resolve, since an inflation would affect many in society who may have no direct relationship with the bank at all—in other words who neither hold its notes nor have demand deposits with the bank. Compensation to the creditors (depositors) only, whose funds have in effect been illegally plundered by the issue of fiduciary media or by the expansion of credit (creation of bank money), would not necessarily provide restitution to all who might suffer from the effects of the

One further point should perhaps be discussed here briefly. Any successful prosecution of a bank for fraud under a 100 per cent reserve law would probably have the effect of rendering the bank untrustworthy in the estimation of prudent investors. If the payment of compensation awarded by the courts does not lead to the bank being forced into liquidation its prospects for continued business would be severely limited. However, in a fallen world where men love sin rather than justice we cannot assume that such prosecution will always result in a bank going out of business. Certainly, severe, sustained or multiple infringements of the law leading to prosecution and conviction would be likely to have a detrimental effect on the bank's reputation and ability to continue trading even if restitution awarded to victims did not lead to closure. However, there are in any society those who cannot secure loans from reputable banks—perhaps because their businesses are considered unlikely to be successful, or because they themselves have bad debts or insufficient security to offer. A bank whose reputation has been tarnished by a successful prosecution for banking fraud and is suffering the effects of distrust by prudent investors may be able to ameliorate its trading position by loaning money to such people at higher rates of interest and by offering higher rates of interest on time deposits. The problem envisioned here is not the uncertainty of the business taken on by the bank or the increased risk to depositors, but simply the fact that a convicted fraud is continuing to trade. The question may arise as to whether such convicted banking frauds should be allowed to continue in business and whether banks should be licensed in some way as a means of controlling this situation and protecting the unsuspecting public.

---

inflation resulting from the bank's abandonment of the 100 per cent reserve requirement. Justice demands that the victims of crime should be compensated, and therefore punishments involving fines paid to the State, while common in modern Western societies, would be unacceptable in principle from a biblical point of view. However, it is impossible to establish with any certainty which individuals without a direct relationship with the bank are the victims of such crimes as debasing the money supply and the extent to which they have been affected. Indeed this is a crime that to some extent affects the whole of society, yet it evidently affects some more than others, and some who are not responsible for the fraud profit from it—e.g. those who secure cheap loans as a result of credit expansion. The task of resolving these problems would be a matter of casuistry to be determined according to biblical principles of justice by the courts. Over time a series of precedents would be set that would greatly ease the burden of determining by whom, to whom and to what extent compensation would be payable in individual cases.

Any call to licence banks, however, should be resisted. Provided appropriate restitution is made and all obligations falling upon a bank as a result of a conviction for fraud are discharged it should be allowed to continue in business if there is sufficient custom to make its continuance possible. There should be free entry into the banking trade just as there should be into any other form of business. No burdens should be imposed on those entering banking other than those of honesty and fairness in the use of weights and measures, which are required in all commercial ventures. Entry into banking should be free from the necessity of obtaining State licences, charters and free from government regulation except for the requirement of honesty and fair weights and measures, which would mean that 100 per cent reserves should be maintained at all times. As in any other business, a bankrupt bank, once it has discharged its debts, may return to business. It is no more reasonable to impose the necessity of obtaining licences and charters in banking than it is in green grocery or any other form of business.

§5
Free Coinage and Abolition of the Royal Mint

Along with abolition of the central bank and the cessation of the printing of fiat paper money by the government or its agents it will be necessary to end all government control of coinage. This means that it would no longer be the responsibility of the government to issue coin in any form. The government mint should therefore be closed. This would also mean the end of "coin of the realm"—i.e. coin that is intended to function within a particular political juris-diction as legal tender. The minting of coin should be the right of all private individuals, companies and groups, but strictly forbidden to the government, whose sole function is the administration of public justice. The role of the government in respect of the minting of coin should be the policing of coinage, i.e. to ensure that coin is of its stated weight and fineness and that those guilty of debasing the coinage are brought to justice and punished accordingly.

The history of government monopoly of coinage is a history of debasement and fraud. Whenever governments have assumed the authority to issue money in any form debasement has usually fol-lowed. Government abuse of standards of fairness and justice in the issuance of money has been relentless throughout much of history. As soon as difficulties arise governments attempt to resolve their problems by granting themselves special powers under which they can legally—though never morally—debase the currency and force people to use this debased currency by passing legal tender laws. As time has passed our governments have ceased to maintain even a semblance of honesty and fairness in their monopoly of the money supply, and the idea that government should not be permitted to monopolise and manipulate the money supply is today considered at best quaint and naïve.

In 1920 the silver coinage in Britain was debased to contain only 50 per cent silver. The last coins to be issued with a content of 92.5 per cent silver were struck between 1911 and 1919.[45] In 1947 silver coin was replaced totally by token coin consisting of 75 per cent copper and 25 per cent nickel.[46] Prior to 1914 gold coin was in circulation in the United Kingdom and Bank of England notes were convertible into gold. The political tension caused by the assassination of Archduke Frans Ferdinand of Austria in June 1914 led to a run on the British pound and the Bank of England reserves fell significantly. As a result the Bank Charter Act of 1844, which limited the amount of fiduciary media that the Bank of England was permitted to issue, was suspended and the Currency and Bank Notes Act was passed authorising the government to issue fiat currency in £1 and 10s notes. A paper currency of 2,500,000 £1 Treasury notes (known as Bradburys, since they bore the signature of John Bradbury, Chief Clerk to the Treasury) was issued by the government. C. R. Josset comments:

Britain, as guarantor, immediately honoured her obligations once the Germans entered Belgian territory.[47] This attempt to invade France by a

---

[45] C. R. Josset, *Money in Britain, A History of the Coins and Notes of the British Isles* (Newton Abbott: David and Charles, 1971), p. 205.

[46] *Ibid.*, p. 213. Those born within the last fifty years who may be tempted to view with incredulity the introduction of gold and silver coins into the economy as common media of exchange should remember that it was within living memory that these were taken out of circulation. Josset remarks: "While most of us have either long since grown accustomed to the disappearance of gold, or perhaps cannot remember its use as legal tender, many will recognise the colour of real silver coins struck up to 1919 and certainly the half-silver coins struck up to 1946. Economists point out the benefits of a token monetary system, while paper money is far easier to carry, but those of us who like to feel that coins should contain their full value in precious metal are reluctant to accept valueless 'silver' coins." (*Ibid.*, p. 226.)

[47] It must be added, however, that in order to honour these obligations to foreign

surprise route, culminated in Britain declaring war on Germany on the day after August Bank Holiday, Tuesday, 4 August 1914. For the remainder of that week the banks and Stock Exchange remained closed. There was much foreboding on the possibility of runs on the banks when they opened on the following Monday, but the situation remained surprisingly calm and after a few hours it was seen that the fears were quite unfounded. The currency and Bank Notes Act proved a successful measure. Although in theory all these notes were convertible to gold [in *theory* only because had everyone claimed their gold there would not have been enough to go round—SCP], the patriotism of the people [why talk about fraud when the victim is a patriot!—SCP] caused them to be accepted even though the majority had not seen paper money before; as banks transferred gold to the Bank of England and accepted paper money in payment, gold virtually disappeared from circulation. In Scotland and Ireland likewise the banks paid in notes only. Nevertheless, it was known that a large quantity of gold coins was still in the hands of the public, which, it was suspected, was hoarding them in the expectation that sovereigns would be of greater value than the currency notes.[48] It was decided to make the melting down of coin an offence and various shipping restrictions were imposed, making it unremunerative to send gold abroad.[49]

Thus our money ceased to be a precious metal-based currency and became instead a paper fiat and token coin currency.

In 1925 Britain went onto a gold bullion standard, which lasted until 1931. The difference between this and the old gold standard was simply that notes could be redeemed for bullion in bars of 400 ounces of fine gold but gold coin did not circulate as a medium of exchange as it had done before 1914. H. O. Meredith describes the situation:

It was not until 1925 that conditions permitted of the restoration advocated. But in that year the Gold Standard Act was passed, giving the country again a gold standard, but with noteworthy modifications upon that

---

governments the British government was quite prepared to dishonour its prior, and greater, obligation to the British people by effectively turning the Bank of England note issue into fiduciary media and by foisting upon the British people a fiat paper currency in the form of Bradburys. These primary obligations of the British government to its people were broken in order to fund the war effort effectively—a war in which the government showed as little concern for the lives of British servicemen as it did for the Bank of England's "promise to pay."—SCP

[48] Obviously these "hoarders" suspected that the government was trying to defraud them. How easy it is to make the victim look like some sort of unpatriotic criminal by accusing him of "hoarding," a practice that in other circumstances would be called saving and rightly held to be prudent and vital to the strength of the economy! Without hoarding (saving) there would have been no wealth for the government to plunder so dishonourably.—SCP   [49] *Ibid.*, p. 207.

before 1914. Gold coins were not again to come into circulation. The actual currency was to remain entirely token, the sovereigns and half-sovereigns being replaced by the Treasury pound and ten shilling notes. It was contemplated that later, as actually came to pass in 1928, the whole of the fiduciary media would be handed over to the Bank of England, which would issue new pound and ten shilling notes. But there was a free market for gold so that there could be no divergence in purchasing power between the paper and the gold it purported to represent. Under the Act the metal could be taken to the Bank of England where the gold was bought at a fixed price per ounce, slightly below its parity with the sovereign. And the Bank of England was bound to sell gold at a fixed price for legal tender money, that is to say, for Bank notes. This price (£3 17s 10½d. per ounce of standard gold) was exactly that of the Mint price of gold. There was parity between the pound and the 113 grains of fine gold that would have made a sovereign. But this gold was sold only in bars containing approximately 400 ounces of fine gold. The gold, therefore, could hardly come into circulation, and we could describe that system as that of a gold bullion standard.[50]

In 1931 a severe run on the Bank of England led to the abandonment of the gold bullion standard. The Bank lost around £32,000,000 in a few weeks. Parliament therefore passed a bill releasing the Bank of England from its obligation to sell gold.[51]

Had government pursued its proper function—i.e. the administration of public justice, which in respect of currency means the duty to prosecute those who use unjust weights and measures or who debase the currency—our currency today would still consist of precious metal or notes fully redeemable in specie. Once government has gained a monopoly control over the currency, however, the temptation to use this monopoly for the government's own ends usually proves irresistible. It is vital for the development of a stable monetary system, therefore, that the minting of coin as well as the issue of paper currency be taken out of the hands of the State altogether and the role of the State in monetary affairs limited to the administration of public justice—i.e. the duty to ensure that fair weights and measures prevail in the minting of coin and that fraud is punished.

The law as it stands today with regard to the minting of coin does not permit private individuals or private mints to issue coin intended to function as money. The Coinage Act 1971 states: "No piece of gold, silver, copper, or bronze, or of any metal or mixed metal, of any value whatever, shall be made or issued except by or

[50] H. O. Meredith, *op. cit.*, p. 404.   [51] *Ibid.*, p. 407.

with the authority of the Mint, as a coin or a token for money, or as purporting that the holder thereof is entitled to demand any value denoted thereon."[52] Those who contravene this section of the Act are "liable on summary conviction to a fine not exceeding £20."[53] The Act also forbids the melting down or break up of any coin that is current in the United Kingdom or "having been current, has at any time after 16th May 1969 ceased to be so."[54] The penalty cited for doing so is a fine of up to £400 or two years imprisonment, or both.[55]

Both aspects of this law, the outlawing of free coinage and the prohibition on the melting down or break up of coin of the realm, constitute a fundamental denial of the individual's freedom over his own property. This law denies to the individual the right to dispose of his own property as he thinks fit and reserves control of the most important form of property in the economy, i.e. the common medium of exchange, solely to the government in order that it might have the ability to debase and expand the money supply for its own ends. Any government that denies the individual's rights of ownership over the money rightfully in his possession, no matter how vociferous it might be in claiming the ideology of freedom, consumer choice and free markets, has in *principle* ultimately denied the individual's right of private ownership over any and all property, since once the government has a monopolistic control over currency it is able to control and expropriate the wealth of the nation. No matter what the private individual has legal possession of or title to, the government is able, by means of monetary debasement, to take his wealth from him. It is for this very purpose that governments demand such monopoly of the money supply. To deny the full rights of ownership over the money in one's possession, the right to dispose of it as one thinks fit, to break it up, melt it down or recoin it, is to deny ultimately man's economic freedom. It is in *principle* to enslave man to the State and an assertion of the power of eminent domain, the doctrine that all property within the nation belongs ultimately to the State, which reserves the right of expropriation. When the conditions are right governments that do not order their affairs by the light of God's law will, notwithstanding their claims to the ideology of freedom, put this principle into operation for their own ends. If the economic history of the twentieth century has taught us anything it is surely this.

---

[52] Coinage Act 1971, Section 9 (1).   [53] *Ibid.*, Section 9 (2).
[54] *Ibid.*, Section 10 (1).   [55] *Ibid.*, Section 10 (2).

It is important, therefore, that the reforms to be implemented in this area, along with limitation of the State's role in monetary affairs to that of the administration of public justice, should be established in law. Reform must ensure that government mints and government fiat money are declared illegal and abolished and the right of free coinage recognised in law.

As with banks, private mints would be businesses subject to company law in the same way that any other commercial enterprise is. There would be no special privileges granted to mints, no officially sanctioned coin of the realm with legal tender status, and no government-granted monopolies or licences. Entry into the business of minting coin would be open to all, the only regulations being those respecting the use of fair weights and measures. Coin would have to contain its stated weight and fineness of precious metal. All attempts to debase coinage would be legally defined as fraud and the perpetrators of such liable to prosecution and to make restitution to their victims according to biblical principles of justice and compensation.

The incentive to maintain fair weights and measures would be provided in the free market by competition. E. L. Hebden Taylor writes: "Any debasement of these private coins would be prosecuted to the limit of the law. Thus, the private mints would find it to their advantage to keep continual watch over each others' gold and silver coins, calling attention to any sign of fraud. By eliminating the present State monopoly of coinage, private competition would act as a safeguard to monetary fraud and the printing of worthless dollar bills."[56]

§6
Tax Reform

The growth of government power and influence over the lives of the British people during the twentieth century has been immense. This growth of the State has meant the increasing politicisation of society. Along with this there has been an inevitable loss of individual freedom, the effect of which has been to change the individual's way of life significantly, indeed to change the essential character of the British way of life nationally. Even on a purely economic level the

[56] E. L. Hebden Taylor, *Economics, Money and Banking* (Nutley, New Jersey: The Craig Press, 1978), p. 92.

effects of this loss of freedom have been enormous, since it has impeded the operation of the free market to such an extent that economic growth and social amelioration in the twentieth century have been substantially curtailed, to the detriment of all in society. The stifling growth of laws and regulations in virtually all areas of life over the past fifty years is now being supplemented on a prodigious scale by the legislature of the European Union. This growth of government influence over and regulation of life has involved also, and inevitably, the growth of both the bureaucracy and the attendant social services deemed necessary to implement government policies and programmes. All this has to be financed of course. As a result, by 1993 British government spending accounted for over 43 per cent of the Gross National Product.[57]

The funds needed to finance this massive government bureaucracy and the allied social service industry—both of which are unproductive from an economic point of view—have been raised by means of various forms of taxation and by public borrowing.[58] This places a heavy burden on the productive sectors in the economy, which create the wealth of the nation. Such a heavy penalising of economic productivity has had serious consequences for the economy since its effect is to create a disincentive to create wealth. As a result, instead of pursuing the acquisition of wealth by means of productivity many turn to political means of acquiring wealth, e.g. by seeking to affect government economic policy via the activities of lobbying groups or union representation, the aim of which is to secure government concessions, special privileges and government subsidies and protection for the companies or industries that are represented by such groups. The purpose of such activities and groups is to *control* the wealth created by others rather than to *create* wealth. Such measures are inevitably irrational and unproductive from the economic point of view and in turn require government funding, which has to be raised by taxation and borrowing, with the consequent monetisation of debt that the latter entails. This further suppresses the incentive to be economically productive and encourages more lobbying for

[57] This figure is based on the 1993 government expenditure figures published by the Central Statistics Office in the *United Kingdom National Accounts*, 1994 Edition (HMSO). Government spending for the year amounted to £272,849,000,000 and the GNP was £633,085,000,000.

[58] In 1991 52 per cent of government revenue was raised by direct taxation and 27.25 per cent by indirect taxation. Public borrowing accounted for 14 per cent of revenues.

government handouts as a means of acquiring wealth. As a consequence the economy is pushed further down a negative economic spiral that ultimately leads to decapitalisation and decline in standards of living and welfare.

The economy cannot sustain this increasing politicisation of society. The goose that lays the golden egg is being strangled to death by taxes. The disincentive to be economically productive that this process creates—that is to say, the incentive to seek control over the wealth that already exists rather than to create wealth—will eventually reach a critical point and the nation will begin to develop economic problems similar to those experienced by many Third World and ex-Soviet nations. Productivity will begin to fall at a rate that will make our present standard of living impossible to sustain. Except where black markets are able to flourish the nation will become almost totally dependent on an economy dominated by State-run—though not necessarily State-owned—industries and programmes (i.e. a fascist State). This will mean the creation of a proletariat that is virtually enslaved to an unproductive and wasteful State-controlled economic system. The consequences of such an organisation of economic life by the State are all too clear from the Soviet debacle. Of course we have not yet reached this stage in Britain, nor generally in the West. But the nation is being prepared for such a scenario with every step towards assimilation into the European super-State that our politicians take. It is vital, therefore, that this trend should be reversed. In order to do this we need to cut off from the State the source of funding that fuels this malady.

Growth of government power and influence, and the army of bureaucrats and ever expanding social services that accompany this process, can only be funded because the government is able to appropriate the wealth of the nation. Without the ability to expropriate the wealth of the individual and thus the resources of the nation the State cannot pursue such totalitarian policies. Assuming that the State does not resort to outright plunder, there are two ways in which it can expropriate the wealth of the nation while maintaining a façade of legality: first, by means of *fiscal* policies, e.g. taxation, and secondly, by means of *monetary* policy, e.g. monetisation of government debt (expansion of the money supply). The latter, as we have seen, is both immoral and extremely damaging in its effects on the economy. Reform of government according to biblical principles must ensure, therefore, that all such methods of raising revenue are proscribed and governments forced to fund their business by means of fiscal policy.

The economic reforms discussed so far in this chapter would have two very important effects on government business that would lead to significant changes in the economy: first, the government would be forced to stop monetising its debt, adopt sound fiscal policies and balance its budget or else declare itself bankrupt. Secondly, government would be forced to raise its revenues by taxation. Taxpayers, therefore, would be able to assess much more easily how much the government is costing them to maintain. If government required greater revenues it would be forced to raise taxes. Since the government would no longer be able to monetise its debt, thereby inflating the money supply and enabling it to make repayment in debased currency, it would be unlikely to borrow, except perhaps in extreme emergencies. Any money the government did borrow would have to be repaid with interest, which would necessitate even higher taxes in the end. This would have the knock-on effect of encouraging the electorate to vote for responsible governments since it would be apparent that it is in the electorate's own financial interests to make sure that the State limited its role and spending as much as possible. Government, therefore, would no longer be able to finance its profligate policies by theft in the form of debased or devalued currency and by monetising its debts. It would be forced to behave honestly and responsibly or face the consequence of losing an election, and in the case of bankruptcy even prosecution and the necessity of making restitution to its creditors. The question still remains, however, as to what the valid limits of government fiscal policy are, that is to say to what extent the State is morally entitled to tax the nation. In order to answer this question we need to understand the biblical teaching on the function and limits of civil government.

The *function* of the civil government according to Scripture is the administration of public justice, the execution of God's vengeance on those who commit evil (Rom. 13:4). And in doing this, the apostle Paul tells us, magistrates are to be servants of God (Rom. 13:6). Thus, the function of the magistrate is to see that crime as defined by God's law is punished, the innocent protected and law and order preserved in society. It is "for this cause,"—i.e. the administration of justice— says Paul, "that we pay taxes," and, in order to drive his point home, he adds that it is the duty of the magistrate to be "continually attending to this very thing," i.e. to this thing and no other (Rom. 13:6).[59] It is for the purpose of upholding justice and punishing criminals, therefore, and not for other purposes, that the magistrate is supported by taxes according to Christian teaching.

The *limits* of the magistrate's authority to levy taxes is established by biblical precedent. As Creator and Sovereign of the universe God possesses eminent domain over the whole earth. As King, God exercises that sovereignty by taxing the increase of man's hands. This tax is a tithe, a tenth of the increase (Lev. 27:30–34, Dt. 14:22). Two important principles follow from this fact: first, the civil magistrate may only levy taxes legitimately on the *increase*, i.e. on net profits. Since God, as Sovereign of the universe, requires a tax on increase only, *a fortiori* the magistrate also may only levy taxes on the increase. The civil government may not tax property and inheritance (cf. 1 Kings 21:1–19). By implication also sales tax is not permissible since it is indiscriminate and therefore cannot be applied in such a way that the biblical requirement of taxing increase only would be satisfied. Secondly, since as Sovereign God requires only a *tenth* of the increase, *a fortiori* no subordinate human authority may claim more than a tenth, nor even a tenth, since to do so would be to claim an authority and jurisdiction over man, God's creature, that is superior or at least equal to God's. For magistrates, kings or civil governments to exact a tithe or more from their subjects, or to tax property and inheritance, is rebellion against God, the rejection of his sovereignty, an assertion of human autonomy and the usurpation of God's authority over man.

This understanding of the limit of the State's authority and power to raise taxes is confirmed by Scripture. The Torah forbade the Kings of Israel to acquire great wealth (Dt. 17:17). The king's economic means, and therefore his power, was limited by God's law. The

---

[59] According to F. Blass and A. Debrunner, Paul uses the Greek term αὐτὸ τοῦτο (translated in Rom. 13:6 as "this very thing") to mean "just this (and nothing else)" (*A Greek Grammar of the New Testament and Other Early Christian Literature* [Cambridge University Press, 1961], p. 151a. Thus, for Paul the function of the State is restricted to that of apprehending and punishing evil doers according to God's law (i.e. as the servant of God). The Bible nowhere gives the State or magistrate a role beyond this limited function. The provision of welfare, for example, is always the responsibility of the family in the first instance, and only where the needy are without family or where the family is unable to provide welfare does it become the duty of the church and those outside the family to provide welfare (cf. 1 Tim. 5:3–8); but never is such a role given to the civil magistrate or State. See Stephen C. Perks, *A Defence of the Christian State*, Appendix A and *passim*.

private property of the people of Israel was protected by the Eighth Commandment, which applied to the magistrate as much as to any other person or institution (cf. I Kings 21:1–19). In I Sam. 8:4–18 an evil and oppressive king—on account of whom the people cry out to God for deliverance (v. 18)—is described as one who exacts a tithe from the people (vv. 15, 17), who taxes property (vv. 14, 16), and who uses conscription as a means of staffing his army and household (vv. 12–14). The kind of State machinery envisioned here—though conspicuously modest compared with modern Western standards—is clearly understood to be beyond what is morally acceptable for a ruler to impose upon his subjects, and there is obviously an element of judgement involved on account of the people's rejection of God as King (v. 7). For the magistrate or civil government to claim an equal share with God, a tithe, is evil and oppressive, and God's judgement on a rebellious nation.

This means that the most that the State may take in taxation is a second tithe, i.e. a tenth of the remainder after the first tithe, which belongs to God, has been deducted from the increase. This puts the total that the State may legitimately claim at 9 per cent income tax. This tax may only be levied on increase, i.e. net income, and therefore the State may not tax property or inheritance without exceeding its God-ordained jurisdiction and authority. For the State to demand anything above this second tithe is to overturn the Christian social order revealed in Scripture. It is also to render unto Caesar the things that belong to God, since God alone has total claim on man's life and property and he requires in tribute 10 per cent of the increase of man's hands.

Because the Bible limits the function of the civil government (the State) to the administration of public justice the level of taxation needed to fund government on the biblical model is far lower than that needed to fund the governments of modern Western States. A taxation level of well below 9 per cent income tax is a realistic and achievable goal for a Christian government that functions within the biblically defined limits of its jurisdiction and authority. Moreover, not only are limited government and limited taxation, and thus greater individual freedom, possible and beneficial to the individual and society generally; they were the norm in Britain until well into the second decade of the twentieth century. A. J. P. Taylor commented on the limited nature of government and the low level of taxation—below 8 per cent of the national income—prior to World

War One, even though government did not confine itself exclusively to the administration of justice:

Until August 1914 a sensible, law-abiding Englishman could pass through life and hardly notice the existence of the state, beyond the post office and the policeman. He could live where he liked and as he liked. He had no official number or identity card. He could travel abroad or leave his country for ever without a passport or any sort of official permission. He could exchange his money for any other currency without restriction or limit. He could buy goods from any country in the world on the same terms as he bought goods at home. For that matter, a foreigner could spend his life in this country without permit and without informing the police. Unlike the countries of the European continent, the state did not require its citizens to perform military service. An Englishman could enlist, if he chose, in the regular army, the navy, or the territorials. He could also ignore, if he chose, the demands of national defence. Substantial householders were occasionally called on for jury service. Otherwise, only those helped the state who wished to do so. The Englishman paid taxes on a modest scale: nearly £200 million in 1913–14, or rather less than 8 per cent of the national income. The state intervened to prevent the citizen from eating adulterated food or contracting infectious diseases. It imposed safety rules in factories, and prevented women, and adult males in some industries, from working excessive hours. The state saw to it that children received education up to the age of 13. Since 1 January 1909, it provided a meagre pension for the needy over the age of 70. Since 1911, it helped to insure certain classes of workers against sickness and unemployment. This tendency towards more state action was increasing. Expenditure on the social services had roughly doubled since the Liberals took office in 1905. Still, broadly speaking, the state acted only to help those who could not help themselves. It left the adult citizen alone.[60]

It is difficult to avoid the conclusion, even from a cursory examination of the evidence, that the growth of big government (totalitarianism), and of socialism generally, has been inversely proportionate to the decline of the Christian faith as a vital force in the life of the nation. Modern British governments take more than four times the amount in taxation that the Lord of all creation requires in tithes. This wealth is expropriated from the nation in various ways: income tax, National Insurance contributions, sales tax, capital gains tax, corporation tax, tariffs, excise duties and public borrowing. The latter, borrowing, represents one of the more absurd aspects of government policy. In 1992 the government raised nearly 11½ per cent of its revenues from borrowing. It spent more on funding this

[60] A. J. P. Taylor, *English History 1914–1945*, cited in Alan Duncan and Dominic Hobson, *Saturn's Children: How the State Devours Liberty, Prosperity and Virtue* (London: Sinclair-Stevenson, 1995), p. vii.

debt in interest payments (7 per cent of total expenditure) than it did on law and order (5½ per cent of total expenditure) and nearly as much as on defence (just over 9½ per cent of total expenditure).[61]

It is essential, therefore, if the nation is to conform to biblical principles of government that taxation should be reformed. The increasing politicisation of life that has occurred over the past century can only be stopped if the funding that supports the level of government that makes it possible is cut off. By limiting taxation to 9 per cent income tax—and this is the maximum permitted by God's word not an ideal target—the State will be unable to pursue its oppressive policies, and State control and regulation of life and society will begin to recede.

But there is more to this than the moral argument, decisive as that argument is. It is just as necessary for *economic* reasons that the State reduce taxation rates to an upper limit of 9 per cent income tax. When the State seizes control of the nation's wealth to the extent that it has done in Britain over the past century economic activity becomes increasingly irrational and standards of living are inevitably affected for the worse. If the nation is to experience once again economic growth and social amelioration on the scale that was achieved in the period of the Industrial Revolution and after—indeed if the nation is even to maintain its present level of economic prosperity—it is essential that taxation should be reformed and reduced to levels that will allow economic initiative to be rewarded and thus flourish.

It will be necessary therefore to abolish inheritance tax, property tax, capital gains tax, graduated income tax, National Insurance contributions, corporation tax and all other forms of direct taxation over and above the second tithe on increase—9 per cent income tax—discussed above, which is the maximum that the State may take. Such taxes are economically irrational since they penalise the creation of wealth and drive those who excel in creating opportunities for economic growth out of the country—in other words they benefit the indolent at the expense of the industrious and therefore discourage the creation of wealth. Furthermore, the amount of revenue that excessive taxation of the "rich" brings into the public purse is quite insignificant. Most tax revenues are raised from the types of taxes typically paid by the middle and working classes. The real purpose of taxing the rich disproportionately is simply to appease the envy

[61] *United Kingdom National Accounts*, 1993 Edition (HMSO).

of those classes that traditionally support socialist governments. Their effect is totally negative and detrimental to economic growth and social amelioration. They are, moreover, in terms of biblical ethics, fundamentally unjust and perverse. It is equally necessary for economic and moral reasons that all forms of *indirect* taxation should be abolished.

These reforms must also embrace all forms of *local* taxation. Local taxes should be limited to raising sufficient revenue to fund the administration of public justice. Public utilities could be privatised or turned into public trusts. As stated above, *overall* taxation, *including* local taxes, should not exceed the value of a second tithe on increase, i.e. 9 per cent income tax. As we have seen, this is because God, who has a prior claim on man's life and wealth, demands only a tithe, 10 per cent of increase. For the State to claim as much or more is an attempt to usurp God's sovereignty over man, society and the nation.

Tax reform on the scale envisioned here would have significant effects on many groups and individuals presently in the employment of government agencies or in receipt of government subsidies and welfare. The end aimed at, however, would be advantageous for all in society—even for the deliberate welfare scrounger since it would force him to work for a living thereby giving him a more useful and meaningful existence. The result would be a more productive economy and higher standards of living across the whole of society. However, this is not to deny that were changes on this scale to be introduced too suddenly they would create a considerable amount of disruption and difficulty for many. It is important, therefore, that such reforms should be introduced gradually into the economy and alternative institutions and welfare organisations—e.g. churches and charities—encouraged to step in and provide essential welfare services for those genuinely deserving of such and who presently rely on State welfare. Only to the extent that this latter development takes place in tandem with government reform and withdrawal from the economy will it be possible to mitigate the undesirable effects of such changes for those who are most vulnerable in society. It is vital that the church, especially, should begin to take its responsibilities in this area seriously by teaching biblical principles of welfare and by providing welfare ministries to those who are genuinely in need and without the support of their family, which is the primary welfare agency in a Christian society (1 Tim. 5:1–16).

Furthermore, as the State withdraws from this area the beneficial effects of increased provision of welfare by the family and by institutions such as the church and Christian charities would be far greater than merely the provision of the necessary level of continuity for the deserving poor. Such a change in administration of alms for the poor and needy would involve also a shift in the predominant philosophy of welfare and a reassessment of the criteria for determining the need for and level of provision required in terms of fundamental Christian values. Such welfare, since it would be administered within a personal and ethically-informed environment, would significantly reduce welfare abuse, which is inevitable with anonymous State welfare programmes. This would release further resources for welfare for those who are genuinely poor and force many to take responsibility for their own lives rather than being dependent on handouts. Such welfare tends also to be improving both morally and economically in its effects on recipients since it is tied— or at least should be tied—to Christian mission (evangelism) and the Christian work ethic—i.e. that those who refuse to work should not eat (2 Thess. 3:10). The effect of abolishing government welfare programmes by cutting off the tax revenues that fund them and replacing them with private and church-run initiatives would be not only to secure a more efficient administration of welfare for the deserving poor. It would also stimulate economic activity (in accordance with Christian principles, e.g. 2 Thess. 3:10) as a means of provision for many of those presently receiving State welfare.[62]

Moreover, by reducing taxation to morally and economically acceptable levels such reforms would alleviate many of the problems of the so-called "poverty trap,"—which could perhaps more accurately be called the "State welfare trap"—since this is partly caused by levels of taxation that penalise people on low wages to such an extent that it is more profitable for them to claim welfare. This in itself would provide a much needed stimulus to the economy as well as helping to alleviate the economic problems caused by high levels of taxation. Instead of a spiral downwards in economic activity and the concomitant increase in claims on government revenue as a means of acquiring wealth we should see in its place a continual spiral upwards based on the creation of wealth—i.e. greater use of human resources and increasing capitalisation leading to higher standards of living. Rather than the short-term impression of prosperity created

[62] See Appendix C, "Help for the Poor and the Meaning of Jubilee."

by government-managed expansion of the money supply, which eventually leads to recession, unemployment etc., the economy would begin to experience a higher rate of real economic growth over the long term.

§7
The End of Government Control and Regulation of the Economy

The sixth and final reform to be dealt with here is not so much a specific reform as a commitment to the process of reform. We have seen that the legitimate function of the State is the administration of public justice—the protection of the innocent and law abiding citizen and the apprehension and punishment of criminals. For this it bears the sword (Rom. 13:1–6), i.e. it has the power of physical coercion. However, this power is exercised legitimately only in so far as it is used in pursuit of the obligations and duties that are delegated to the State by God's word. Of the 613 laws in the Torah only a comparatively small number require enforcement or enjoin punishment by the civil authorities. And in none of these do the civil authorities act as an agency of welfare, education, art, commerce etc. The role of the civil government is one of administering justice. For the State to enter into these areas of welfare, education and commerce with the power of the sword and enforce State-run programmes funded by taxes is to overturn the social order revealed in God's word and the law that God has given to govern and protect that order. When government exceeds the bounds of and limitations on its authority as established in God's word it ceases to act with divine approbation and authority.

Furthermore, if the civil government is to administer public justice properly, fairly and effectively, it must be impartial in its deliberations and judgements; that is to say it must be a *disinterested* party. Once the civil government exceeds the bounds of its legitimate authority as a ministry of public justice and becomes involved in areas of private and public life over which God's word has instituted alternative forms of government—e.g. family, church, economy—it ceases to be a dis-interested party and will in its deliberations and judgements have respect to its own interests, thereby violating its duty to administer justice impartially. That is to say, it will, to the extent of its interest in any particular sphere, cease to act impartially, and this will inevitably result in the maladministration of justice (corruption). There is no middle way for the State to avoid this problem. Any incursion into spheres of human life and society by the State that are not undertaken strictly with the aim of impartially administering public justice between third parties will adversely affect the State's ability to administer justice in those areas. This is so with regard to the economy as with any other sphere of life.

As an example of the kind of problems that are created by the State's illegitimate interference in spheres outside its own jurisdiction as a ministry of public justice we shall look at education. Education is an economic good subject to supply and demand just like any other good. Many may find this fact unacceptable. "Education is too important to be left to the market" some will say. On the contrary, education is too important *not* to be left to market forces. In any case, there are economic goods that are far more vital to life than education, and yet the State does not take away our freedom to purchase them on a free market. Food, for instance, is far more vital and basic to life than education. Yet we all buy our food on the open market without being dictated to by the government.[63] For the government to step in and regulate the nation's diet by law would be considered by most people an intolerable denial of individual freedom and an abuse of the State's power and authority. And the consequences of such interference are only too obvious from the debacle that has befallen the ex-Soviet nations. Food is an economic good *because* it is so important.

Likewise, education, because it is so important, is a scarce economic good for which people are prepared to exchange other scarce economic goods via a common medium of exchange. When the State takes control over and monopolises education this fact of life is not abolished by any means. We shall either purchase education in a

---

[63] To *some* extent this is no longer true since the European Union has restricted the free market for foodstuffs in member countries by the imposition of import tariffs. In some cases foods that used to be common in the UK are now considered luxuries for the average family due to the imposition of as much as a 100 per cent tariff on products coming from countries outside the European Union. The countries from which many of these foods used to be imported had long-established trading links with the UK that were based on free market exchange. These markets have in many cases now been replaced by government rigged European markets. For more on this see Chapter One, pp. 39–43. Most people, however, would consider this restriction of freedom unjust and unnecessary and would prefer a free market for foodstuffs, and indeed for other kinds of economic goods, unhindered by European Union policy.

free market or else the government will purchase it for us with funds raised by taxation and in the process take away our freedom to determine what kind of education our children will receive. Education remains an economic good that we pay for in both cases, but in the latter case we have to pay far more for less, and our freedom to choose what *kind* of education our children receive is denied us.

When the State passes a law requiring all citizens to provide their children with a certain degree or kind of education it has already distorted the operation of the free market for the provision of education by interfering with the balance between supply and demand. Having passed a compulsory education law the State then finds that some are unwilling to educate their own children and unwilling or unable to pay the fees necessary to send their children to school. This necessitates further action on the part of the State if the law is to be upheld. But unlike law that is negative, i.e. aimed at eliminating evil,—e.g. "thou shalt not murder"—positive law requiring citizens to perform some form of social good as defined by modern social theory is much more difficult and problematic to enforce. Someone who steals, once convicted, can be forced to make restitution or placed in servitude until he has worked off his debt to his victim. A murderer can, and should, be put to death, thus ridding society of evil. The remedies for such crimes are not difficult to determine and are comparatively straightforward to administer. But the State cannot force parents to offer a level of education for their children that they consider themselves incompetent to provide, nor force them to send their children to a school whose fees they cannot afford or refuse to pay. The State must, therefore, if it is to follow through consistently with its compulsory education law, provide grants from the public purse to such schools as will take the children of those who will not, or cannot, educate their children and cannot afford, or will not pay, to send them to fee-paying schools. But then this will be seen as unfair in that some have to pay school fees or educate their children at home while others have a free ride at the expense of the taxpayer. The numbers of those willing to pay will decrease and State funding in the form of scholarships, grants and assisted places will become the order of the day for formerly private schools. This will of course lead to State regulation in one form or another. Eventually a State education system will be established and taxes raised to fund it from the whole population, regardless of who uses the State system.

This is essentially how the State educational system has developed in Britain. The State system may even become compulsory, and all private and public[64] schools outlawed.[65] Educational standards are then set according to bureaucratic criteria, not the economic criteria of providing an education that meets the demands of consumers (i.e. fee-paying parents). The result is the corruption of the market for education and the denial of economic freedom in the provision of education: first, the State's interference in education, the provision of an economic good for *some* that is free *at the point of delivery*, but paid for by the levying of taxes on the whole population, besides being a denial of the God-given freedom and responsibility of parents, is a fundamental injustice to those who derive no benefit, for whatever reason, from the State's provision of education. Furthermore, this injustice is perpetrated by the very institution that above all others has the duty to eliminate and rectify such injustice: the State.

Second, the establishment of the State schooling system distorts the market for education to such a degree that it cannot function as a market at all at many levels. The provision of State education that is free at the point of delivery prices most of the State system's private competitors out of the market for those with average and low incomes. Because there are no tax concessions for those not using the State system these people are doubly in difficulty if they wish to educate their children privately, since their means of providing for their children's education has been confiscated by the government to support the State schooling system. Private schooling then becomes affordable only for the wealthier members of society.

Third, another aspect of this distortion of the market for education is that private schools and teachers who do not wish to work in the State system are forced out of the market since they cannot offer their services free of charge as the State schools do. Teachers who would otherwise have provided a valuable service to the community

[64] In Britain a public school is a private establishment that receives public funding in some form, e.g. through grants for scholarships or for any other purpose whatsoever. The term was coined before the State system came into existence to distinguish those private schools that received some form of public funding from those that did not. Most private schools in Britain today are public schools since they receive public money in some form, which may be provided, for example, through the assisted places scheme. The development of the State system has rendered the terminology somewhat confusing.

[65] Some Labour and Liberal Democrat politicians in Britain are committed to the outlawing of all forms of private education, and the vociferous supporters of this viewpoint are legion among the socialist parties of various colours.

in a free market for education are forced to seek employment in State schools,[66] even though they may not agree with the ideology of State-funded and State-controlled education, nor with its philosophy of education, code of practices and religious perspective.[67]

Fourth, the *quality* of education provided in State schools is also inferior for many reasons, most of which can be put down to the fact that the system is a government-controlled bureaucracy. For example, much time and energy is diverted away from essentially educational matters into paper work designed to satisfy the bureaucratic requirements of government departments and inspectors.[68] Political considerations may also bear upon the kind of service teachers are expected to provide. A related problem for the teaching staff is that they are expected to act as social workers and ideal substitute parents for those in society who refuse to shoulder their responsibilities as parents and who wish to leave virtually the whole task of raising their children to school teachers. All this takes time and energy away from the essential task of providing an education, and these problems are greatly exacerbated for State school teachers by the high ratio of pupils to teachers in most State schools.

Furthermore, since the bureaucratic method of management is utterly unsuited to economic enterprise the provision of State schooling is far more expensive than the private alternative would be were it permitted to function in a non-State-regulated free market economy, although the population generally may be unaware of this due to funding of the State system being raised by taxation along with a host of other services provided by the State. The ever growing

[66] Where there is no State provision of education the market and charitable foundations are able to provide for the educational needs of society more than adequately, even for the poorer classes in society. This fact has been borne out by research into the provision of education in nineteenth century England before the 1870 Education Act. See E. G. West, *Education and the Industrial Revolution* (London and Sydney: B. T. Batsford Ltd, 1975), and *Education and the State: A Study in Political Economy* (Indianapolis: Liberty Fund, [1965] Third Revised Edition, 1994).

[67] On the religious perspective of the secular humanist ideology underpinning the State education system see Stephen C. Perks, *The Christian Philosophy of Education Explained* (Whitby, England: Avant Books, 1992), Chapter Two and *passim*.

[68] The National Curriculum is a good example of this. Most teachers, if they follow the rules required for the implementation of the National Curriculum and the proper administration of the SATs tests, have little time left for teaching. The bureaucratic administration of these State regulations takes up an inordinate amount of time and as a result the education of pupils suffers. This is a good example of the universal rule that bureaucracy is not a suitable form of management in an economic enterprise.

bureaucratic tier of management has to be funded and this makes the whole system vastly more expensive. The result is a poorer quality of education and dissatisfied parents. Instead of being educated pupils are subjected to the latest educational theories and programmes devised by State bureaucrats and progressive educationalists, the main effect of which seems to be the steady growth of illiteracy in society and the continual downgrading of academic standards. It would be wrong to think that this situation necessarily represents a failure on the part of the teaching profession, as politicians would perhaps like us to believe. Rather, the problem is that the provision of education is not suited to bureaucratic government management and suffers from the irrationalities that such a system of administration inevitably enforces upon what is essentially an economic enterprise.[69] In short, State education is uneconomic, wasteful, inefficient and fails in large measure to deliver the product. The growth, in recent decades, of illiteracy in Western societies such as Britain[70] and the United States,[71] which have developed highly bureaucratised State education systems over the past century, is ample testimony to this fact.[72]

The same kinds of arguments are relevant to the provision of

[69] On the problems of the bureaucratic method of management as applied to economic enterprise see Ludwig von Mises, *Bureaucracy* (Spring Mills, Pennsylvania: Libertarian Press, Inc., [1944] 1983).

[70] It is a misconception encouraged by socialist ideology that prior to the advent of State education the vast majority of the working class in Britain were uneducated ignoramuses. On the contrary, the level of education provided by private fee-paying and charitable schools for the majority of the working classes in Victorian England prior to the 1870 Education Act was above the world average by *today's* standards. A comparison of contemporary popular literature with that of the nineteenth century suggests that general standards of literacy are now lower than they were in the nineteenth century, despite the fact that more money is now being spent on education by the State than at any other time in our history. The State did not create an education system so much as take over an exceptionally successful private system of schooling that already existed, which was created by a Christian society. For more on this see E. G. West, *Education and the Industrial Revolution*.

[71] On the situation in the USA see Samuel L. Blumenfeld, *The New Illiterates* (Boise, Idaho: The Paradigm Company, [1973] 1988).

[72] In State schools much of teachers' time is taken up with fulfilling government requirements for paperwork instead of teaching. If teachers do this work out of school hours at home—and many do—they often work well over a 50 hour week. Likewise, much of the so-called long holidays that teachers are deemed to have is taken up with bureaucratic paperwork and planning for the next term. Much of this work is not necessary for educational purposes. On the contrary, its real purpose is to demonstrate the government's commitment to educational reform, which is often Messianic in its aims. This has been particularly the case since the introduction of the National Curriculum in the UK.

other economic goods by the government, e.g. health care, social services, public works and utilities, welfare etc. It is important therefore that the government should withdraw from all such involvement with the economy and restrict itself to the administration of public justice. It can only do this properly and effectively if it is disinterested and impartial in its relationships with the economy and indeed with any other aspect of life in which it has the responsibility to administer justice.

The privatisation of nationalised industries begun during the 1980s should, therefore, be continued, rationalised and extended to include areas such as education and welfare. The proceeds from the sale of nationalised industries should be used to reduce the national debt. In particular, privatisation should not take the form of turning a government-created and nationalised monopoly into a private monopoly, and care must be taken to ensure that in the privatisation of nationalised industries the creation of free market conditions and competition is prioritised. The public is not served, nor justice done, when a vast private monopoly simply replaces a public monopoly. Conditions must be created in which competition and free entry into previously government-controlled or unionised industries is possible. Only when the government has withdrawn from involvement in the economy will it be able to pursue impartially and fairly its own duties and obligations as a ministry of justice.

Examples of injustices perpetrated by the civil government when it enters into spheres of life for which God has ordained alternative forms of government that are independent of the legitimate function of the State could be multiplied. The essential point is that government should be limited to the administration of public justice. When government fails to observe its legitimate boundaries justice is the first casualty because the State ceases to be an impartial judge in its administration of justice. The usual term for this is *corruption*. The pursuit of justice in society by the civil government is too important to be compromised in this way and therefore the process of reform set forth above must be pursued vigorously until the limits of government power and authority are reduced to that of the impartial administration of public justice.

CHAPTER SIX

CONCLUSION

§1

Economics and the Moral Order of Creation

THERE are essentially two kinds of argument for reform of the economy as outlined in the previous chapter: first, there is the moral argument. The Bible requires that in all economic transactions just weights and measures should be used (Lev. 19:35–37; Dt. 25:13–16). These laws are direct and admit of no extenuating circumstances in which they can be set aside. To break them is to sin against God and injure one's neighbour. Biblical ethics demands that those who transgress these laws should make restitution to their victims, that is to say restore what was stolen, or the value of what was stolen, plus compensation of between a fifth and five times the value of what was stolen, depending on the nature of the crime (Ex. 22:1, 7–9; Lev, 6:1–5; Num. 5:6–7). In principle the Bible also forbids multiple indebtedness (Ex. 22:25–27). Furthermore, the Bible does not permit the State to exact a tithe—i.e. a tenth of increase—from its citizens. The taxes it raises must therefore be less than a tenth of the increase. God takes a tithe, a tenth of the increase. For the State to take a tenth is to claim equality with God. For it to take more than a tenth is to claim that its jurisdiction over man is superior to God's. The most that the State may legitimately take, therefore, is a *second* tithe, a tenth of the remainder of the increase after the deduction of the first tithe, which belongs to God (1 Sam. 8 and 9 cf. Dt 17:14–20). Moreover, the State may not tithe or tax inheritance, nor assume the power of eminent domain without incurring the wrath of God (1 Kings 21). The power and authority of the State is thus very limited in the Bible, its function being that of administering public justice (Rom. 13:1–6). In short, from the biblical perspective the State has neither sovereign power nor sovereign jurisdiction over the nation. Sovereignty belongs to God alone and all power and authority vested in the State, as in the church and the family, is limited and governed by God's word. The moral argument for the reforms set out above is thus very strong.

Secondly, there are economic arguments for these reforms. The business cycle has become a major problem in Western economies. The continual swing between booms (periods of inflation, easy credit and imprudent expansion of businesses, resulting in a massively debt-laden economy) and slumps (periods of recession, high interest rates, bankruptcies, unemployment etc.) is crippling the economy. These cycles are the result of the inflation of the money supply by the banks, deficit financing on the part of government and the false climate of economic prosperity and growth that this creates. Such attempts to stimulate and control economic growth have had serious consequences that politicians and their economic gurus have not been able to predict or control. The damage inflicted upon the economy in terms of bankruptcies, unemployment etc. has been enormous. There is always a heavy price to be paid for the creation of a false climate of economic prosperity in this way since it is generated by the creation of money, not by the creation of real wealth. The result, inevitably, is a period of recession in which society readjusts to the *real* and much lower level of economic growth that underpins the economy. The recession of the early 1990s was much longer and far deeper than politicians and economists anticipated when it first began to bite in 1989. This indicates that the real level of inflation—i.e. expansion of the money supply—that prevailed throughout the 1980s was far higher than government retail price indexes suggested.[1] Of course, there are other problems and causes involved in the creation of such recessions, but inflation of the money supply has been the main culprit for the economic vandalism that has been inflicted upon the nation during the past half century.

But there is a further, much more damaging effect of these booms. The corruption of the price mechanism that occurs during periods of high inflation leads to the uneconomic—i.e. less productive or even unproductive and wasteful—use of the available scarce resources needed for the creation of real wealth and economic growth. As a result the capital base of the economy is not growing in proportion with the demands that society is increasingly making upon it. This trend, if it continues unchecked, will eventually lead to dire circumstances, since the constant consumption of the capital base necessary

[1] On inflation of the money supply and its relation to the retail price index see p. 141ff.

to maintain economic growth will ultimately result in the decapital-isation of society. This problem, exacerbated by a decrease in the growth of the population necessary to sustain current levels of social welfare, is already facing the nation and causing difficulties for governments of both left and right wing parties. Examples of such difficulties include the recurring problems of funding for such essen-tials of welfare as health care and education. When the wealth finally runs out even the semblance of a prosperous industrialised society will be gone. Britain will find itself on the economic scrap heap that has been the lot of ex-Soviet socialist States for many years.

Britain faces this scenario at the beginning of the twenty-first century far more keenly than most people suspect. Pan-European socialism administered by a centralised bureaucracy in Brussels will herald an economic decline for the nation that will make the recession of the early 1990s seem insignificant by comparison. If the current attempts of politicians to bring Britain into political union with the rest of socialist Europe are successful this decline will be swift and our ability to extricate ourselves as a nation from the European economic debacle will have gone. Much political ground has been covered in Britain in the process of European political assimilation over the past decade. Even a mere ten years ago some of the proposals for European assimilation now being considered would have been unthinkable.

Although these are two distinct arguments for reform of the economy—the moral and the economic—we must not think that they are totally unrelated. The world is not a product of blind impersonal forces but the creation of a holy God. The cosmos has been created to serve a purpose, namely to reveal and glorify God. Science studies the mechanisms of second causes and therefore describes the forces and laws of nature in terms of depersonalised cause and effect relations.[2] This is, of course, right and proper within the narrow

---

[2] Science is a *descriptive* discipline. It does not seek to *define* phenomena, but simply to describe and explain them in terms of cause and effect. The attempt to define is a religious and philosophical undertaking. When scientists assume that their descriptive discipline is able to define the meaning of phenomena they inevitably run into trouble, going beyond the bounds of scientific enquiry in an attempt to apply the scientific method to problems for which it cannot yield an appropriate answer. The result is that scientists tend to combine and confuse philosophy with science, often without a sufficient appreciation of the epistemological principles underpinning *either* discipline to do justice to the issues involved with the task of defining phenomena. Modern science, and this is particularly true of the exact sciences, is simply not equipped to perform the function, previously allotted to the

parameters of the scientific disciplines themselves. It was the Christian faith that freed the study of natural phenomena from the debilitating influence that animism in its various forms exerted for so long upon man's efforts to understand the world in which he lives. "The biblical revelation of creation out of nothing in actual historical fact" writes E. L. Hebden Taylor "provided the intellectual as well as religious conditions for the birth of modern science in Western civilization alone."[3] Only in the cultural matrix of Western Christendom, which has been heavily influenced by the biblical world-view, has man developed "faith in progress, confidence in the lawfulness and rationality of the universe, appreciation of the quantitative method, and a depersonalized view of the process of motion in the universe, all qualities which are the main features of the scientific quest,"[4] in sufficient measure to make modern science possible. As a result the natural world ceased to be seen as an irrational environment continually influenced by a myriad divinities all exerting their will upon mankind through the elements in contrary ways, thereby controlling his destiny. Instead it became the arena of man's dominion, to be investigated, understood and exploited for the benefit of mankind and the greater glory of God. Yet we must also remember that science is an abstraction of one aspect of reality from the totality of life, which finds its ultimate purpose and meaning in the creative act of a rational, law-giving God. It is man's purpose in the whole of life to serve and honour God as Creator, Lord and Saviour. This purpose for man is to be realised in his economic life no less than in his devotional life, and God has so ordered his creation that man might rationally and purposefully pursue this calling and thereby bring the whole earth under the rule and government of Jesus Christ. This

---

"queen of the sciences" (theology), that modern Western society demands of it. Science can only describe; it cannot define since definition is outside the scope of its method. Therefore it cannot provide mankind with the answers to questions of *meaning* and *purpose* that he so desperately seeks.

[3] E. L. Hebden Taylor, "The Reconstruction of Modern Science in Terms of the Biblical Life-and-World View" in *Calvinism Today*, Vol. III, No. 1 (January 1993), p. 7*b*.

[4] *Ibid.* Taylor is here summarising the argument set forth by Stanley L. Jaki in *Science and Creation: From eternal cycles to an oscillating universe* (Edinburgh: Scottish Academic Press, 1986). On the birth of modern science within a specifically Christian cultural matrix see R. Hooykaas, *Religion and the Rise of Science* (Edinburgh: Scottish Academic Press, [1972] 1984) and Stanley L. Jaki, *op. cit.* On the rise of the scientific world-view within a specifically Protestant context see Peter Harrison, *The Bible, Protestantism and the Rise of Natural Science* (Cambridge University Press, 1998).

is the meaning of the cultural mandate given to mankind at creation (Gen. 1:28) and the Great Commission given by Christ to his disciples at his ascension (Mt. 28:18–20). The cosmos, therefore, is not impersonal and the laws of nature, which are simply descriptions of the mechanisms that govern second causes, are not independent impersonal aspects of an autonomous universe. The cosmos is created by God, belongs to him and exists in all its minutest detail to serve his purposes. It is therefore intensely personal,[5] and all cause and effect relationships of second causes are related teleologically to the creative will of God.[6] This is as true of economic phenomena as it is of every other kind of phenomenon in the created order.

[5] Cornelius Van Til, *The Defense of the Faith* (Philadelphia, Pennsylvania: Presbyterian and Reformed Publishing Company, 1976), p. 42. See also G. North, *The Dominion Covenant: Genesis* (Tyler, Texas: Institute for Christian Economics, 1982), Chapter 1, "Cosmic Personalism," pp. 1–11.

[6] It might be objected that what I have conceded above by arguing that only in Western Christendom did man develop an understanding of the depersonalised process of motion in the universe, appreciation of the quantitative method and confidence in the lawfulness and rationality of the universe in sufficient measure to make modern science possible, I have taken away by relating all events in the universe teleologically to God's will. However, the animistic and Christian views of ontology are radically different and it is this difference that accounts for the birth of science in Western Christendom and its "stillbirth," to use Jaki's term, in those cultures that have not developed under the dominating influence of Christianity. In the animistic perspective all being is one, with god or the gods at the top of the chain of being and amoebas at the bottom. Mankind is somewhere in between the two. In this perspective the gods are part of the universe; they are of the same being with the rest of the universe. The Christian perspective or biblical world-view, however, posits an absolute distinction between the Creator and the creature, i.e. between created being and the uncreated being of God, who governs his creation by his creative word. The Bible tells us that God upholds the universe continually by the word of his power (Heb. 1:3). The Christian God, however, is a rational, law-giving God, not the capricious god of the Moslems and the pagans. He governs the cosmos not by whim but by means of law. This government of the cosmos by God, in which cause and effect can be observed and identified as the means by which God governs his creation (second causes), contrasts sharply with the world-view of animism in which capricious spirits control the natural phenomena to which man is subject. In such a perspective the world is not a rationally ordered environment subject to the laws of creation (cause and effect), which man can understand and harness for his own advantage and to the greater glory of God. Therefore man survives not by exercising dominion over the natural world, which is his calling in the divine order of things (Gen. 1:28), but by placating the spirits that are thought to control it. The abandonment of animism for the biblical world-view led mankind from a condition of subjection to the natural world to a position of dominion over the natural world, a position in which he is able to exploit the world for God's glory and for the benefit of mankind and the natural world itself. This was the meaning and intent of the creation mandate given to mankind at creation (Gen.1:28; see also note 7 below).

Furthermore, because the God who created the cosmos is a holy God, a righteous God, and because the cosmos is a revelation of his Godhead and exists to glorify his name, the created order is also for man an intensely *moral* environment. Man also is part of the created order, but unlike any other aspect of the created order man is made in the image of God, and therefore all that man is, does, thinks and desires is moral in nature. Man either seeks in all things to honour God as Creator and Lord or rebels against his Creator and rejects the God-created and God-ordered nature of the world in which he lives. This moral rebellion, which begins with spiritual apostasy,—the rejection of God's word as authoritative and the ultimate standard of human behaviour, man's rule of life—leads to the practical manifestation of evil throughout the whole of man's life and in all that he touches. Wherever fallen man goes and in whatever he does, he seeks to overturn God's created order and impose his own fallen understanding of life and his own sinful will upon the creation he has been given to rule over. But this rebellion can only end in frustration and failure, since God's creation is a revelation of his glory and exists to serve his purposes. Man cannot overcome or negate by his sin and abuse of God's world the purpose it serves in God's creative plan. He must either submit and honour God or be crushed by a world that exists to serve God and will serve God notwithstanding man's corrupt attempt to pervert that purpose.

The attempt to create economic prosperity by printing money is a good example of man's desire to impose his own autonomous will upon the world in defiance of God and contrary to the clearly revealed order of creation. Men desire prosperity, but instead of pursuing this by means of honest hard work and thrift they seek to create it as if by magic through printing paper money. This is an attempt to short-cut reality as God has created it, indeed to re-create it according to man's own will,—wealth without effort! But reality denies to man such phantasies because it exists to serve and glorify God, not to satisfy the sinful desires of men. Money is not the source of wealth. Work is the source of wealth in the world that God has created, a world in which man is commanded to work six days of the week. Money is merely a means of exchanging the various kinds of wealth created by work.

The consequences man suffers from abandoning principles of justice in economic affairs, therefore, are not merely the result of impersonal cause and effect relations on the level of second causes, but also moral consequences, the judgements of a personal and righteous God who punishes man for his wickedness and has so ordered his creation that man cannot sin with impunity.[7] Indeed, it is because the creation reveals the glory of God and exists to serve his purposes that man cannot escape the consequences of his sin. Try as he might, man cannot escape the moral order of creation.

If man is to achieve economic prosperity, therefore, he must behave with integrity in the market place. He must deal justly, using fair weights and measures, not seeking to benefit himself by cheating his neighbour. His pursuit of profit, economic growth and social amelioration must be based on rational principles of economic activity, and in the world that God has created, a world that reveals God's creatorhood and declares his glory, those rational principles of economic activity are based on the Christian virtues of honesty, hard work and thrift. If man would achieve economic growth and social amelioration, therefore, he must seek to transform society by pursuing the Christian ethic in all his activities, and this means

[7] The Westminster Confession of Faith expresses the relation between God's eternal decrees and second causes in the following way: "God from all eternity did, by the most wise and holy counsel of his own will, freely and unchangeably ordain whatsoever comes to pass; yet so, as thereby neither is God the author of sin, nor is violence offered to the will of the creatures, nor is the liberty or contingency of second causes taken away, *but rather established*" (Chapter III.i). In other words God's eternal decree is accomplished not against but rather through the operation of second causes, whose nature and purpose in the divine order of creation is thereby established, rendering God's creation a rational, regular and ordered universe that can be understood and relied upon by mankind. Only in this biblical perspective is the universe demystified and yet still imbued with ultimate meaning and purpose, and this is why historically modern science has developed within a specifically Christian cultural matrix. In sharp contrast to this biblical world-view is the animistic perspective of paganism (cf. note 6 above), which renders the natural world irrational, and the impersonalism of the modern evolutionary perspective, which renders the natural world meaningless. Both these perspectives are extremely detrimental to the development of the kind of world-view that made the scientific task possible. Under the influence of the former man sees his only means of ameliorating his conditions in life as the placating of the gods and spirits that he believes control the natural world. Under the influence of evolutionism modern science is veering off fatally into science-phantasy and adopting cosmogonies and cosmologies that differ from the fables of the ancient world only in the degree to which they employ twentieth-century jargon to mask their pseudo-science. Hence, just as it was only within the context of a Christian world-view that modern science was born and able to develop, so also only a return to the Christian world-view can save science from the "blind alleys" and "murky backwaters," to use Jaki's words, that led to the ignorance and scientific stagnation that prevailed in the ancient world. See Stanley L. Jaki, *Science and Creation*, cited above, and *The Road of Science and the Ways to God* (Edinburgh: Scottish Academic Press, 1978).

pursuing economic activity according to the principles of justice and honesty set down in God's law. This involves loving one's neighbour as oneself, since the *Christian* work ethic requires "the lawful procuring and furthering the wealth and outward estate of ourselves *and others*," as the Westminster Shorter Catechism puts it. As we have seen, it is the capitalist system based on the Christian work ethic that is alone able to achieve this twofold purpose. This has been borne out by history. It is only as the Christian religion has been embraced by the Western nations and lived out in the daily lives of their peoples that the benefits of economic prosperity that we enjoy and so much take for granted in the West have become available to mankind.

Modern Western society, however, is in the process of abandoning the Christian ethic, and the consequences of this have been enormous not only in terms of morality but in economic terms as well. This is because the economic life of man is inextricably tied up with his moral behaviour and his view of the nature and meaning of life. The answer to man's economic problems therefore is not simply a mechanistic change in the way he does business. Sin cannot be remedied by mere technology, much as our politicians and economists are committed to the idea that it can. Only as man is reformed inwardly, in the heart, and turns away from his sin to embrace the truth incarnate in Jesus Christ, and hence his true purpose in life, will he understand the necessity of pursuing God's will in the whole course of life, including his economic life. Until men are transformed inwardly by the grace of God they will not be able to transform their cultures nor their economies, since they will not *desire* to change the way they behave. Society will continue to grope around in darkness, stumbling from one folly to the next in a moral and economic decline that becomes exponential with every crisis the nation faces. But once changed, once touched by the grace of God, that change must work itself out in the whole fabric of man's life and culture, and in every detail of his economic life no less than in church, devotional and family life. It is only as this inward transformation wrought by the Holy Spirit in men's hearts becomes a reality once again in the life of the nation that we can expect outward transformation of our culture. But such outward transformation does not happen automatically. It must be implemented by faithful men and women seeking to work out their salvation with fear and trembling (Phil. 2:12).

It is imperative, therefore, that Christians should not view the gospel of Jesus Christ as concerned only with eternal salvation, a saved soul, and in the meantime waste their lives. God has put man on the earth for a purpose, and he has redeemed his people that they might fulfil that purpose by dedicating themselves and their lives to God's service in the task of transforming their cultures. This transformation begins in man's heart, but it must not stop there. It must go on to manifest itself in the whole of man's life, including his economic life.

§2
British Decline and the European Union

But there is far more to be considered here than merely economics. The decline of honesty and integrity in economic affairs is an indication of a far greater apostasy in the life of the nation and is itself an example of God's judgement upon men for their worship of the creature rather than the Creator (Rom. 1:18–32). God is not mocked. Spiritual apostasy is the cause of the economic problems faced by modern Western nations. The decline that has overtaken Britain in recent years—and I include as part of this decline our alliance with an ever-growing centralised European super-State and the disastrous effects this is having on society, not only economically but legally and socially—is surely a judgement upon the nation for its apostasy from the Christian faith. Those who doubt this must remember that judgement seldom comes upon men and nations in the supernatural way that it is often thought to do. Judgement comes slowly, little by little, and people fail to realise the gravity of the situation or see the hand of God at work. They do not repent, and their stubbornness only exacerbates the situation and aggravates their guilt. Their eyes are blinded by their foolishness and so they stumble on into worse folly.

On two occasions in the twentieth century Britain waged war on an enemy bent on creating the kind of European hegemony that our politicians are now pursuing. What has so changed that what we previously fought against we now willingly throw ourselves into? Surely not the issues. All that is of advantage in a European market and in free trade between the nations of the European Union can be achieved without the kind of European super-State that our politicians are now contemplating, and on a vastly greater scale, with greater advantages not only for Western European trade but for world trade, including trade with those Third World and Eastern European countries we hear so much about, which are seldom helped by Euro-socialist dumping policies. But the advantages to be gained by such free trade both within and outside Europe are a bulwark against the kind of European Union that our Euro-bureaucrats are intent on creating.

Of course, Hitler was a monster: he tried to commit genocide. It is assumed that our new enlightened socialist world, unlike that of Hitler and Stalin, does not go in for this any more, so a European super-State is now acceptable to many. Such thinking is easily shown to be superficial. Those who think that a repeat of the past is impossible need look no further than the nationalist conflicts that followed the break-up of what was formerly Yugoslavia. And anti-Semitism is not far from the surface in modern Europe either. In a centralised European State the ability of those who find such ideologies hateful to defend persecuted minorities—and it is not in-conceivable that Christians should eventually find themselves in this category—will be severely limited. Such prospects may seem incred-ible today, but a brief look back in history will teach us otherwise. With the increasing decline of the Christian faith both in Britain and in Europe, we cannot rely on a future in the Union that will guarantee those freedoms and rights that only the prevalence of a *Christian* culture has created and sustained.

The writing is on the wall, but our politicians have not seen it yet. When they do, like Belshazzar, they will be unable to do anything about the mess that their failure to serve the living God has created. It has been said that history repeats itself, the first time as tragedy, the second time as farce. Undoubtedly, the European Union is a farce, perhaps even a tragic farce. But the nation will not survive its alliance with Europe unscathed, certainly not in its present form. Our politicians are about to sell our birthright for a mess of European pottage. When they do we shall be given up to a fate that the British nation fought so hard against and prayed so earnestly to be delivered from. But this will be no more than the nation deserves for its apostasy and its treading underfoot of God's word.

It is the long-term future therefore that Christians must look towards. Nothing happens in the history of men or nations that is not in the plan of God for the establishing of his kingdom. Nations and civilisations rise and fall according to God's will. British society is surely ripe for judgement, but what will the Christian's attitude be to the justice of God?

Judgement is God's action of overturning what is bad to make way for his kingdom. Therefore Christians must rejoice at God's omnipotent power and his judgement on those who oppose his authority and rule. Christians are the heirs of God's kingdom, the ones who are to inherit the earth. Therefore we must put our hands to the plough and start building for the future. We must also remember, however, that judgement begins at the house of God; and just as Israel disobeyed and was sent into captivity, likewise we also may face servitude in the Babylon of the European Union until the church has learned once again to face up to its responsibility to honour God in all things.

REFORM OF
LIMITED LIABILITY LAW

AMONG those who have called for reform of the economy along the lines set out in Chapter Five there are those who have also argued for the abolition of the limited liability status of joint-stock companies as a necessary concomitant of such reforms. As we shall see, R. J. Rushdoony links the development of limited liability and the growth of a fiat money economy and in *The Politics of Guilt and Pity* he entitled the chapter on limited liability "Limited Liability and Unlimited Money."[1] Likewise, Gary North in *An Introduction to Christian Economics* wrote: "Monetary inflation, multiple indebtedness, and limited liability are an unholy economic trinity; they are eroding the very foundation of Western culture."[2] These are strong words indeed against limited liability, since although there are in the Bible specific laws addressing the debasement of money and multiple indebtedness there are none that explicitly address the kind of limited liability granted to joint-stock companies in modern Western law. The issue is much more complex than that. Nonetheless, although the Bible does not contain explicit laws addressing this issue it does give general principles and case laws from which the limits of a company's or individual shareholder's liability can be deduced. A careful study of the biblical material relevant to this issue would, I believe, yield neither the conclusion that shareholders of joint-stock companies should be held liable beyond the nominal value of their shareholding in *all* circumstances where the company's actions or failure to act have led to justifiable claims for damages, nor that limited liability status should be accepted in its present form, since both fail to apportion liability for damages in the way that biblical law suggests that it should be apportioned.

Limited liability law restricts the liability of a shareholder in a

---

[1] R. J. Rushdoony, *The Politics of Guilt and Pity* (Fairfax, Virginia: Thoburn Press, 1978), pp. 254–262.

[2] Gary North, *An Introduction to Christian Economics* (The Craig Press, 1973), p. 18.

joint-stock company to the nominal value of his shareholding. In the event of a limited company being forced into liquidation in order to pay off its debts the shareholder may lose the whole or part of his investment, since the company's assets will be sold and the proceeds used to reimburse its creditors. But that is the limit of his liability. If the sale of the company's assets does not raise sufficient funds to clear the company's debts the shareholder is not obligated to reimburse the company's creditors out of his own private estate, as would be the case if he were a partner in a non-limited liability company that was forced into liquidation. He would not run the risk of personal bankruptcy therefore.

There are three kinds of limited liability company: the *private* company, the *public* company and the company *limited by guarantee*. The private limited company is more restricted in its ability to raise capital than the public limited company since the maximum number of shareholders permitted by law is fifty, its shares are not quoted on the Stock Exchange and transfers of shares have to be approved by the directors. In addition, the controlling shareholders are often required by banks to give personal guarantees for any debts incurred by the company. This latter fact goes some way to mitigating the effects of the limited liability status granted by law to private limited companies. The public limited company, by comparison, can raise capital by means of public subscription, its shares are traded on the Stock Exchange and their sale does not have to be approved by the company's directors. Shares in a public company are thus more liquid. Companies limited by guarantee are normally non-profit making or charitable organisations. They have no share capital and the liability of their directors is limited to a fixed, usually nominal, amount of money.

The term limited liability can be used in a much broader and looser sense than this however. Because man is a finite being his liabilities are limited. Man's knowledge is not exhaustive; he has to live and work within the limits of his knowledge. The fact that man's knowledge is limited means that his liabilities are of necessity limited also. In this broader sense man's liabilities are limited by many things. For example there are *natural* limits to man's liability: e.g. death limits man's liabilities. There are also *man-made* limits to his liabilities: for example, contracts may limit a man's liability. Insurance companies may write clauses into life insurance policies limiting the liability of the insurance company under certain circumstances. A common contractual limitation in life insurance policies stipulates that if the insured commits suicide within a certain number of years after taking out the policy the company is not liable to pay out. Such contracts bring us into the realm of legal limitations on man's liability. But man's liability is also limited by God's law. There are thus *divine* limits placed on man's liability.[3] However, it is with the restricted and narrower use of the term that we are concerned here, i.e. with the term as it is applied in law to joint-stock companies whose shareholders' liability is restricted to the nominal value of their shareholding. The purpose of this chapter is to establish from biblical principles and criteria the extent of the validity or non-validity of this modern idea of limited liability as it is applied to joint-stock companies in law. It is important that this restricted use of the term is kept in mind and not confused with the more general notion and alternative uses of the term.

It has been argued that limited liability is in the first place unjust, since it shifts liability from those who are responsible for a company's actions to innocent parties. Second, limited liability separates property from control and ownership from management, resulting in the separation of management from responsibility. Shareholders become interested not in ownership and responsible management of the company but simply in the drive for more profits. Third, this leads to a greater tendency for companies to assume debt, make risky investments and undertake risky business projects. Since the conse-

---

[3] I am concerned here with man's liability to other men in economic matters. What is said here, therefore, should not be taken as necessarily applicable in strictly *criminal* matters. For example, limitations on man's liabilities arising from sabbath-year release of debt and manumission would not be applicable to someone making restitution for theft or fraud. Neither am I dealing with man's liability before God as a sinner under the sentence of God's law. It is a fundamental axiom of Christian theology that God holds man accountable for his sin and that his liability to eternal punishment for the transgression of God's law is unlimited precisely *because* man is unable to make sufficient amends for his sin, which, of course, has infinite consequences. Only in Christ is man's unlimited liability for sin before God removed since Christ, as the God-man, has made a propitiation that is sufficient to atone for man's sin and thus able to discharge the debt incurred by it. Regarding this R. J. Rushdoony writes: "The covenant-breaker, at war with God and unregenerate, has an unlimited liability for the curse. Hell is the final statement of that unlimited liability. The objections to hell, and the attempts to reduce it to a place of probation or correction, are based on a rejection of unlimited liability" (*The Institutes of Biblical Law* [Presbyterian and Reformed Publishing Company, 1973], p. 668). It would not be valid, however, to apply this or similar arguments to economic relationships between men since God's law clearly establishes limits to man's liability in such cases.

quences of bankruptcy are borne only partially by the company, its creditors having to bear any loss above the value of its assets, there is an incentive for companies to assume debt that they cannot clear by the sale of their assets in the event of failure. Shareholders without limited liability to protect them, however, would likely be more concerned about the kind of risk taking the company engages in, the amount of debt it assumes and more generally that it has a responsible management team. These concerns would be expressed at shareholders' meetings by the dismissal of incompetent or irresponsible directors and the appointment of a prudent and trustworthy management. At such meetings shareholders would be concerned about protecting not only their investments but also their personal estates and reputations. Limited liability, by protecting shareholders from the more unpleasant and economically ruinous consequences of risky and imprudent enterprises undertaken by the company encourages irresponsibility on the part of shareholders—many of whom may not even turn up for shareholders' meetings—and greater risk taking and imprudent investment by the company's management. With companies that are not granted limited liability status shareholders have to protect themselves by ensuring that the company acts responsibly and is able to clear any debts it has incurred by the sale of its assets and therefore without calling on the personal estates of its shareholders should it be forced into liquidation.

Rushdoony argues the case for complete abolition of the limited liability status of joint-stock companies. He makes the point that although there is limited liability status for companies in modern Western society, the individual, by comparison, is subject to almost unlimited liability by the law: "Today, the law penalizes the individual with almost unlimited liabilities, so that every kind of insurance is necessary for the individual as homeowner, driver, and parent (in the event that his child blackens a bully's eye). On the other hand, corporate irresponsibility is fostered by limited liability laws which, over a period of time, separate property from control, ownership from management, and management from responsibility."[4] Rushdoony goes on to state the problems with limited liability very clearly:

Liability is inescapable; by limiting the liability of the company which contracts a debt, or permits a fraud, the liability is then passed on to innocent parties. Limited liability thus shifts responsibility away from the responsible

----

[4] *The Politics of Guilt and Pity*, p. 252.

to society at large. A partner or shareholder in a company will exercise cautious and conscientious control over his company, if his liability for the debts and frauds of that company are not limited to the extent of his investment. The result is sound, moral, and careful management of a company by the actual owners. But, with limited liability, a premium is placed on profit irrespective of responsibility. The shareholder is less concerned with buying responsible ownership and more concerned with buying a share in profits. And then, as the state further protects the shareholder against liabilities in his irresponsible pursuit of profits, the shareholder becomes less and less concerned with the responsible and moral management of his company.[5]

Furthermore, "The limited liability company has an advantage over the company without such protection. Having limited responsibility for its debts, it is free to take chances which a fully responsible company will not take: the limited liability [company] has state protection in its risk-taking which the other companies do not have."[6]

Likewise, E. L. Hebden Taylor in *Economics, Money and Banking* argues that limited liability "must be abolished so that all investors are forced to assume full responsibility for the companies in which they own shares. Such a drastic step would make all shareholders attend the annual meetings of the companies in which they now hold shares and keep track of what the managements of such companies are doing."[7]

The effects of limited liability, argues Rushdoony, are twofold:

The *first* effect of limited liability was the progressive separation of ownership from responsibility, of management from property. Burnham called it the "managerial revolution," without analyzing its origins in limited liability. Berle has also described it as a revolution, one in which a group of executives control a corporation whose owners have retained little power over their property: "the historic [*sic*] field of responsibility—a group of financially interested stockholders to which each corporate management must account— is progressively being eliminated." . . . There is a divorce of individuals from economic initiative; there is now "power without property," i.e., without responsible individual ownership; persons and organizations other than owners control or manage property. The stockholders, technically owners, "have the right to receive only. The condition of their being is that they do not interfere in management."[8]

---

[5] *Ibid.*, p. 256f. [6] *Ibid.*, p. 258.
[7] E. L. Hebden Taylor, *Economics, Money and Banking* (Nutley, New Jersey: The Craig Press, 1978), p. 92.
[8] *The Politics of Guilt and Pity*, p. 258f. The quotations are from Adolf A. Berle, Jr., *Power Without Property* (New York: Harcourt, Brace, 1959), pp. 56 and 59.

The *second* effect of limited liability is that it has "assured a greater readiness by corporations to assume debt. After all, the homes and incomes of those involved are not at stake, but only their limited investment."[9] Furthermore, Rushdoony argues that the accumulation of corporate debt is geared to the process of inflation. Limited liability and an inflationary economy go hand in hand and feed on one another. "The effect of this [limited liability] has been to replace a hard money economy with an inflationary credit economy. It is interesting to note that both paper money and limited liability became entrenched in the United States after the Civil War."[10] Hence North's insistence that inflation, multiple indebtedness and limited liability are an unholy alliance that threatens the foundation of Western culture.

A related problem is that by providing shareholders with a degree of immunity from the consequences of the irresponsible actions of the company, limited liability also helps to impede the efficient and prudent allocation of scarce resources within the economy, since companies may take risks and engage in debt-financed enterprises that would not otherwise have been practicable and that assume a level of economic prosperity within society that is in fact illusory. This factor is more prominent during periods of economic boom when cheap loans and easy credit are available in abundance. The resulting adjustments that have to be made when recession hits the economy generally lead to an increase in company bankruptcies. The shareholders benefit during the boom from the expansionary and irresponsible actions of the company and when recession hits the economy they are able to get away with the loss of their investment only, which by then, as a result of inflation, is worth much less than when originally invested anyway. In other words, in an inflationary economy the short-term profits that can be made as a result of irresponsible expansion and the debt-financing of enterprises may well sufficiently exceed the shareholder's initial investment to compensate him more than adequately for the limited loss involved should the company be forced into liquidation when recession hits the economy. The effects of such irresponsibility, however, do not simply disappear; they are passed on to others in the form of bad debts and unpaid bills for capital and services supplied to the company before it is declared bankrupt. Limited liability thus contributes to the general economic vandalism generated by the business cycle.

[9] *The Politics of Guilt and Pity*, p. 260.   [10] *Ibid.*

These are important arguments that demand serious consideration. The irresponsible use of wealth will ultimately lead to economic
decline and limited liability encourages such irresponsibility, or at least
helps to protect shareholders from the more severe effects of such
irresponsibility. The case against limited liability must be considered
seriously therefore and weighed against the biblical material relevant
to the issue.

More recently, however, Gary North has changed his mind on
this issue and no longer sees limited liability as part of an unholy
economic trinity that threatens Western culture. In his book *Tools
of Dominion* North argues that limited liability has good precedent in
God's law. North writes: "Certain kinds of economic transactions that
limit the liability of either party, should one of them go bankrupt,
are valid." For example: "a bank that makes a loan to a church to
construct a building cannot collect payment from individual members,
should the church be unable to meet its financial obligations."[11] He
then claims that "The same sorts of limited liability arrangements
ought to be legally valid for other kinds of associations, including
profit-seeking corporations, limited partnerships, or other private
citizens who can get other economic actors to agree voluntarily to
some sort of limited liability arrangement."[12] North claims that he
has come to this conclusion by a "careful" consideration of "the legal
implications of the imposition of unlimited personal liability on church
members for the decisions of pastors and church officers."[13] He then
poses the question "Could the church function if every member were
made potentially liable to the limits of his capital for the illegal activity
of the church's officers?" However, the case of an individual church
member is very different from that of a shareholder in a joint-stock

---

[11] Gary North, *Tools of Dominion* (Tyler, Texas: Institute for Christian Economics,
1990), p. 473.   [12] *Ibid.*, p. 474.
[13] *Ibid.*, p. 474, note 37. North does not actually say that he has changed his
mind at this point, but rather states his disagreement with Rushdoony on the issue.
Neither does he rehearse the reasons that Rushdoony advances for abolishing limited
liability nor the fact that he formerly espoused Rushdoony's position. Furthermore,
North not only disregards the arguments advanced against limited liability by
Rushdoony, but also rides roughshod over the biblical material with which he is
dealing. The impression this creates is that North is anything but "careful" from
an exegetical point of view, which is surely not an insignificant point in a commentary.
His handling of the issue seems to be attended by a cavalier attitude to the text
and sloppy thinking all round. This is indeed a pity since heretofore North's skill
in handling economic matters from a biblical perspective has, in my opinion, been
unparalleled.

company. The two are certainly not analogous. A church member does not own part of the church nor does he draw dividends from it, and except in "democratic" churches he is not responsible for the actions of the church leadership. Furthermore, North demolishes his own case by arguing, correctly in my opinion, that a wise banker would not loan money to the church and would instead advise individual members to finance the church's needs by remortgaging their houses and then donating the borrowed money to the church, thus placing the liability for the debt with individual church members on whom the bank can foreclose if they default on repayment. North comments that this "makes church members personally responsible for repayment . . . Members cannot escape their former financial promises by walking away from the church."[14] The remortgaging scheme for making funds available to the church, North continues, "keeps the church out of debt as an institution, which is godly testimony concerning the evil of debt (Rom. 13:8a)."[15] Evidently then, for North, individual church members *should* bear the responsibility for securing debt in regard to a church project; it is the institution that should be protected not the individual member. But this contradicts his former statement that individuals should *not* be held liable. North's argument here is confused and inconsistent. This simply demonstrates, however, that the analogy between the church and the joint-stock company does not hold. It is illogical therefore to deduce the liabilities of shareholders in a company from the individual personal liabilities involved in church membership. North is a high churchman who likes to argue that membership in the church is not voluntary, but rather the commandment of God. Given that perspective, how then can he argue that the same principles of personal legal liability arising from membership of a church are applicable to a voluntary association such as a joint-stock company? His argument breaks down completely. But even leaving aside this argument, since not all Christians would argue that membership of a church is not voluntary,[16] membership of a church, or indeed of a

---

[14] *Ibid.*, p. 473, note 36.

[15] *Ibid.* This is quite the point: the church should not contract debt in any case. If, however, it does contract debt that it is not subsequently able to repay there is no reason morally why the creditors should not recover their money from those responsible for authorising the debt.

[16] Membership of the church is not voluntary from the point of view of man's responsibility before God, but it is voluntary from the human and social point of view, at least in the modern world—in former centuries when recusancy laws were

youth club, social club or bingo club, is an entirely different matter from share-ownership in a company. North's argument for limited liability revolves around faulty exegesis and faulty logic.

Unfortunately, North does not help his case by mixing arguments regarding limited liability in the narrower sense as applied to joint-stock companies whose shareholders' liability is restricted to the nominal value of their shareholding with examples of other kinds of limited liability such as an employer's liability regarding the risks knowingly taken by an employee doing a dangerous job and the contractual limits placed on an insurance company's liability by an insurance policy. The latter two cases are of an entirely different order from that of the former, and the conflation of these disparate kinds of restriction on a company's liability in the same argument only serves to confuse the issue of whether limited liability as applied to shareholders of joint-stock companies is morally valid and sanctioned by biblical law.

Furthermore, the question at issue between those who would abolish limited liability and North, who wishes to keep it, is not whether there should be limits or no limits to man's liability, but *at what point* man's liability should be limited. North is correct when he argues that "Man is a limited creature. His knowledge is therefore limited. Because his knowledge is limited, God limits man's legal liability."[17] But this is a much more general notion of limited liability than that indicated by the term as it is applied to joint-stock companies. It would have been helpful if North had kept this stricter meaning of the term in mind when voicing his disagreement with Rushdoony. Those who advocate abolition of limited liability law as it applies to the shareholders of a company are not doing so on the premiss that man's responsibility is *un*limited, but rather on the premiss that the point at which his liability should cease must be governed by biblical principles and priorities. Without limited liability status as it is presently granted by law the maximum limit of the liability of individual shareholders in a bankrupt company would be determined not by the nominal value of their shareholding but by the extent of the company's debts and bankruptcy law,—that is to say a bankrupt company that could not clear its debts by the sale

---

common it was a different matter of course. Nevertheless, it should not be forgotten that membership of the church of Christ is not necessarily coterminous with membership of a specific denomination or institution.

[17] *Tools of Dominion*, p. 471.

of its assets would be forced to call upon the private estates of its shareholders, who would have to make repayment, if necessary, up to the point of having to declare themselves bankrupt. Thus, the shareholders' liability is limited ultimately by bankruptcy law not limited liability law as it now exists.

Rushdoony argues that this is a reflection of biblical law, which required that at the end of every seventh year all debts should be cancelled (Dt. 15:1–2). He cites H. B. Clark: "Modern statutes of limitation and bankruptcy acts fulfill the purpose of the ancient law of sabbatical release—the former by forbidding the bringing of an action upon a debt after a certain number of years and the latter enabling a debtor to turn over his property in satisfaction of his debts."[18] Rushdoony adds the comment that "The modern statutes are thoroughly secular and profane in intention, however, and, while derived from the Biblical sabbath law of release, are alien in spirit from it."[19] Rushdoony later restates the point that bankruptcy laws reflect the biblical principle of sabbath release from debt and makes an additional observation on the protection they afford to the family: "Modern bankruptcy laws, despite their abuses, reflect not only the Biblical sabbatical release on debts, but the preservation to the wife and family of the home from the claim of creditors."[20] Those who have, following Rushdoony (and North himself in his earlier writings), argued for the abolition of limited liability laws are not arguing that man's liabilities are unlimited, therefore, but simply that the modern practice of limiting a shareholder's liability to the nominal value of his shareholding should be abolished. A shareholder's liabilities would be limited by bankruptcy law, which reflects the biblical principle of sabbatical debt release.

The difference between North and those who wish to abolish limited liability is thus not that the former accepts the validity of limited liability while the latter insist there should be no limits to man's liability. It is rather a difference over the point at which a shareholder's liability should be limited legally. North desires that shareholders' liability be limited to the nominal value of their investment. Rushdoony insists that shareholders should exercise responsible ownership and that limited liability discourages this and should be abolished. Instead the shareholder's liability would be limited by

[18] H. B. Clark, *Biblical Law* (Portland, Oregon: Binfords and Mort, 1943), p. 156 [§268], cited in R. J. Rushdoony, *The Institutes of Biblical Law*, p. 145.
[19] *The Institutes of Biblical Law*, p. 145.   [20] *Ibid.*, p. 380.

bankruptcy law. This would force shareholders to exercise responsible ownership over the company.

A careful consideration of the biblical laws governing the responsibilities of ownership suggests, however, that neither of these two positions is entirely correct, and that they both contain important elements of the biblical position while rejecting other equally important biblical principles.

The biblical case laws relevant to the responsibilities and liabilities of ownership of property are given in Exodus 21:28–36 and 22:5–6. Neither these nor any other laws in the Bible address the modern concept of share-ownership directly, but the principles involved are applicable to joint-stock companies by way of extension. Indeed, these case laws set down the only principles from which we can determine from a biblical perspective what the liabilities of share-ownership should be.

If an ox gore a man or a woman, that they die: then the ox shall be surely stoned, and his flesh shall not be eaten; but the owner of the ox shall be quit. (Ex. 21:28)

But if the ox were wont to push with his horn in time past, and it hath been testified to his owner, and he hath not kept him in, but that he hath killed a man or a woman; the ox shall be stoned, and his owner also shall be put to death. If there be laid on him a sum of money, then they shall give for the ransom of his life whatsoever is laid upon him. Whether he have gored a son, or have gored a daughter, according to this judgement shall it be done unto him. If the ox shall push a manservant or a maidservant; he shall give unto their master thirty shekels of silver, and the ox shall be stoned. (Ex. 21:29–32)

And if a man shall open a pit, or if a man shall dig a pit, and not cover it, and an ox or an ass fall therein; The owner of the pit shall make it good, and give money unto the owner of them; and the dead beast shall be his. (Ex. 21:33–34)

And if one man's ox hurt another's, that he die; then they shall sell the live ox, and divide the money of it; and the dead ox also they shall divide. (Ex. 21:35)

Or if it be known that the ox hath used to push in time past, and his owner hath not kept him in; he shall surely pay ox for ox; and the dead shall be his own. (Ex. 21:36)

If a man shall cause a field or vineyard to be eaten, and shall put in his beast, and shall feed in another man's field; of the best of his own field, and of the best of his own vineyard, shall he make restitution. (Ex. 22:5)

If fire break out, and catch in thorns, so that the stacks of corn, or the standing corn, or the field, be consumed therewith; he that kindled the fire shall surely make restitution. (Ex. 22:6)

It is clear from these laws that in the biblical perspective the major criterion for determining an individual's liability arising from ownership of property is the extent of his knowledge of the consequences of his actions or failure to take action. If a man's actions or failure to act have consequences that he cannot reasonably be expected to foresee his liability for damage inflicted on the property or lives of others is limited. In this case North's observation is correct: "Man is not to be judged by standards that could apply justly only to an omniscient being."[21] If on the other hand a man knows that his actions or failure to act are dangerous and likely to result in injury to others or damage to their property he is held liable to compensate the victim fully for his loss, and in the case of the death of a victim the maximum penalty of death is available. Quite clearly, therefore, biblical law establishes cases in which the financial liabilities arising from ownership of property are limited to the value of the property involved or even less than the value of the property involved. It also establishes cases in which liability is *not* limited to the value of one's investment and in which restitution must be made in full.

We shall now look more closely at these cases, extend the principles involved to other possible similar cases, and then consider how they might be applied to modern joint-stock companies and their shareholders.

Case *a.*—An ox that has no previous record gores a human being to death. The owner had no prior warning of this since the animal had previously been docile. The owner's liability in this case is very limited; in fact the limit of his liability is the nominal value of his investment since the ox is put to death and cannot be sold for meat. The Bible clearly establishes here a case of limited liability to some extent analogous to the kind of liability imputed to shareholders of a limited company. The difference, however,—and it is a significant difference—is that limited liability is not a status applicable in all possible eventualities. The limit of the owner's liability, in other words, is not established by the granting of a legal status but in terms of the particulars of an individual case in which a claim might be made against the owner.

Case *b.*—An ox that has no previous record gores another ox to death. The owner of the goring ox must sell it and split the price between himself and the owner of the dead ox. They then divide the dead ox between themselves. In this case the liability of the owner

---

[21] *Tools of Dominion*, p. 472.

of the goring ox is limited to *less* than the nominal value of his investment since the costs incurred by the incident are borne equally by the two parties involved, the victim as well as the owner of the goring ox. The owner of the dead ox receives compensation only to half the value of the live ox plus half the value of the dead ox. Generally speaking, the market value of a goring ox will be lower than that of a docile ox and thus the compensation received by the victim may well be less than half the value of his loss. If the ox that gored is a prize bull, however, he might possibly gain more than this.

Case *c.*—Suppose, however, that a previously docile ox gores two oxen to death. The Bible does not address this case specifically, but the principles for determining the limits of the owner's liability and the just settlement of any claim arising from it are already given in case *b*. The live ox is sold and the price split three ways, one part going to each of the three parties involved, or in the case that the two dead oxen are owned by the same person two parts going to the injured party, and the dead oxen are similarly split three ways. In this case the compensation received by each of the parties involved from the sale of the live ox is less than in case *b*, i.e. each party receives only a third of the proceeds from the sale of the live ox compared with half the proceeds in case *b*, and each party receives a third of each of the two dead oxen. Were each dead ox to be split equally between its owner and the owner of the goring ox the latter would come off better than the injured parties, since each party would receive a third of the value of the live ox, but the owner of the goring ox would receive half of both dead oxen, whereas the injured parties would receive only half a dead ox each. In case *b* each party receives an equal share of the proceeds of the sale of the live ox and an equal division of the dead ox. In order for this proportionality to be maintained in case *c*, therefore, the dead oxen must be split equally between all the parties involved. The liability of the owner of the goring ox is in one sense greater in that he receives less from the division of the price of the live ox than in case *b*, but the compensation awarded to the injured parties is correspondingly less than in case *b* also.

In these cases the liability of the owner is clearly limited and the criterion for determining this limitation of liability is the extent of the owner's knowledge. Man is a finite creature; he cannot be expected to predict the future and he is not to be judged as if he could. His liability is therefore restricted by the limits of his knowledge. The case is far different, however, where the owner had prior knowledge that an ox was dangerous.

Case *d.*—An ox that is known to be dangerous and whose owner has been warned and yet still does not take sufficient care to restrain it, so that it gores a free man, woman or child to death. This is clearly a case of criminal negligence. The owner's liability is established by means of the biblical principle of justice: "life for life" (Ex. 21:23). In this case provision is made for the death sentence to be commuted to financial compensation (a "ransom," v. 30). The citing of the death penalty, however, serves an important purpose in establishing the ultimate limits of liability arising from ownership of property. If in certain cases a man may be liable to forfeit his life, then he is, *a fortiori*, liable to forfeit his property in order to compensate his victim, and possibly even his freedom since he may be forced to sell himself into servitude in order to raise sufficient money to pay the ransom determined by the court (Ex. 21:2 cf. Lev. 25:39–41, Dt. 15:12–14). In compensating a victim's family for his death the owner of the goring ox with a reputation would be expected to pay in full whatever the court determined as an appropriate ransom.[22] His liability, therefore, is certainly not limited to the nominal value of his investment. In the case where an ox with a reputation gored a slave to death the amount of compensation was fixed at thirty shekels of silver and paid to the slave's owner not to his blood relatives.[23] According to Keil and Delitzsch thirty shekels of silver was probably the price for the redemption of a slave, that of a free man being fifty shekels of silver (Lev. 27:3).[24]

If the owner had attempted to restrain the animal securely, however, and the rope broke or the ox escaped in some other way, it would be up to the court to determine whether the owner had

[22] In determining the amount of compensation payable by a poor man the court would have to take into account the maximum sum he would be likely to raise by selling himself into bondage and fix the ransom at a level that would not exceed this plus the value of his property.

[23] In a sense when a man became a slave he effectively became a covenant member of his master's family and thus the compensation was paid to the head of the victim's covenant family, which in this case was the slave's owner. Still, leaving aside this argument, the master has property in his slave and therefore compensation is owed to him (see John Murray, *Principles of Conduct* [London: The Tyndale Press, 1957], pp. 96–102).

[24] C. F. Keil and F. Delitzsch, *Biblical Commentary on the Old Testament* (Wm B. Eerdmans), *The Pentateuch*, Vol. II, p. 136. Cf. John Calvin, *Commentaries on the Four*

taken reasonable precautions within the limits of his knowledge.[25] If he were found to have acted responsibly and could not have foreseen that the rope would break the case would be resolved as a case involving limited knowledge as in case *a*.

Case *e*.—An ox that is known to be dangerous and whose owner has been warned and yet still does not take sufficient care to restrain it, so that it gores another ox to death. The owner of the goring ox must pay full compensation for the value of the dead ox, which then becomes his. Again, the owner's liability is not limited. If the dead ox is a prize bull he must pay the full value.

Case *f*.—Someone opens or digs a pit and leaves it uncovered or without a fence around it and an ox or a donkey falls in and as a result dies (cf. Dt. 22:8). This case is treated like those in which the owner of an ox that is known to be dangerous does not restrain it properly, since it is reasonable to expect the one who leaves a pit uncovered to foresee the possible consequences of doing so. It is within the limits of human understanding to calculate the dangers posed to others by leaving a pit uncovered. The one who leaves the pit uncovered is thus liable to pay full compensation to the owner of the dead animal, and keeps the dead animal himself.

Case *g*.—An ox that is known to be dangerous and whose owner has been warned and yet still fails to take precautions to restrain the animal, so that it gores to death *two* oxen. This case, as with case *c*, is not directly addressed in the Bible, but the principles for determining the owner's liability are contained in case *e*, and it is a simple matter to apply them in this case. The owner of the goring ox must pay full compensation for both dead oxen and keeps the dead animals, the sale of which may help to defray the costs of compensating the victims.

Case *h*.—An ox with a reputation for goring whose owner has been warned and still does not take care to restrain the animal properly, so that it gores *five* oxen to death. This is an extension of case *g*. The owner of the goring ox must pay compensation in full to the victims. However, suppose he is poor and he has to sell

---

Last Books of Moses Arranged in the Form of a Harmony (Grand Rapids, Michigan: Wm B. Eerdmans), Vol. III, p. 45.

[25] Cf. G. North, *Tools of Dominion*, p. 472f. North does not consider in this case whether or not the owner of the ox has taken reasonable precautions within the limits of his knowledge as a criterion for determining liability and simply assumes that the broken rope case is an argument for limited liability *per se*.

his possessions to raise enough to compensate his victim. He may get something from the sale of the dead oxen, which would help, but even then he is not able to make restitution. His only recourse would be to sell himself into bondage to raise the money needed to compensate his victims. Suppose, however, that even this does not raise enough money to pay full compensation to the victims. He is still in debt to his victims. The maximum period of bondage into which a Hebrew could sell himself was seven years (Lev. 25:39–43). The maximum period for which a Hebrew could be in debt was also seven years (Dt. 15:1–2).[26] Moreover, the actual period of bondage or debt might be considerably less than this since manumission and cancellation of debt occurred every seventh year. If a Hebrew obtained a loan or sold himself into bondage three years after the last sabbatical year of release the maximum period he would serve or be in debt would be four years. The implication of this for the matter under consideration here is that if the poor man could not raise the full amount of compensation by selling his property and then selling himself into bondage, the victims would have to settle on the maximum that he could raise in this way. Even if they were to hold the remainder against him as a debt while he was in bondage it would automatically be cancelled at the next sabbatical year, which would coincide with his manumission. This is to some extent analogous to modern bankruptcy law, the most significant difference being that modern bankruptcy law does not provide for the bankrupt to sell himself into bondage. The liability of the goring ox's owner is not limited to the nominal value of his investment, but it is ultimately limited by the sabbatical year of release.

Case *i.*—Someone allows his animals to graze another man's field or vineyard, or starts a fire that spreads to another man's property. These are laws relating to accidental damage to property caused by one not exercising proper caution. The compensation payable by the offending party to his victim is simple restitution. There is no limitation of liability such as that granted to joint-stock companies in modern Western law for the one who causes the accident, since the consequences of allowing one's animals to graze in another man's field or of lighting a fire without taking precautions to ensure that it does not spread can be expected to be foreseen. The perpetrator

---

[26] The sabbath-year release of debts referred to charitable loans made to those who were poor not to commercial loans of the type contracted in the modern business world. There were no commercial loans of the latter type in ancient Israel. I agree

would thus be liable to the full value of the damaged property, and he would have to make restitution out of his own estate or, if this were insufficient to pay off his debts, sell himself into servitude until the next sabbatical year of release, at which point his liability would cease. This case is analogous to case *f* since the outcome of such negligence is foreseeable. Application of the principles of liability set forth in case *i* to modern joint-stock companies is fairly straightforward. Shareholders of companies that were required to pay compensation as a result of such accidents would be responsible for ensuring that the victim was fully compensated for his loss. If the company were unable to pay such compensation either some or all of its assets would have to be sold in order to raise the funds necessary or the shareholders would have to raise sufficient funds between them from their own estates, and their liability would not be limited except by bankruptcy law.

It is clear from these cases that the Bible limits man's liabilities but not in the way that modern limited liability law restricts the liabilities of shareholders of joint-stock companies. The most important point thrown up by a consideration of these cases is the criterion used to determine the extent of one's liability arising from the ownership of property, viz. the extent of the owner's knowledge. Limited knowledge brings limited liability. But cases *d, e, f* and *i* demonstrate that this principle cannot be abused to the extent that the owner of property need only be ill-informed of the consequences of his actions or failure to act in order to avoid the responsibilities of ownership. Thus cases *d* and *e*, involving an animal with a reputation for goring, case *f*, involving an uncovered pit, and case *i*, involving accidental damage to another's property by straying cattle or fire, place limits on the application of the limited knowledge principle. That is to say, the limited knowledge principle is not applicable where an owner can be reasonably expected to foresee the possible dangerous consequences of his actions or failure to act and the damage it might cause to others' property or lives, even though he may not have fulfilled that expectation, i.e. even though he may be ignorant of his responsibilities. In other words, biblical case law establishes the possibility of *negligence* as a criterion for determining the extent of liability as well as the criterion of *extent*

---

here with Gary North that the provisions of Deuteronomy 15 regarding the sabbath year release of debt do not apply to modern commercial loans. See Appendix B.

of knowledge. In fact the negligence principle establishes the limits of the extent of knowledge principle.

The issues involved in reform of limited liability company law from a biblical perspective are, therefore, much more complex than a simple choice between limited liability (using the term in the strict sense as applied to joint-stock companies) and unlimited liability. The cases in which, in terms of biblical criteria, a modern limited company might be held to be genuinely in ignorance regarding the possible consequences of its actions or failure to act and thus in which its shareholders' liability is limited to the nominal value of their investment are far less numerous than those in which the shareholders would be held liable beyond the value of their shareholding. Furthermore, in those cases in which a company acted in ignorance the maximum liability of the shareholders in financial terms might be considerably *less* than the nominal value of their shareholdings. For example, a company that buried toxic waste knowing the dangers this posed to others' property and lives, or at least in a situation where it might reasonably be expected that the company's managers could calculate the risks involved, would be liable to pay full damages in terms of biblical criteria and its shareholders would be expected to contribute from their private estates if the sale of the company's assets failed to raise sufficient funds to compensate the victims. On the other hand, a drug company that issued a drug that was genuinely believed to be beneficial and safe within the limits of knowledge available at the time, and that was confirmed to be safe within the limits of the knowledge then available by independent sources, but was subsequently shown to have serious side-effects might, according to biblical principles, have no liability at all, i.e. in case of death (case *a*),[27] or only limited liability, which would in financial terms be less than the total value of the company's assets,—e.g. in the case of serious injury the company would be forced to liquidate its assets and distribute the proceeds between its victims and shareholders, the

---

[27] In case *a* the goring ox is put to death. In the example used here of a chemical company releasing a drug that caused death there is no equivalent to the death of the ox except withdrawal of the drug from the market. If it were argued that the company should be put to death in the sense of being forced to close down, the victim's family would still receive nothing from the sale of its assets. This is, however, a pure type, as is the following example using case *c*, and in reality the situation would likely be more complex, involving elements of both cases *a* and *c*. This would require liquidation of the company's assets but only the injured parties would receive compensation, not families of dead victims.

shareholders receiving between them a one part share of the proceeds (case *c*). Neither of these scenarios would conform to current practices of compensation by limited liability companies. Evidently, therefore, there is need for reform of limited liability law as it presently exists.

The question now arises as to how the biblical criteria for determining the extent of liability arising from ownership of property might be applied to modern joint-stock companies. It is clear from a consideration of the biblical evidence that a blanket limitation of the shareholder's liability to the nominal value of his investment, such as that granted in modern limited liability law, in many cases is subversive of justice since it legally relieves companies of their moral responsibility to make full compensation to those adversely affected by their actions or failure to act where biblical principles of liability and restitution demand that they should. From the biblical perspective, therefore, the case for abolition of the limited liability status of joint-stock companies, at least as it presently exists, is a strong one. One the other hand, it would be equally unsatisfactory from the biblical perspective to expose shareholders to the same variety of liabilities that would arise in a modern Western society if limited liability were simply abolished entirely. Along with the abolition of current limited liability laws, therefore, it would be necessary to establish some way of limiting the liabilities of shareholders where such limitations could be justified on biblical grounds. Reform must be aimed at protecting shareholders where their liability is genuinely limited in terms of biblical criteria as well as forcing them to honour their obligation to compensate their victims fully where such limitations are not applicable. However, it would be very difficult, probably impossible, to incorporate such limitations into the legal structure of a company in the way that modern limited liability law does. It would seem that the only way of applying biblical principles of liability to joint-stock companies would be through the courts on a case by case basis in which the extent of a company's liability is established on the merits of each individual claim or group of claims arising from the same incident. Reform of limited liability law, therefore, would need to entail both the abolition of the limited liability status of companies as it presently exists in law and the recognition in law of biblical principles governing the limitation of liability arising from ownership of property. This would protect individuals and companies from claims for compensation that could not be justified on biblical grounds or were in excess of the amounts that would be granted as a result of the application of the biblical principle of limited knowledge.

Conclusion

Although there are no proof texts that directly address share-ownership as practised by modern joint-stock companies the biblical principles relevant to the responsibilities and liabilities of ownership of property generally support the conclusion of R. J. Rushdoony and E. L. Hebden Taylor—and even G. North in his earlier writings— that the limited liability status of modern companies should be abolished. It would not be valid to conclude, however, that shareholders in joint-stock companies should therefore bear unlimited liability for the actions of the company in *all* circumstances involving valid claims against the company for compensation. The extent of a company's liability arising from any particular case would have to be determined on its own merits by the courts in terms of the application of the biblical principles of extent of knowledge and negligence.

Although limited liability law as it presently stands is contrary to biblical principles of justice in many cases and thus in need of reform, it is not as serious in its effects on the economy as the problems arising from the debasement of currency and multiple indebtedness. It is doubtful that it is undermining the foundations of Western culture, though in many cases it does unjustly undermine the moral requirements of responsible ownership and the biblical requirement that compensation be made in full to those adversely affected by a company's irresponsible actions or failure to act responsibly. Reform must lead to the recognition in law of the biblical principles of limitation of liability arising from ownership of property; it must also enable these principles to be applied effectively in practice by the courts.

This would mean that the maximum liability of shareholders in a joint-stock company would be limited by bankruptcy law and that where their liability is restricted as a result of limited knowledge it might be fixed in financial terms below, and possibly significantly below, the nominal value of their shareholding. These reforms would engender responsible attitudes to ownership on the part of shareholders while at the same time protecting companies from the unfair and unscrupulous claims for compensation that they would likely incur in modern Western societies without the protection of limited liability status.

A   CHRISTIAN   VIEW   OF   INTEREST

UNTIL the Reformation the church had almost universally condemned the taking of interest on pecuniary loans of any kind, whether for consumption or commercial purposes. The accepted teaching of the church throughout the Middle Ages had been that usury, meaning simply what we today call interest, is against both divine and natural law.[1] At the Council of Vienna in 1311, for example, Pope Clement V had even threatened with excommunication magistrates who passed laws permitting usury or who failed to repeal such laws within three months. As Eugen von Böhm-Bawerk remarked, however, "There was only one opponent that the canonist doctrine had never been entirely able to subdue, and that was economic practice itself. In the face of all the penalties of earth and heaven which were provided, interest continued to be offered and taken. This was done partly without disguise, partly under the manifold forms which the inventive spirit of business men had devised for slipping through the meshes of the prohibitionist laws in spite of all their casuistry. And the more flourishing the economic conditions of a country, the more strongly did practice oppose the dominant theory."[2]

§1
The Origin of the Mediaeval Church's Teaching on Interest

The mediaeval church's teaching on usury was ostensibly based on the Old Testament ban on Israelites charging interest to their fellow Israelites. But the fact that, rather inconsistently, the church's pro-

---

[1] The canonists of the twelfth century did legitimise certain types of financing operations that were designed to circumvent the ban on usury. To the profit made on these kinds of transaction the term *interest* (from the Latin *interesse*, *to be between*) was given, while all other kinds of profit from the loan of money were considered usurious.

[2] Eugen von Böhm-Bawerk, *Capital and Interest* (South Holland, Illinois: Libertarian Press, 1959), Vol. I, p. 16.

hibition was not applied to lending of a non-pecuniary kind—e.g. goods, houses—indicates that the church's teaching here originated from a source other than the Bible, since where interest or usury is prohibited in Scripture it is prohibited on all kinds of loans— money, food, houses, livestock etc. This is because in reality there is no difference between the increase gained from lending money (interest) and that made from lending goods (rent). As with so many other doctrines of the mediaeval church its teaching on usury was derived from the pagan Greek philosopher Aristotle.

It was Aristotle's defective view of trade that was the origin of his disapproval of interest. Aristotle considered that there were two uses of a thing, the proper use and the improper use: "Of everything which we possess there are two uses: both belong to the thing as such, but not in the same manner, for one is the proper, and the other the improper or secondary use of it. For example, a shoe is used for wear, and is used for exchange; both are uses of the shoe. He who gives a shoe in exchange for money or food to him who wants one, does indeed use the shoe as a shoe, but this is not its proper or primary purpose, for a shoe is not made to be an object of barter. The same may be said of all possessions, for the art of exchange extends to all of them . . ."[3] The proper use of the shoe is to wear it, and the improper use is to exchange it for other goods. Trade, for Aristotle, is the acquisition of wealth by the improper use of things and thus unnatural. One who makes his living from trade rather than from the management of house and land is therefore despised and censured: "Of the two sorts of money-making one . . . is a part of household management, the other is retail trade: the former necessary and honourable, the latter a kind of exchange which is justly censured; for it is unnatural, and a mode by which men gain from one another."[4] It follows naturally from this premiss that the most despicable and unnatural form of trade is that of lending money at interest since this is totally divorced from the "natural" use of anything. Hence Aristotle continues his diatribe against trade: "The most hated sort, and with the greatest reason, is usury, which makes a gain out of money itself, and not from the natural use of it. For money was intended to be used in exchange, but not to increase at interest. And this term usury [τόκος], which means the birth of money from money, is applied to the breeding of money

---

[3] Aristotle, *Politics* (Oxford: Clarendon Press, 1905, translated by Benjamin Jowett), p. 41. [4] *Ibid.*, p. 46.

because the offspring resembles the parent. Wherefore of all modes of making money this is the most unnatural."[5]

This Aristotelian theory of interest was taken up wholesale by the mediaeval church and baptised by a superficial appeal to the Old Testament ban on charging interest to the poor, although sound exegesis of the relevant biblical texts would have shown that Aristotle's argument against usury cannot be sustained by Scripture, which sets forth a much more specific ban that is narrower in its application. From the Christian point of view, therefore, if Aristotle's argument were correct it would prove too much. In fact it would render the biblical teaching itself, first, unjust, because biblical law permitted the Hebrews to charge interest on loans to foreigners, and secondly, inconsistent and contradictory, because in no sense did it permit them to defraud foreigners by means of a form of trade that is in principle unjust and unnatural. Any appeal to Scripture to support the mediaeval church's teaching on interest that does not address these

---

[5] *Ibid.* Böhm-Bawerk sums up Aristotle's position in the following way: "Money is by nature incapable of bearing fruit. The lender's gain therefore cannot come from any economic power inherent in money, but only from a defrauding of the borrower. Interest is therefore a gain got by abuse and injustice" (Böhm-Bawerk, *op. cit.*, p. 11). This summary of Aristotle's view of interest has been criticised on the grounds that Aristotle did not argue that money is incapable of bearing fruit. Paul Mills writes: "Much of the subsequent discussion of Aristotle's position is based on the misconception that the philosopher thought that since money was 'barren,' it could not naturally reproduce . . . However, this is a parody of Aristotle's views. Instead of claiming that money is barren and that therefore interest contravenes natural law and is immoral, Aristotle's argument is that money *can* be made fruitful but that this subverts the original purpose for which money was brought into existence—namely to act as a medium of exchange. The affront to nature comes in the use of money for a purpose for which it was not intended. Whilst Aristotle readily conceded that it was not necessarily wrong to use an object (such as a shoe) for a purpose other than its primary one (*Politics*, 1257a), it was because lending at interest *had* to be motivated by the desire to profit from an exchange of money that made it unnatural, and therefore immoral" (Paul S. Mills and John R. Presley, *Islamic Finance: Theory and Practice* [Macmillan Press, 1999], p. 109f.). There are two points to be made here: first, Aristotle does condemn the use of objects for exchange whose primary function is not to act as an object of barter (e.g. a shoe). He says unequivocally that such exchange, i.e. trade, is "justly censured" because it is unnatural and "a mode by which men gain from one another." Thus, second, although Mills is correct in saying that Aristotle did not deny that money can be made to bear fruit, this fact is without significance for the critique of his view of interest. Böhm-Bawerk's conclusion that for Aristotle the charging of interest is a defrauding of the borrower, a gain got by abuse and injustice, is entirely correct. Aristotle states that it is *unnatural* for money to increase at interest. Lending at interest is an improper use of money for Aristotle because money is meant to function as a medium of exchange.

two crucial points fails to do justice to the texts and for this reason alone falls to the ground. The scholastic arguments for prohibiting interest were really philosophical not exegetical. This was the weakness of the mediaeval church not only here but in many other areas of doctrine also, since an interpretation of the Christian religion that was heavily syncretised with pagan Greek philosophy came to dominate the intellectual life of the church and, along with the heavy accent on the authority of tradition, overruled Scripture as the supreme authority in doctrine and practice. Under these conditions it is not surprising that the biblical teaching on interest lay submerged under the spurious casuistry of the schoolmen for many centuries.

§2
The Reformation

At the Reformation, however, there was a renewed commitment to Scripture as the supreme and binding authority over the life of man, both as an individual and as a member of society. Scripture took its rightful place above tradition in the Reformed churches and through biblical exegesis it filled the place once occupied by philosophy in the mediaeval church. With the Reformers there began a thawing of the old mediaeval canonist attitude towards the taking of interest. In the first sermon of the third of his five *Decades* of sermons Heinrich Bullinger, the Swiss Reformer and successor of Ulrich Zwingli in Zürich, sets forth the doctrine that usury itself is neither unlawful, dishonest nor condemned by Scripture. For Bullinger it is only the abuse of the practice that has made the name of usury dishonest. He defines usury as rent, as Scripture does (Lev. 25:35–38; Dt. 23:19–20) and sees no reason why "a good Christian and an honest man may not reap some lawful commodity of the hire of his money, as well as of the letting or leasing of his land." Bullinger then gives the following example to show that usury *per se* is not oppressive or dishonest: "It is in the power of him which so letteth out his money, with that money to buy a farm, and so to take the whole gain to himself; but now we see that, in letting the other [the borrower] have it, he granteth him the use of his money, whereby he [the borrower] is a very great gainer. This fellow, to whom this sum is lent, or otherwise given upon covenants of contract, doth with the money get some stay of living, with the revenue whereof he nourisheth all his family, paying to his creditor the portion agreed on; of which when he hath once made a full restitution, he maketh the living his own for ever, and acquitteth himself from the yearly pension [i.e. the payment of interest]. In this kind of covenanting no man I think, will say, that the poor is oppressed, when the thing itself doth rather cry, that by such usury the poor is greatly helped. Usury therefore is forbidden in the word of God, so far as it biteth (for here I use the very term of the scriptures) his neighbour, while it hindereth him, or otherwise undoeth him."[6] Bullinger did maintain, however, that it is the duty of the magistrate to protect the poor by setting a lawful rate of interest. Where such a lawful rate of interest is lacking creditors are to be guided by the Golden Rule as a means of setting a fair rate of interest.

Likewise, Calvin cautiously relaxed the prohibition on usury, claiming that "if we should totally prohibit the practice of usury, we would restrain conscience more rigidly than God himself."[7] He demonstrated the error of the mediaeval church's teaching by attacking the argument used by Ambrose and Chrysostom that money is sterile: "How do merchants increase their wealth? By being industrious you answer. I readily admit what even children can see, that if you lock your money in a chest, it will not increase. Moreover, no one borrows money from others with the intention of hiding it or not making a profit. Consequently, the gain is not from the money but from the profit."[8] Calvin also argued that interest on money loans is no different from interest on the loan of goods (rent): "The pretext that both St. Ambrose and Chrysostom cite is too frivolous in my judgment, that is, that money does not engender money. Does the sea or the earth [engender it]? I receive a fee from renting a house. Is that where money grows? Houses, in turn, are products of the trades, where money is also made. Even the value of a house can be exchanged for money. And what? Is money not more productive than merchandise or any other possession one could mention? It is

---

[6] *The Decades of Henry Bullinger* (The Parker Society: Cambridge University Press, [1549] 1851), Third Decade, First Sermon, Vol. II, p. 42.

[7] *Calvin's Ecclesiastical Advice* (Edinburgh: T. and T. Clark, 1991), p. 139. This and the following quotations from this book are taken from a letter from John Calvin to one of his friends contained in the *Corpus Reformatorum* volume 38, part I. There is disagreement as to who the recipient was. According to H. M. Robertson, "Professor Hauser has shown conclusively that Claude de Sachins was the enquirer to whom Calvin's reply was addressed" (*Aspects of the Rise of Economic Individualism* [Cambridge University Press, 1933], p. 115).

[8] *Calvin's Ecclesiastical Advice*, p. 141.

lawful to make money by renting a piece of ground, yet unlawful to make it from money? What? When you buy a field, is money not making money?"[9] Calvin concludes that "although at first such subtleties appear convincing, upon closer examination they evaporate, since there is no substance to them. Hence I conclude that we ought not to judge usury according to a few passages of scripture, but in accordance with the principle of equity."[10]

Calvin then gives an example to demonstrate his argument: "Take a rich man whose wealth lies in possessions and rents but who has no money on hand. A second, whose wealth is somewhat more moderate—though less than the first—soon comes into money. If an opportunity should arise, the second person can easily buy what he wants, while the first will have to ask the latter for a loan. It is in the power of the second, under the rules of bargaining, to impose a fee on the first's goods until he repays, and in this manner the first's condition will be improved, although usury has been practiced."[11] The wording here is not altogether clear but what Calvin seems to be saying is that the second person, upon making a loan to the first, is allowed to require him to mortgage some of his goods as security for the loan and then charge rent on the mortgaged goods until the loan is repaid.[12] It is clear from this that Calvin, quite correctly, identifies this rent as usury; and although this usury is for the use of goods, not money, it is considered acceptable under the rules of bargaining. Since rent (usury on loaned goods) is not evil *per se* neither is usury on money. Calvin drives his point home: "Now, what makes a contract just and honest or unjust and dishonest? Has not the first fared better by means of an agreement involving usury by his neighbor than if the second had compelled him to mortgage or pawn his goods? To deny this is to play with God in a childish manner, preferring words over the truth itself. As if it were in our

---

[9] *Ibid.*   [10] *Ibid.*

[11] *Ibid.*

[12] In his commentaries on the law Calvin gives a similar example: "If any rich and monied man, wishing to buy a piece of land, should borrow some part of the sum required of another, may not he who lends the money receive some part of the revenues of the farm until the principal shall be repaid? Many such cases daily occur in which, as far as equity is concerned, usury is no worse than purchase. Nor will that subtle argument of Aristotle avail, that usury is unnatural, because money is barren and does not beget money; for . . . the purchaser of the farm might in the meantime reap and gather his vintage." (*Commentaries on the Four Last Books of Moses arranged in the form of a Harmony* [Grand Rapids, Michigan: Eerdmans], Vol. III, p. 131)

power, by changing words, to transform virtue into vice or vice into virtue. I certainly have no quarrel here."[13]

Following Scripture, however, Calvin maintains that interest on loans should not be taken from the poor and needy, and furthermore, that the wealthy should be ready and willing to lend to such. We must not mistake Calvin's motives here. He had no liking of usury and was not in any sense led to this position by self-interest. He did not approve of lending at interest as a form of livelihood[14] and says "it would be desirable if usurers were chased from every country, even if the practice were unknown."[15] But as a pastor and exegete of God's word he had to set aside his own preferences and expound what the Bible teaches, and he plainly states the matter when he says "I should, indeed, be unwilling to take usury under my patronage, and I wish the name itself were banished from the world; but I do not dare pronounce upon so important a point more than God's words convey."[16] Unfortunately, Calvin, like Bullinger, accepted the idea that the State may determine the rate of interest and advised that this should not be exceeded.[17] In this respect Bullinger and Calvin retained an element of mediaeval thinking on economic matters and went beyond Scripture since there is no biblical justification for the idea that the authorities may establish a legal rate of interest to which moneylenders must restrict themselves rather than charging the market rate of interest.

By today's standards Bullinger's and Calvin's views on usury may seem somewhat unexceptional and overly cautious, even strict. But in the sixteenth century their teaching on this subject was revolutionary and represented a significant advance on the muddled economic thinking and faulty exegesis of the mediaeval canonists and schoolmen.

From the Reformation onwards teaching on interest within the Reformed communities slowly began to express a more biblical emphasis and interest *per se* was no longer considered evil and prohibited. For example, the English Puritan divine Richard Baxter, in his *Christian Directory*, published in 1673 but originally written in 1664–65, argued that usury as such is forbidden neither by natural law nor by the law of Moses or any positive command of Christ; usury may be taken, therefore, except where it is against justice or

[13] *Calvin's Ecclesiastical Advice*, p. 141f.   [14] *Ibid.*, p. 142.   [15] *Ibid.*, p. 140.
[16] *Commentaries on the Four Last Books of Moses*, Vol. III, p. 132.
[17] *Calvin's Ecclesiastical Advice*, p. 142.

charity.[18] Likewise, Francis Turretin, in his *Institutio Theologiae Elenc-ticae*, published in 1679–85, gives a systematic defence of usury, arguing that all usury, with the exception of that exacted on a poor loan, is neither prohibited by the law nor opposed to equity and honesty.[19] Eventually, under pressure from the world of commerce, even the Roman Catholic Church—always more sensitive to influences other than the teaching of Scripture—relaxed its condemnation of usury.

§3
Recent Opposition to Interest

More recently, however, a number of voices have been raised against usury (interest) within Christian circles. Two groups, one in the United States and one in Britain, both seeking to apply Old Testament law as a model for the organisation of modern society, have advocated a total ban on interest, arguing that this is the correct interpretation

[18] Richard Baxter, *A Christian Directory or Body of Practical Divinity* (London, 1673), Part IV, ch. xix, Tit. 4.—"Cases of conscience about lending and borrowing," Question 12. To the question "When is usury sinful?" Baxter answers: "When its against either Justice or Charity: 1. When its like cheating bargaining, which under pretence of *consent* and a form of Justice doth deceive, or oppress, and get from another that which is not *ours* but *his*. 2. When you lend for increase where charity obligeth you to lend freely: Even as it is a sin to lend expecting your own again, when *Charity* obligeth you to *give* it. 3. When you uncharitably exact that which your brother is disabled utterly to pay, and use cruelty to procure it, (be it the Use, or the principal). 4. When you allow him not such a proportion of the gain as his labour, hazard or poverty doth require; but because the money is yours, will live at ease upon his labours. 5. When in case of his losses you rigorously exact your due, without that abatement, or forgiving debts (whether *Use* or *principal*), which humanity and charity require. In a word, when you are *selfish* and do not as, according to true judgement, you may desire to be done by, if you were in his case." (Richard Baxter, *Chapters from A Christian Directory* [London: G. Bell and Sons Ltd, 1925], p. 127f.)

[19] Francis Turretin, *Institutes of Elenctic Theology* (New Jersey: Presbyterian and Reformed Publishing Company, 1994, translated by George Musgrave Giger), Vol. 2, p. 126. Turretin argues that the legitimacy of usury is founded (1) upon necessity and utility; (2) upon natural equity; (3) upon just gratitude to the creditor; (4) upon Christian charity, since not to charge usury would amount to assisting others at the expense of one's own family and this contradicts 1 Tim. 5:8 and 2 Cor. 12:14; (5) from a comparison with other contracts, e.g. rents on houses, farms, tools etc.; and (6) because limitations on lawful usury are established in law by the civil authorities. Turretin, like Bullinger and Calvin before him, argues that the Mosaic ban on usury relates only to charitable loans given to the poor (*ibid.*, p. 126f.).

of the biblical teaching. The American group, coming from within the Reconstructionist or Theonomy movement, has correctly identified interest and rent as the same phenomenon but has advocated as a result the abolition of rent as well as interest, considering both to be immoral and unjust.[20] The arguments on interest put forward by this group are confused and misleading and have been answered by Gary North in his book *Tools of Dominion*.[21] The second group, based in Cambridge, England, is the Jubilee Centre, directed by Michael Schluter, and is familiar in Britain for its stance and campaigning on the Sunday trading laws issue. The Jubilee Centre sponsored the "Keep Sunday Special" campaign. Unfortunately, the Jubilee Centre seems to be influenced by a collectivist philosophy of society, and though claiming to develop a biblical perspective on social order would validate the use of government agencies to enforce its own version of a Christian social order on the nation to a far greater extent than can be justified by exegesis of Scripture, something the Centre tends not to do, preferring to promote government measures to achieve the structural reforms deemed necessary in society by the Jubilee Centre's own interpretation of the biblical social paradigm.[22] The use of a "ladder of abstraction"[23] to determine the meaning and purpose of biblical law, rather than exegesis, is perhaps one of the major flaws of this approach.[24] Both groups appeal to

[20] The position of this group has been set forth in S. C. Mooney, *Usury, Destroyer of Nations* (Warsaw, Ohio: Theopolis, 1988).

[21] G. North, *Tools of Dominion: The Case Laws of Exodus* (Tyler, Texas: Institute for Christian Economics, 1990). The reader is directed to this book for a critique of Mooney's position.

[22] See for example Schulter's suggestions for strengthening the extended family in *Family Roots or Mobility?* (Cambridge: Jubilee Centre Publications Limited, 1986), pp. 13–16. Schluter's answer to the decline of the extended family amounts to promoting government policies aimed at restricting individual freedom of mobility. Not only are such government policies not to be found in the Bible; the story of Abraham gives us an example that diametrically contradicts Schluter's theory about the extended family and the need to restrict mobility. This shows a selective use of Scripture that distorts the biblical record in the interests of Jubilee Centre ideology.

[23] The Jubilee Centre people seem to be aware of the problems with the use of a "ladder of abstraction" and in some of their publications and lectures have pointed out what they consider to be faulty conclusions derived from such an approach—i.e. those conclusions that differ from their own. In spite of this, however, they continue to use this approach, assuming that their own conclusions are valid. The only way to correct the errors accruing from the use of this approach is exegesis, but if exegesis is done properly in the first place there is no need for the "ladder of abstraction" as a primary feature of one's hermeneutic.

[24] Another problem with the Jubilee Centre's approach to the application of biblical law is a conspicuous lack of attention to the covenant in Scripture—surely

Scripture, specifically the Old Testament, as the basis of their views. The Jubilee Centre is generally much looser and more selective in its appeal to Old Testament law—though at the same time much more literalistic in its interpretation in places—than the Theonomy or Reconstruction movement. The US based group has also maintained its position against all forms of interest, including rent, by the selective use of Scripture, but its concern is much narrower than that of the Jubilee Centre.

§4
The Old Testament Ban on Interest

In view of this resurgence of interest in ethical questions regarding the validity of usury it will be necessary to look in more detail at the relevant biblical texts and the various interpretations made of them. The law relating to usury is set forth in the following passages:

If thou lend money to any of my people that is poor by thee, thou shalt not be to him as an usurer, neither shalt thou lay upon him usury. (Ex. 22:25)

And if thy brother be waxen poor, and fallen into decay with thee; then thou shalt relieve him: yea, though he be a stranger, or a sojourner; that he may live with thee. Take thou no usury of him, or increase: but fear thy God; that thy brother may live with thee. Thou shalt not give him thy money upon usury, nor lend him thy victuals for increase. (Lev. 25:35–37)

Thou shalt not lend upon usury to thy brother; usury of money, usury of victuals, usury of any thing that is lent upon usury: unto a stranger thou

---

a fundamental flaw in any attempt to assess the meaning and purpose of biblical law for society since the covenant is the organising principle of Scripture, both in soteriological and social matters. This neglect of the covenant is accompanied by the use of the term "relational" to define biblical ethics. It seems that "relational" ethics is a substitute for the covenant as the organising principle of Christian ethics. The problem is that it is difficult to see in this idea of relationalism anything more than a concession to fashionable late twentieth-century feminist ideas about how individuals in a society should relate to each other. It would be absurd to deny that biblical ethics deals with interpersonal relationships, but it does so within the context of the covenant. The covenant is surely the overarching structure in terms of which biblical ethics is to be understood. Any approach to biblical ethics that fails to recognise the importance of the covenant in Scripture is likely to lead to a distortion of the biblical perspective since the covenant is the biblical paradigm, to use Jubilee Centre terminology, in terms of which both individual and social ethics find their context and meaning.

mayest lend upon usury; but unto thy brother thou shalt not lend upon usury: that the Lord thy God may bless thee in all that thou settest thine hand to in the land whither thou goest to possess it. (Dt. 23:19–20)

In these texts there are two words used for usury or interest: *neshek* and *tarbith*. *Neshek* comes from the verb *nashak*, meaning *to bite, vex, oppress, lend on usury* or *exact interest*. *Neshek* is thus a bite. The etymology of the word suggests that the interest was taken in advance; for example the debtor might agree to repay sixty shekels while receiving only forty shekels from the lender.[25] A modern example of the kind of interest represented here is that taken on a bill or promissory note that circulates prior to its date of maturity at less that its face value. The difference, or discount, gained by a trader in such bills when a bill matures is his bite or percentage of its value. *Tarbith* is derived from the verb *rabah*, meaning *to be* or *become many, numerous, to increase, multiply*. *Tarbith* thus means increase. A related word is *tarbuth*, meaning *progeny*. *Tarbith* represents the kind of interest we normally associate with lending money, i.e. increase on the principal loaned out. Too much importance should not be attributed to the difference between these two words however. The phenomenon of interest involved in both cases is the same, the difference being only one of method of calculation and payment. *Neshek* is used in all three texts cited above. *Tarbith* is used only in the Leviticus text, which reads literally "you shall not take from him bite (*neshek*) or increase (*tarbith*)" (v. 36).

The Authorised Version causes problems with these texts by translating two Hebrew words by the same English word, the effect of which is to create a contradiction in the English version. In Lev. 25:35 the Hebrew word *ger* is translated as "stranger." In Dt. 29:20 *nokri* is also translated "stranger." Thus, it appears in English that the Bible says both that strangers must not be charged interest and that they may be charged interest. However, the Hebrew word *ger* (from *gur*, meaning *to sojourn, dwell*) in Lev. 25:35 should be translated "sojourner"[26] and the word translated as "sojourner" by the Author-

---

[25] G. A. Barrois, "Debt, Debtor" in *The Interpreter's Dictionary of the Bible* (Nashville: Abingdon Press, 1962), Vol. I, p. 809b cf. Roland de Vaux, *Ancient Israel, Its Life and Institutions* (London: Darton, Longman and Todd, 1961), p. 170.

[26] In the Old Testament *ger* "designates an alien or immigrant in the process of becoming assimilated" (M. H. Pope, "Proselyte" in *The Interpreter's Dictionary of the Bible*, Vol. 3, p. 921b). The LXX translates the word as προσήλυτος. This Greek term means "one who has arrived, a stranger" (Abbott-Smith) but is used in the New Testament to designate converts to Judaism (Mt. 23:15). The Hebrew, *ger*, itself underwent the same change in meaning and is used in the Mishnah of converts.

ised Version, *toshab* (from *yashab*, meaning *to sit, dwell, inhabit*), should be translated as "settler." The word *nokri* (from *nakar*, meaning *to estrange, alienate*) in Dt. 19:20 may be translated "stranger" or "foreigner."[27] This produces the following results:

And if your brother becomes poor and cannot support himself among you, then you shall help him, the sojourner and the settler too, that he may live with you. (Lev. 25:35)

You shall not charge interest to your brother, interest on money, interest on victuals, interest on any thing that may earn interest. You may charge interest to a foreigner, but you shall not charge interest to your brother ... (Dt. 23:19–20)

The Bible is thus very clear, in spite of the Authorised Version's mistranslation: it was permissible to charge interest to foreigners, i.e. those who were strangers to Israel's culture and way of life, but not

---

The rabbis distinguished two types of proselyte, the *ger tsedeq*, proselyte of righteousness, who was circumcised and partook fully of the Jewish cultus, and the *ger hashsha'ar*, proselyte of the gate (cf. Ex. 20:10 and Dt. 5:14), or *ger toshab*, resident alien (cf. Lev. 25:35, 47), who, though uncircumcised, kept what the rabbis believed were the seven laws of the Noachian covenant mandatory for all Gentiles (B.T. 'Abodah Zarah 64*b*–65*a*: there was some dispute over this definition however), i.e. the requirement to administer justice (or of obedience to authority), to refrain from blasphemy, idolatry, adultery, murder, theft and the eating of flesh cut from a living animal (B.T. Sanhedrin 56*a*), or possibly flesh with the blood still in it (cf. Acts 15:29).

[27] *a.* The word *nokri* should not be understood to mean *citizen of another State*, however. *Nokrim* were *strangers* to Israel, people who were not assimilated into Jewish culture. Those who were assimilated into Jewish culture were not foreigners (*nokrim*) even if they were citizens of other non-Jewish States. For example, in the diaspora many Jews became citizens of foreign States, but they did not assimilate with the pagan cultures into which they had been deported. The Old Testament ban on interest meant that Jews who were citizens of Israel could not lend at interest to poor Jews who were citizens of Babylonia since the latter were brothers or kinsmen (*'achim*) not strangers or foreigners to Israelite religion and culture. Their citizenship was irrelevant. Jewish citizens of Babylonia, however, were permitted to lend at interest to their Gentile neighbours—unless of course they were proselytes or God-fearers—even though they were citizens of the same State, since the latter were not brothers or kinsmen, but rather strangers (*nokrim*) to Israelite religion and culture. The Bible is not addressing issues of citizenship in the modern sense. Failure to appreciate this point has led some to conclude that the ban relates to citizens of the same State (see the discussion at note 55 below). But this is to read modern ideas of citizenship back into the text and cannot be supported exegetically.

b. There are no exegetical grounds for S. C. Mooney's assertion that *nokri* refers only to the original inhabitants of Canaan who were displaced by the Israelites (*op. cit.*, pp. 148–151). Furthermore, his assertion that interest is an inherent evil that God permitted the Hebrews to commit as a means of judging the inhabitants of to fellow Israelites, sojourners and settlers—those who lived with the Jews and were prepared to assimilate with their culture.

The Authorised Version uses the term *usury* in all three texts. This has led to some confusion and debate over the definition of terms. It has been common for many years for a distinction to be made between interest and usury, the term *usury* being reserved for rates of interest that are considered exorbitant or illegal and the term *interest* for rates that are considered legal and within the bounds of fairness, however that should be conceived. This distinction goes back to the canonists of the twelfth century, who used the word interest (from the Latin *interesse*, meaning *to be between*) to denote the profits made on certain kinds of financing operations and credit transactions designed to circumvent the general prohibition on usury.[28] The dis-

---

Canaan is ethically flawed, and moreover quite novel. To my knowledge it has never before been claimed by Christians that God sanctions the committing of evil as a means of pursuing justice—i.e. judging the wicked. On the contrary, the witness of the whole of Scripture is that we are not to render evil for evil (Rom. 12:17). The answer to evil is *always* the administration of justice. Israel was the instrument of God's justice in his judgement upon the corrupt inhabitants of Canaan. It makes no ethical or theological sense to argue that God sanctioned the committing of acts that were inherently evil as a means of executing his justice upon the Canaanites. Mooney cites the opinions of Luther and Ambrose to support his argument, but it is not certain from the passages he cites that they were arguing the same point, though the difference may be subtle. Mooney *denies* that exacting usury from the Canaanites, which he must perforce admit was permitted to the Jews, was an exception to what he regards as the inherent evil of usury. Likewise, he denies that the execution of a murderer is an exception to what he claims is the inherent evil of killing. Mooney writes: "Usury exacted from the foreigner does not imply that usury is not inherently evil, just as the carrying out of the death penalty does not imply that killing is not inherently evil. The command to execute a murderer is not to be taken as an 'exception' to, or 'qualification' of the commandment 'you shall not kill'. In the same way, usury is an inherent evil that is not 'qualified' by permission to practice on foreigners" (*ibid.*, p. 151). Mooney's position here is at best confused and involves a fundamentally distorted view of the relationship between God's justice and his providential government of the creation, resulting, it would seem, in some form of abstraction similar to Kant's categorical imperative—e.g. usury is always evil; divine approbation does not qualify this general principle, therefore God, by permitting usury as a form of judgement on the Canaanites, permitted the Jews to commit acts that are inherently evil. It cannot be argued from his citations of Luther and Ambrose that they were also pursuing this line of thought. The biblical approach is simply to accept that since God is righteous and just and permits interest to be taken from the Canaanites, the charging of interest in this instance is a righteous (just) activity involving no sin, which is precisely the point of Ambrose's argument cited by Mooney.

[28] Harold J. Berman, *Law and Revolution: The Formation of the Western Legal Tradition* (Cambridge, Massachusetts: Harvard University Press, 1983), p. 249.

tinction, however, is quite arbitrary and without any validity other than that of usage and custom. In view of the fact that the distinction is misleading it would be preferable to ignore usage and tradition. There is in reality no difference between interest and usury; they are merely different terms for the same thing. G. North uses the term *usury* for interest charged on charity loans, regardless of the rate charged, and the term *interest* for increase on all other loans, again regardless of the rate charged. This too, in my judgement, is incorrect, at least from the biblical point of view, though not as misleading as the former usage. Whether interest and usury mean different things due to usage throughout history and whatever nuances may be brought to bear on their meanings as a consequence of their differing etymologies is quite irrelevant for my purposes here, since it is the *biblical* notion of requiring an increase on or bite out of the principal loaned that is in view. Call it interest or usury, it refers to the same phenomenon.[29] For our purposes here, therefore, I shall treat the terms as equivalent in all respects.

Whereas the Decalogue sets forth general principles, the context of biblical case law is specific, since its purpose is to explain the general principles of God's law by applying them to the concrete circumstances that faced the people of Israel. In this way the people of Israel were left in no doubt as to the meaning and application of the Decalogue. There is no virtue in reading back into Scripture practices and circumstances that were unknown to the people of Israel in those times and that the case law did not address. Such a procedure is anachronistic and can lead to serious misunderstanding of the text. Yet this is how teaching on the ethics of usury has often been handled. The correct procedure is to start with Scripture, with exegesis, and develop an understanding of the context, the concrete situation that Scripture addresses, and then apply the biblical teaching to *equivalent* circumstances in the modern world. Where this procedure is inverted the biblical teaching is often distorted and consequently its application to modern society is faulty.

In order to understand the meaning and purpose of the Old Testament ban on usury it is necessary to understand what kind of loans were generally incurred by the people of Israel at that time.

---

[29] Other than on this particular point, which is purely semantic, I am in agreement with G. North on the subject of interest. I prefer to equate the two terms. Thus, I believe there is legitimate and illegitimate interest, and legitimate and illegitimate usury in terms of God's law. Cf. the relevant sections in North's book *Tools of Dominion*.

In the first place it must be recognised that commercial loans of the kind generally incurred in modern business practice—i.e. non-charitable secured loans—were unknown among the people of Israel at this time. A primitive agricultural community of the kind that existed in Israel in early biblical times had no need of commercial loans of this kind to finance its economy. Commerce among the Jews in this period seems to have been very minimal and, with the exception of Solomon's merchant navy and trade with King Hiram (1 Kg. 5; 9:26–28; 10:11–29), foreign trade was not common.[30] King Jehoshaphat's attempts to rebuild a merchant navy came to nothing (1 Kg. 22:48, 2 Chron. 20:36–37). The economy was based almost exclusively on agriculture. Loans in this period were made primarily to the poor in order to provide the borrower with the necessities of life during a period when he and his family would otherwise have starved.

Second, consumer loans of the type common in modern Western societies—i.e. loans to finance acquisition of luxuries or goods that are not essential for basic needs—were also unknown at this time. Third, borrowing was generally considered a practice to be avoided if at all possible. The Bible teaches that "The rich ruleth over the poor, and the borrower is a servant to the lender" (Pr. 22:7). Furthermore, being in a position where one had sufficient means to lend to those in need was considered a blessing from God. Thus Dt. 15:6 states: "For the Lord thy God blesseth thee, as he promised thee: and thou shalt lend unto many nations, but thou shalt not borrow; and thou shalt reign over many nations, but they shall not reign over thee" (cf. Dt. 28:12). Being in the position of having to borrow was an undesirable condition and debt was to be entered into only when there was no alternative. Loans were measures that the poor

---

[30] Writing in the first century A.D. the Jewish historian Josephus says: "As for ourselves, therefore, we neither inhabit a maritime country, nor do we delight in merchandise, nor in such a mixture with other men as arise from it; but the cities we dwell in are remote from the sea, and having a fruitful country for our habitation, we take pains at cultivating that only. Our principal care of all is this, to educate our children well; and we think it the most necessary business of our whole life, to observe the laws that have been given us, and to keep those rules of piety that have been delivered down to us. Since, therefore, besides what we have already taken notice of, we have had a peculiar way of living our own, there was no occasion offered us in ancient ages for intermixing among the Greeks, as they had for mixing among the Egyptians, by their intercourse of their exporting and importing their several goods; as they also mixed with the Phoenicians, who lived by the sea-side, by means of their love of lucre in trade and merchandise." (*Against Apion* [Whiston's translation], Book I, paragraph 12. Cf. Alfred Edersheim, *Sketches of Jewish Life in the Days of Christ* [Grand Rapids, Michigan: Eerdmans, 1988], pp. 199–212.)

were forced to take when there was no other option open to them. Someone requiring a loan was, for whatever reason, in desperate circumstances and without sufficient savings or non-essential possessions that he could sell in order to obviate an emergency, his only hope being to tap the resources of someone more wealthy than himself by means of a loan. Hence the rich are exhorted to lend to those in need: "If there be among you a poor man of one of thy brethren within any of thy gates in the land which the Lord thy God giveth thee, thou shalt not harden thine heart, nor shut thine hand from thy poor brother: but thou shalt open thine hand wide unto him, and shalt surely lend him sufficient for his need, in that which he wanteth [i.e. lacks]." Even when the year of Jubilee was close at hand and the probability was that a debtor would not be able to repay his loan before the year of release of debts the wealthy were commanded to be generous and lend to the poor (Dt. 15:9–10). On the other hand, failure to pay one's debts when this becomes possible is considered a mark of wickedness: "The wicked borroweth, and payeth not again: but the righteous showeth mercy, and giveth" (Ps. 37:21). And a man might have to sell himself into servitude to pay off his debts (Lev. 25:39–41, cf. Neh. 5:4–5).

Fourth, the nation of Israel at this time was primarily an agricultural society and the most common reason for having to borrow during this period was the failure of crops (Neh. 5:2). During such times it would be the poorer families, those who did not have sufficient grain stored to carry them over the lean years or alternative forms of wealth that could be sold in order to buy grain, that would suffer the most. Hence when the crops failed or during years when the harvest was poor they would be forced to borrow from the more wealthy members of the community. Alternatively, they might sell themselves into bondage until the next year of Jubilee (Lev. 25:39–41). Both options would be considered only by the very poor. Possibly, as G. North maintains, these two practices were formally and contractually linked, the criterion for obtaining an unsecured interest-free poverty loan being the willingness of the debtor to sell himself into servitude until the next year of Jubilee in order to redeem his debt should he be unable to make repayment by any other means.[31]

Fifth, during the period of the second temple oppressive taxation was also a problem that created hardship for the poor and led to

---

[31] G. North, *op. cit.*, pp. 713–718. This was possibly a definitive feature of a non-interest bearing charitable loan. The nature of the pledge required as security for

the necessity of both borrowing and the selling of family members into service to raise enough money to survive (Neh. 5:1–5). Nehemiah rebuked the nobles and rulers of Israel for exacting interest on loans from their fellow Israelites (Neh. 5:6–13), but clearly the situation was again one of famine and poverty, and was in part caused by excessive taxation.

The biblical ban on charging interest is not a total ban however. The Bible distinguishes between those from whom interest may be taken and those from whom it may not be taken. The basic distinction is between the Jew and those Gentiles who were permanent members of the Jewish community, and foreigners. Lev. 25:35 makes it clear that not only Jews but sojourners and settlers in Israel were also to be treated like fellow Jews and interest was not to be exacted from them. Sojourners and settlers were resident aliens who chose to live in Israel. They were people who, first, placed themselves under the law of God—at least formally in all the demands that it makes upon the external actions of man and his relationships with others—and thus, secondly, were prepared to assimilate with the culture of Israel. In other words they were God-fearers. An analogy could be drawn between such and many in the Christian societies of the West in previous centuries who, though not regenerate believers, were none-theless highly Christianised, i.e. assimilated into a Christian culture to the extent that they behaved like Christians in terms of morality and thought like Christians, having a common Christian world-view. The Bible commands that such sojourners and settlers in Israel were to be treated equally under the usury law with native-born Hebrews (Ex. 12:49, Lev. 24:22, Num. 15:16, 29) and therefore they were not to be charged interest on loans. In Dt. 23:20, however, we are told that Jews were permitted to charge interest to foreigners. The Jews were permitted to exact interest from those who were members of an alien culture, and no restrictions whatsoever were placed upon the taking of interest from such.

Some important conclusions regarding the ethics of taking interest follow from this discussion: first, the Old Testament ban on interest

---

a charitable loan and the rules governing such pledges were also important features that help to define charitable loans and distinguish them from the kind of commercial borrowing that is common in modern Western societies. The pledge offered as security for a charitable loan was inalienable. A man who is in need of a poverty loan is by definition unable to offer as security for the loan assets that can be sold in order to compensate the creditor should he be unable to repay the loan before the year of release of debts. See note 14 on p. 107f.

is not general in nature. The ban is always issued in a qualified form. In Ex 22:25 and Lev. 25:35–37 it is limited to the poor Israelite and settler, and in Dt. 23:19–20 simply to the Israelite. The Scriptures nowhere forbid lending at interest in general terms but always lending at interest *to some particular class of persons.* The law, in other words, is not given as a general ban such as "you shall not kill," which is qualified by certain exceptions such as the execution of murderers, kidnappers or in the defence of judicially innocent human life. It is always given as a specific ban on taking interest from particular types of people. Thus Calvin writes: "But those who think differently, may object, that we must abide by God's judgment, when He generally prohibits all usury to His people. I reply, that the question is only as to the poor, and consequently, if we have to do with the rich, that usury is freely permitted; because the Lawgiver, in alluding to one thing, seems not to condemn another, concerning which He is silent."[32] Since there is no general ban on taking interest in the Bible the purpose of exegesis in regard to these laws is to show where the restriction applies. In expounding the relevance of the law for modern society it is then necessary to identify *equivalent* circumstances in modern culture to those addressed by the law, since it is there that the ban has its application.

If, however, it is assumed that the ban is general in nature, with possible exceptions, the purpose of exegesis will be to show where those exceptions apply. The two approaches will yield very different conclusions. The former demonstrates where there are specific restrictions; i.e. interest is *permissible* in *all* circumstances *except* this or that, whereas the latter will only show that certain cases are excepted from the general ban, i.e. interest is *not* permissible in *any* circumstances *except* this or that. The prohibition under the latter interpretation is much more extensive and universal than under the former. It is important, therefore, that the nature of the ban be established at the outset. As we have seen, the ban is never stated in a general or universal form, that is to say it is never given as a general principle, but always in the form of a case law demonstrating a specific restriction. The permission to take interest from foreigners is not an exception to a general ban on charging interest; rather, the restrictions on taking interest from fellow Israelites and settlers are exceptions to a practice that is in all other circumstances permissible.

Thus, second, interest *per se* is not evil or unjust. The Jews were

---

[32] *Commentaries on the Four Last Books of Moses*, Vol. III, p. 131.

never permitted to act unjustly towards foreigners. All human actions are required by God to conform to the ethical norms revealed in his word, and this general principle applies to all human relationships, whether they are relationships with one's family, neighbours or foreigners. Indeed, the Torah specifically requires that one's relationships not only with one's friends and neighbours but also with one's enemies should be regulated by justice and compassion (Ex. 23:3–5). There is in Scripture a distinction placed between foreigners and fellow Israelites in the matter of charging interest, but there is no double standard of ethics. The Bible does not require strict adherence to ethical standards between believers but relax this requirement in relationships between believers and non-believers or foreigners. If interest were wrong *per se*, intrinsically evil, however, this would be the case precisely. The only alternative would be for the Jews to be forbidden to charge interest to foreigners also. But the Bible permits this. All notions of interest being intrinsically wrong or evil, therefore, must be set aside. Not only is there no biblical justification for such an idea; it makes complete nonsense of biblical teaching on the ethics of charging interest. Scripture teaches that the taking of interest is ethically acceptable but that there are certain exceptions to this, situations in which it is wrong to take interest, namely when the loan is a charitable loan given to help a poor fellow Israelite or God-fearer in his distress.

Third, neither is the taking of interest on charity loans or loans to the poor forbidden *in principle*. The ban is more specific than this. The biblical law prohibits the taking of interest on loans to specific categories of the poor, namely Israelites, settlers and resident aliens. It would, therefore, be quite acceptable for a Jew living in a foreign country, which was much more common after the diaspora, to take interest on loans made to poor Gentiles. Furthermore, there would be no sabbath-year release of debt required on these loans (Dt. 15:3). The charging of interest on such loans is not immoral or evil; it is permitted by Scripture. The ban on interest relates to poor loans made to believers and those who are prepared to live under the external demands and requirements of the faith, for such were the resident aliens and settlers, who, by their willingness to live in Israel, put themselves under the ethical demands of the covenant, at least in the outward conduct of their lives. The distinction between those from whom interest may be taken and those from whom it may not be taken is a *religious* and *cultural* distinction. Interest may be charged on loans made to foreigners and those who refuse to place themselves under the law of God, even if they are poor. The believer has a duty to help those in need, the destitute and the poor, if he is able to do so. This duty extends to foreigners and non-believers, but the charging of interest on loans to such is not prohibited and no disapprobation should be attached to the practice.

Fourth, that interest *per se* is not evil or forbidden is corroborated by the fact that Israel's being in a position to lend to many nations— at interest—is considered a *blessing* that God will bestow upon the nation if the people are faithful to his covenant: "For the Lord thy God blesseth thee, as he promised thee: and thou shalt lend to many nations, but thou shalt not borrow; and thou shalt reign over many nations, but they shall not reign over thee" (Dt. 15:6, cf. 28:12). Since the Bible teaches that "The rich ruleth over the poor, and the borrower is servant to the lender" (Pr. 22:7) the making of interest-bearing loans to Gentiles was a principal and peaceful means by which the people of God were to extend their dominion over the earth. Being able to lend at interest to Gentiles, therefore, was both a blessing for the Jews and a means of dominion over the ungodly sanctioned by God's righteous law for the glory of his name.

§5
Later Rabbinic Teaching on Interest

Although commerce was comparatively minimal in the early history of the people of Israel, when their livelihood was based principally on agriculture, the Babylonian captivity brought this period of relative isolation to an end. Jewish communities grew up in all the great commercial cities of the ancient world. As a result the Jews were well placed for commercial activities of all kinds and it seems that the Jews of the diaspora were indeed largely reliant on commerce for their livelihoods.[33] Since the law permitted Jews to charge interest on loans to foreigners we can assume also that interest-bearing commercial loans were made by Jews to Gentiles.

However, the rabbis continued to prohibit interest on all loans to fellow Jews, even in commerce and business,[34] though as we have

---

[33] W. H. Bennett, "Trade and Commerce" in James Hastings, ed., *A Dictionary of the Bible* (Edinburgh: T. and T. Clark, 1902), Vol. IV, p. 805*b*.

[34] This can be accounted for by the Pharisaical tendency to place a fence around

seen the Torah did not address the issue of non-charitable commercial loans. It will be useful therefore to look briefly at how the rabbis interpreted this ban since their observations throw some light on what would be involved in taking the ban as a general prohibition and how this would affect commerce and trade in the modern world.

First of all the rabbis interpreted the ban on interest between Jews and settlers to apply not only to payments in money or the specific goods lent but also to gifts given to the lender either before or after contracting a loan, since these are considered inducements or rewards for the loan and therefore constitute a form of interest.[35] The mere giving of information—which, after all, is vital to entrepreneurial activity (creation of wealth)—to a creditor who would not otherwise have had such information is considered usurious.[36] Thus, any form of advantage gained by a creditor from a debtor is treated as interest.

Second, another area where the Old Testament ban on interest would apply were it to be understood as a general ban—and one involving a practice that is very common in Western society today— is given by the rabbis, namely the practice of discounting prices for on the spot cash payments. The Mishnah reads:

RENT MAY INCREASE, BUT NOT THE PURCHASE PRICE, E.G. IF A MAN RENTS HIS COURT, AND SAYS TO HIM [THE TENANT], "IF YOU PAY ME NOW [FOR THE YEAR], YOU CAN HAVE IT FOR TEN SELA'S[37] PER ANNUM; IF MONTHLY, AT A SELA' PER MONTH"—THAT IS PERMITTED. IF HE SELLS HIS FIELD, AND SAYS TO HIM [THE PURCHASER], "IF YOU PAY ME NOW, IT IS YOURS FOR A THOUSAND ZUZ;[38] BUT AT HARVEST, FOR TWELVE MANEHS"[39]—THAT IS FORBIDDEN.[40]

---

the Torah (Aboth, Chapter I, 1), i.e. to go beyond the plain teaching of Scripture in an effort to guard oneself from inadvertently transgressing the Torah's commands. More often than not, however, this procedure led to the idolising of mere human laws and the setting aside of God's law (cf. Mk. 7:8–13). Thus the rabbis taught: "My son, be more careful in [the observance of] the words of the Scribes than in the words of the Torah, for in the laws of the Torah there are positive and negative precepts; but, as to the laws of the Scribes, whoever transgresses any of the enactments of the Scribes incurs the penalty of death. In case you should object: If they are of real value why were they not recorded [in the Torah]? Scripture stated, '*Of making many books there is no end*'" (Rabbi Dr I. Epstein, ed., *The Babylonian Talmud* [London: The Soncino Press, 1938], *Seder Mo'ed*, Vol. II, Erubin 21b, p. 149).   [35] *Ibid.*, *Seder Nezikin*, Vol. I, Baba Mezi'a 75b (p. 434).   [36] *Ibid.*

[37] A *sela'* was a coin worth four denarii.

[38] A *zuz* was a coin equal in value to a denarius.

[39] A *maneh* was a weight in gold or silver equal to a hundren common shekels, worth a hundred *zuz*. Twelve *manehs* was thus worth 1,200 *zuz*.

[40] *Seder Nezikin*, Vol. I, Baba Mezi'a, 65a (p. 382f.).

The Gemara (commentary) on this text explains: "What is the difference between the first clause and the second?—Rabbah and R. Joseph both said: Rent is payable at the end [of the year]; hence, since it is not yet time to claim, it is not payment for waiting, but this [a *sela'* per month] is its actual value; and as for his proposition, IF YOU PAY ME NOW [FOR THE YEAR], YOU CAN HAVE IT FOR TEN SELA' PER ANNUM, he is favouring him with a cheaper rent [than normal]. But in the second clause, the reference is to purchase, where the money is immediately due; therefore [the higher price] is payment for waiting, which is forbidden."[41] This principle was also recognised by the canonists of the twelfth century, who maintained that the sale of goods on credit for a higher price than cash sales was usurious.[42] Thus, the Old Testament ban on interest would, where applicable, render such cash discounts unacceptable. This would have significant repercussions for modern retailing practices were the ban judged to be a general ban and applicable in modern society. To this we should add that all bills of exchange that circulate at a discount prior to their date of maturity fall into this category also.

Third, of great significance for the modern world of business, were the Old Testament ban to be considered applicable to commercial loans, would be the Rabbinic observation that contracts for futures may lead indirectly to the taking of interest. The Babylonian Talmud states: "Our Rabbis taught: One may not contract for commodities until the market price is out; once the market price is established, a contract may be entered into, for even if one [the vendor] has no stock, another has. If the new supplies were at four [*se'ahs*[43] per *sela'*] and the old at three, a contract may not be made until the price has been equalised for the new and the old."[44] H. Freedman comments: "New supplies were cheaper, because they were not yet fully dried. Now the purchaser, though paying early, does not receive the wheat until that too becomes old, and if he contracts for the whole at the price of the new, he receives interest. Therefore he must wait until the same market price is fixed for both."[45] Here the kind of interest envisaged is not direct interest—i.e. a fixed rate of return on a loan—but indirect interest as a result of speculation. Such profits arising from speculation are considered usurious nonetheless since

[41] *Ibid.*, (p. 383).

[42] Harold Berman, *op. cit.*, p. 249. This theory, however, was abandoned by the canonists in the latter part of the thirteenth century (*ibid.*).

[43] A *se'ah* was a measure of capacity.

[44] *Seder Nezikin*, Vol. I, Baba Mezi'a, 72*b* (p. 420).   [45] *Ibid.*

they come within the rabbinic—and economically sound—maxim that all payments for waiting for one's money constitute interest.[46] The kind of interest contemplated and forbidden here is precisely the kind of profit earned by those who deal in futures. Under the application of the Old Testament ban on interest to commercial transactions, therefore, markets for futures, at least in their present form, would not be permissible.

Those who see the Old Testament ban as a general ban on interest in all circumstances should be aware of the consequences of such an interpretation. The implications would be far reaching for the economy, both for the way it functions and for its productivity and efficiency. For instance, the effect of outlawing profits made in markets for futures would be to make the quoting of prices of raw materials and semi-manufactured goods to be delivered at a later date impossible and this would in turn lead to greater uncertainty and fluctuations in retail prices. Of course this is essentially a pragmatic argument and it is not being suggested here that such arguments should be allowed to determine one's ethics. But it is important also that we should understand the implications of an ethical stance on a given issue.

§6
The Parable of the Talents

By New Testament times banking and interest-bearing loans were well enough established facts of commercial life in Israel for Jesus to have based one of his parables on the practice. Though the rabbis continued to condemn the taking of interest from fellow Jews on all loans—commercial as well as poverty loans—the New Testament makes no comment on the practice in relation to commerce other than what can be inferred from the Parable of the Talents (Mt. 25:12–30, Lk. 19:11–26).

It has been claimed both that the Parable of the Talents legitimises the taking of interest on commercial loans[47] and that it does not do so.[48] It is difficult to determine from the parable alone whether

---

[46] "R. Nahman said: The general principle of usury is: All payment for waiting [for one's money] is forbidden." (*Ibid.*, 63*b*, p. 378).

[47] G. North, *Honest Money* (Tyler, Texas: Dominion Press, 1986), p. 70f.

[48] S. C. Mooney, *op. cit.*, p. 110–113; Michael Schluter, *The Old Testament Ban on*

interest-bearing commercial loans are permissible in terms of biblical ethics. One's interpretation of the parable will largely be determined therefore by whether one views the Old Testament ban as a general ban or a specific ban on interest. As we have already seen, the exegetical case for the ban being general in nature is very weak whereas the case for the ban being specific and limited to the cases cited is very strong. If we accept the latter on exegetical grounds the Parable of the Talents simply corroborates the conclusion that the ban on interest in the Old Testament did not address commercial loans. On this premiss it is quite legitimate to argue that the parable legitimises interest on loans made for purely commercial purposes. Thus, G. North writes: "Jesus was affirming the legitimacy of both profit through trade and the normal rate of return which is secured by lending money. The two forms of activity are not the same, as the parable indicates, but both are legitimate."[49] If, on the other hand, we ignore the exegetical case for the ban being specific and treat it as a general ban on interest, the parable becomes more difficult to explain, since the master, who required at least that his money be loaned out at interest, is clearly to be identified with Christ.

In order to circumvent this problem S. C. Mooney attempts to interpret the parable in such a way that lending at interest is not condoned by the master. This idea is far-fetched but it will be instructive to look at the argument in more detail in order to demonstrate the difficulties with this kind of interpretation. Mooney writes:

Here is what the servant who has hidden the money said to the master in the parable, "Master, I knew you to be a hard man, reaping where you did not sow, and gathering where you scattered no seed. And I was afraid, and went away and hid your talent in the ground . . ." (Matthew 25:24, 25) In Luke (19:21) this servant calls the master an "exacting" man . . . Now what does the master say concerning the servant? "You wicked, lazy slave" (Matthew 25:27), and "You worthless slave" (Luke 19:22). It is evident that these are incompatible evaluations. Is it really a great problem to decide whose words are truth? If it already has been said that the master represents Christ, would it not be inconsistent to doubt the evaluation he gives of that servant? If His evaluation is accepted, and we come also to view this one as a worthless, wicked, and lazy slave, then how much stock would we put

---

Interest: Its Relevance for Reform of Britain's Industrial Structure in the 1980's (Cambridge: Jubilee Centre Publications Ltd, 1984), p. 4f.

[49] G. North, *Honest Money*, p. 70.

in his image of the master? Not a great deal at all. Does Jesus reap where He has not sown, or take up where he has not laid down (steal)? We know that this is untrue. Then why do some read the remainder of the master's comments as though he were admitting that the slave was right? He says, ". . . you knew that I reap where I did not sow, and gather where I scattered no seed? Then you ought to have put my money in the bank, and on my arrival I would have received my money back with interest." (Matthew 25:26, 27). What the master is saying here is something like, "If that really is what you thought of me, then this is what you would have done . . ." Indeed, the Luke version comes very close to saying it just that way when the master says, "By your own words I will judge you, you worthless slave . . ." (19:22). It is only by the word of the slave that the master is those evil things, never by any admission of the master. The word of the slave does not determine that the master is evil, rather the slave, by his own words, has proven himself to be evil, for the master is good definitively.[50]

On this interpretation the master is *not* saying that the servant should at least have loaned out the money at interest but only that *if* the master was as corrupt as the servant *claimed* he was he should have lent it out at interest—a corrupt practice according to Mooney. However, the text does not say "thou *thoughtest* that I reap where I sowed not," but "thou *knewest*" etc.[51] Mooney's claim that the words of Luke, "out of thine own mouth I will judge thee" (v. 22), suggest the former interpretation is not sustainable: first, the adjective used of the master by the servant (αὐστηρός) does not imply corruption, which is what we should expect if Mooney's interpretation were correct. The word means simply *hard, severe, strict*. The English word *austere* is derived from this Greek term. To have a code of conduct

---

[50] S. C. Mooney, *op. cit.*, p. 111.

[51] The verb used in both texts (Mt. 25:26 and Lk. 19:22) is ᾔδεις, 2nd pers. sing. pluperf. of οἶδα (2nd perf. from the obsolete present tense εἴδω), meaning *to have seen* or *perceived* and hence *to know, have knowledge of* (Abbott-Smith). This verb is used in the perfect tense with the sense of the present tense. That is to say it represents a present state based on the acquisition of knowledge in the past. The pluperfect thus has the sense of the imperfect. Hence, the lazy servant knew that the master reaps where he has not sown because he has observed the master doing precisely that in the past. According to Liddell and Scott the perfect tense of this verb always means *to know*. It is not possible to translate this verb as "thought," especially since on Mooney's interpretation it would have to mean "thought erroneously"—i.e. on Mooney's interpretation ᾔδεις would have to mean "you were deceived," the very opposite of what in fact it does mean—and nothing in the context suggests that to do so would yield a more reasonable interpretation. Mooney is forced into twisting the meaning of the word used in the text by his own preconceptions and as a consequence distorts the context. His interpretation is based on eisegesis (reading into the text what one wishes to find there) rather than exegesis (bringing out of the text what it actually says).

that is austere certainly does not imply moral corruption; rather the opposite. But on Mooney's interpretation lending money at interest is an evil form of gain—indeed Mooney equates it with theft—practised by those who are morally corrupt. Second, even if we accept, for the sake of argument, that the Old Testament ban is general in nature, this in no way casts these words of Luke in a different light, nor can it justify changing "knew" to "thought" or "believed"—incorrectly on Mooney's interpretation. Third, to come *close* to putting the words in a form that would support Mooney's interpretation is not the same thing as putting them in a form that does in fact support his interpretation. Mooney's interpretation is contrived. The most straightforward interpretation of the words is simply that the servant knew the truth about his master and therefore what he did was inexcusable. His punishment is therefore just. The words in Luke 19:22 will not bear Mooney's interpretation, and to change "knew" to "thought" is simply a distortion that creates problems with the logic and internal consistency of the interpretation, as we shall see.

Fourth, Mooney thinks that the parable teaches that taking interest is something that only hard and evil men do and that the servant's estimation of his master's demands was incorrect—that is to say that the master was not hard, that he did not reap where he had not sown nor gather where he had scattered no seed. To interpret the parable in any other way would, for Mooney, imply that Christ is a hard and unscrupulous master. But neither exegesis of the text nor the logic of Mooney's argument will bear out this interpretation. As to the former, the text clearly indicates that the servant's estimation of his master's demands is correct.[52] As regards Mooney's logic, if we accept that the master is not evil, which is quite true, it simply does not follow that the slave's assessment of his master's actions upon his return is incorrect. On Mooney's interpretation we should expect the master to show mercy to the slave,

---

[52] *a.* See the discussion at note 51 above.

b. If it should be objected that in that case Christ is portrayed as unjust because he reaps where he has not sown, which constitutes theft according to Mooney, (*op. cit.*, p. 111), I answer that God demands perfect obedience to his law from those in whom he has not sowed the seed of faith by the work his Spirit, i.e. special grace, whereby alone men are enabled to repent and obey God, and that all such as are without that special grace, both Gentile *and* Jew, will be judged according to the law and condemned for their sin. If the master is unjust here in the Parable of the Talents for reaping where he has not sown, therefore, the implication is that God is unjust in his condemnation of the wicked and thus the pedagogical purpose of the parable is defeated or at least severely confused.

since he was not really the hard man that the slave claimed he was. But in fact he does not show mercy and instead punishes the slave, the very thing that the slave feared in the first place. Thus, the internal logic of this interpretation falls apart. The slave's assessment of the master is correct therefore; the slave is wrong only in calling his master hard rather than just. And surely this is the point: non-believers complain at God's justice when it is meted out to them and call it injustice.

Fifth, Mt. 25:27 militates against Mooney's interpretation of the parable since the phrase "thou oughtest" in "thou oughtest therefore to have put my money to the exchangers" is, as Leon Morris points out, "a strong term; the master is thinking of the easiest way of getting a profit, and at the very least this is something that the man was under obligation to do."[53] Good stewardship of the resources committed to us, the point of the parable, requires at the very least, other things being equal, that we lend out our money at interest—unless of course it is loaned to the poor believer or God-fearer—since it is then put to productive use that will benefit others and ourselves rather than being buried in the ground where it will do no one any good.

Michael Schluter also treats the Old Testament ban on interest as general in nature and sees the granting of permission to Jews to exact interest from foreigners as an exception to this general principle. "There is only one exception" writes Schluter, "that is, loans to foreigners. These are people outside Israel's borders. The resident alien or refugee is included among those who may not be charged. The ban on interest between citizens of a State is given as a universal absolute. There seems no way to avoid this conclusion. Perhaps it should even be regarded as a structural evil, in the same category as death."[54] The claim that the ban is a universal absolute for citizens of a State, however, cannot be supported from Scripture. As we have seen the Torah permitted Jews residing in Gentile countries where they were citizens to take interest from Gentiles on *all* kinds of loans, and Jewish residents in Gentile nations were forbidden by the same law from taking interest on loans to poor Jews resident in Palestine, even though they were citizens of another State.[55] Even if we accept

---

[53] Leon Morris, *The Gospel According to Matthew* (Eerdmans and Inter-Varsity Press, 1992), p. 631.   [54] Michael Schluter, *op. cit.*, p. 2.

[55] Schluter says: "Historically, Jews have only applied the ban to loans among themselves rather than applying it to loans to any within the countries within which

the idea that the ban on interest is a general principle with certain exceptions, it would not be valid to conclude, as Schluter does, that the ban relates to citizens of a State. The Bible clearly contradicts such a notion by permitting Jewish citizens of Gentile States to lend to Gentile citizens of such States. Even if the ban were to be understood as general in nature, there is a clearly stated exception to it (Dt. 23:20) that contradicts Schluter's argument.

Schluter goes on to consider the Parable of the Talents and claims that it does not relax the Old Testament's universal and absolute ban on interest between citizens of a State:

they have resided. Perhaps they have never fully identified with the countries where they have resided outside Israel, but in any event it has been a major factor in their unpopularity." (*ibid.*, p. 6n.1.) This is misleading however. Of course the Jews did not identify with the Gentile nations into which they were deported. They were required by God's word not to assimilate with idolatrous pagan cultures, and this applied in the diaspora just as much as in their homeland. Schluter understands the Hebrew word *'ach* (*brother* or *kinsman*) to mean *citizen* in the modern sense. He also understands the word *nokri* (*stranger* or *foreigner*) to mean simply *citizen of another State* (see above note 27*a*). But this is at best anachronistic. It also confuses one's citizenship with one's cultural identity, a serious error. Even in the modern world one can be a citizen of a State without sharing the cultural identity of the indigenous population. Culture is primarily a *religious* phenomenon and by no means coterminous with citizenship. Citizens of a State have a common culture only when they share a common faith, since culture is very largely the external form of religion. A State may comprise many societies with disparate cultures. The word *society* comes from the Latin noun *societas*, which means *fellowship, union*, or *communion*, and is cognate with the verb *socio*, meaning *to do* or *hold in common, to share*. The people of Britain were for centuries bound together by their common faith in the Triune God of Scripture, and thus British society found the purpose and meaning of life in terms of a Christian world-view. Those who are part of Muslim and Hindu communities in Britain today are part of different societies with their own cultures, though they may be citizens of the same State. Dt. 23:19–20 is not addressing the modern idea of citizenship of a secular State, as Schluter supposes, but the religious and social issue of how the Israelites were to relate to their kinsmen and those who were assimilated into their culture and in what way this differed from their relationship with those who were members of an alien culture. This issue stands on its own quite apart from the modern secular idea of citizenship of a State. Christians today who live in non-Christian countries, like the Hebrews of Old Testament times, are morally required to maintain their cultural identity and resist all temptations and pressure to assimilate with pagan cultures. The *only* legitimate means of achieving cultural identity with the people of such nations is through conversion of the indigenous culture to the Christian faith. A first step in this process—especially where the preaching of the gospel is severely restricted—might legitimately be for Christians to exercise rulership over non-believers by means of trade and commerce (economic power), including the practice of usury, a peaceful means of conquest (Pr. 22:7). This course of action is sanctioned by the Bible. Thus, the reason the Jews loaned money at interest to Gentiles in whose countries they resided is simply that the Bible specifically permitted them to do so.

Nothing in the N[ew] T[estament] relaxes the ban on interest. It is often argued that in the Parable of the Talents Jesus allows interest for business dealings, differentiating commercial loans from the exploitation by money lenders referred to in the Mosaic law. However, careful scrutiny of the passages does not allow this way out. Firstly, to base a major change in the Law on the detail of a parable is not generally regarded as permissible in biblical interpretation; it is surprising how readily it has been accepted in this case. Secondly, the words which Jesus actually puts in the mouth of the Master are these: "You bad and lazy servant. You knew, did you, that I reap harvests where I do not sow and gather crops where I do not scatter seed? Well then, you should have deposited my money in the bank and I would have received it all back with interest when I returned["] (Matt. 25:26, 27). Interest is regarded by the Master as reaping where one has not sown, rather like the current bank advertisement which shows a man asleep and with his feet up, who is said to be "busy earning 8.75%" on his money. This is hardly a view of interest which should encourage Christians to promote interest-lending. Nor can we even be certain that the bank referred to in the parable would be lending money to fellow Israelites. Knowing the influence of the Pharisees and their addiction to the detail of the Law, it is more likely that any banks in Jesus' day would have been lending to foreigners, so that the Master in the story is only encouraging the servant to lend within the framework laid down by the Law. If any lesson can be deduced from the story, it would be that lending at interest is better than just hoarding gold, but that it is still very much a second best to direct investment.[56]

All four points made here fail to prove the basic contention, namely, that the parable does not permit interest-bearing commercial loans, and the overall argument is unconvincing—a fact that Schluter as good as admits at the end. The first argument, namely, that to base a major change in the law on the detail of a parable is not good hermeneutics, is in itself a valid point. But in this context it begs the question. This argument is only valid if the interpretation of the parable as permitting interest-bearing commercial loans is indeed a major change in the law—in other words if it can be conclusively proved that the Old Testament ban is an absolute universal ban prohibiting interest on all types of loans, including commercial loans, between citizens of a State. Schluter's argument assumes the truth of the point to be proved. But as we have seen, the point cannot be proved. On the contrary, exegesis of the relevant texts shows that the laws prohibiting interest are case laws addressing specific circumstances. Hence, to interpret the parable as permitting interest-bearing commercial loans is *not* a major change in the law.

[56] *Ibid.*, p. 4f.

Schluter claims that "nowhere do the Law or the prophets separate out some lending and make it legitimate because it is between contracting parties of equal financial strength, or because it may be classified as productive investment."[57] However, this is true only because such commercial loans were not a feature of Israel's primitive agricultural economy. To apply case laws that deal with the specific and concrete circumstances of Israelite society in early biblical times to practices that were then unknown is not legitimate unless there is some general principle underpinning those laws (general equity) that is relevant to the new cases and can be applied to them.

For instance, the case law requiring the Hebrews to put fences around their roofs to protect life (Dt. 22:8) is not applicable to houses with sloped roofs since they are not lived on as are flat roofs. But the general equity of the law applies to other constructions such as bridges, stairways etc. But this is not the case with the case laws prohibiting interest since the Bible makes it clear that in other cases familiar to the Jews—e.g. lending to foreigners—interest is permitted. The general principle of an absolute and universal ban on interest cannot be extrapolated from the case law, since such a principle is not embodied in the law. Were such a principle of general equity— i.e. justice—embodied in the ban on usury it would clearly be in conflict with the fact that the law permitted Jews to lend at interest to foreigners. Since the general equity of the law would apply to foreigners just as much as to Israelites,—otherwise the whole notion of general equity would be meaningless—the inescapable implication would be that the Bible itself, in permitting Jews to exact usury from foreigners, is unjust. And of course, this would in turn mean that God himself is unjust, since not only has God permitted his people to practise such a perverse and unjust form of trade; he has also promised to bless them with success in it if they obediently serve him before all else. This would be not only for God to condone the sin, but also to reward it. It is not possible to draw such a principle of general equity from the ban on usury, therefore, without destroying the coherence of biblical ethics and indeed without impugning the very character of God as a righteous and just lawgiver. However, the general principle, "thou shalt not kill" is embodied in the law requiring fences around flat roofs. We are *always* required to preserve judicially innocent human life where possible, since this is the meaning of "thou shalt not kill." But the ban on interest, as we have seen,

[57] *Ibid.*, p. 4.

is not an application of the general principle "thou shalt not steal" since if interest *per se* were theft, it would not be permissible to make interest-bearing loans to foreigners. The specific ban on interest is an embodiment of the requirement to show charity to fellow believers and God-fearers. In other words, the interest ban embodies a principle of *charity* not a principle of justice,[58] and of course, as one would expect, given this fact, there is no judicial penalty for failure to fulfil this law of charity—i.e. it does not come within the scope of the magistrate's duty to enforce public justice and punish criminals because failure to obey this law is not a crime.[59] Yet the fact that the law embodies a principle of charity rather than of justice does not mean that it is not *morally* binding in the context in which it is given. God will certainly judge those who refuse to abide by his word and obey this commandment. The point is that such charity is not required, legally or morally, in cases outside the scope of the commandment's particular terms of reference, i.e. fellow Jews, sojourners and settlers—those who are prepared to live under the external requirements of the covenant. The same degree of charity is not required in the believer's relationship with those outside the faith.

Take the following analogy: I am required to feed and clothe my children, i.e. provide for their welfare. The Scripture says I am worse than an infidel if I fail to do this (1 Tim. 5:8). But I am not required to feed and clothe all and sundry in the same way. If I sell clothes I may make a profit out of my customers—indeed, only as I do make a profit am I able to fulfil the Bible's command to provide for my own dependants. In making a profit from the sale of clothes to such people I do them no injustice, though if I were to help a poor man by giving him some clothes I should be showing

---

[58] According to Richard Baxter, "there is no doubt but the whole controversie is resolved into this last question, whether all Usury be against Justice or Charity to our neighbour. *Justice* obligeth me to give him *his own*: Charity obligeth me to give him more than his own, in certain cases, as one that love him as myself. That which is not against *Justice*, may be against *Charity*: But that which is against Charity, is not always against Justice strictly taken. And that which is an act of true Charity, is never against Justice: Because he that giveth his neighbour *more* than his own, doth give him *his own* and *more*. There is a *Usury* which is against *Justice* and *Charity*. There is a *Usury* which is against *Charity*, but not against meer *Justice*: And there is a Usury which is against neither *Justice* nor *Charity*." (Richard Baxter, *Chapters from A Christian Directory*, p. 124f.)

[59] On the difference between sin and crime as it relates to the function of the State in enforcing public justice see Stephen C. Perks, *A Defence of the Christian State* (Taunton: Kuyper Foundation, 1998), *passim*.

mercy. Similarly, I am obligated by God's law to provide a godly education for my children, but this obligation does not extend to all who need educating, i.e. to those outside my family. My obligation to provide for my own household in these matters is not based on some general principle that requires me to provide for everyone else in the same way, much less does it require the State to exercise this obligation for me or for society generally by funding welfare programmes with taxes levied on my family's income,—income that I need in order to fulfil my obligation to my family properly. The ban on interest embodies a similar principle of charity and no more necessitates a universal prohibition on interest than my duty to feed, clothe and educate my children at zero profit requires me to feed, clothe and educate the whole neighbourhood on the same basis.[60]

The principle is this: Old Testament law is valid and applicable to contemporary society provided it is applied to a *comparable* situation. We do not put fences around our roofs since we do not live on them. But we do put railings along bridges and on stairways. The law has to be applied to comparable circumstances. The fact that the Bible permits the charging of interest in many circumstances—e.g. to foreigners, and even on mercy loans to foreigners—should give us reason

---

[60] *a.* This analogy is not perfect of course. I am the legal guardian and covenantal head of my family and deprivation of a dependant's vital needs (i.e. those that preserve life) when he could not provide these for himself would constitute a crime, i.e. a sin that should be dealt with by the courts. This is not the case with usury on mercy loans to fellow believers, though of course the moral strictures may be equally as strong.

b. It is worth noting here that although the Bible demands that parents provide food, clothing and education for their children, i.e. that they provide for their welfare, failure to do so properly, though worthy of the strongest moral strictures (1 Tim. 5:8), is not a matter of public justice that can be enforced through the courts— unless of course such failure is the result of or involves some crime to which the Bible appends a judicial penalty that must be enforced by the State. That is to say, the obligation incumbent upon parents to educate their children does not imply a reciprocal right to be educated that can be legally defined and protected by the magistrate. Neither was failure to make interest-free loans to poor fellow Israelites a matter of justice that could be settled in court. Rather, it was a matter that God dealt with by means of his providential government of the universe, i.e. by means of blessing and cursing. The ban is not a matter for State action, but rather a matter of personal self-government. The excessive concentration on rights in modern Western society, rather than on duties and obligations, is a perverse development that characterises modern man's atheism, his search for deification, and a substantial cause of confusion and ruin for our traditionally Christian legal system. For example, modern compulsory education laws can only be made effective by suspending the basic rights, freedoms and obligations of parents and ultimately by the funding of State education with taxes—i.e. theft (see pp. 208–212 above).

to be very cautious about extrapolating from these specific case laws to generalities. Commercial lending was not the issue being addressed but rather the poor and needy fellow believer. In a society without commercial loans it would be irrelevant for the law or the prophets to make the distinction that Schluter mentions.

Schluter's second argument, that reaping where one has not sown is a view of interest that should not encourage Christians to promote lending at interest, is similar in nature to Mooney's argument discussed above, namely, that exacting interest is the practice of hard and unscrupulous men, incompatible with the Christian virtues, and falls to the ground for the same reasons. The third argument, that Jewish banks were influenced by Pharisaic principles and thus encouraged lending at interest only to foreigners, may well be correct, but if commercial loans are not banned by the biblical case laws it changes nothing. The Pharisees bound many laws of their own devising upon the people. They were notorious for making a fence around the Torah,[61] yet neglected the weightier matters of the law (Mt. 23:23). This argument still assumes that the Old Testament ban is general in nature and thus presupposes the point to be proved. If this is not so it matters not how the Pharisees ran their banking business. Furthermore, this argument contradicts the second argument. They are alternative interpretations that cannot be squared with each other since the argument that lending at interest *per se* is unethical would, if true, make lending to foreigners unethical also.

The fourth point made by Schluter is odd in that it seems to reduce to insignificance if not absurdity the previous three points. If the lesson to be deduced from the parable is that "lending at interest is better than just hoarding gold, but that it is still very much a second best to direct investment," then in order to show that lending at interest is wrong it would have to be shown that hoarding gold—i.e. saving—is also wrong. The latter is a completely different subject, however, and to argue that the Bible forbids the hoarding of gold (saving) as a premiss for denying the validity of lending at interest would surely stretch the credulity of the most ardent opponent of usury. We cannot save our gold and we cannot lend it out at interest. The only alternative is to spend it all as soon as we get it or else give it all away immediately, since even direct investment involves a certain amount of long-term planning and thus hoarding (i.e. saving). I suppose this has a certain logic from a socialist point of

---

[61] Aboth, Chapt. I, sec. 1. See above note 34.

view—i.e. money is evil *per se*, get rid of it[62]—but it hardly leads to productivity, capitalisation, and economic and social progress, and, moreover, as a result flies flat in the face of the teaching of the parable.

On the other hand, following the logic of the argument, if hoarding gold is morally legitimate then lending at interest on a commercial basis is also morally legitimate. No disapprobation is imputed to the taking of interest *per se* therefore. The encouragement to use one's wealth in a more productive form of investment might be a valid principle of Christian stewardship, though not in all circumstances (cf. Calvin's argument above). I have no problem with drawing this lesson from the parable: it is internally consistent as well as consistent with the argument that interest-bearing commercial loans are not outlawed in Scripture.

§7

Some Practical Considerations

Before drawing this discussion of interest to a close there are a few other points that should be made, which, while outside the scope of the discussion strictly speaking, do have some practical relevance. In the Bible the Christian is encouraged to avoid borrowing if at all possible, whether at interest for commercial and consumer purposes, or because of poverty without paying interest: "Owe no man any thing, but to love one another" (Rom. 13:8). Thus, while it is acceptable to lend at interest on non-charitable commercial loans, and to make interest-free loans to those in need who are of the faith, it is undesirable to borrow under any circumstances. All borrowing is to be avoided by the Christian if possible. This is not always possible, especially in the matter of housing, but it is a goal to aim at. Nonetheless, there are priorities in the Christian life, and getting out of debt may not be the most important. For instance, in a culture where the market for rented accommodation is extremely limited (as it is in Britain) and where it is virtually impossible to save up for

---

[62] Although socialists sometimes talk as if money were evil in this way, in fact they *never* act in conformity with such sentiments. Their sole purpose in life seems to be to get their hands on other people's money. Money is evil for socialists, therefore, if it is other people's money. This discrepancy between ideology and practice indicates the true motive behind socialist ideology: envy. See Helmut Schoeck, *Envy, A Theory of Social Behaviour* (London: Secker and Warburg, 1969).

a house because of inflation and the consequent ever escalating cost of housing, it is more important that the family has a home of its own to live in than that the mortgage is dropped. (In many places in Britain the only alternative to buying a house with a mortgage is to be dependent on the State for housing, certainly an option not to be preferred above taking on a mortgage.) Mortgages may be necessary therefore, and as long as the Christian keeps the general injunction to stay out of debt in mind he should not feel guilty about having a mortgage *per se*. Some advocate paying off the mortgage as soon as possible, and in principle this is good advice. But there are priorities in life. If paying off the mortgage in ten years instead of twenty years is going to mean that one has insufficient funds to provide a good Christian education for one's children, it would seem better to let the mortgage run a few more years, other things being equal. A Christian education for one's children, either at home or at a good Christian school, takes priority over paying off the mortgage early in my opinion. These are, of course, matters that each individual believer and Christian family must determine for themselves, but it is important not to overstress the issue of mortgage debt at the expense of issues that take priority over it. On the other hand *all* kinds of consumer debt should be avoided.

The general principle to be aimed at is to get out of debt as soon as possible, since "The rich ruleth over the poor, and the borrower is servant to the lender" (Pr. 22:7). Being in a position to lend is a blessing, and a willingness to lend to the poor and those in need is the mark of a righteous man (Ps. 37:25–26). Christians are to be in positions of dominion and leadership, ruling over the earth for the glory of God, and thus borrowing is to be avoided. The Bible teaches that lending at interest is a means of dominion over the ungodly.

Conclusion

To summarise: loans in the Bible relate primarily to the poor and needy who, in order to sustain themselves in difficult times, have to resort to borrowing. The law prohibits the taking of interest from the poor and needy Israelite or God-fearer (settler). The ban on interest is not a general or universal ban, and interest may be taken from foreigners. Interest is thus not evil or unjust in itself, though it is wrong to take interest from poor believers and God-fearers who are prepared to live under the external demands of the covenant. Being in a position to be able to lend to those in need, and to non-believers at interest, is a blessing that God bestows upon a covenantally faithful people. The Bible does not specifically address the question of modern commercial and consumer type loans. Interest-bearing commercial and consumer loans, therefore, are not banned by biblical law and the Parable of the Talents corroborates this interpretation. Christians, however, should generally seek to avoid all debt if possible, whether interest-bearing or non-interest-bearing.

HELP FOR THE POOR
AND THE MEANING OF JUBILEE

§I

Misconceptions of the Jubilee Principle

It has been fairly common among Christians who have sought to develop a biblical perspective in terms of which to address the problems of modern economies to see in the Jubilee land-lease laws of Leviticus 25 a paradigm for some form of wealth redistribution programme. At least this has been the case in Britain, where some form of socialism has been adopted by most Christians as the type of economic organisation of society that comes nearest to fulfilling what is considered to be Christian ideals of economic behaviour. It is assumed that the restoration of ancestral lands every fifty years in the Mosaic economy constituted primarily a form of "social justice"[1] in which those who had over the years acquired wealth through the purchase of land were required to redistribute that wealth, in the form of land, to the poor. The Jubilee has thus been

[1] The idea of "social justice" is in fact a modern one stemming from the ideology of socialism. The notion was unknown in biblical society where justice, or right-eousness—they mean the same thing in the Bible and both are used to translate the Hebrew word *tsedeq*—was understood to be adherence to God's law. In the Bible the administration of justice is the sphere of the State's legitimate activity where there are penalties attached to transgressions of the law—i.e. where *crime* has been committed—or where adjudication is necessary to determine whether or not crime has been committed. Compassion for the poor and needy is the duty of the church and of private individuals and the family. The Bible maintains a separation of powers and functions between the institutions of church, family and State,—and this is true of the Old Testament also in spite of much talk of the old covenant nation being an "undifferentiated" society. The role of each of these biblical institutions has boundaries and limits. To speak of "social justice" is to confuse and combine the different social functions of these institutions and to place in the hands of the State, which bears the sword to enforce its judgements, the role of ensuring that society acts with compassion—as conceived by those in office—towards the needy. The ideology of "social justice" is not found in the Bible and cannot be squared with the Christian faith. The term "social justice" is really no more than a synonym for wealth redistribution and economic equality used to disguise the notion it represents—

seen as a form of capital redistribution as well as general wealth redistribution. This is, however, a mistaken idea. The Jubilee was not essentially about the redistribution of wealth, capital or otherwise, and the benefits accruing from the Jubilee land laws were not directed to the poor since the rich stood to gain also and, as we shall see, many of the poorest in society stood to gain nothing or even lose what little they had as a result of the implementation of the Jubilee. Yet in spite of this the idea has persisted. For example, Alan Storkey writes:

> It was a fundamental tenet of the Mosaic law that as people naturally became poor through various processes, some accidental and some involving exploitation, they were to be helped. They were not only to be helped through various neighbourly activities, but also through state activity. In the Mosaic law this was far more radical than anything we would envisage now. It was basically a redistribution of *wealth*, especially land, whereas we tend to limit redistribution to income and leave wealth relatively untouched. (*cf.* Leviticus 25 and Deuteronomy 15). This was a matter of law and of state control, and it seems inevitable that Christians who take the biblical teaching about the poor seriously must be committed to a fairly radical view of wealth redistribution through legislation and the state.[2]

In spite of the claim made here there is no biblical evidence to support the notion that the Jubilee laws of Leviticus 25 or the sabbath remission of debt and manumission laws of Deuteronomy 15 constituted a form of State-controlled or State-enforced wealth redistribution.[3] These texts, therefore, certainly do not commit Christians to taking seriously a radical programme of wealth redistribution through legislation enforced by the State as a means of helping the poor. It is of course true that the Bible requires the wealthier members of society to help the poor. This will not be contested at all here.

---

which is an essential aspect of the socialist agenda. The idea of "social justice" is a form of "double speak" used to introduce socialist ideology slowly and subliminally into the world-view and social life of the nation. The Bible is certainly concerned with justice, but it knows nothing of the modern notion of "social justice." See Appendix D, "Social Regeneration and Political Idolatry."

[2] Alan Storkey, *A Christian Social Perspective* (Inter-Varsity Press, 1979), p. 309.

[3] This is not an uncommon assumption. See Appendix D, "Social Regeneration and Political Idolatry" for a more detailed discussion of this problem. The prevalence of ideas such as "social justice," the right to economic equality and socialism generally, and the existence of the Welfare State for over fifty years in Britain, are no doubt the reason that such assumptions are so easily read into Scripture. It might fairly have been expected, however, that an author seeking to develop a *Christian* social perspective would have taken care to avoid such an error.

What will be contested is that it is the role of the *State* to enforce this kind of welfare by means of wealth redistribution programmes. Of the 613 laws in the Torah only a small number relate to the role of the magistrate or civil government. Most require individuals to govern *themselves* and their families in terms of just principles of behaviour and compassion for the poor as expounded in the Torah. God judged Israel for failing in this respect, but the Torah does not require the State to rectify this failure through wealth redistribution programmes, nor is it ever asserted by the prophets, who revealed God's will to the nation, that the State was required to take action on behalf of the poor or that God's anger was kindled because the State had not provided welfare programmes or wealth redistribution programmes for the poor. Certainly, State-enforced wealth redistribution was not a feature of the model of social organisation set forth in the Torah, and there are no texts in Scripture, including Lev. 25 and Dt. 15, that will, when correctly exegeted, lend credibility to such a notion.

§2

Jubilee and the Distribution of Wealth

As far as the redistribution of wealth within society is concerned, the Jubilee land laws meant that all land sold in Israel was sold on a forty-nine year or less leasehold basis. In this sense, therefore, there was no difference between the Jubilee provisions and modern leasehold purchase of property. The real meaning and significance of the Jubilee lay in its typological nature. The Jubilee land-lease provisions, however, were *not* a measure to help the poor: first, the Jubilee restoration of ancestral lands involved only the descendants of the original Israelite settlers. Those who were immigrants, whether proselytes or settlers, were not affected, and immigrants were usually among the poorest members of society.[4] If a proselyte living in Israel were desperately poor the Jubilee land laws would not help him at all. There is no law requiring that land be given to those who were not descendants of the original settlers no matter how poor they were, and this is simply because the purpose of the Jubilee was not to redistribute wealth or to make it possible for the poor to "start again,"

[4] David Chilton, *Productive Christians in an Age of Guilt Manipulators* (Tyler, Texas: Institute for Christian Economics, 1985, Third Edition), p. 158.

as it has sometimes been argued. A by-product of the Jubilee inheritance laws may have been that *some* of the poor were able to start again, but that opportunity was not available to all. Any help the poor may have had from the Jubilee, therefore, was not based on some ideal of wealth redistribution or economic equality, which is unknown in the Bible. Rather, the Jubilee land provisions could only help certain of the poor in a way that was quite incidental to their main purpose, and even then only on a purely non-egalitarian basis, namely, *inherited privilege*, something that hardly fits well with modern socialist ideals of equality, "Christian" or otherwise.

Furthermore, the Jubilee legislation might actually exacerbate the poverty of some. Suppose for instance that a poor proselyte family moves into the land. The first generation manages to lease some land on which to make a meagre living. But over the years the harvests do not enable the family to capitalise itself to the extent that it will be able to lease another piece of land on which to earn a living after the Jubilee. When the Jubilee is announced this poor family becomes landless, and its latter condition is worse that its former. In this case the Jubilee actually redistributes the land away from the poor, possibly to a much wealthier family. Such cases demonstrate clearly that the purpose of the Jubilee land provisions was not the redistribution of wealth and that its meaning is to be found elsewhere.

Second, those who received back their ancestral lands were the rich as well as the poor. These were *inheritance* laws, not welfare laws. They protected a family's inheritance, and this was so for the rich no less than for the poor. Third, a man may have grown very rich during the fifty years between Jubilees, rich in sheep, cattle, livestock of all kinds, as well as in gold and silver. When he returned any leased land to the hereditary owners the wealth he had accumulated on the land remained his own. The wealthy kept their wealth and were not required by the Torah or the State to redistribute it to the poor. Of course, there was the requirement that the rich help the poor and less fortunate, and they were morally required to pay their tithes, part of which went to help the poor. But the civil government or State was given no mandate to ensure that they did so; it was a responsibility that they were to shoulder themselves before God through the use of their poor tithe and through charitable giving. God's law demands that the wealthy should be compassionate to the poor; it does not give the State the duty or right of enforcing such compassion.

Fourth, after the Jubilee a man was free to acquire again the land he had previously leased, or other lands, if the owners were prepared to lease them; and if he were rich enough before the Jubilee he could easily do this since the Jubilee did not affect his accumulated wealth. From the point of view of the distribution of wealth in society, therefore, there was no difference between the case of a man who acquired land by lease in Israel and that of a shop owner in modern Western society when the lease on his shop comes to an end. He either re-purchases the lease or leases premises elsewhere. The owner of the lease is at liberty to re-sell, to raise the price, or to keep the land for his own use. No State welfare or wealth redistribution programme is implied by this arrangement today, and neither was it in ancient Israel.

Fifth, as a form of wealth or wealth-producing capital the actual land inherited by the descendants of the original Israelite settlers became increasingly meaningless with each succeeding generation. The Jubilee land-lease arrangements were mandatory only in Israel itself. They did not apply to land acquired and held outside Israel, nor did they apply to property within Israelite *cities* either. The one exception to the latter was property owned by Levites, who retained the right of redemption at any time in all Levitical cities irrespective of whether those to whom they had leased their property were poor or rich (Lev. 25:32). Furthermore, as the population grew the portion of land available to those who inherited decreased accordingly since primogeniture was not practised and the land was divided between the inheriting children,[5] with a double portion only going to the eldest (Dt. 21:15–17, Num. 27:1–11). Yet the Hebrews were told that if they

---

[5] The speculative statement of Roland de Vaux that "Probably only the movable chattels were shared, and the house, with the ancestral holdings, would be allotted to the eldest, or at least not divided" (Roland de Vaux, *Ancient Israel, Its Life and Institutions* [London: Darton, Longman and Todd, 1962], p. 53) is contradicted by Dt. 21:15–17, which stipulates that eldest should receive a double portion of the inheritance only, and by the case of the daughters of Zelophehad, who had no sons (Num. 27:1–7). Numbers Rabbah XXI.12 states: "Moses brought their case before the Lord. The Holy One, blessed be He, answered him: The daughters of Zelophehad speak right. This indicates that the Holy One, blessed be He, acknowledged the justice of their words. Thou shalt surely give them (XXVII, 7). Give them, He implied, moveables and the share of their father's birthright in the property of Hepher. They took three shares, viz. the share of their father who had been among those who came out of Egypt, and his share with his brothers in the property of Hepher from which, having been a firstborn, he took two portions" (Numbers Rabbah [London: The Soncino Press, 1983], p. 839). It is clear from this that both chattels *and* land were divided between the inheriting children with only

obeyed God's law God would prosper them and multiply them greatly—indeed this was the promise made to Abraham. The significance of the inherited ancestral land therefore decreased over time as a form of wealth in the context of an increasingly prosperous society. The Jubilee land provisions were not a measure aimed at providing capital for the poor of succeeding generations to enable them to start again. The Bible makes it clear that there ought to have been no poor among the people of Israel, but it did not require State-enforced and State-controlled wealth redistribution programmes as a means of achieving this goal. Rather, such prosperity was to be the blessing of God on an obedient society (Dt. 15:4–6), which included obedience to those commandments stipulating that the wealthy should show compassion to the poor. However, the more numerous the people became the less the effects of the Jubilee land provisions featured as the basis of their prosperity. The significance of the Jubilee, therefore, was far from the welfare system it is supposed by many to have been. Even if it could be argued that the Jubilee was a form of wealth redistribution or welfare arrangement—which I deny—it was an increasingly *inadequate* one as time passed even for the privileged ones who benefited from it.

§3
Help for the Poor: Private or State-Controlled?

Few Christians, if any, would deny the fact that the Bible requires the better off and wealthier members of society to help the poor and helpless. Mercy and charity are very clearly required and commanded by God's law. What is denied here, and with biblical precedent, is the idea that the *State* has the right to determine *who* should be helped, *how much* should be given and *what kind* of help they should receive. What is also denied is that the State has the right to take upon itself the function of an organisation for collecting and administering the funds needed to help the poor. In short, the State does not have the right to usurp the individual's responsibility to help the poor and to tax him so heavily in order to fund its own welfare programme

---

a double portion being allotted to the eldest (cf. Babylonian Talmud, Kiddushin 42a–42b [pp. 210–211 in the Soncino edition] and Baba Bathra 71a [p. 281]). Primogeniture does seem to have been practised in the earlier patriarchal period however (Gen. 25:27–34 and possibly 21:9–14; Gen. 27:1–40 cf. 49:1–28).

that he is barely able to provide for his own family without resorting to State welfare, let alone provide for those who are poorer and needier than himself by means of personal charitable giving. Such tax-funded State welfare programmes *create* the very kind of dependency and powerlessness that biblical charity is aimed at removing and that is rightly seen as so debilitating.

Of course, the Bible does give laws governing charity, but it does not give the State the right to administer or police those laws. It has already been stated that there are 613 laws in the Torah and of these only a comparatively small number have judicial penalties attached to them or require administration by the State. The basic principle of biblical law is *self*-government under God. If people will not govern themselves properly according to God's law how can they be expected to elect a government that will do it for them? The whole argument for "Christian" socialism is an argument for the *abdication* to the State of the personal responsibility that God's word requires of man. But if Christians will not shoulder their personal responsibilities what makes them think that others, and non-believers at that, will do it for them? All that the abdication of personal responsibility to the State creates is the abuse of power.

The Bible requires families to care for their own, and where this is not possible it is the duty of private individuals and groups, and of the *church* to provide for them—that is precisely the purpose of the diaconate. Unfortunately many Christians have not only surrendered the family's responsibilities to the State along with control of many other areas of "secular" life, but also an important area of the church's responsibility. The State exacts a quadruple tithe (and more) from the taxpayer in order to finance this illegitimate business. On the leftovers it now receives the church is finding it difficult to survive. This is a judgement on the church and the nation for its infidelity to the law and gospel of God.

Christians should not complain that the State provision of welfare is un-Christian in its emphasis and philosophy since the State has stepped in where the church has abdicated its God-given duty. Had the church remained faithful to its divine mission the kind of welfare provided now by the State would have been provided by the church from a Christian perspective and within the context of a Christian environment, and it would have been able to screen out welfare abuse more effectively than the State by applying Christian work ethics as a basis for its assessment of those in need.

Neither does the answer to poverty lie with Christianising the State—though of course the State should be Christian for the proper reasons. It lies rather in the provision of *Christian* charity through individual and family care for those in need, through the ministry of the church, since this is part of the church's God-given function, and in removing welfare from the orbit of the State's authority and responsibility. In the Bible the State is the ministry of public justice; when it becomes a ministry of welfare, education, employment etc. it ceases to function properly in its God-given role, and justice and mercy are both compromised. No wonder the modern State cannot cope with the breakdown of law and order in society! It is hamstrung in this area by its near total involvement in all other areas of life.

Of course in the Mosaic economy there were gleaning laws, which embodied an important principle. There are equivalent situations and circumstances in modern society where some form of gleaning could be provided, even in built-up cities and urban areas. But in the society of Old Testament Israel the civil magistrate did not run gleaning programmes. The provision of gleaning was required as a moral responsibility of those who farmed the land, but it was not policed by the State. The fact that some may have abandoned their responsibility to provide opportunities for gleaning did not mean that the State should assume the responsibility, since that would simply lead to another form of abuse. The answer to the failure of personal responsibility in any area of life is not for the State to step in and take over man's responsibilities. To expect the State to step in every time men abandon their duties is to embrace totalitarianism as the only way to organise society in a fallen world, since men continually fail in their duties. Freedom is not cheap. We can face our responsibilities and the consequences of our failures as *free* men or we can sell ourselves into slavery to the all-powerful predestinating State. To require the State to step in every time men fail is to idolise the State. It is to require the State to save mankind from the consequences of sin and failure, and this inevitably leads to the regulation of every aspect of man's life by the State. It is the rejection of God's providence, of God's predestination, and the preferment of State control over man's life. It is, in short, to ascribe the role of God to the State and thus a form of idolatry.

A social order is not defective in its obligations to the poor just because it does not require the *State* to administer charity to the poor. But the arguments for socialism, "Christian" or otherwise—whether or not its devotees use the *term* socialism—always assume that it is. But in fact the contrary is true. When the State interferes in welfare private charitable activity decreases since the funds needed and available to finance charity are plundered by the State through taxation. Furthermore, tax revenues do not simply go to relieve the same needs that individual private charities would have relieved had they received the funds. They are channelled by the State to very different ends, by no means all or even most of which are welfare for the *deserving* poor: first, there is the vast and ever growing State bureaucracy—an inefficient and blundering edifice by anyone's standards. It costs millions to finance the administration of this delinquent State welfare bureaucracy. There is no incentive for those who work for it to minimise costs of administration since, unlike private charities where workers are often genuinely motivated by compassion for those whose needs they are attending to, the State welfare business is staffed by bureaucrats working their way up their career structures, with all the usual industrial costs and inefficiencies that are involved in State-run industries. This bureaucratic tier of State management is immensely expensive to maintain. By contrast private decentralised charity is far more efficient since it does not have the massive overheads of the State bureaucracy and is able to screen out spongers without violating anyone's "rights" as a citizen.

A good example of this contrast is the difference between the USA and Britain. There are far more funds available across the whole spectrum of charitable aims in the United States than there are in Britain, with its ineffective and wasteful State welfare programme, because the population is not taxed so heavily to pay for the bureaucracy. It is also a good deal cheaper to live in the United States than it is in Britain since we pay vastly inflated prices for the basic necessities of life just for the privilege of being a party to the European economic debacle. This latter fact, which is always the case in a socialist economy, means both that it is more difficult for the poor to make ends meet than it need be and that it is more difficult for those who are not poor to help the needy since there is less discretionary income left over from their salaries after the State has taken its "share."

Second, private decentralised charity raises the distressing question of *who* the deserving poor are, and who determines who they are. Socialists hate this of course. As stated above, private charities are more effective in screening out spongers. By contrast, State provision of welfare is subject to abuse by those who can manipulate the political system in order to secure funds for individuals and groups that are not legitimate recipients of welfare in terms of biblical criteria. This includes people who get themselves into economic hardship by mismanaging and wasting their resources and who subsequently refuse to take advice about budgeting, as well as those who are on drugs or who gamble and drink their incomes away and refuse to reform their habits or seek help that will lead to reform. At the very least private charity can offer help with strings attached so that instead of merely providing funds to fuel bad habits the recipients can be obliged to receive corrective help. State welfare is notoriously inadequate in this area. Millions of pounds are spent on spongers and those who will not try to change or agree to receive help aimed at correcting their ways, as well as on those who refuse to work even though they are able-bodied—to say nothing of deliberate and organised welfare fraud.

On top of this there is the ever changing definition of poverty, which is always subject to abuse by politicians who can make political capital out of poverty and by interest groups that can milk this fact for their own ends. No doubt the term poverty will soon be applicable to those who are deprived of such essentials of modern life as video machines and computer games—television is already considered an essential of modern life, lack of which is deemed a factor in the definition of poverty.

The Bible teaches that "if anyone will not work, neither let him eat" (2 Thes. 3:10). Of course this does not apply to those who *cannot* work, whether through physical ailment or genuine lack of opportunity, but there is far less of the latter than is often thought. Often shop keepers cannot get staff because those unemployed people who are available for work can claim more State welfare as unemployed persons than they would earn at work. Such attitudes are also to be found in high unemployment areas. As a consequence a good deal of State welfare is taken up with providing for the lazy rather than for the poor. This is not only immoral but also irrational from the economic point of view, since those with shops and businesses have to pay high taxes and rates (local property and business taxes), which are used to fund welfare for such people. Such businesses often cannot pay higher wages precisely because they are taxed so heavily and have to pay high rates to fund the welfare given to those who are available for work but refuse to work because they can claim more money in welfare payments if they are unemployed than they could earn at work.

Third, it is also more difficult for a person to live off private charity because it is not anonymous and it is not something one has a right to. Private charity is therefore not only more efficient in terms of administering funds. Because it is more personal it generates a feeling of obligation and responsibility in the recipient, who is likely to work to free himself of his dependence on others more than one who is able to claim anonymous State welfare, to which he is deemed to have a right. This creates an incentive for those needing charity to work to support themselves, thereby releasing funds for more needy people. The end results of private decentralised charitable aid are therefore far more effective than those achieved by State welfare.

Fourth, people who give to private charities are more likely to make sure that the organisations receiving their funds administer them in a way that is consistent with their own beliefs. Christians give to Christian charities that offer help within a Christian environment and from a Christian perspective, and thereby proclaim the gospel in a practical way. State welfare seeks to be religiously neutral and amoral. Although this is not possible, the fact that many think that it is means that State welfare is certainly not offered on a *Christian* basis. In fact it is given on a secular humanist basis, which is *anti*-Christian.

If it is argued that the provision of charity and help for the poor cannot be left to individuals, families and the church for fear that this will be inadequate, how can it be argued that it should be left to the State, since the administration of welfare by the State fulfils society's obligation to care for the poor far less satisfactorily in terms of biblical criteria than does private charity? The fact that society does have an obligation to care for the poor, which is to be fulfilled in terms of biblical criteria, means that it cannot be left to the State. God's providence is not defective. Yet in his providence God has left helping the poor to the church, the family, and to private individuals and groups, not to the State. To argue that this is not good enough is to argue that God's providence, his government of the world, is inadequate. To abdicate one's responsibilities to the State when there is no biblical warrant is to question God's providence as well as his revealed order for society. It is to say that it is not sufficient to leave care of the poor to God's providentially appointed means, i.e. church, family and private charity, but that his providence should be supplemented, indeed replaced, by State welfare programmes. This is to place the State in the role of the church as the dispenser of God's mercy. It is the church's commission to preach the gospel, and also to heal the sick and care for the poor and needy. The apostles did not subsequently relegate the latter to the State.

§4
"Christian" Socialism

Many Christians have embraced some form of socialism, especially in Britain, where socialist ideals pervade society and have been institutionalised by both the State and the church. Nevertheless, socialism cannot be squared with Scripture. This does not necessarily imply that those who hold these views are not Christians, and someone's standing before God should not be judged simply on that basis. However, this should not obscure the fact that such views are *sinful* and that those who hold them should *repent* of their sin. This sin manifests itself on two different levels.

First, the problem in Britain is that the whole socialist way of thinking has become so ingrained in our culture that many Christians are unaware of the degree to which it colours their reading of the Bible. Nor are they aware that the Bible addresses these issues decisively and offers an obedient way to think about them. Many simply assume, because they have been told this for so long by the clergy, that the Bible does not say anything directly about social, political and economic issues, or that what it does say is only Old Testament stuff and not for the modern Christian, and therefore they imbibe the humanist alternative without giving the biblical teaching a second thought. The only Christian teaching deemed to be relevant is that the wealthy do have a responsibility to help the poor. *How* that responsibility is to be realised is not thought to be a legitimate question to ask of the Bible. Instead, it is simply assumed that the responsibility lies with the State. At the very least this apathy to biblical teaching needs to be repented of.

Secondly, however, the problem goes deeper than this for many, though not all. The psychological mainspring of socialist ideology in British society today is *envy*[6] and hatred of privilege. This is evident in the taxation rates. The rich are taxed so heavily not because this

---

[6] On the effects of envy in society see Helmut Schoek, *Envy: A Theory of Social Behaviour* (London: Secker and Warburg, 1969).

brings vital revenues into the Treasury—it brings in very little actually, and most revenues come from the middle classes, who are always the ones to suffer from both right- and left-wing taxation policies. The rich are taxed so heavily because it is thought that they are not morally entitled to have a better standard of living and therefore should not be allowed to enjoy their wealth. However much socialists preach about equality and dress it up in Christian sounding jargon the fact is that at the bottom of it many are envious of those who are better off than themselves. Therefore they vote for govern- ments that will appease their envy-ridden psyche by penalising the rich, even though this produces no real material benefit for themselves or society, and indeed even hinders economic progress for society as a whole by discouraging those with capital from investing in British industry and business.

The church of course used to preach against envy, which was considered one of the seven deadly sins. Today, however, it is unusual to hear envy preached against. Why? Because socialism has turned envy into a virtue and the clergy, by and large, have swallowed socialism lock, stock and barrel. And this is so for many Christians also. "Christian" socialists are not lily-white when it comes to their professed concern for the "poor," even though their motives may not be as black as their more consistent non-believing comrades. Envy is sin, and it motivates not a few "Christian" socialists in their economic and political views. That does not mean that they are damned. It does mean that they should repent of their sin. As for social*ism*, its consistency with the biblical teaching on compassion and care for the poor in society has yet to be demonstrated. Capitalism can certainly be abused, but it is not in *principle* unbiblical or unjust. Indeed, the prevalence of the Christian world-view in a nation will lead to the economic organisation of society on a capitalist model, as it did after the Reformation in northern Europe. Socialism, however, is unbiblical and unjust in *principle*, and no amount of good intentions will make it a fitting ideology to be embraced by those who claim the name of Christ and stand for justice and against oppression. The original authors of modern socialism were certainly not Christians but rather social revolutionaries attempting to bring about the demise of Christendom. The founders of modern socialism saw Christianity as a great evil. Are we now to believe that somehow Marx merely wanted to develop a social theory that would enable men to be good Christians and fulfil their duty to the poor properly?

To see the Jubilee provisions as a form of wealth or capital redistribution is to read an essentially modern idea back into the text of Scripture. It is the result of faulty exegesis, or perhaps a total lack of exegesis, and the desire to find biblical justification for an unbiblical and anti-Christian ideology. It is also the result of a failure to understand the effects of the outworking of socialist principles on the economic, political and historical levels. Socialist societies have never achieved the Utopian ideal of redistribution of wealth and economic prosperity that has so often been claimed for them by the theorists of socialist ideology. The economic growth and social amelioration experienced in the West since the Reformation has been the result of the economic organisation of society on the capitalist model, and this was only made possible historically with the rise of the Protestant Christian nations of northern Europe. The Reformation brought a decisive break with feudalism for those nations that embraced it. The Protestant doctrine of the priesthood of all believers and a proper understanding of the Christian's *calling* in all walks of life, the acceptance of the doctrine of the cultural mandate and the legitimacy of man's dominion over the world replaced the ignorance and superstition that had characterised so much of life in the mediaeval period. Exponential economic growth and social amelioration were present typically where the Reformation was embraced, and typically lagged behind in those nations that rejected the Reformation. The emergence of these economically strong Christian nations was the result of people turning to the Bible as the rule of man's life, the light by which society was to order its ways. Had institutions such as the Jubilee been essentially socialist wealth or capital redistribution programmes applied to all nations in every age the economic history of the West would have been a very different and considerably depressing story.

§5
The Meaning of Jubilee

But if the Jubilee was not about wealth redistribution, then what was it about? In other words, if the Jubilee was simply a date for terminating a lease why should it foreshadow the redemption that is in Christ Jesus or be the occasion for celebration of the good news of salvation (Luke 4:18–19) that the New Testament seems to suggest?

This is an important question, and it is the failure to provide an adequate explanation for the meaning of the principles set forth in the Jubilee that has led to the abuse of the Jubilee in an ad hoc fashion to justify so many kinds of wealth redistribution programmes by Christian socialists. It is to this question that we shall now turn.

The core of the Jubilee was deliverance and restoration, both in the practical concrete sense of release from debt and restoration of ancestral land, and in the eschatological sense of pointing to Jesus Christ, who sets the believer free from the burden of sin and restores him to covenantal fellowship with God, with all that that entails. The Jubilee was thus *typological* in that the release from debt and restoration of ancestral lands pointed to the work of Christ.

The Jubilee restoration of family lands established the principle of the *inviolability of inheritance*. This might incidentally bring economic advantages and benefits or it might not, since, for example, with an increasing population the economic benefits to be derived from the Jubilee would be very diluted—remember, the Jubilee land regulations applied only to rural land, not city land and buildings, and were limited to Israel, a relatively small geographical area. Moreover, those who had their ancestral lands returned to them might also have to release land to other families. Any advantage to be gained from the Jubilee might be cancelled out. In fact, as we have already seen, some might lose out to a considerable extent, even though poor.

There are two aspects to this inheritance law: (1) the *principle* of inviolability of inheritance, and (2) the *specific conditions* under which this principle was enacted in Israel. Clearly, the specific conditions given in the law are limited to Israel. Since the Jubilee did not affect land acquired by the Hebrews outside Israel, indeed not even city land within Israel, there is no basis for the application of these lease restrictions to modern society. That is to say, the *specific* provisions of the Jubilee land-lease laws had a limited application even to the people of Israel and even in the land of Israel itself. Unlike the law generally, the Jubilee land laws did not address Gentile nations nor are the Gentiles ever considered guilty of breaking them. This point is not made on the basis of some dispensational hermeneutic, but simply on the basis of a consistent reading of the Mosaic code itself.

The general principle however, i.e. inviolability of inheritance, remains applicable, just as the general principle of the sacrificial law— that there is no remission of sin without the shedding of blood— remains in force even though the old covenant sacrificial rituals themselves are no longer practised. The expropriation of legitimate inheritance by the State is thus outlawed. All legitimate taxes, e.g. tithes, in the Bible are levied on *increase*, not property *per se* or inheritance. Over and above this, however, there is an eschatological doctrine of inheritance involved here, and it is this that is of primary importance for the typological nature of the Jubilee inheritance law. The eschatological doctrine of inheritance is a much neglected theological concept; possibly it has never been fully and properly developed by Christian theologians. It is closely linked with the doctrine of adoption, which is also a much neglected doctrine—the Westminster Confession of Faith is untypical in including a chapter on adoption.

As joint-heirs and members of the family of God by adoption Christians have an inheritance that is imperishable. Under the old covenant this inheritance was set forth typologically in the land of Israel. The Jubilee restoration of ancestral lands every fifty years pointed to the fact that this inheritance is inalienable. The people of Israel were under the tutelage of this kind of typology, as a child who is under age is under a tutor, until the appointed time when God sent forth his Son to redeem his people. Now, however, in Christ the believer has come of age and thus enters into his inheritance (Gal. 4:1–5). As Christians the inheritance that the Jubilee typology pointed to is ours. Just as we fully partake of the benefits of Christ's atonement and no longer look to the sacrifice of bulls and goats, so also we look to the inheritance that is ours in Christ and not to the land of Israel. We fully partake of Christ's inheritance as joint-heirs with him. We are not under the types that set this forth, the Jubilee, but rather experience the actual fulfillment of what the Jubilee pointed to: salvation in Christ and joint-heirship with him. Since it is the whole earth that the Father has given to the Son as his inheritance (Ps. 2; 37:9; 115:16; Mt. 5:5; Rom. 8:15–17), it is the whole earth that believers inherit as members of the family of God by adoption through faith in Christ. With the coming of Christ and Pentecost the gospel is preached to the whole world, Gentile as well as Jew, and the promises and blessings of the covenant are made available for all nations. The whole earth is to be conquered for Christ through the preaching of the gospel.

The specific provisions of the Jubilee land law related to Israel as the chosen nation under the tutelage of types. These specific provisions are, therefore, like all typological law, of limited duration.

They function until what they foreshadowed comes. They cease to be observed in the same way once Christ has come. But, just like typological atonement law relating to the sacrifice of bulls and goats, the general principle underpinning the Jubilee typology is permanently put into force by the coming of the one whom it foreshadowed. Christ's coming necessitates both that the specific provisions relating to Israel as a nation under the tutelage of types cease and that the general principles underpinning them are permanently enforced. For example, Christ's coming brought the sacrifice of bulls and goats to an end because he made a perfect sacrifice of permanent validity for all time. But the fact that he came and made a blood sacrifice for sin established permanently the principle underpinning the old covenant sacrifices, namely that without the shedding of blood there can be no forgiveness.

Thus, although the general principles underpinning typological law continue, the specific regulations cease. At the destruction of Jerusalem in A.D. 70 the nation of Israel as a geo-political power ended, and along with this the specific provisions of the Jubilee land law came to an end also. The body of Christ, as the household of God by adoption through faith in Christ, inherits the benefits and privileges of Israel. The general principles of the Jubilee law continue however. Just as the necessity of an atonement for sin continues so also the general principle underpinning Jubilee land law, i.e. the inviolability of inheritance, continues, but now it is transformed by the coming of Christ.

What does this mean? It means that the earth belongs to the rightful heirs, to those who through faith in Christ and obedience to his word shall rule over it to the glory of God by bringing all things under the dominion of the Lord Jesus Christ. Christ taught this: "Blessed are the meek: for they shall inherit the *earth*" (Mt. 5:5); "Go ye therefore, and teach all nations, baptising them in the name of the Father, and of the Son, and of the Holy Ghost: Teaching them to observe all things whatsoever I have commanded you" (Mt. 28:19–20). The Jubilee land provisions taught that the land belongs to God and that his people cannot be disinherited. The typology of the Jubilee pointed to the fact that the whole earth belongs to God and has been given to Christ as his inheritance and to all those who by faith look to him for salvation, those who are members of God's family by adoption. This fact became a historical reality with the coming of Christ. All power and authority in heaven and on earth has been given to Christ and he is now claiming his inheritance through the preaching of the gospel (Mt. 28:18–20). Christ cannot be disinherited, nor can his people: "Of the increase of his government and peace there shall be no end" (Is. 9:7). The earth must be possessed and subdued by the rightful heirs. God will accomplish this for his own glory: "The zeal of the Lord of hosts will perform this" (Is. 9:20).

The principle underpinning the Jubilee land provisions is still in operation, but not in the way that it was under the specific provisions of the typological law. The principle of inviolability of inheritance means that the State has no authority to expropriate the wealth of the people by means of inheritance taxes. It may only levy taxes on the increase. The earth belongs to Christ and to those who are adopted into the family of God through faith in Christ and who are consequently joint-heirs with Christ (Mt. 5:5, Rom. 8:16–17). For the State to expropriate this inheritance, which though it is an eschatological promise is also a tangible and real inheritance of the physical earth in history (cf. Ps 115:16), is sacrilege. The State may only levy taxes according to principles laid down in God's law, which restricts taxation by the State at the most to a second tithe on the increase.

Conclusion

The Jubilee land law represented the *passing on* of a specific form of wealth, namely *inheritance*, by what is in the Bible the fundamental economic unit in society and the provider of the welfare and education of its members: the family. As the basic economic unit in society it is the duty of the *family*, not the State, to provide welfare, education and health care for its members. When the State expropriates the wealth of the family through inheritance tax, death duties etc. it makes it impossible for the family to do this. Hence for Christians to use the Jubilee as a rationale for advocating State-enforced wealth redistribution programmes is to stand the Jubilee on its head, to contradict and overturn the very purpose for which it was given. The requirement that the people of Israel were to help those less fortunate than themselves was to be put into force through the family's stewardship of its resources and also to some extent through the church's ministry to the poor. This pattern for social order is repeated in the New Testament (1 Tim. 5:3–16). The Jubilee land law guaranteed the passing on of inheritance to the basic economic unit of society: the family. It was the responsibility of the family then to provide care for the less fortunate and the poor, and also the responsibility of the church—which is funded by the family through the tithe—where the poor have no family or where the family is not able to provide for its own. For the State to expropriate a family's inheritance by means of inheritance taxes and death duties or by means of any other form of wealth redistribution is therefore theft and the overturning of the general principle underpinning the Jubilee land law.

The eschatological doctrine of inheritance, typified by the Jubilee, means the joint-heirship of the whole earth by those who are adopted members of God's family through faith in Christ. The earth belongs to Christ and to his people. It may not be expropriated by the State or by heathen nations, and moreover, the whole earth must submit to this fact: "Be wise now therefore, O ye kings; be instructed, ye judges of the earth. Kiss the Son, lest he be angry, and ye perish from the way, when his wrath is kindled but a little. Blessed are all they that put their trust in him" (Ps. 2:10–12 cf. Ps. 149).

SOCIAL   REGENERATION
AND   POLITICAL   IDOLATRY

THE Puritans who emigrated to New England in the early seventeenth century did so, according to John Winthrop in his "A Model of Christian Charity" speech on board the *Arbella*, to "seek out a place to live and associate under a due form of government both civil and ecclesiastical."[1] Their purpose was "to improve our lives to do more service to the Lord and to comfort and increase the body of Christ of which we are members, so that ourselves and our posterity may be better preserved from the common corruptions of this evil world in order to serve the Lord and work out our salvation under the power and purity of his holy ordinances."[2] They saw their experiment in the wilderness as the setting up of a city on a hill, an example of a people who in all areas of life and on all levels of society looked to God and his word as the governing principle of life, and to the religion it set forth as the unifying principle in society.

This was the attempt to work out in practice the Scriptural injunction to "Let your light so shine before men, that they may see your good works, and glorify your Father which is in heaven" (Mt. 5:16), and is the duty of all Christian peoples and nations. Of course, such a society is a beacon on a hill only to the extent that it does radiate, in all its institutions and in all aspects of its life, that light of God's word without which both the individual and society must continually grope in darkness and ignorance, a condition that inevitably leads to the depth of depravity and debauchery. Such was the way of life that characterised the ancient world, a way of life that the emerging Christian church showed to be so degraded by the brilliance of its light, transforming as it did both individual lives and societies. Such also is the way of life that is, sadly, beginning

[1] John Winthrop, "A Model of Christian Charity" in *1493–1754: a New World*, Vol. I of *The Annals of America*, ed. Mortimer J. Adler (Chicago: Encyclopaedia Britannica, 1968, 18 vols), p. 114, cited in Terril Irwin Elniff, *The Guise of Every Graceless Heart: Human Autonomy in Puritan Thought and Experience* (Vallecito, California: Ross House Books, 1981), p. 5.   [2] *Ibid.*

to characterise Western society. This is because the Christian religion has been cast aside and, as a consequence, public institutions and private lives have been stripped of those life-giving principles that made the Protestant nations the greatest force for progress and social amelioration in human history.

To the extent that this beacon on a hill was doused by human corruption, sin and disobedience, it could not claim to be truly representing and manifesting the pure pattern set forth in God's word of the covenanted society to which all men and societies must aspire to conform. And doubtless no society in history will manifest that purity in its entirety. Hence no society can claim to be the kingdom of God on earth. Nevertheless, all societies must strive to manifest the kingdom of God, and they must strive to do so in their public institutions no less than individual believers must strive to do so in their personal lives. The public institutions of society must express the corporate faith that unites the nation.

This corporate faith must express itself throughout the whole fabric of human society, and it is the calling of the Christian to pursue and work for such a reformation of church and society. As to the *means* to be employed in the pursuit of this purpose, we find ourselves in a situation in which the idolatry of political power and political institutions by modern society—the constant desire for government intervention and the provision of cradle to grave welfare by the State—so easily overwhelms the minds of even Christians and influences their attempts to articulate a *Christian* understanding of social regeneration, that anyone seeking to apply the biblical pattern for the reformation of society, and particularly reformation of its public institutions, must continually run the gauntlet of the church as well as the non-believing world. Since the Enlightenment even the Reformed churches have, by and large, swallowed this political camel and now strain at the gnat of reforming society according to God's word, an ideal that their oft praised but, at least when it comes to social issues, seldom listened-to Puritan forefathers would have recognised as the inescapable duty of all Christian peoples.

Modern humanism sees the State, as the embodiment of the idea of human society, as the agency that must effect social transformation. It is the idolatry of the church in our age that this apostate principle is accepted almost without question by Christians. The idea that the *individual* primarily bears the responsibility to fulfil his God-given and biblically-defined duty to affect society by the way he thinks and lives in all aspects of his life, through his family, church, vocation etc. is seldom voiced in our politically overactive society. Of course, political institutions must be reformed according to God's word also, by those who are called to office and by the electorate in their selection of candidates for office. And for those who are called to public office this involves limiting the role and power of civil government so that its actions fall within the boundaries set forth in God's word. This will take the Christian politician down a very different road from that of his non-believing colleague. For the secular humanist there is no power or authority higher than man. The State, as the ultimate human authority, must become the all powerful predestinating agent that plans, regulates and controls man's life according to the good it deems to be in society's best interests to pursue. If there is need of reformation and transformation in society, it is the State that must plan and accomplish it.

But this leaves God and his will for man totally out of the picture. God's revealed will as set down in his word, the Bible, ceases to be "the most valuable thing that this world affords." Wisdom now comes not from God but from man. Law becomes an expression of man's desires and will, not God's absolute justice.[3] As the ultimate authority in society the State gives meaning and purpose to society and to the nation, and thus if there is to be social change or regeneration it must be initiated by the State and carried out according to State decrees and planning. For the godless humanist society the State is the origin of, agent in, and reference point for all social change and regeneration, since it is the guardian of society's good and the source of social well-being. In such a society the State is required by the people to fulfil, and assumes the authority and power to fulfil, all those aspirations of prosperity, economic security and well-being that in the Christian society one looks to God for. This is simply to say that for the secular humanist society the State assumes all the functions and responsibilities that in the Bible are attributed to God. The State becomes, by popular consent, self-consciously or unselfconsciously, the god to which society attributes ultimate power and authority.

This philosophy can be observed being worked out in practical terms in many ways and on many levels in British society. For example, the Department of Trade and Industry takes upon itself

---

[3] See Stephen C. Perks, *Christianity and Law: An Enquiry into the Influence of Christianity on the Development of English Common Law* (Whitby: Avant Books, 1993).

the initiative to stimulate and promote economic regeneration in inner cities and other economically "deprived" areas by means of tax-incentives and government grants to businesses moving into these areas. It is automatically assumed by many, including Christians, that the State's role in this kind of social regeneration is legitimate and even necessary without further consideration.

Yet the Bible nowhere ascribes such a role to the State and most emphatically ascribes it to God (Dt. 28). For the Christian, social amelioration is not achieved by empowering the State to raise taxes that can be redistributed to the poor. Rather it is the fruit of a nation's obedience to God's law. This means that the true nature of these social ills is not *economic*, as we are constantly being told by politicians and economists, but *ethical*. They are the result of *moral* failure, the abandonment of moral principles and rules of behaviour that God has promised will guard and protect a society's freedom and prosperity. When society turns its back on these Christian principles and laws it invokes the Creator's wrath and brings upon itself all those political and economic ills that the Bible affirms are the lot of the godless society.

The humanist State's answer to this situation amounts to throwing public money at spiritual and social problems that can only be remedied by obedience to God's word. This is a form of mammonism. Indeed, at the end of the day the only power that the State has to affect the economy for good outside its biblically defined role as a ministry of public justice is the power of money (and stolen money at that since from the biblical point of view the vast majority of taxes are raised illegitimately). This is an inappropriate answer to a misconceived problem that can only end in more of what it is ostensibly designed to eradicate. But godless men who consider biblical morality to be obsolete impute to money all the power and authority that the Bible ascribes to God. Money has become their god to the ruin of their souls and the ruin of society (1 Tim. 6:10). But unlike the God of the Scriptures, whose yoke is easy and whose burden is light, the yoke of the humanist State is a heavy yoke that will crush its people, since it can finance its megalomania only by taxing and controlling its citizens totally. The modern socialist pre-destinating State has in a very real sense institutionalised mammon as man's ultimate good, since the redistribution of wealth and the creation of money is seen as the answer to all the problems and social ills that blight the nation.

For the Christian, however, the agent of social transformation and regeneration is not the State. The State has a role to play in the proper ordering of society for sure; but that role is defined biblically as a ministry of public justice, an earthly representative of God's justice. It has the obligation to enforce those laws that God has given it the authority and power to uphold. Its authority extends thus far and no further, and for the State to extend its power further than that biblically defined role is tyranny and the usurpation of God's authority over men. For the State to assume the role of social regenerator is to play god. It is rebellion against the one who alone can regenerate society and whose word must govern all aspects of society, including the role of civil government and the boundaries of its authority.

Christians must learn from God's word that they have a duty to pursue godliness in all areas of life, and to do so in a way that conforms to God's revealed pattern for man's life. This includes the duty to develop and manage public institutions in accordance with God's word. Not only must we pursue scriptural *goals*; we must use *means* to achieve those goals that are in conformity with God's revealed will for man as set forth in the Christian Scriptures. There may be many very great evils in society, but the magistrate may only act to prosecute those who commit *crimes*, i.e. transgressions of God's law that Scripture places within the orbit of the magistrate's authority. And he *must* act to prosecute those who break the laws that God has placed within his sphere of authority.[4] When the magistrate does not act in this biblically defined way justice is aborted and crime— viz wrongdoing that the magistrate has a responsibility under God's law to punish—is institutionalised by the very authority whose duty it is to see that it is rooted out. At the same time areas of responsibility that lie totally outside the magistrate's sphere of authority in terms of God's word are hijacked by the apostate State, resulting in oppression. Society is then turned upside down: justice is called injustice and men are denied their freedom under God. Yet crime goes unpunished, even rewarded. As an example of the perverse logic of this apostasy we may cite the fact that in most Western countries one may murder one's unborn children with impunity and yet meet with insuperable problems created by State bureaucrats and regulators if one tries to give them a Christian education by home-

---

[4] On the Christian doctrine of the State, its function, power and jurisdiction, see Stephen C. Perks, *A Defence of the Christian State* (Taunton: Kuyper Foundation, 1998).

schooling them. In such a society men are free to sin, but not free to be righteous. God's word requires that men be free to be righteous and hence free to give their children a Christian education without fear of oppression. It also denies man the freedom to commit crimes. This is precisely the meaning of Rom. 13:1–6. Yet modern Western society is called enlightened and the pattern set forth in God's word ancient and barbarous.

That Christians should have fallen pray to this political idolatry is particularly grievous since it is only through their witness, their testimony to the truth and their willingness to work for reform according to God's word that society can be transformed according to the pattern of social order revealed in Scripture. God, who is the agent of true social transformation, works through his church, the body of Christ on earth, in bringing the kingdoms of this world under the rule of his Son and heir. When the church herself is under the spell of idolatry how can the nation escape the judgement of God? It cannot. In Britain approximately 200,000 unborn infants are murdered every year, and the Bible tells us that "blood it defileth the land: and the land cannot be cleansed of the blood that is shed therein, but by the blood of him that shed it" (Num. 35:33). The Bible also tells us that "judgement must begin at the house of God: and if it first begin at us, what shall the end be of them that obey not the gospel of God" (1 Pet. 4:17).

It is important that Christians should work for the reform of civil government in order that such crimes might be proscribed and punished. It is equally important that the civil government should be denied the authority to use its power in any way that takes it beyond its biblically defined role as a ministry of public justice and into areas of individual or corporate life for which God has instituted alternative forms of government—e.g. education and welfare, which in the Bible are entrusted to the family and the church. The illegitimate exercise of State power in such areas always leads to injustice and tyranny. This requires at the same time, of course, that those individuals and institutions to whom God has committed the tasks of education and welfare should once again fulfil their responsibilities. The work of social transformation is a necessary task that every Christian should take seriously in an apostate society. But it must be carried out by God's instituted means. This is where men have the duty to apply God's word to their individual callings, to their families and to their churches. In this process the role of the State is severely limited by God's word, which requires individuals, families and churches to shoulder their own responsibilities. The role of the State is almost entirely negative, namely, to create the conditions of peace and order under which individuals, families and churches are able to fulfil the positive role that God has ordained for them. It is these institutions of family and church along with the individual that are primarily responsible for the task of influencing society for good by promoting the spiritual well-being, economic growth and social amelioration of society. The State's role under God's law is that of punishing the wrongdoer and securing for the law-abiding citizen the freedom to pursue his calling before God.

When Christians do speak of the necessity of reforming society according to the word of God they are sometimes misunderstood to mean that the *State* should set about the task. While it is certainly true that the State should be reformed according to God's word the notion that the State should reform society generally is not Christian. Rather, individuals, families, churches, businesses etc. should reform *themselves* according to God's word. The biblical model for society sets forth the principle of limited authority within each God-ordained institution and sphere of life. The State, therefore, should only act to re-establish justice when crime has been committed. This point, however, has often been lost on Christians who have come to view the State in the same idolatrous way that the majority of non-believers view it. In the highly politicised culture of modern society many cannot conceive of the transformation of society by any means other than that of State planning and control, and this is a political idolatry in terms of which everyone who speaks of social change is judged. Most people, including perhaps the majority of Christians, simply never consider that there is an alternative way to go about it.

Christians must reject this political idolatry. In its place the biblical emphasis on the necessity of *self*-government and transformation of society by the individual, the family and the church must be revived. Only as individuals, families and churches learn to govern themselves according to God's word and teach this godly self-discipline to their children will society be able to free itself from the tyranny and oppression of totalitarian government, because people who are unable to govern themselves according to God's word are, for the same reasons, unable to elect a civil government that will govern in its own sphere according to God's word.

The nation must be weaned off its dependence on the State for welfare and economic prosperity. This process must begin with the development of the biblical ethic of self-government under God's law, the strengthening of the welfare institutions of the family and the church and the safeguarding of their independence from government control. Only as individuals, families and churches begin to fulfil their God-given roles in society according to God's word shall we begin to see the limiting of the State to its proper function as a ministry of public justice. The process of social transformation must begin in the individual believer and go on to manifest itself in all aspects of his life—in the family, church, business etc. and, as a limited part of the whole of life, in the political sphere also. To expect the State to accomplish all of this by political fiat is idolatry, the abandonment of personal responsibility under God and the enthroning of the Molech State as man's sovereign, the one to whom he must look for his ultimate good and well-being. The Bible rejects such a role for the State. It is the usurpation of God's authority and the substitution of political totalitarianism for the biblical covenantalism in which each God-ordained institution—family, church, civil government—receives a mandate from God's word to perform specific roles in society and is delegated limited authority to pursue that mandate according to God's law.

To seek government intervention for all the ills that have arisen in society because men have refused to shoulder their God-given responsibilities is the perverse characteristic of a society that looks only to political idols for deliverance from the problems and difficulties of life. It is the denial of the total jurisdiction of the sovereign God of Scripture and his law over the nation's life and institutions. Such a society is in rebellion against the biblically defined social order set forth in God's word. While the Christian must, if he is to be faithful to the word of God, maintain the necessity of the God-ordained and scripturally defined role of the magistrate as a minister of public justice—i.e. as a protector of the innocent and a terror to the evildoer (Rom 13:1–6)—he must never fall into the trap of looking to the State to cure all those social ills that God alone can and does promise to eradicate by his chosen means (institutional or otherwise) in the covenantally faithful community. To do so is political Messianism, not Christianity. The Christian must seek instead to work out his salvation in all areas of life, in his private, family, church, social and political life, and seek to reform all these according to God's word. He must pursue faithfully the righteousness of God before all else and seek to bring the whole of life under the covenant of redemptive grace that God has established with his people in Jesus Christ. This is the biblical antidote to the political idolatry that is now so rampant in the nation. As the Christian pursues this goal he can be confident that God will bless his faithful endeavours (Is. 65:23–24); and the society that seeks to be bound together in such a task and to manifest that way of life in its institutions as a corporate expression of its faith in the triune God of Scripture can be confident that God will make it a city on a hill, a light to the nations, where men will come and learn the law of God and from which the light of the gospel will be shed abroad.

This is no idle dream. It has been the reality of Western nations in times past—never perfectly of course. It has already been said that no Western nation can claim to be or to have been the kingdom of God on earth. But we can say that in the Protestant nations of the past the purposes of God for mankind and for human *society* have been manifested in such a way that the promises of Psalm 149 have become a reality in their history.

To deny the possibility of manifesting the kingdom of God at the national level, however imperfectly, is to deny the possibility of progress in the fullest sense of the term and to close one's eyes to the facts of Christian history over the past two millennia. To abandon the goal of transforming society according to the word of God through the working out of our salvation in all areas of life is not only to run away from the work of God in history, it is to deny to our children the freedom that was purchased for them by the blood of Christ and confirmed in the blood of countless martyrs throughout the history of the nation. It is, in short, the denial of a glorious future for the sake of a little ease in the present. It is cowardice in the face of the enemy.

The rebuilding of the nation in terms of the Christian faith will not be easy. We can expect tribulation in this life. But this is the task to which we are called as the people of God and joint-heirs with his Son (Mt. 28:19–20).

APPENDIX E

WEALTH, POVERTY AND
THE RICH YOUNG RULER

THE incident of the rich young ruler who came running to Jesus to ask what he must do to obtain eternal life (Mt. 19:16–26, cf. Mark 10:17–27, Luke 18:18–27; see also Dt. 15:4–6) is commonly understood to teach how dangerous great wealth is to the soul, and how those who possess great wealth are less likely to understand their need for a saviour. It is argued that the comfort and ease that riches bring blunt one's awareness to the human condition and hence one's awareness of man's plight before God and the need for sin to be dealt with in Christ if man is to be reconciled with God. There is, consequently, in the minds of many Christians a good deal of suspicion of those who possess great riches and also profess faith in Christ. This incident of the rich young ruler is seen as validating this kind of suspicion and is in turn usually explained primarily in terms of the dangers of wealth in respect of one's eternal condition. I believe this is a misconception. This chapter will attempt to show that the story of the rich young ruler is not primarily about the dangers of wealth and that to bring this modern perspective to this text and interpret the incident in terms of it is to misuse Scripture in such a way that the original point of the story is lost. The story is thus used wrongly to support the idea of the virtue of poverty, which, in its modern form, is basically a romantic notion foreign to the Bible.[1] On the contrary, what the Bible here teaches is that those who were deemed the most likely to obtain eternal life in terms

[1] The rejection of wealth as inherently evil and the idolising of poverty as a virtue in itself has, of course, had a long history in Christendom. It was a common feature of the many heretical sects that flourished in the Middle Ages as well as being common in the early period of various monastic orders such as the Franciscans. But it has not usually been considered an essential mark of orthodoxy. Even the Franciscan doctrine of poverty was eventually condemned by Pope John XXII, who declared the assertion of Christ's absolute poverty heretical, thereby destroying the basis of the Franciscan ideal. In some respects, given the unorthodox bent of much of modern Christianity, the prominence of this kind of thinking in the modern church is merely the most recent manifestation of this heretical influence (a corresponding

of the understanding of the disciples were unable to obtain it as the result of their own human achievements, and further, that those who were considered most likely to inherit the kingdom of God were the morally upright and *wealthy*, since their wealth was considered a blessing from God and a form of divine approbation of their moral rectitude. The point of the story is to impress upon the disciples that if this rich young ruler could not count on receiving an eternal reward for his righteousness—for he was a righteous man, i.e. an upright and God-fearing man, otherwise he would not have come to Jesus and asked the question—then no one could on the basis of mere morality and self-righteousness, least of all the disciples, among whom were represented some of the worst elements of society—e.g. tax collectors, zealots. And indeed this lesson was brought home to the disciples, since they are told that what is impossible with men is possible with God. In other words, it is only by means of the righteousness of God through faith in Jesus Christ that anyone is able to enter into eternal life (Rom. 3:22).

It is important, therefore, if we are to understand the text properly, that we appreciate the biblical teaching on wealth and examine also the kind of perception that the disciples were likely to have had on the question of wealth and riches in relation to one's standing with God. The purpose of the story is to show that their perception was wrong. But this perception of the issue was radically different from the modern perspective, which sees *poverty* rather than wealth as a testimony of one's virtue.

§1

Some Preliminary Observations

Before looking more closely at the biblical teaching on wealth as it is represented in this story, however, we should observe, first, that however one views this incident it is undeniably true that simply

---

influence in much of the modern church, again shared with many mediaeval heretical sects, is millennarianism in its various forms). According to Gordon Leff "the veneration of poverty, in addition to being one of the hallmarks of most heretical movements, provided them with what may be called an historicism: an historical justification of their opposition to the church" (G. Leff, *Heresy in the Later Middle Ages* [Manchester University Press, 1967], Vol. I, p. 9; see also *ibid.*, pp. 51–255. See also Norman Cohn, *The Pursuit of the Millennium* [London: Temple Smith, (1957) 1970], *passim*).

keeping the commandments is not sufficient if one is to enter into eternal life. A better understanding of the biblical teaching on wealth and of the perspective of the disciples will not alter this fact, nor will it alter the fact that this rich young ruler was not prepared to sacrifice all he had for Christ, and this showed clearly his idolatry of riches. All this is granted, and I shall not gainsay. But these points have been made many time before and I shall not dwell on them. This is not meant to imply that these considerations are unimportant; far from it, they are essential points of the biblical doctrine of salvation and necessary warnings against the idolatry of riches. However, these are not the only points relevant to a proper understanding of the text and they are not the primary focus of what is under consideration here. Instead I shall look at this incident in terms of the biblical teaching on wealth and from the perspective of the disciples themselves and the view of wealth that was contemporary with their generation, which formed the backdrop to their understanding of the issues involved. This should help us to avoid reading modern ideology into the text, and thereby misunderstanding its true meaning.

Secondly, although Christ shows us that keeping the commandments is not sufficient if one is to inherit eternal life, neither does he teach that keeping the commandments is not necessary. The fact that obedience to God's law cannot secure eternal life is not an argument for not being obedient, and Christ does not here relax the necessity of keeping the commandments. Obedience to God's law is still required by Christ: "if thou wilt enter into life, keep the commandments" he says. True, this does not save men from their sins (i.e. justify them before God), but it is necessary. Christ says "except your righteousness shall *exceed* the righteousness of the scribes and Pharisees, ye shall in no case enter into the kingdom of heaven" (Mt. 5:20). The pursuit of godliness through obedience to God's law is not set aside by Christ. This is because the doctrine of salvation by faith alone implies also the doctrine of sanctification, just as does the doctrine of election or predestination (Eph. 1:4). The one is impossible without the other (Rom. 8:29–30). It is only those who are sanctified from sin and who seek after righteousness in terms of the requirements of God's law (Rev. 12:17) that are shown in the end to be chosen in Christ before the foundation of the world and therefore saved by grace through faith alone without the works of the law. Therefore, granted that keeping the commandments does not save us, neither are we saved without works.

We must look now at this incident and attempt to understand what prompted the disciples to ask the question "Who then can be saved?" since in our own culture this question would not have been asked. Our modern world-view would have had no difficulty with the idea that the rich cannot enter into eternal life. It is assumed as an axiomatic truth that, if anything, riches *dis*qualify one from obtaining eternal life. The question would not have been raised today. We must, therefore, attempt to understand the incident in context. Only then shall we be in a position to understand what the Scripture teaches; and only then shall we be able to apply it to ourselves and to our own culture and understand what it is saying to us. In doing so, however, we must look not only at the context of Scripture itself, but examine the preconceptions that we ourselves bring to Scripture, since we must divest ourselves of these preconceptions and adopt the preconceptions of Scripture if we are to understand Scripture aright.

§2
The Biblical Background to the Incident

(a) *The biblical teaching on wealth and poverty*

Deuteronomy 15:4–6 teaches that wealth and prosperity are the norm for a covenantally faithful community. This teaching is further spelt out in detail in the Scriptures (cf. Dt. 28). The obedient society will be a prosperous society, a wealthy society in every way. And it is certainly no sin to aim to better one's economic conditions and increase one's wealth and prosperity provided this is done in a lawful way. The Westminster Shorter Catechism states: "The eighth commandment requireth the lawful procuring and furthering the wealth and outward estate of ourselves and others." We are also told in Scripture that the Lord delights in the prosperity of his servants (Ps. 35:27). But this teaching needs to be understood in the light of other biblical teachings that set it in its proper context.

First, the pursuit of wealth is not to be our *primary* goal in life. Our first purpose is to serve God and glorify him. Of course, seeking our own prosperity is quite consistent with this, but it must not come before it. Thus, Christ teaches: "seek ye first the kingdom of God, and his righteousness [or *justice*, which is what the word means]; and all these things shall be added unto you" (Mt. 6:33). We are called first and foremost to be faithful, not successful.

Second, faithfulness, as Scripture teaches, leads to blessing and prosperity, both in the spiritual and material sense: "there shall be no poor among you; for the Lord shall greatly bless thee in the land which the Lord thy God giveth thee for an inheritance to possess it: *Only if thou carefully hearken unto the voice of the Lord thy God, to observe to do all these commandments which I command thee this day*" (Dt. 15:4–5). The promise of blessing and prosperity is conditional upon the covenant faithfulness of God's people. If we are faithful success is a blessing for which we can thank God with a good conscience.

Third, wealth in Scripture does not mean simply material possessions, property and personal chattels, as it does in modern Western society. Children, for instance, were considered a form of wealth, for so they are (cf. Ps. 127:3–5). In some cultures still children are considered a superior form of wealth to material possessions, and indeed they are. Western society is very poor in this respect, since many children are literally thrown down the drain in the abortion clinics. This is not only murder, it is the despising of God's blessing; it is an anti-life mentality that is tantamount to spitting in the face of God. Children are wealth, and the Hebrews were promised that if they were faithful their women would not miscarry, nor their animals, and they would be a fertile people living in a fertile land flowing with milk and honey. Fertility was a basic blessing that produced wealth in the form of children, offspring of animals and abundance of crops. The lack of it was a curse. Of course, in a primitive agrarian society fertility must be considered the most important form of blessing without which there would be no kind of wealth whatsoever. And doubtless sociologists would explain the significance of fertility in the Bible simply in such terms. I do not believe, however, that the importance of fertility in Scripture, especially human fertility, can be explained simply in terms of the necessities of a primitive agrarian society. The Bible is a pro-life book because its author is pro-life. Mankind has been commanded to multiply and fill the earth not merely out of necessity for the preservation of the species, but because the God we serve delights in the *creation* of *life*, and human beings are created in his image and are to extend his kingdom over the face of the earth. Life is the greatest form of wealth, and Christ came that we might have life more abundantly (Jn 10:10).

Fourth, the eradication of poverty is part of the cultural mandate given to mankind and the Great Commission given by Christ to his disciples (Gen. 1:28; Mt. 28:18–20). And this has been demonstrated by Christians throughout history. Wherever the Christian faith has gone it has been a force for good in lifting people out of the poverty and misery that idolatry and disbelief inevitably bring upon mankind. It is the Christian nations that have brought relief and medicine to the heathen Third World. The eradication of poverty is an aspect of the church's dominion in Christ.

Fifth, this promise of prosperity to the faithful is not a promise to particular individuals that obedience to the commandments will lead automatically to their being able to make a personal fortune and retire at the age of thirty. To treat this promise as an individual formula for financial success is to misunderstand it and abuse it. God is not a slot machine to be worked over. This promise is a *culturally conditioned* promise. It is a covenant promise made to a covenantally faithful *community* or *nation*. What has been said here should not be understood as condoning or promoting the so-called "health and wealth" gospel that has become popular in some churches. This notion is at best a simplistic misconception of what the Bible teaches about the blessings of faithfulness. To read this ideology into Scripture is to assume a kind of individualism that is foreign to Scripture and to the covenantalism of Scripture. This kind of individualism is a significant departure from the covenantalism of the Bible. The church has, to a great extent, lost touch with the cultural dimension of the faith. Because of this many people misinterpret biblical doctrines that have an important bearing on social and cultural issues. As a consequence, the beliefs they hold are often an ugly caricature of what Scripture teaches.[2] The promise of prosperity held out in the Bible has reference to the long-term social and economic progress reaped

[2] It is perhaps worth noting here that the "poorer than thou" mentality of many Christians who seem to view poverty as a virtue is simply the mirror image of the "health and wealth" gospel, and based on the same inadequate reading of Scripture. Failure to take cultural factors into consideration when assessing the biblical teaching on the blessings of wealth must lead either to the "health and wealth" doctrine or to the "poverty is a virtue" mentality, since Scripture is decontextualised and forced into an individualist framework that distorts its meaning. Given such a hermeneutic, one must conclude either that the Deuteronomic teaching means that God will always and under any conditions bless his people with health and wealth, or that the warnings of the prophets against ill-gotten wealth mean that wealth as such is evil and hence that poverty is the only human condition consistent with true spirituality. A good example of this false dichotomy is afforded by James Barr, a fundamentalist liberal, who claims that "The ethical judgement and ethos of many parts of the Old Testament contains a strong eudaemonistic element, if we may so call it, a stress in the family and its cohesion, and on the wealth and prosperity with which great

by a *society* that orders its life by the light of God's word. The prosperity promised to the faithful in Deuteronomy is a social phenomenon (cf. 2 Chron. 24:20). It is a promise to societies and nations that are in covenant with God.

Historically this has become evident in the Western world, which has broadly—though not perfectly—been built on Christian foundations. The poorest of people in the West are wealthier than many in the Third World. Western societies have a very high standard of living, and this is because God has blessed and prospered Christian nations.

The promise of prosperity in Dt. 15:4–6 and 28:1–14 should not be understood in an individualistic way since its terms of reference, its implications and the demands it makes for its fulfillment, are

---

men like Abraham and Job are rewarded. In Jesus' teaching these considerations are greatly minimized. The family is a threat to one's obedience to God, one has to be ready to drop one's obligations to it, rewards are not to be expected in this world, riches are a danger and a temptation, and the obedient must expect suffering, persecution and loss . . . [I]it seems simply impossible to suppose that in his basic ethical values Jesus is following the guidance of the main currents of the Old Testament" (*Holy Scripture: Canon, Authority, Criticism* [Oxford: The Clarendon Press, 1983], p. 17). Both the "poverty is a virtue" and the "health and wealth" interpretations falter at the same point, the societal or cultural dimension of life, but lead to diametrically opposite viewpoints. This is because from a purely individualist perspective we are faced in Scripture with two seemingly contradictory teachings. On the one hand we are confronted by the promises in Deuteronomy that God will bless his people if they are faithful. But on the other hand we have the statements in the Prophets and Wisdom literature lamenting the fact that the righteous struggle in poverty and experience persecution while the ungodly prosper, adding field to field, in spite of their evil ways. If we take the cultural dimension into account, however, this apparent contradiction disappears. The promise of prosperity in Deuteronomy is addressed to the nation. If the nation obeys it will prosper at the hand of God. But if the nation disobeys and turns away from God's law, from righteousness and justice to corruption and wickedness, evil men will be able to rise to prominence in society and exploit and persecute the poor and righteous. Thus we have the warnings of the prophets against those who disregard the law of God and oppress the poor. In such a situation the righteous are not able to rise precisely because they are righteous and they are persecuted because they represent opposition to the prevailing wickedness of society. Hence the righteous and the poor groan under the heavy yoke of the wicked. Only as the nation forsakes its wickedness and returns to God and to his law will the promises of Deuteronomy again become a reality, since they are addressed to a redeemed and covenantally faithful nation. It is the societal factor that puts both the Deuteronomic promises and the warnings of the prophets into context. The warnings of the prophets and lamentations of the righteous and poor under the oppression of the ungodly do not contradict the promises of Deuteronomy. On the contrary, they confirm and bear testimony to the historical reality and inevitability of the curses threatened in Deuteronomy against an ungodly society that turns away from the law of God.

cultural and affect the whole of society. It is a cultural phenomenon.[3]

Sixth, it must be remembered that this promise of prosperity in Scripture is not the promise of economic *equality*. The idea of economic equality, which is idolised so much in the modern world, is foreign to Scripture. The Bible never promises economic equality to the faithful. Nor does the Bible require that society enforce economic equality by means of progressive taxation or government-enforced wealth redistribution programmes—taking from the rich by force to give to the poor. Charity is commanded in Scripture, but no agency is given the right to enforce the redistribution of wealth from the "haves" to the "have nots." Charity is voluntary giving to those in need. State-enforced wealth redistribution is theft, and no amount of legislation or the use of euphemisms such as "progressive taxation" or the "Welfare State" can alter that fact. Prosperity is promised to the faithful society, but this promise does not include, much less demand, economic equality. The Bible demands and requires that all men be equal before the *law*. But it does not require *economic* equality to be enforced by society or by individuals or groups within society. The promise in Deuteronomy is one of prosperity to a covenantally faithful society, not of economic equality to individuals within that society.

Bearing these qualifications in mind, we can see that because of this positive biblical teaching on wealth and because wealth was accepted as a good thing in itself, the existence of great wealth and of rich individuals, even in comparison with the rest of society, was not considered a bad or odious thing by the disciples. It was not automatically assumed that because a man was rich he had alienated, expropriated or oppressed the poor. Such oppression certainly did occur, and the prophets warned the nation of Israel against it. But it was not assumed that riches were necessarily the result of oppression. Quite the reverse. The biblical world-view accepted wealth as a blessing and considered those who possessed great riches, provided they were not ill-gotten, to be people whom the Lord had blessed, as indeed they were. Surely, such people had a responsibility to think of others and a duty to help the poor. But wealth and prosperity were seen as good, and wealthy men were not viewed with suspicion in the way that they are by Christians in modern Britain. Right-

---

[3] Max Weber's sociological analysis of the roots of capitalism, *The Protestant Ethic and the Spirit of Capitalism* (London: George Allen and Unwin), is a good starting point for those who wish to study this further in the context of Western society.

eousness and great riches were not considered inconsistent or irrec-
oncilable.

(b) Examples from Scripture

Abraham, we are told, "believed in the Lord; and he counted
it to him for righteousness" (Gen. 15:6, cf. Rom. 4:3). Yet Abraham
was a very rich man: "and Abram was very rich in cattle, in silver,
and in gold" (Gen. 13:2). Abraham did not acquire his wealth through
oppression. It was a blessing from God, and the Lord said to Abraham
"Fear not, Abram: I am thy shield, and thy exceeding great reward"
(Gen. 15:1). Again, take Job. Job was a fabulously wealthy man; indeed
we are told that he was "the greatest of all the men of the east"
(Job 1:3). Yet we are also told that Job was a man who was "perfect
and upright, and one that feared God, and eschewed evil" (Job 1:1).
And though God tested him to prove his faithfulness, and took away
all his possessions and wealth, and all his family save his wife, and
then even his health, Job did not turn away from God, but praised
his name. And in the end Job was blessed by God, and we are told
that "the Lord turned the captivity of Job . . . the Lord gave Job
twice as much as he had before" (Job 42:10). Both Abraham and
Job were eminent men of God in the Old Testament, yet they were
incredibly wealthy, and their wealth is attributed to the favour and
blessing of God upon them. So, we can see that although serving
God is not a guaranteed means of accumulating great personal
wealth, neither is the possession of great wealth inconsistent with faith
in God. Indeed, it is to be seen as God's blessing upon those who
serve him, provided it is not ill-gotten. Thus we are told in Proverbs
that "The crown of the wise is their riches" (Pr. 14:24).

Given this positive biblical teaching on wealth it is not unrea-
sonable that wealth and prosperity should have been associated with
God's favour in the minds of the disciples. Such a view was generally
accepted by the Jews at this time. For example, in the tractate Aboth
in the Mishnah we find the following statement: "Whoso fulfils the
Torah in the midst of poverty, shall in the end fulfil it in the midst
of wealth; and whoso neglects the Torah in the midst of wealth, shall
in the end neglect it in the midst of poverty."[4] Here wealth is

---

[4] *The Sayings of the Fathers with an Introduction and a Commentary by J. H. Hertz* (London:
East and West Library, 1952), p. 59 (4:11). R. Jonathan, to whom the saying is
attributed, was a disciple of R. Akiba (d. 135 A.D.).

associated with faithfulness and zeal for the Torah, and poverty with apathy and indifference to it. This saying is a good indication of the perception of wealth that was common in the Jewish culture of first century Palestine. Such a perception throws considerable light on the disciples' reaction to the incident of the rich young ruler.

(c) *Misapplication of the biblical teaching*

But this perception of wealth as a dispensation of God's favour is likely to assume too much of the outward circumstances of an *individual's* life. Men can misunderstand this teaching and come to terribly wrong conclusions. It is possible that having accepted this positive view of wealth some will then argue that poverty is *necessarily* God's judgement on *individuals* regardless of the circumstances surrounding them. This is wrong. Generally speaking poverty *is* a judgement. In the national or cultural context poverty is a curse from the hand of God because of society's infidelity to his word. But this cannot be said of *individual* cases as if there were a simple cause and effect relationship between the two that operates in the same way under all circumstances, since in a godless society a faithful man may be poor because he is faithful. His poverty may be the result of persecution. Of course, individuals *may* be poor as a result of God's curse. There may be some element of wilful disobedience involved in their lifestyle that inevitably results in poverty. A man may be poor because he is lazy and will not work, in which case his poverty is his own fault. But men may be poor also through no fault of their own. We must distinguish between the poor properly so called, the deserving poor, and the lazy parasite who refuses to work. But one cannot simply argue that poverty is *necessarily* the result of individual sin and hence a punishment from the hand of God. In individual cases, therefore, one's economic circumstances cannot be used as a *test* of one's faithfulness to God, since individual circumstances can be affected by any number of other factors that may significantly modify our understanding of the general principles underlying cultural economic conditions.

But this is precisely what men often do. They use an individual's outward conditions as a test of his standing with God. Job's comforters said that calamity had come upon Job because of his sin. They said, in effect, "God will surely bless his servants and curse his enemies"— and generally speaking this is so from the cultural or social perspective. It is an indisputable lesson of history. But they then said "Ah! Job is suffering because he is under the curse of God," which was not true. He was suffering precisely *because* he was a righteous, God-fearing man. They failed to appreciate, first, the fact that the biblical promise of blessing and prosperity is culturally conditioned, and secondly, that wealth or the lack of it is only one factor in the equation of an individual's personal circumstances and standing with God. They came to a false conclusion about the cause of Job's suffering. But we can see how this misapplication of a culturally conditioned promise made to a covenantally faithful nation was misused and condensed into a *test* of personal faithfulness in the individual.

(d) Summary

To summarise briefly: first, it is not being said here that in individual cases prosperity is never the result of personal faithfulness to the covenant nor that poverty is never the result of disobedience. God may and does bless individuals who are faithful to the covenant with great wealth and prosperity, and he may curse the ungodly individual with poverty. My point is simply that he may not in both cases, and that one's individual economic condition may be affected by other factors outside of one's personal faithfulness to the covenant. Second, other things being equal, i.e. given a general cultural faithfulness, I believe that God will provide for his people very generously in terms of outward economic conditions. We serve a generous God who delights in the prosperity of his people. Third, this does not imply economic equality. It implies, basically, a high standard of living and better health, the eradication of disease and a high fertility rate, all factors that the Western—i.e. Christian—nations have experienced in far greater measure than other cultures. God has kept his promises to Christian nations. Fourth, given an adverse cultural situation, i.e. general cultural unfaithfulness, God's people can expect to suffer, both materially and in other ways. And of course, it should not be forgotten that God's people can be party to national apostasy themselves, as modern Western churches have demonstrated only too well. In such cases judgement must begin at the house of God (1 Pet. 4:17 cf. Heb. 10:30).

Hence, the wealth question is a complex one, and the biblical teaching on wealth is complex. Riches are a blessing from God, and they *may* be a sign of God's favour upon individuals. Riches may also be the result of wickedness and oppression, and such ill-gotten wealth is condemned in Scripture. But the possession of ill-gotten wealth is a curse rather than a blessing because it will lead eventually to judgement. Likewise poverty *may* be the result of God's judgement upon individuals, but it may not be. Bearing in mind these qualifications we can say generally, i.e. in terms of cultural and social analysis, that poverty is a curse and the judgement of God, and prosperity the blessing and favour of God.

(e) *The incident in context*

In the light of all this we can well understand the disciples' preconceptions about the rich young ruler who came running to Christ to ask what he must do to obtain eternal life. Here was a man, they thought, who was supremely blessed by God; he was a ruler of Israel (Luke 18:18), he kept all the commandments, and he was a very wealthy man. And his wealth was perceived as an indication of God's favour towards him, a divine approbation of his righteousness. Surely, if anyone could obtain eternal life it was this man. He qualified perfectly, or so they thought. Surely this man would be accepted by God. These were the preconceptions of the disciples. But no! He lacked a vital qualification. This shocked the disciples. "Who then can be saved?" they asked. If such a man could not be saved what chance was there for a band of fishermen, ex-tax collectors and ex-zealots? And so Jesus presses the lesson home in no uncertain terms. It is impossible for anyone to obtain eternal life except through faith in Jesus Christ who made a perfect blood sacrifice of himself on the cross as an atonement, to appease the divine justice on behalf of those who put their faith in him.

This is the biblical context of the incident. It was a significant incident because it picked out the kind of person the disciples thought most likely to inherit eternal life as a result of one's own righteousness. The purpose of this incident, therefore, is not to teach that it is difficult for a *rich* man to obtain eternal life; rather, it is to teach that it is impossible for *any*, rich *or* poor, to obtain eternal life. The rich man is picked out as an example simply because he would have been considered the most likely to qualify for eternal life in the minds of the disciples. No one, therefore, is saved except through faith in Christ, which should produce the fruit of obedience to Christ. The rich young ruler showed his lack of faith by his lack of obedience to Christ. He would not sell what he had and follow Christ when called upon to do so.

§3
The Modern Perception of the Issues Involved

Our modern perspective is very different from that of the disciples. We have had a hundred or more years of socialism in Britain, and over the past fifty years socialism has become institutionalised in the British establishment. We think of wealth and poverty in a different way. Many people assume that wealth can only be gotten by oppression, extortion and expropriation—and doubtless to some extent it is true that wealth is accumulated in this way in modern society, though popular representation of *who* is being oppressed and who is doing the expropriating and extorting is often seriously inadequate and misleading, if not totally mistaken. And there is also a good deal of inverted snobbery and romanticism about poverty. Poverty has become virtuous of itself in the minds of many, and those who are poor, or rather claim to be poor, or to whom poverty is imputed by groups that can make political capital out of the existence of poverty, are considered to be innocent victims of oppression and beyond criticism. The poor can do no wrong in the eyes of many, and if they do it is put down to deprivation and blamed on a society that fails to maintain economic equality. Socialist politicians often plead economic inequality as the main cause of—and sometimes even justification for—crimes against property by those deemed to be living below the poverty line. Yet the existence of economic inequality in society by no means implies the existence of poverty. In reality poverty would have to be determined by criteria that are not affected by the existence of economic inequality.[5] Yet constantly the envy-

---

[5] Whether someone has more than me has no bearing whatsoever on whether I am poor or not. And if I am poor the fact that everyone else has no more than me in no way means that I am no longer poor. Economic inequality does not necessitate the existence of poverty, nor does economic equality define poverty out of existence, although if the logic of socialist thinking were correct we should have to conclude that it does, an absurdity so obvious that only those blinded by envy could fail to notice it. In fact in many primitive cultures that are deemed among the very poorest on the earth there is virtually complete economic equality. Indeed, this is where all socialist ideology must take us ultimately, namely, universal poverty. The continual penalising of those who attempt to better their economic conditions by those envious of anyone with a higher standard of living than their own only

motivated politics of socialism assumes that the existence of economic inequality means poverty for many. The poor are defined simply by the fact that they do not have the same standard of living enjoyed by the wealthier members of society.

In this kind of propaganda two serious errors are generally made: first, there is no recognition of the fact that one's perception of poverty is highly relative to the culture in which one lives and therefore that it means different things in different cultures and to different people. Secondly, no attempt is made to distinguish between the deserving and the undeserving poor. There is a deliberate confusion about *what* poverty is and *who* the poor really are, which is to the advantage of those who created the confusion, since their purpose is not to help the deserving poor but to despoil the wealthier classes of their wealth under the pretence that they have expropriated it from the poor. This perspective, however, is motivated largely not by a real concern for the poor but by envy, and envy, as the Scriptures teach, is sin.[6] In the resulting clamour and race to wreak vengeance on the "oppressors" the so-called "oppressed" have become the oppressors, and the "expropriated" have become the expropriators.

The problem with this modern perspective is that when it is brought to the Scriptures without recognition of the radically different perspective of the Bible, it is simply read into Scripture and as a result the message of the Bible is distorted. This kind of misreading of Scripture, along with a myopia for the social and cultural dimensions of the Christian faith, has resulted in a major perversion of the Christian world-view. In Britain, for instance, Christian social thought is almost synonymous with socialism. But this kind of thinking is a form of idolatry. Socialist ideology cannot be used as a hermeneutic for reading Scripture without seriously distorting what Scripture teaches. We must, therefore, seek to understand the Scriptures in context. In the particular context of this incident, this means ridding ourselves of the idea that wealth *per se* is a form of theft or oppression, or the result of oppression, and that poverty is virtuous of itself.

---

leads to the failure of all productive work beyond the provision of the bare necessities of life, i.e. subsistence living. It is precisely this envious attitude and the corresponding fear of envy that it provokes that accounts for the abject poverty prevailing in many primitive societies. For more on this see the work referenced in note 6 below.

[6] For an excellent analysis of the problem of envy and the devastating consequences it has on society see Helmut Schoeck, *Envy: A Theory of Social Behaviour* (London: Secker and Warburg, 1969).

There are many examples of how this kind of wrong thinking and reading of modern ideology into Scripture can lead to sin within the church, and to wrong attitudes between believers. A good example of this was a church (known to this writer) that prided itself on its working class ethos. It would permit only those whom its members perceived to be working class people to become members. To be working class was *the* thing. Wealthy people, which in biblical times would have included Abraham, Job, David *et al.*, and middle class people—who were also considered to be too wealthy for their own good—were shunned because wealth was deemed inconsistent with righteousness. The working classes were considered to be the "poor in spirit" of whom Christ spoke in Mt. 5:3.[7] The implication is that righteousness is a working class phenomenon. Such an attitude does not demonstrate the righteousness commanded in the Bible however.

§4
Application

When we come to the application of this Scripture, therefore, something strange happens. As it stands this story fails to have anything like the impact in modern Western society that it had on the disciples. Given the modern perspective and world-view it does not seem astonishing that a rich man should not obtain eternal life. We have been taught to believe that the rich, least of all, can expect to obtain an eternal reward. The poor are the righteous, the virtuous, in the socialist world-view of our day, and they are the ones who are deemed worthy of an eternal reward, if any. So this incident fails to have the impact on us that it originally had on the disciples.

But the problem is much worse than this. Because there is so much ignorance of the biblical teaching on this subject, and because the modern perspective is so often read into Scripture, the incident is used to teach something that is not only beside the original point and anachronistic, but *contrary* to Scripture. This Scripture is used to manipulate the wealthy, or those who are perceived to be wealthy,

[7] This is a Marxist reading of Scripture however. In reality being working class or middle class has very little to do with income as such and more to do with one's *attitude* to wealth and the way one uses one's income. Many so-called working class families have higher incomes than many considered to be middle class. In such cases the higher standard of living apparent in middle class families has to do with the responsible use of money and management of resources.

by provoking misplaced feelings of guilt for the fact that they enjoy a good standard of living, which in truth is a gift from God to be received with thanks and enjoyed for his glory. This Scripture has been used to promote a "poorer than thou" mentality and to malign and manipulate those with wealth into supporting government policies that are clearly condemned in the Bible as theft, policies relating both to the State-enforced redistribution of wealth in our own society and to foreign aid given to the Marxist regimes of Third World countries, which only misuse the funds they receive to further oppress their peoples and promote economies of waste and destruction. It is interesting to note that during the Ethiopian famine, which received widespread television coverage in the West, the Ethiopian Marxist government spent £35,000,000 on a colour television system and millions of pounds on a whisky gala.[8] This was in 1984 when there was mass starvation among the rural population and civil war in twelve of the country's fourteen provinces, which also consumed precious resources needed to get the country back on its feet economically.

Such wickedness is common in Third World countries. Yet many Christians, both in the First World and the Third World, accuse the West of causing such Third World poverty.[9] We are told by many Christians that it is our duty to support these Third World socialist governments and revolutionary movements with aid because socialism is a more just and virtuous form of social arrangement and nearer the "Christian" ideal. Our own government is lobbied to provide ever increasing amounts of aid for these irresponsible regimes. In the advertising literature for a book dealing with the Third World published by one popular Christian publishing house, for instance, we are told that "We are all in some way responsible for the plight in which the Third World finds itself."[10] Doubtless the "all" refers

[8] This information is taken from a lecture given by Yonas Deressa, Director of the Ethiopian Refugee Education and Relief Organisation, at a special White House Briefing sponsored by the Ethics and Public Policy Centre in the U.S. on February 1st, 1985. The lecture was reprinted in *Biblical Economics Today* vol. VIII, No. 3 (Tyler, Texas: Institute for Christian Economics, 1985).

[9] See for instance Allan A. Boesak, *Comfort and Protest* (Edinburgh: The Saint Andrew Press), p. 67.

[10] This is not Ronald Sider's book *Rich Christians in An Age of Hunger*, but one of the books subsequently published on the back of the overexcited and misplaced feelings of guilt generated by it in some Christian circles. One wonders what the publishers did with their profits or whether the author donated his royalties to the government of some Third World nation. With socialists it always seems that it is

to those living in the West. Seldom is the Third World itself deemed to be in any way responsible for its plight. Such literature is common, and invariably the basic aim is to make Westerners feel guilty for the high standard of living they enjoy. Such a mentality is foreign to Scripture and a misrepresentation of biblical teaching. Its pervasiveness shows to what extent many Christians who would reject Liberation Theology have in fact adopted a social theory that, when stripped of its pietistic evangelical sentiments, is hardly distinguishable in any real sense from that advocated by Liberation theologians.

If we wish to have some idea of the original impact that this incident had on the disciples we must realign our perspective. People in twentieth-century Western societies would understand the point of the incident more clearly if they were to recognise that it is harder for a *poor* man to enter the kingdom of heaven than it is for a camel to go through the eye of a needle. Only then would they begin to understand the significance of what Jesus said. Wealth debars a man from entering the kingdom of heaven no more than poverty. It is *sin* that bars men from entering the kingdom of God, and sin can only be dealt with by Christ's substitutionary death on the cross. A man's *attitude* to wealth may bar him from entering the kingdom of God, for example when it is sinful and idolatrous, as with the rich young ruler. So also, a man's attitude to poverty may bar him from seeking the kingdom of God—e.g when it is sinful and seeks justice merely in terms of class warfare and idolises an ideology that is motivated by envy.

Conclusion

It is not wealth *or* poverty that makes one acceptable or unacceptable to God. It is *sin* that makes mankind unacceptable to God, and it is only by the removal of that sin that man can be reconciled with God. In the sacrifice that Christ made at Calvary there is an effective atonement for sin before God. We are accepted by God only in Christ, and whether we are rich, middle class, working class, or poor, we must seek to live our lives in obedience to his word. "There is

---

the other person who is not giving enough and that redistribution of wealth is therefore not a matter of personal responsibility and compassion. Rather, the *State* should redistribute people's wealth for them. In other words "If there is a need, the State should take the money from *you* to remedy it, not me."

neither Jew nor Greek, there is neither bond nor free, there is neither male nor female: for ye are all one in Christ Jesus" (Gal. 3:28). We should not make distinctions based on such things as outward estates in our fellowship with other Christians. We must accept believers in Christ because they profess faith and manifest their faith by their works, and on this basis alone.

APPENDIX F

MAX WEBER AND
THE PROTESTANT DOCTRINE
OF THE CALLING

Max Weber wrote that the word *calling* is known "only to the languages influenced by the Protestant translations of the Bible."[1] This term, he continued, "expresses the value placed upon rational activity carried on according to the rational capitalistic principle, as the fulfillment of a God-given task."[2] Thus, the word has a strong religious connotation. This point is significant for a proper understanding of the emergence of the economically strong Protestant nations of the West over the past four centuries. According to Weber "if we trace the history of the word through the civilized languages, it appears that neither the predominantly Catholic peoples nor those of classical antiquity have possessed any expression of similar connotation for what we know as a calling (in the sense of a life-task, a definite field in which to work), while one has existed for all predominantly Protestant peoples. It may be further shown that this is not due to any ethnical peculiarity of the languages concerned."[3] This Protestant concept of the calling was essential to the thesis set forth in Weber's famous essay *The Protestant Ethic and the Spirit of Capitalism*, and its importance has been stressed in this book. Although it has been controversial and challenged by some[4] Weber's thesis has never been successfully refuted and it remains an abiding landmark in the historiography of the rise of Western capitalism.

The appearance of this concept of the calling at the time of the Reformation was no coincidence. It was the necessary concomitant of the Protestant doctrine of the priesthood of all believers. Prior to the Reformation the Roman Catholic notion of priesthood as a

[1] Max Weber, *General Economic History* (New Brunswick and London: Transaction Books, [1927] 1981), p. 367.   [2] *Ibid.*

[3] Max Weber, *The Protestant Ethic and the Spirit of Capitalism* (London: George Allen and Unwin [1930], Counterpoint edition, 1985), p. 79.

[4] See for example H. M. Robertson, *Aspects of the Rise of Economic Individualism* (Cambridge University Press, 1933).

special ecclesiastical vocation had prevailed throughout Christendom. If one was to dedicate one's life to the service of God this invariably meant entering the church and taking "holy orders." The sharp division between the secular and the sacred emptied secular occupations of any meaning as a form of Christian service. Salvation was administered to the laity by the priesthood and the layman's duty was to be content to make confession and receive the sacraments as a faithful member of the Roman Church, by means of which he would receive eternal life. With the Reformation all this changed. For the Reformers and Puritans no amount of reliance on what was considered to be essentially a magical rite, i.e. the Mass, and mere membership of the outward, visible church would guarantee the individual's salvation. Personal faith and obedience to God's word as the fruit of such faith were considered necessary if a man is to obtain salvation. If the doctrine of the priesthood of all believers meant that each man must manifest this personal faith and obedience in his daily life, then the doctrine of the calling provided the believer with the arena in which he could exercise that faith by dedicating the whole of his life in every detail to the service of God.

The gulf between the secular and the sacred was thus closed and the whole life of man, including his occupation or form of livelihood, became an opportunity for the believer to work out his salvation with fear and trembling (Phil. 2:12), thereby proving his election by divine grace. As Weber put it, with the emergence of the Protestant concept of the calling "at least one thing was unquestionably new: the valuation of the fulfilment of duty in worldly affairs as the highest form which the moral activity of the individual could assume. This it was which inevitably gave every-day worldly activity a religious significance, and which first created the conception of a calling in this sense."[5] The effect of this conception of the calling on the economies of the Protestant nations was the rationalisation of economic activity on the basis of the Christian ethic of honesty, hard work and thrift. The result ultimately was the transformation of the economic landscape of northern Europe.

It is true that most of the elements of economic activity necessary for the development of a capitalist economy of the modern Western kind were to some extent already present before the Reformation, if only in seminal form. This led Lewis Mumford to claim that "Max Weber's thesis, that Protestantism played a prime part in the con-

[5] Max Weber, *The Protestant Ethic and the Spirit of Capitalism*, p. 80.

ception and development of capitalism, has become current during the last generation. In view of the patent facts of history, this belief is as strange as it is indefensible: for it assumes that modern capitalism did not take form until the sixteenth century; whereas it existed as a mutation at least three centuries earlier and by the fourteenth century it pervaded Italy: a country where Protestantism has never been able to gain a hold."[6] But this is not only to misread history; it is also to misread Weber's thesis concerning the genesis of modern Western capitalism. Weber claimed not that Protestantism brought these elements into existence, but that the Protestant faith created for the first time an ethic of rationalisation, i.e. of subordination of the acquisitive impulse to rational economic principles based on the Protestant worldly asceticism, which led to the *development* of modern capitalism. Weber wrote:

On the other hand, however, we have no intention whatever of maintaining such a foolish and doctrinaire thesis as that the spirit of capitalism . . . could only have arisen as the result of certain effects of the Reformation, or even that capitalism as an economic system is a creation of the Reformation. In itself, the fact that certain important forms of capitalistic business organization are known to be considerably older than the Reformation is sufficient refutation of such a claim. On the contrary, we only wish to ascertain whether and to what extent religious forces have taken part in the qualitative formation and the quantitative expansion of that spirit over the world.[7]

As we have already seen Weber did claim that "in modern times the Occident has developed, in addition to this [viz the activity of the capitalistic adventurer—SCP], a very different *form* of capitalism which has appeared nowhere else: the rational capitalistic organization of (formerly) free labour."[8] Furthermore, the Puritan "emphasis on the ascetic importance of a fixed calling provided an ethical justification of the modern specialized division of labour. In a similar way the providential interpretation of profit-making justified the activities of the business man."[9] What Weber claimed, therefore, was that "One of the fundamental elements of the spirit of modern capitalism, and not only of that but of all modern culture: rational conduct on the basis of the idea of the calling, was born—that is what this discussion has sought to demonstrate—from the spirit of

[6] Lewis Mumford, *The Condition of Man* (London: Secker and Warburg, 1944), p. 159.

[7] Weber, *The Protestant Ethic and the Spirit of Capitalism*, p. 91.

[8] *Ibid.*, p. 21, my italics.   [9] *Ibid.*, p. 163.

Christian asceticism."[10] Moreover, Weber showed that for the Puritan "this ascetic conduct meant a rational planning of the whole of one's life in accordance with God's will. And this asceticism was no longer an *opus supererogationis*, but something which could be required of everyone who would be certain of salvation. The religious life of the saints, as distinguished from the natural life, was—the most important point—no longer lived outside the world in monastic communities, but within the world and its institutions. This rationalization of conduct within this world, but for the sake of the world beyond, was the consequence of the concept of calling of ascetic *Protestantism*."[11]

Among the Puritans this Christian ethic led to the rationalisation of life in this world for the sake of the world beyond, and this meant inevitably also the rationalisation of economic life. The Puritan looked to God's blessing on his business activities as evidence of his salvation, as he looked to God's blessing in every other part of life as evidence of his salvation. He sought in business, as in all other things, to rationalise his conduct, to be productive and successful, but always this rationalisation of his conduct was based on the Christian ethic. He sought profit not for the sake of profit, by any means and at any cost, but rather as evidence of God's blessing, as a divine testimony of his being in a state of grace. Thus, the Christian ethic and the rationalisation of life that accompanied it was brought to bear upon economic activity. This rationalisation of life according to the Christian ethic was the Puritan's calling, his duty in life, and the means by which he sought confirmation of his divine election by grace in accordance with the teaching of Scripture (cf. 2 Pet. 1:4–11). It was the rationalisation of economic conduct within this world but for the sake of the world beyond that led to the expansion of the spirit of capitalism throughout Protestant Europe.

Without the Protestant concept of the calling this process of economic rationalisation would have been significantly less developed in Western economies. The various elements of modern capitalistic enterprise, although already in existence in various forms at the time of the Reformation, would not have been harnessed so as to produce the kind of economic growth and social amelioration that was achieved historically in the Protestant nations following the Reformation. The Protestant doctrine of the calling, which was based on the doctrine of the priesthood of all believers, was thus the catalyst that led to the development of modern Western capitalism. Before

[10] *Ibid.*, p. 180.   [11] *Ibid.*, p. 153f., my italics.

the Reformation, argued Weber, traditional attitudes had prevented this vital development from taking shape:

Traditional obstructions are not overcome by the economic impulse alone. The notion that our rationalistic and capitalistic age is characterized by a stronger economic interest than other periods is childish; the moving spirits of modern capitalism are not possessed of a stronger economic impulse than, for example, an oriental trader. The unchaining of the economic interest merely as such has produced only irrational results; such men as Cortez and Pizarro, who were perhaps its strongest embodiment, were far from having an idea of a rationalistic economic life. If the economic impulse in itself is universal, it is an interesting question as to the relations under which it becomes rationalized and rationally tempered in such fashion as to produce rational institutions of the character of capitalistic enterprise.[12]

The answer to this interesting question Weber found in the Protestant asceticism and its doctrine of the calling. The difference between the "capitalistic adventurer," who finances wars and activities "directed to acquisition by force, above all acquisition of booty,"[13] and the Protestant merchants and traders of seventeenth- and eighteenth-century England was that the acquisitive impulse was subordinated by the latter to a process of economic rationalisation based on the moral dictates of the Protestant ethic. The two were worlds apart. It was the Protestant concept of the calling and the Protestant ethic or "worldly asceticism" that accompanied it that made the all-important difference to the way economic enterprise was conducted in the Protestant nations of northern Europe. As we have seen, modern Western capitalism was based on "the rational capitalistic organization of (formerly) free labour." The kind of economic enterprise undertaken by the "capitalistic adventurer" was not the distinctive feature of what we today know as Western capitalism, and due to its essentially irrational nature such enterprise does not lead to the kind of economic growth and social amelioration experienced by the Protestant nations after the Reformation.[14] The wealth tapped by men such as Cortez and the conquistadores "flowed through Spain,

---

[12] *General Economic History*, p. 355f.

[13] *The Protestant Ethic and the Spirit of Capitalism*, p. 20.

[14] This is not to say that the Protestant nations were without those who undertook economic enterprises of a predominantly irrational and exploitative nature geared to acquisition by force. The voyages of Francis Drake and Walter Ralegh and other privateers of the time are good examples of just the kind of enterprise engaged in by Weber's capitalistic adventurers. But such enterprise was not what characterised Western capitalism under the influence of the Protestant doctrine of the calling; rather

scarcely touching it, and fertilized other countries, which in the 15th century were already undergoing a process of transformation in labour relations which was favourable to capitalism."[15] The wealth acquired by the Catholic nations from the Americas was not directed to rational capitalistic enterprise of the Western kind. It thus flowed away from these nations to the Protestant nations where entrepreneurs were engaged in economic activity of a more rational nature.

The ethic upon which this rationalisation of economic activity was based was the Christian ethic of honesty, hard work and thrift in a life directed to activity with a purpose, namely that of rendering service to God in the fulfilment of one's calling. According to Weber, although asceticism had existed in many religions the world over, and had even produced great achievements of various kinds, it had never developed in the way that Protestant asceticism developed after the Reformation, but remained instead essentially a "virtuoso religion" that failed to determine everyday ethics.[16] This was so also in Christendom in the mediaeval period, even though life in the monasteries was characterised by rational activity: "In that epoch the monk is the first human being who lives rationally, who works methodically and by rational means toward a goal, namely the future life. Only for him did the clock strike, only for him were the hours of the day divided—for prayer. The economic life of the monastic communities was also rational. The monks in part furnished the officialdom for the early middle ages; the power of the doges of Venice collapsed when the investiture struggle deprived them of the possibility of employing churchmen for overseas enterprises."[17] But, says Weber,—and this is the important point—"the rational mode of life remained restricted to the monastic circles."[18] The dichotomy between sacred and secular, which characterised mediaeval Christendom under the influence of Roman Catholicism, cut the layman off from developing a Christian notion of calling in all walks of life.

The Reformation broke decisively with this system:

The other-worldly asceticism came to an end. The stern religious characters who had previously gone into monasteries had now to practice their religion in the life of the world. For such an asceticism in the world the ascetic dogmas of Protestantism created an adequate ethics. Celibacy was not

---

it was the *rationalisation* of the acquisitive impulse according to the Protestant ethic that characterised Western capitalism.   [15] *General Economic History*, p. 353.
    [16] *Ibid.*, p. 364.   [17] *Ibid.*, p. 365.   [18] *Ibid.*

required, marriage being viewed simply as an institution for the rational bringing up of children. Poverty was not required, but the pursuit of riches must not lead one astray into reckless enjoyment. Thus Sebastian Franck was correct in summing up the spirit of the Reformation in the words, "you think you have escaped from the monastery, but everyone must now be a monk throughout his life."[19]

The dichotomy between the sacred and the secular was abandoned and the doctrine of the priesthood of all believers brought spiritual meaning to the daily life and routine of each believer. Now each man was required to render a rational service to God by dedicating the whole of life—at church, at home and at work—to God and by conforming in every detail of his life to the will of God as revealed in his word (Rom. 12:1–2). "Christian asceticism, at first fleeing from the world into solitude, had already ruled the world which it had renounced from the monastery and through the Church. But it had, on the whole, left the naturally spontaneous character of daily life in the world untouched. Now it strode into the market-place of life, slammed the door of the monastery behind it, and undertook to penetrate just that daily routine of life with its methodicalness, to fashion it into a life in the world, but neither of nor for this world."[20] Hence for the Protestant the "only way of living acceptably to God was not to surpass worldly morality in monastic asceticism, but solely through the fulfilment of the obligations imposed upon the individual by his position in the world."[21] Thus was born the Protestant conception of the calling, a belief that has had profound effects upon the every-day life of men in the Protestant nations. Owen Chadwick summed up the impact on society of the Protestant doctrine of the calling: "The Reformation made all secular life into a vocation of God. It was like a baptism of the secular world. It refused any longer to regard the specially religious calling of priest or monk as higher in moral scale than the calling of cobbler or prince. Christian energy was turned away from the still and the contemplative towards action. The man who would leave the world turned into the man who would change it."[22]

Weber ends his *General Economic History* on a note of pessimism, observing that the religious impulse of the early capitalist period has been lost:

[19] *Ibid.*, p. 366.
[20] *The Protestant Ethic and the Spirit of Capitalism*, p. 154.   [21] *Ibid.*, p. 80.
[22] Cited in Peter S. Heslam, *Creating A Christian Worldview: Abraham Kuyper's Lectures on Calvinism* (Eerdmans/Paternoster Press, 1998), p. i.

The religious root of modern economic humanity is dead; today the concept of the calling is a *caput mortuum* in the world. Ascetic religiosity has been displaced by a pessimistic though by no means ascetic view of the world, such as that portrayed in Mandeville's Fable of the Bees, which teaches that private vices may under certain conditions be for the good of the public. With the complete disappearance of all the remains of the original enormous religious pathos of the sects, the optimism of the Enlightenment which believed in the harmony of interests, appeared as the heir of Protestant asceticism in the field of economic ideas; it guided the hands of the princes, statesmen, and writers of the later 18th and early 19th century. Economic ethics arose against the background of the ascetic ideal; now it has been stripped of its religious import. It was possible for the working class to accept its lot as long as the promise of eternal happiness could be held out to it. When this consolation fell away it was inevitable that those strains and stresses should appear in economic society which since then have grown so rapidly. This point had been reached at the end of the early period of capitalism, at the beginning of the age of iron, in the 19th century.[23]

Weber is essentially correct in his analysis here. It needs to be added, however, that the church itself must bear much of the responsibility for this. Since the rise of the Enlightenment Christians have, by and large, abandoned the world and retreated into an extreme form of pietism. This pietism is effectively the Protestant equivalent of the monastery. In spite of the fact that modern Protestantism has retained the verbiage of the doctrines of the priesthood of all believers and the calling the reality is that in practice these doctrines have been abandoned. Rather than taking the faith into the world and bringing all things under the influence of rational Christian activity, the Western church in the twentieth century turned instead to private devotion and "spiritual" exercises as the only means of living acceptably to God in this corrupt world. This is the very antithesis of the Protestant conception of the Christian's calling so clearly analysed by Max Weber in *The Protestant Ethic and the Spirit of Capitalism*. As a result the acquisitive impulse in our society has again moved towards economic activity of an essentially irrational and speculative nature,[24] even involving the pursuit of "fiscal booty

[23] *General Economic History*, p. 368f.

[24] Weber makes an interesting observation about capitalist society that has lost the sense of calling as a religious imperative: "Where the fulfilment of the calling cannot directly be related to the highest spiritual and cultural values, or when, on the other hand, it need not be felt simply as economic compulsion, the individual generally abandons the attempt to justify it at all. In the field of its highest development, in the United States, the pursuit of wealth, stripped of its religious and ethical meaning, tends to become associated with purely mundane passions, which

by exploitation of subjects,"[25] though in the West this has not usually been of a militaristic kind but rather by means of political manipulation. The prospect for Western society under such a reversion to pre-Reformation methods of satisfying the acquisitive impulse is indeed a depressing one that has increasingly been realised over the past century. Rational capitalistic activity according to the Christian ethic has been replaced by socialism and by large-scale political capitalism, which resembles the kind of capitalism described by Weber more in appearance than it does in substance and is in reality more akin to fascism.[26] Both these forms of economic organisation are inevitably irrational and indeed destructive of the kind of capitalism that emerged in the Protestant nations of northern Europe after the Reformation.

The answer to this sad retrogression, however, lies not with science or technology, nor with the development of advanced econometric models and political control of the economy according to the dictates of macroeconomic ideals. Rather, it lies with the church, since only as Christians once again seek to bring all things into subjection to Christ and to live rationally according to his word will the Christian ethic necessary to redeem economic enterprise from an otherwise inevitable decline be revived in Western society.

---

often actually give it the character of sport." (*The Protestant Ethic and the Spirit of Capitalism*, p. 182)
    [25] *Ibid.*, p. 20.   [26] See p. 74ff. above, "Economic and Legal Ownership."

HOW TO WALK WITH GOD
IN OUR CALLINGS
A Sermon by William Bridge

[THE following sermon by William Bridge is reproduced here to illustrate the Puritan conception of the Christian calling to which Weber attributed such a vital part in the development of Western capitalism. William Bridge (1600–1670) was a leading Puritan divine of his day. He was a member of the Westminster Assembly, one of the "dissenting brethren," and frequently preached before the Long Parliament. In 1662 he was ejected from his living at Great Yarmouth under the Act of Uniformity. This sermon is reproduced from volume five of *The Works of the Reverend William Bridge* printed by Thomas Tegg in 1845 and reprinted in 1989 by Soli Deo Gloria Publications.]

"Brethren, let every man wherein he is called therein, abide with God."
—1 COR. 7:20.

IN this chapter the apostle speaks to a case of conscience, whether it be lawful for the believing wife to depart from the unbelieving husband; which he resolves negatively, ver. 10. "If the unbelieving will depart, let him depart," saith the apostle, ver. 15, but the believer may not depart; which he persuadeth unto by divers arguments. The first is taken from the profit or good that the believer may do by his continuance, ver. 16, "For what knowest thou, O wife, whether thou shalt save thine husband." The second is taken from the call of God unto that condition, ver. 17, "But as the Lord hath distributed unto every man, as the Lord hath called every man, so let him walk:" and this is our duty; for, says he, "So I ordain in all the churches." Why, but suppose a man be called being a servant, is he to abide therein? Yes, says the apostle, ver. 20, "Let every one abide in the same calling wherein he was called." Art thou called being a servant? care not for it, but if thou mayest be made free use it rather; for, ver. 22, "He that is called in the Lord, being a servant, is the Lord's freeman;" only saith he, "Ye are bought with a price, be not ye the servants of men," serving men only, but the Lord in them. And so, brethren, let every man wherein he is called, abide with God by calling: so that apostle doth understand that state and condition wherein God hath placed us. We do ordinarily take the word *calling* for our civil employment, and outward occupation; but the apostle takes it here for our outward state and condition, yet not excluding but including the other, for there is no state or condition that we are called unto, but some occupation, employment, or calling, is to be used therein; and therefore in speaking to one of these, I shall speak to both. And so the doctrine is this:

That it is the duty of every man to abide or walk with God in his calling; take calling for your state or condition, or take calling for your ordinary way of employment, the doctrine is true, that it is our duty to abide or walk with God in our calling. It is commanded ver. 17, "As the Lord hath called every one, so let him walk." It is commanded again ver. 20, "Let every man abide in the same calling wherein he was called." And it is commanded again ver. 24, "Brethren, let every one," &c. Surely therefore there is some great concernment in this. And ver. 20 he saith, "Let every man abide;" but in ver. 17 he saith, "As the Lord hath called every one, so let him walk;" and saith the text, "Here let him abide with God." Plainly then, it is the duty of every man to walk or abide with God in his calling. For the prosecuting of which I shall labour to shew you:

First, That it is a great mercy for a man to be placed in a good, lawful, and honest calling. A good calling is a great mercy.

Secondly, That a man being so placed, is to abide therein.

Thirdly, That it is our duty to walk with God in our calling.

Fourthly, What a man should do, that he may walk with God in his calling.

Fifthly, I shall give you some motives and encouragements to provoke you to this work, of walking with God in your callings.

First, therefore, I say, a good calling is a great mercy. It is a great mercy for a man to have an honest, good, and a lawful calling: whether you take the word *calling* for the calling of condition, or for the calling of employment, it is a great mercy to be planted in an honest and lawful calling. For,

This was the condition of Adam in the state of innocency; then the Lord set Adam for to till the ground: he gave him an employment in the state of innocency, and there was nothing given him in the state of innocency but mercy. Whatever God called him to, or put him upon before the fall, was mercy. Now in that state God put an employment upon him. Employment did not come in by the fall; it is not a badge of that conquest that the devil made upon us by the fall: therefore an honest calling is a great mercy. For thereby,

A man is kept from idleness. Idleness is the nurse of all wickedness: our vacation is the devil's term. *Homines nihil agendo, &c.:*[1] Men by doing nothing learn to do evil. Idleness, saith the heathen,[2] is the burying of a living man. *Hic situs est.* When a great senator of Rome would go live privately in his country house, that he might be more retired, Seneca coming by, said, *His situs est;* Here lies such a man: as you say over a tomb, Here lies such a man, and there lies such a man, so said he, *Hic situs est Vacia;* Here lies Vacia; for idleness is the burial of a living man, but what more contrary to man than to be buried alive. Now the honest lawful employment or calling will keep ever from idleness. Yea,

Thereby also a man shall be kept from busy-bodiedness and too much meddling: the more idle a man is, the more apt he is to be too busy and meddling with others' matters. Mark, therefore, I pray, how they go together in 2 Thess. 3:11: "We hear that there are some which walk among you disorderly, working not at all, being busy-bodies." Working not at all, and yet overworking, being busy-bodies; how should this be cured? Why, saith he, in the next verse, "now them that are such, we command and exhort by our Lord Jesus Christ, that with quietness they work and eat their own bread." Either a man must eat his own bread or he will eat another's; if he eat another's constantly that will be uncomfortable; if he would eat his own bread, then let him work; if he do not work when he should, he will be at work when he should not; he will meddle with others' matters, and be a busy-body. "Now, therefore, I command and beseech you in the Lord (saith the apostle), that every one work." Thus shall a man be freed from busy-bodiedness. Yea,

A lawful honest calling both of condition and employment is God's ground. As no calling is the devil's ground, so a good and honest calling is God's ground. As an unlawful calling is the devil's ground, so a lawful calling is God's ground. And look when a man is out of his calling and place, he may then say. What do I here

---

[1] Homines nihil agendo mala discunt egere.—Sen.
[2] Otium est vera hominis sepultura.—Sen.

on the devil's ground? and look when a man is in his place and calling, then he may say, What doest thou here, Satan, tempting me? this is none of thy ground, this is God's ground to me. And so it is, indeed, for there God will appear to men. God did appear to shepherds, bringing the news of Christ's birth; but where did he appear to them, but in their calling? They were keeping sheep, and suddenly they heard a noise of heavenly angels. He did appear to Peter and Andrew in their callings to follow Christ; but where did he appear to them, but in the way of their callings? They were casting their nets into the sea, and Christ came and said to them, "Follow me, and I will make you fishers of men." Calling ground is appearance ground; there God appears unto his people. Surely, therefore, it is a great mercy to be on this ground, to have an honest and lawful calling and employment. And that is the first thing,

Secondly, A man having an honest and good calling, he is to abide therein. "Let every one abide therein," saith the apostle here, again and again. Now for the opening of this I shall briefly speak unto these four things:

1. That there is an aptness in us to change or lay down our callings.

2. That it is not absolutely unlawful so to do.

3. Yet ordinarily a man is to abide in his calling, and not readily to be removed from it.

4. I shall answer to some objections or cases of conscience about the change or relinquishment of our calling.

1. Therefore there is an aptness in us to change or lay down our calling, &c. Why should the apostle three times, one after another, call upon us to "abide in our callings?" And if ye look into 2 Thess. 3, ye shall find that as soon as the apostle had commanded the Thessalonians to work, and eat their own bread by working, verse 10, he presently adds, "But ye, brethren, be not weary of well doing." Why so? But because there is an aptness in us, and an itching disposition to leave and desert our calling.

2. But it is not absolutely unlawful for a man to leave or change his calling. This in some cases thou mayest do, says Peter Martyr, *modo teipsam non quæras, vel timere agas,* so that you do not seek yourself, nor be rash therein. For possibly a man may be qualified for higher employments than his own calling bears. In this case, David left his calling of a shepherd and became a king; Amos left the calling of a herdman and became a prophet; the apostles left the calling of

their fishing and became apostles. Possibly a man may be qualified for better and higher employments, and in that case it is lawful to change or leave his calling.[3] Or,

Possibly a man may see the same hand of God leading him out of his calling which he did bring him into it. So when Noah had the same command to go out of the Ark that he had to go in, then he went out, but not before, though the waters were gone off the earth. Now sometimes a man may hear the same voice of God leading him out of his calling, which he did bring him in, and in that case it is lawful to leave or lay down his calling. Or,

Possibly the porter that standeth at the door of a man's calling may let him out; there are porters which God hath set at the door of every condition: if a man be a single man, and would change his condition, and his parents are unwilling, then he may not go out of that calling or condition, for the parents, which are the porters of the door, do not open to him. There are porters at the door of every condition; possibly this porter may open the door, and then it is lawful for a man to change or lay down his calling. Or,

Possibly a man may be forced through want, to change or desert his calling. Paul though a preacher and apostle, was sometimes forced to work with his hands. And though Masculus was a good and excellent preacher, yet he was sometimes forced to work, and to dig in the city ditch or moat, for his living.[4] Possibly I say, a man through urgent necessity and want, may be forced to leave or desert his calling; and then, in that case, it is lawful for him to do it: so that it is not absolutely unlawful for a man to change or lay down his calling. Yet,

3. Though it be lawful in some case to do so, yet ordinarily a man is to abide in his calling, and not readily to be removed from it: for a good calling is the Lord's gift.

It is God that calls a man to that state, condition, or employment. Now a man should not readily leave or desert that calling or employment which God hath called him to, or owned and blessed him in. For how do I know whether God will own or bless me when I shall desert that calling, wherein he hath appeared unto me. It

[3] Si ad magistratus vel ecclesiæ regimen adcersitus fueris justa ratione, tum tuipse non est qui te transferas ex una vocatione in aliam sed a Deo promoveris. Sic ab arato ad consilium voleris romdis.—Pet. Mar. in cap. p. 96.

[4] Idem statuendum est, cum aliqua gravi necessitate compelleris, et subeas non as conditiones.—Pet. Mar. ibid.

is my duty to follow God, and not to go before him; as God hath distributed to every man. As the Lord hath called every man, so let him walk. God doth distribute and carve out our callings for us. Has the Lord therefore called me to a place or employment, then am I with thankfulness to walk therein. It is not for the private soldier, saith Peter Martyr, to appoint his own station; but look where he is set by his commander, there he is to abide. Has the Lord therefore set me in this or that calling or employment, then am I to wait on God, and abide in it, and not readily to be removed from it.

There is no calling either of employment or condition, but God may be served and enjoyed therein. No calling or employment so mean, but a man may honourably serve, and comfortably enjoy God therein. Art thou called being a servant, care not, saith the apostle; why? For he that is called being a servant, is the Lord's free man, verse 22. Likewise also, he that is called being free, is the Lord's servant. I remember I heard a preacher say some twenty-five years since, that a man is never ashamed of his calling, though it be never so mean, but a man is ashamed of his sin, although he be never so great. If, says he, you call a man tinker or cobbler, yet he is not ashamed thereof, because it is his calling; but if you call a man drunkard, or adulterer, he is ashamed thereof, because that is none of his calling. A man may honourably serve God in his calling, though it be never so mean, and he may comfortably enjoy God in his calling although it be never so great.

4. But that is the reason why I would lay down my calling, because I cannot serve God so well therein. I meet with my temptations, provocations, and impediments, which hinder me in the service of God; if I were free from this calling, then I should be more free for God, and should be more free from those snares and provocations that I now meet with. But for the answer:

Are you sure of that? Luther tells us of a certain man that was given to anger, and to avoid provocation, he would go live alone, as an hermit; and going to the well with his pitcher, somewhat displeased him, and he threw down his pitcher, and broke it in anger; which when he had done, and reflecting on himself, and his own actions, he said, Well, now I see it is not in my condition, but in my heart and self, that doth cause anger and provocation; therefore I will return to my calling again. And when men speak at the rate of that objection, what do they do, but lay the fault of their anger and provocation upon their condition, and excuse themselves? But our Saviour saith, That that comes from within, that defiles a man, not that which comes from without. It is not the condition, or the place, or the employment, or calling, that defiles the man, but that that comes from within, that defiles the man. Mr. Greenham[5] being asked whether a man might avoid the doing of a thing whereunto he is called, because he feels corruption in himself, said he, In avoiding society, you shall cover, but not cure your infirmities; and though you depart from men, you cannot go out of yourself; it is not the use of the creatures, but the love of the creatures, that hinder from good. I never look, said he, for a better estate than that wherein I am; but oft prepare for a worse. And I pray tell me, beloved, was not Joshua, when Moses died, and he was to lead the people into Canaan, a man of great employment? "Yes even then," saith the Lord to him, "this book of the law, shall not depart out of thy mouth, but thou shalt meditate therein day and night," Josh. 1:8. And was not David a man of great employments? Yet, says he, "At evening, morning, and at noonday will I pray, yea seven times a day; yea, I meditate on thy law all the day long." Surely therefore our hindrance to good, doth not lie in our calling, place, or employment; but it lies within ourselves. And therefore why should we lay down our callings to be rid thereof.

5. But this is not my reason, I know that a man may serve God in the worst of honest callings, but callings are made for maintenance. Now I have enough to maintain myself and mine; and therefore why may not I now lay down my calling?

Because you are mistaken. A calling is not only to maintain yourself and your family, but it is an ordinance of God to preserve and keep you from idleness: whereby you are not only to maintain yourself, but to help others, and therefore ye find that Paul saith, "he wrought with his hands;" not only to maintain himself but others. "You know (says he) yea, yourselves know, that these hands have ministered to my necessities, and to them that were with me," Acts 20:34. He did not only work occasionally to maintain himself, but others also. And if ye look into Eph. iv., the same church that he spake to in Acts xx., ye shall find that he layeth his injunction on them and us: "Let him that stole steal no more, but rather let him labour, working with his hands the thing that is good, that he may have to give to him that needeth," verse 28. Surely therefore a calling is not only appointed to raise a maintenance for ourselves: and

[5] Greenham on calling.

therefore, though you can live, and have outward means enough to maintain both you and others, yet you may not therefore leave or desert your calling; it is that trust that God hath committed to you, and you must make good your trust.

But though I may not leave my calling altogether, yet may I not leave it for a time, that on the week-day I may go and hear and enjoy ordinances?

Yes, surely, for man is not made for the calling, but the calling is made for man. Ye read of a converted woman in John iv., that when she had a taste of Christ's preaching, she left her pitcher or pail, and went and called others to hear the same. And so, though you do not break your pail or pitcher, yet you may leave your pail or pitcher for a time, to tend on the words of Christ. Did not the Jews go up three times a year to Jerusalem from their several habitations, employments, and callings? Is it not said, "That the converted Jews did continue daily with one accord in the temple, and breaking bread from house to house?" Acts ii. 46. Indeed God will have mercy and not sacrifice; but though ye may not leave or lay down your callings readily, yet for a time you may leave them, that you may attend on the ordinances. But though you may so leave your callings for a time, yet you must abide therein with God. And so I come to the third general, which is this:

Thirdly, That it is our duty, or the duty of every man to walk with God in his calling, not barely to abide therein, but to abide and walk with God therein. For thus,

It was so from the beginning. Adam had a calling, even in the state of innocency, but therein he was to walk with God.

And if a man do not walk with God in his calling, how can he walk with God at all. A man is not said to walk with God because he prays in the morning or evening; walking is a constant thing. Now it is the duty of every man to walk with God; and therefore it is his duty to walk with God in his calling.

Thereby a man is distinguished from the world and the men of the world. A man is not therefore one of another world, because he deserts his calling that he may give himself unto his devotions: for the monks, and nuns, and anabaptists, should be men and women of another world; he is a man of another world, "that doth use the world as if he used it not." Christ himself was in the world, "but not of the world." And if you would not be of the world, you must not go out of the world, but you must walk with God in the world.

Hereby you shall be distinguished from the world, and men of the world. Now it is our duty so to walk, as that it may appear that we are not of this world. Therefore it is our duty to walk with God in our callings, not only to abide therein, but to walk with God therein.[6]

This is that which will sweeten and elevate your callings: every thing is raised or depressed as God is present with it or absent from it. Bethlehem was but a little city, therefore says the prophet Micah, chap. v. 2, "Thou Bethlehem, though thou be little amongst the thousands of Judah;" yet, Mt. 2, it is said, "And thou Bethlehem art not the least." Why? Because Christ was born there. Look what place, or town, or condition that is where Christ is, though it be little in itself, yet it is raised by him. The more, therefore, that you walk with God in your calling, the more your calling is sweetened and elevated. And yet further,

Every man is as he is in his calling; and man hath no more grace than he may or can use in his calling; and though I have all parts and gifts, so as I can remove mountains, yet if I be not gracious in my calling, all is nothing, my parts and gifts are but as sounding brass and as tinkling cymbal. My calling is that ground whereon I am to plant all my gifts and graces. If I have grace, it will appear in my calling: every man is as he is in his calling. Surely, therefore, it is not only our duty to abide, but to abide and walk with God in our callings. And that is the third general.

Now, by way of application, I might speak something in reference to every branch of the doctrine. If a good calling be a great mercy, then why should not parents provide honest callings for their child, and children be thankful to God and their parents for such provision? And if it be our duty to abide with God in our callings, then why should not every man be contented with his condition, whatever it be, though it be never so mean? And if it be our duty to walk with God in our callings, then why should we not make it our business, not to be rich by our callings, but to walk with God in our callings. But you will say,

---

[6] At hodie summa habeter pietas, si quis domi relectis liberis at exore aut etiam grandævis parentibus, vel Hierosolymam adeat, vel in monasterium; vide quo impudentiæ ventum est ecclesia, Christi, nec in pari proxsus dementia decipiunt hodie at catebaptistæ, relictis enim uxoribus liberis et familiis (tanquem attoniti et fanatici homines circumstant, atque ita se pomariam regni Christi propagularos dejerunt; tum interim rem familiarem concoquent subvertantque, totam et ecclesiam Christi miris modis obturbent.—Bullinger in 1 Tim. 5:8.

Fourthly, What should a man do that he may walk with God in his calling? This is of daily concernment. How should we, therefore, so walk in our callings, that we may walk with God in our callings?

I answer negatively and affirmatively.

Negatively. If you would walk with God in your calling, you must not be ignorant of the way of your calling; for if you take up a calling, and are ignorant of the way and mystery thereof, you may tempt God therein. "The wisdom of the wise (saith Solomon) is to direct his way," his own particular way. Every man should be the master of his art.[7] Possibly a man may step into a calling both of condition and employment before he knows the way and the manner of it. But as in marriage, though the parties meet in the flesh without any sanctified means, yet if God afterwards give them grace to live holily together, he sheweth that not only their corrupt meeting is pardoned, but that now they are blessed. So, though a man enter into a calling without gifts at first, yet if afterwards God furnish him with able gifts, he doth not only shew his former sin, in running into that calling, is pardoned, but that he is blessed. But if an man be not the master of his art, and gifted for his calling, then he leaves God therein, and doth not walk with God.

If you would walk with God in your calling, you must not be negligent in your place and calling. Diligence in our calling is commanded, commended and rewarded in Scripture. It is commanded: "Whatever is in the power of thy hand I [sic] do, do it with all thy might;" "Be not slothful in business, go to the pismire, O sluggard." It is commended: "He that is diligent in his business shall stand before princes." And it is rewarded: "For the diligent hand maketh rich." Now if God doth command, commend, and reward diligence in our calling, then surely you cannot walk with God and be negligent therein.

If you would walk with God in your calling, you must not deal unjustly or unrighteously in your callings with men. "God hath shewed thee, O man, what is good," saith the prophet Micah vi. 8. "And what doth the Lord require of thee, but to do justly, and to love mercy, and to walk humbly with thy God?" Plainly, then,

---

[7] Q. Quænam requirunt ad honestam vocationem honeste exercendum? R. 1. Requiritur peritia. 2. Attentio ad officia propria. 3. Sedula diligentia. 4. Providentia in opportunitate commoda observanda. 5. Fortitudo et constantia in difficultatibus superandis. 6. Moderatio appetitionis lucri. 7. Religiosa sanctificatio omnium laborem.—Ames Cas. consc. lib. v. cap. 46.

a man cannot walk humbly with God that doth not deal justly and righteously with men in his calling.

If you would walk with God in your calling, then you must not be too familiar with your calling. God hath given you a calling that it may be a nurse to you, and your grace. Children sometimes are so fond of their nurse that they regard not their parents; and if you be too fond of your calling, you will forget the God of your calling. "Let him that marrieth be as if he married not (says the apostle), and he that useth the world as if he used it not." You will go with an apron into your shop that you may keep your clothes clean, and hath your soul as much need of an apron when you are in your shop and your calling. If the ivy clings too close unto the oak, it hindereth the growth of the oak; so if your callings cling too close to you, and you to your callings, it will hinder your spiritual growth. The world may be well used at a distance: it is not evil to meddle with the world, but to mingle with it. Would ye, therefore, walk with God in your place, then you must not be too familiar with the world and the things thereof. This negatively. Now

Affirmatively. If you would walk with God in your place and calling, then you must observe what those snares and temptations are that are incident unto your calling, and take heed thereof; such there are, for says the apostle, chap. vii. 23, "He that is unmarried, careth for the things that belong to the Lord, how he may please the Lord; but he that is married careth for the things of the world, how he may please his wife." And this saith he, verse 35, "I speak for your own profit, not that I may cast a snare upon you, but for that which is comely, and that you may attend upon the Lord without distraction." Plainly, then, there are snares and temptations that are incident unto all, and the best conditions and callings; and if we would attend unto God without distractions, we must observe what these snares and temptations are, and take heed thereof.

If you would walk with God in your calling, then you must live by faith in your callings. "For by faith Enoch walked with God." "And the life that I live in the flesh, I live by the faith of the Son of God." Thereby you shall be kept from covetousness and love of the world. "This is our victory, whereby we overcome the world, even our faith." Thereby you shall be contented with your condition, whatever it be; thereby you shall be able to leap over a wall, and over all those difficulties that you meet with in your callings; thereby you shall live sweetly and graciously in your calling, and walk with

God. Now if you would live by faith in your calling, then you must have an eye to God's commandment, promise, and providence. You must go to your callings as to God's ordinance; otherwise you cannot look with both eyes to God, but with one eye to the world, and with the other to God. But you see that he hath taught us, that you cannot look with one eye to heaven, and with the other eye to the earth; but if you will look to the heavens, both eyes will look to heaven. So if you will look to God, you must look with both eyes to God. The way, therefore, to look with both eyes to God in your calling, is to go to your calling as to God's ordinance; and because faith and the promise are as buckle and clasp, the one cannot be without the other. Therefore you must observe those promises that are made to your calling, and rest thereon. And because God doth sometimes guide us by his eye in the way of our callings, therefore you must have an eye to providence; and whatever you do in the way of your calling, you must quietly leave the issue of it and success to God. And thus shall you live by faith in your calling, and so walk with God in your place.

If you would walk with God in your calling, then whatever you do therein, do all to the glory of God. "Whether you eat or drink, (saith the apostle) do all to the glory of God." If I work in my calling for mine own profit only, then I walk with myself therein; but if I do all for God's glory, not mine own profit, then I walk with God in my calling.

If you would walk with God in your particular calling, then be sure that you so manage your calling, that your general calling may not be an hindrance, but an help unto your particular; and thus your particular calling may be no hindrance, but an help to your general calling. Woe to that calling that eats up prayer. The particular and general callings are joined together by God: "Those that God hath joined together, let no man put asunder." Be sure, therefore, that your general calling be an help to your particular, and your particular no hindrance to your general. Thus shall you walk with God in your calling. And,

If you would walk with God in your calling, then be sure that you turn as God turns, sweetly complying with his dispensations in the way of your calling. If two men walk together, when one turns the other turns, and if one do not turn as the other turns, they cannot walk together; but if one turns as the other turns, then they walk together. So in our walking with God, it may be God's dispensations in my calling are comfortable, then am I to rejoice and to praise the Lord. It may be God turns and his dispensation is sad, in the way of my calling; then am I to humble myself before the Lord, and to comply with his dispensation; which if you do in your calling, then shall you walk with God therein. Yet,

If you would walk with God in your calling, then you must judge of things in your calling, as God judges, and measure things by his bushel. We are very apt to measure and judge of things in our callings, by the verdict of the means and second causes: if the means and second causes smile, then we smile, though God frown; if the means and second causes frown, then we frown, though God smile: if the second cause be big, and promise a great mercy or blessing to us, then in the strength of the second cause, we promise it to ourselves, though God threatens the contrary; if the second cause or means threaten a misery, then in the strength thereof, we threaten ourselves with that misery, though God promise the contrary blessing. This is not to walk with God in our callings. He that walks with God in his place and calling, must judge and measure things according unto God's verdict. But,

If you would walk with God in your place and calling, then you must spiritualize your particular calling with heavenly things, and the things of God; not put all upon a morning and an evening prayer, but your particular calling must be sprinkled with holy meditations and gracious speeches. Thus it was with Abraham's servant when he went for Rebecca, he sprinkled his service with meditation, prayer, and godly speech. And if ye look into Judges 5. ye shall find that upon a gracious victory that God gave to his people, it is said, ver. 11, "They that are delivered from the noise of the archers, in the places of drawing of water, there shall they rehearse the righteous acts of the Lord," Not only at their church meetings, and in prayer or duty, but while they are drawing of water. Thus our particular calling is to be sprinkled with heavenly things; and if you do thus, then shall you walk with God in your calling. And oh, that there were an heart in us all, thus to walk with God in our callings. This is every man's work, and every day's work. Now, therefore, that you may do it, give me leave by way of motive, to leave these few considerations with you.

If you walk with God in your particular calling, God will walk with you in your general calling. Is it not a great mercy to meet with God in your prayers and duties; if you go up to him in your particular callings, he will come down to you in your general. Then shall your calling be a blessing to you indeed, and you shall have another, further and greater reward than the wealth of your calling. "Servants obey your masters in all things, not with eye-service as men pleasers, but in singleness of heart, fearing the Lord," Col. 3:22. "And whatever ye do, do it heartily, as to the Lord, and not unto men," ver. 23. "Knowing that of the Lord ye shall receive the reward of the inheritance; for ye serve the Lord Christ." It seems then, by this scripture, that though a man be a servant, yet therein he may serve the Lord, and walk with God; and if he do so, he shall not only have wages from his master, but of the Lord he shall receive the reward of the inheritance. Now he is best paid, which the Lord pays; the Lord will not only give him his outward wages, but an everlasting inheritance. Oh, what a good thing it is to walk with God in our callings. Yea,

Thereby the knots and difficulties of your calling shall be taken off, and your way made easy; that God whom you walk with in your callings, will lift you over all the stiles that are in your callings. If a child walk with his father in the fields,when they come to a high stile, the father lifts him over it. So if you walk with God in your callings, then he will lift you over all stiles and difficulties of your callings. Yea,

Thereby you shall be kept from the sins and temptations of your calling. A man's calling is like to a great log or piece of timber in a green field; look upon the field, and you see it all green and handsome, but take up the log or timber that lies in the midst thereof, and there you find worms, and sows, and vermin that do breed under it. So look upon a man's carriage, and generally it is very green, civil and handsome; but if ye look under his calling, you will find nothing but sows, worms, and vermin. Now this walking with God in your calling, will keep you from the vermin of your callings. Yea,

Thereby shall your way of godliness be convincing and winning. "As God hath distributed to every man, as the Lord hath called every man, so let him walk and abide with God," saith the apostle in this chapter. Why so? "For what knowest thou. O wife, whether thou shalt not save thine husband;" or, "how knowest thou, O man, whether thou shalt not save thy wife?" Yea, says the apostle Peter, "Likewise ye wives, be in subjection to your husbands, that if any obey not the word, they also without the word, may be won by the conversation of the wives," 1 Peter 3:1. It is not therefore a morning or evening duty, though that is good, that is so winning; but a constant walking with God in our places and callings, is convincing and winning. Yea,

Thereby also you shall be fit to die, and leave all the world with ease. The more a man runs his heart into the world in his calling, the harder it will be to die; and the more a man walketh with God in his calling, the fitter he will be to die, and to leave all the world with ease. Now therefore as you do desire, that you may be fit to die, that your ways of godliness may be convincing and winning, that the knots and difficulties of your callings may be taken off, that your callings may be a blessing to you indeed, and that God may meet and walk with you in your general calling, labour more and more to abide and walk with God in your particular calling; which that you may do, labour to be master of your art, be diligent in your place, deal not unjustly with men in your calling, be not too familiar with your callings, but keep your due distance from them; observe what the temptations and snares are, that are incident, and take heed thereof; labour more to live by faith in your calling; let not your general eat up your particular, nor your particular destroy your general. Whatever you do in your calling, "do all to the glory of God," be sure that you turn as God turns, give when he gives, measure all things in your callings by his bushel, and be sure that you always sprinkle your outward employments with some heavenly refreshments. And thus brethren, "Let every one wherein he is called therein abide with God." For it is the duty of every man to abide and walk with God in his calling. And thus I have done with this argument, How to walk with God in our callings.

GLOSSARY OF TERMS

Accepting house. An institution specialising in guaranteeing ("accepting") *bills of exchange* (q.v.), for which it will charge a commission of about ¾ per cent of the value of the bill. Accepting houses are usually *merchant banks* (q.v.). Bills accepted by an accepting house (bank bills) will be traded at less discount than those accepted only by a trader (trade bills); hence the willingness of those holding bills of exchange to pay for their being underwritten by an accepting house.

Balance of payments. An account of the financial transactions of the nation as a whole with the rest of the world. The balance of payments account is broken down into the *current account* and the *capital account*. The current account consists of the *visible trade account* (see *visibles*) and the *invisible account* (see *invisibles*). The visible account shows the relation between total exports and imports of visibles, i.e. physical goods such as manufactured and semi-manufactured products and raw materials. In 1989 total exports (credits) of visibles amounted to £92,526 million, and total imports (debits) of visibles amounted to £115,683 million. The difference between these two figures is often called the *balance of trade*, which in 1989 showed a deficit of £23,112 million. This is called an "unfavourable balance of trade." An excess of visible exports over visible imports is called a "favourable balance of trade." This terminology is misleading, however, and is derived from the Mercantilists (protectionists) of the sixteenth and seventeenth centuries (see *balance of trade*; see also note 37 on p. 35f.).

The invisible account consists of services such as banking, insurance, tourism, shipping, profits earned abroad and interest payments. In 1989 total provision of these services by UK residents to foreign countries (credits) amounted to £108,530 million, and total provision of these invisibles to residents of the UK by foreign residents (debits) amounted to £106,268 million. There was thus an invisible balance of £2,262 million, i.e. an invisible surplus. The combination of the visible and invisible accounts gives the balance of payments on current account, which in 1989 amounted to a current account deficit of £20,850 million (sometimes the term *balance of trade* is applied to this overall balance of payments on current account, i.e. visible *and* invisible trade).

The *capital account* is an analysis of lending and borrowing between the UK and the rest of the world, including lending and borrowing between the UK government and the governments of other countries. The *long-term capital account* records foreign investments in the UK (credits) and UK investments abroad (debits). The *short-term capital flows* records short-term money flows between the UK and other countries: e.g. foreign deposits in British banks and loans to the UK from overseas (credits), and UK deposits in overseas banks and loans by the UK to overseas countries (debits). The capital account also records the sale and purchase of gold and foreign currency reserves by the Bank of England. In 1989 the UK capital account balance showed a surplus of £4,341 million.

When all sections of the balance of payments are tabulated together there should be a balance, i.e. debits should equal credits. However, due to errors in collecting the data necessary to compile the balance of payments account a *balancing item* is included to correct such errors in the accounts (in 1989 the balancing item amounted to £16,509 million).

The political obsession with the balance of trade, and more generally with the balance of payments on current account, is often represented as legitimate concern for the British economy. However, the fears that generate this obsession are political in origin not economic. Politicians generally seem to think that an overall deficit in the balance of payments on current account is disadvantageous for the economy. This is not so. Politicians often misunderstand the economic realities of the situation, sometimes because they are blinkered by ideology, often because they simply do not understand economics. Sometimes the fear of a deficit in the balance on current account is motivated by the prospect of increased foreign investment in the UK and foreign ownership of UK industries and assets. This is a *political* neurosis however, not an economic problem, since such investment creates jobs for UK residents and leads to the creation of wealth and better standards of living (see "International Trade" in Chapter One). From the economic point of view, therefore, foreign investment in the U.K. performs the same function in the domestic economy that exports perform.

Balance of Trade. The balance between exports and imports of *visibles* (q.v.) over a given year. Sometimes the term is used to refer to the balance of payments on current account (see *balance of payments*). The term *balance of trade* relates only to imports and exports of certain types of goods and services. It is a misleading term and its careless use by economists and media pundits has caused much confusion among people who are uneducated about economic matters —particularly politicians. The term *balance of visible trade* or *balance of payments on current account* should be used to denote the ideas often represented by the term *balance of trade*.

Bank money. Money created as a result of bank loans being credited to demand deposit accounts. This is money that exists only in the form of numbers in bank accounts and circulates by the writing of cheques (cf. *clearing system*).

Bank rate. See *minimum lending rate*.

Bill of exchange. A written order signed by the party issuing it (the drawer) requiring the party to whom it is addressed (the drawee) to pay a sum of money to a specified person or bearer (the payee) on a particular date, usually in three months time. These bills must be "accepted," i.e. endorsed, by the borrower (the party on whom they are drawn), after which they can be traded at a discount. Bills of exchange are a form of near-money since they are very liquid (i.e. easily exchanged for cash). A bill may also be accepted by an *accepting house* (q.v.). Bills accepted by an accepting house (bank bills) will be traded at less discount than those accepted only by a trader (trade bills). Bills of exchange are sold by the banks because of their liquidity. Bills of exchange are of three kinds: commercial bills (bills drawn on firms), local authority bills (bills drawn on local authorities), and *Treasury bills* (q.v.).

Boom. The early part of the *business cycle* (q.v.), characterised by inflation, easy credit, business expansion and a general but false perception of economic prosperity.

Business cycle (or trade cycle). An economic cycle that involves in the early part of the cycle increased economic activity (e.g. establishment of new companies and businesses and the expansion of existing firms), easy credit, increased consumer spending, debt-financed expansion of enterprise, and the general perception of prosperity. This first part of the cycle is called a *boom* (q.v.) and is later followed by a *slump* (q.v.), i.e. a period of high interest rates, business failures and bankruptcies, high unemployment, recession and depression. Business cycles are caused by *inflation* (q.v.). The new money creates a false impression of economic prosperity that stimulates economic activity and consumer spending. As prices rise, however, economic reality begins to catch up with people and the false climate of prosperity vanishes. People find that they are no better off in real terms than they were before. In fact, they find that they are worse off, since the false climate of prosperity has led to a greater consumption of scarce resources on non-essentials—i.e. "living it up"— than was prudent. As a result people and firms have to economise and reduce spending. In other words, as a result of the uneconomic (i.e. wasteful) use of resources in the period of inflation (the boom period) there is less capital to sustain economic growth in more basic and essential areas. Society has to readjust to this new situation in which there are less resources available in the economy. Standards of living fall and the economy goes into recession.

If the monetary authorities wish to avoid the problems associated with a recession after a period of inflation they may continue to inflate the money supply. But the inflationary process becomes exponential with each new injection of money into the economy. Recession is postponed for a short time but eventually the consequences become more serious and destructive to the economy. If the authorities continue inflating the money supply regardless of the consequences the economy begins to experience hyper-inflation and eventually goes into *crack-up boom* (q.v.), i.e. demonetisation of the currency and flight into real goods as a means of economic exchange (barter trading).

Capital. The stock of material resources at the disposal of an individual, company or society used to produce goods and satisfy wants. Capital is classified as *fixed* capital, *working* or *circulating* capital, and *specific* capital. Fixed capital consists of resources whose function does not change essentially through use, e.g. factories, buildings, machinery and equipment used in the manufacture of goods and provision of services. Working capital consists of goods that are in the process of being manufactured, e.g. stocks of raw materials and semi-finished goods, and finished goods stocked by manufacturers, wholesalers and retailers. Specific capital refers to goods and resources that can only be used for the purpose for which they were originally designed.

Capitalisation. The process of accumulating capital. When a company or individual makes a profit from an economic enterprise this profit, or part of it, can be used to acquire more capital, which can then be put to further productive use. As productivity increases more consumer goods become available to more people at lower prices. The more capitalised a society becomes, therefore, the higher its standard of living will be. A highly developed process of capitalisation is a feature of capitalist, free market economies. Capitalisation is less developed in socialist economies. The latter rely more on State investment in capital than on private investment, and this is achieved by redistributing the existing stock of wealth rather than by creating new wealth that can be invested in capital. Since in socialist societies there is not the same scope for personal initiative that can be rewarded economically, private investment is not well developed and the capital equipment deployed by industry tends to be old fashioned and behind the times compared with that available in capitalist societies. Hence the lower standard of living experienced by such societies generally.

Capital market. The market for medium- and long-term debt consisting of institutions and firms such as the commercial and merchant banks, issuing houses, the Stock Exchange, building societies and insurance companies.

Cash. Cash is any form of money that is widely accepted as a means of payment not involving credit, e.g. Bank of England notes and coin of the realm (cf. *legal tender*). However, cheques for small amounts are often now considered cash as well since bankers' guarantee cards ensure that up to a certain amount a cheque will not bounce, i.e. the bank guarantees that up to a certain amount it will honour a cheque even if there are insufficient funds in the account on which it is drawn to cover it. In the banking system the commercial banks' balances with the Bank of England are also considered cash since the bank of England can always supply the banks with its own banknotes in exchange for these deposits. In our modern economy, therefore, cash can also be defined as *a liability of the Bank of England*.

CGBR. The central government borrowing requirement, i.e. the total amount of borrowing needed to fund the central government *deficit* (q.v. See also *PSBR*).

Clearing system. An arrangement whereby the *settlement banks* (q.v.) settle claims against each other. Suppose at the end of the day bank A has received cheques drawn on bank B for £100, and bank B has received cheques drawn on bank A for £120. The two sums are offset against each other and the net amount of £20 owed by bank A is paid to bank B. The efficiency of the clearing system can be better illustrated with an example using three banks. Suppose bank

A owes bank B £200, bank B owes bank A £100, and bank B owes bank C £100. All three debts can be cleared if bank A pays bank C £100. This payment is made by debiting bank A's balances at the Bank of England and crediting the money to bank C's balances at the Bank of England.

Crack-up boom. As hyper-inflation begins to make economic calculation in terms of money increasingly difficult and unreliable people stop exchanging goods and services via the previously accepted medium of exchange (money) and resort to alternative forms the value of which is not being debased. The result is demonetisation of the currency. Barter takes place where formerly exchange would have been by means of money. This situation is called crack-up boom.

Currency. What people accept and use as money (from the Latin *curro*, meaning *to run*, because it circulates from hand to hand in exchange for goods and services). Usually, but not necessarily, currency is the official money of a country or State, i.e. its legal tender. In the U.K. currency consists of Bank of England notes, coin of the realm and Scottish banknotes—though the latter are not legal tender anywhere in the UK, including Scotland.

Decapitalisation. The process by which a society consumes, instead of putting to productive use, the stock of wealth needed for capital investment if standards of living are to rise (cf. *capitalisation*). Socialist societies are characterised by decapitalisation to various degrees since the aim of socialist economic policy, theoretically, is to raise standards of living for the poor by means of government *control* and *redistribution* of the nation's wealth rather than through the *creation* of wealth. Capitalist policy, on the other hand, aims at raising the standard of living of everyone, not by means of government control of the existing stock of wealth, but by permitting and encouraging people to *create* more wealth in a free market economy. The two policies yield contrary results. Though socialist economic policy, ostensibly, is concerned with helping the less fortunate and poor in society, its actual effect is to hinder wealth creation and retard economic growth for the very people it is supposedly designed to help. Furthermore, the consumption mentality that is inevitably associated with socialist economies, i.e. the desire to get one's hands on and consume one's "fair" share of the wealth available in society, leads to a drastic decrease in the rate of *capitalisation* (q.v.), since wealth is redistributed from those who know how to use it productively in order to create wealth, to those who seem to know only how to consume it. The resources that should be used for capitalisation—i.e. the creation of more wealth—or at least a large proportion of these resources, are therefore redirected away from the process of wealth creation into direct consumption. This process of consuming the resources needed for investment in capital if standards of living are to rise is called decapitalisation.

Deficit. A shortfall between receipts and expenditure that has to be funded by borrowing. Since government borrowing is linked to the money supply governments generally use the government deficit as a means of influencing and controlling the economy in accordance with government policy.

Deflation. A contraction of the money supply (cf. *inflation*).

Demand deposits. Bank deposits that can be drawn upon instantly by the depositor (e.g. current accounts, which can be drawn upon instantly by writing cheques).

Depression. A severe *recession* (q.v.).

Discount (of bills). A deduction from the face value of a bill when purchased before its date of maturity. Discount in this sense is a form of *interest* (q.v. See also *rediscount*).

Discount market. Prior to March 1997 the discount market was a group of firms, most of which were authorised banks and all of which were members of the London Discount Market Association, that traded in short-dated bills, e.g. Treasury bills, and had a direct dealing relationship with the Bank of England. The discount market lent to the government by buying Treasury bills and financed its business by borrowing at very low rates of interest from the banks. If the banks were forced to call in loans to the discount market the discount houses could apply directly to the Bank of England to rediscount *eligible paper* (q.v.) or lend against its security. It was through the discount market, therefore, that the Bank of England acted as the lender of last resort to the banking system and was able to influence interest rates generally. (The Bank of England did not lend directly to the banks but provided money to the banking system as lender of last resort via the discount houses.) If the Bank of England wanted to raise interest rates it could create the conditions necessary to force the banks to call in loans to the discount market. For example, a substantial increase in the sale of medium- and long-dated government securities in open market operations by the Bank of England will lead to money being withdrawn from the banks by those who purchase the securities. This will reduce the banks' balances with the Bank of England. Since the banks' balances with the Bank of England are part of their reserve assets this would force the banks to call in loans to the discount market in order to replenish their reserves. This in turn forced the discount houses into the Bank, i.e. it forced the discount houses to borrow from the Bank of England at a penal rate of interest. This higher rate of interest was then passed on to the banks, which bought Treasury bills from the discount market because of their liquidity. The discount market was thus a buffer institution between the Bank of England and the banks (see "The Modern Banking System" in Chapter Four). By the mid-1990s, however, the number of discount houses had declined considerably and in March 1997 the Bank of England declared itself ready to enter into a direct dealing relationship with a much wider range of financial institutions than those previously operating in the discount market. The Bank is now prepared to deal directly with banks, building societies and securities firms provided certain supervisory and functional criteria are met, the chief criterion being that such firms must be able to maintain an active presence in the money market. Firms with a direct dealing relationship with the Bank of England are now called "counterparties" by the Bank. There is still a discount market in the sense that the Bank of England continues to rediscount eligible bills in its money market operations; but it has also broadened the range of money instruments with which it will now work. Much of the Bank's money market operations are now conducted in *repos* (q.v.).

Economic rationalisation. The *Concise Oxford Dictionary* defines economic rationalisation in the following way: to "make (a business etc.) more efficient by reorganising it to reduce or eliminate waste of labour, time, or materials." Economic rationalisation is the process whereby a business or enterprise is subjected to rational economic principles with the aim of maximising efficiency and thus increasing output. It is the increased output—i.e. creation of extra wealth— that is important. Were it not for this the Luddites might have had a valid point. Of course, an individual firm might not increase output itself as a result of pursuing economically rational practices. It may simply reduce its costs. But in a free market order these savings will benefit the economy as a whole, since they will either be passed on to customers in the form of lower prices or else passed on as increased profits or dividends to the owners or shareholders, who will either reinvest or spend the money in the economy. Other things being equal, therefore, the money saved by such rationalisation will find its way into the economy and stimulate output elsewhere even if it does not stimulate output in the particular firm or industry in which the rationalisation has been achieved. Economic rationalisation thus leads to greater *capitalisation* (q.v.) and hence to economic growth and social amelioration. The abandonment of economically rational practices—a feature of socialist economies in various degrees—leads to waste of labour, time and resources, and therefore to *decapitalisation* (q.v.) and economic decline.

Economic rationalisation was the distinctive feature of the kind of capitalism that developed in the Protestant nations after the Reformation. Max Weber contrasted this kind of capitalism, which he saw as the outworking of the Protestant asceticism or ethic, with the kind of capitalistic acquisition that has existed in all kinds of societies throughout history, including pre-Reformation Europe, which was "predominantly of an irrational and speculative character, or directed to acquisition by force, above all the acquisition of booty, whether directly in war or in the form of continuous fiscal booty by exploitation of subjects" (*The Protestant Ethic and the Spirit of Capitalism*, p. 20). Weber referred to those who pursued economic acquisition in this way as "capitalistic adventurers." A good example of such exploitation of subjects by fiscal booty was the system of monopolies that existed in England under the Tudor and early Stewart monarchies. The selling of monopolies was often a means of raising government revenue or of granting privileges to favourite courtiers. Walter Ralegh, for instance, a good example of Weber's "capitalistic adventurer" in every way, grew rich on the wine monopoly, receiving thereby the right to charge every wine merchant in England one pound per annum for the right to retail wine.

Eligible paper. First class securities (e.g. Treasury bills, bills of exchange accepted by an accepting house or a British bank, and British government stock with five years or less to maturity) that the Bank of England will rediscount or against the security of which it will lend money to the *discount market* (q.v.).

EEC. The European Economic Community, originally an economic trading area that came into existence on 1 January 1958 as a result of the signing of the Treaty of Rome in 1957. The six countries that signed the Treaty in 1957 were France, West Germany, Italy, Belgium, the Netherlands and Luxembourg. Britain joined the EEC in 1973. The purpose of the EEC, ostensibly, was the elimination of all obstacles to free trade between the member nations. Yet throughout most of the 1970s and 1980s non-tariff barriers to free trade between member nations increased and member States sought to protect their own domestic industries. In 1992 the Single European Act came into force, which committed the member nations to a "single market." However, since then it has become apparent that the main driving force behind the EEC is the desire on the part of certain member countries to create a political union. The passing of the Maastricht Treaty effectively meant the surrender of the member nations' political independence to the government of the European Community, which then became the European Union. The Maastricht Treaty came into force with difficulty in some member nations, and was ratified in others (e.g. Britain) with an "opt out" clause for the "social chapter," which committed the European Union to radical socialism. Britain eventually signed up to the social chapter after the election of a new Labour government in 1997. There is little doubt that the authority surrendered by member nations to the central government of the European Union as a result of the signing of this treaty, and hence the Union's power over member States, is such that a "United States of Europe," i.e. a pan-European super State, is now in the making. The political philosophy of those in control of the Union is socialist through and through and governments of member States, even if they are eager to move away from such socialism, as the British government claimed to be in the 1980s, have now lost the power to act in any way that is significantly out of step with European policy made in Brussels. It is ironic, however, that a Conservative government, under Edward Heath, took Britain into the EEC, and another Conservative government, under John Major, ratified the Maastricht Treaty, when the political philosophy driving the European Union is the very opposite of what is in the UK espoused as Conservative political philosophy.

ERM. The *exchange rate mechanism* of the EMS (European Monetary System). The ERM was an agreement between certain members of the European Monetary System to keep the exchange rates of their currencies within certain ratios relative to other currencies in the ERM. It was a test mechanism for a pan-European super-currency, which came into being in 1999 with the creation of the euro. Britain joined the ERM in October 1990 and left it in September 1992 after the price of sterling fell below its permitted exchange rate ratio. Currency speculators were blamed for the demise of sterling as a member of the ERM and its devaluation. A little reflection will show this to be unfair however. Markets reflect the value of the commodities offered for sale on those markets relative to other commodities. If the exchange rate of sterling is falling to such an extent that it cannot maintain its place in the ERM the fault lies not with those who trade in the markets, who simply express by their sales and purchases the value of the currency relative to other currencies, but with the authorities who have devalued the currency in the first place by their inflationary mismanagement of the economy.

Furthermore, as the then Governor of the Bank of England, Robert Leigh-Pemberton, made clear in a speech given on 8 October 1992, currency speculators were not solely nor even mainly responsible for the loss of confidence in sterling: "I well understand the widespread distaste at images of dealers gloating over the quick profits they had made at the expense of the nation. But don't be misled into thinking that this is the whole picture. It is in fact a caricature. Much of the selling—almost certainly *most* of the selling although it is difficult to demonstrate—originates with corporate treasurers or fund managers who are seeking to *protect* the value of their assets, or those of their employers, clients and customers—including depositors and investors—against devaluation, often in relation to foreign currency liabilities. When there is a clear risk that a currency will lose 5 or 10% of its value overnight there is inevitably a rush for the exit, some of it *by* the banks but much more *through* the banks, which anyway have prudential limits on the open position (i.e. the speculative position) they can take against sterling. There are, of course, those who are simply taking a gamble, some on a very large scale. But while they can accelerate or accentuate a problem—acting as a catalyst, if you like—it is implausible to see straight market speculators as the arbitrary *origin* of a problem in the markets; you have to remember that, if they get it wrong, they can easily lose as much as they hope to gain." (*Speech given by The Rt Hon Robin Leigh-Pemberton Governor of the Bank of England at the CBI Eastern Region Annual Dinner on Thursday 8 October 1992* [released as a press notice by the Bank of England at 19.30 hours, Thursday 8 October 1992])

In any case, floating exchange rates are more honest and preferable to fixed exchange rates, which are in fact fixed only because governments, via their central banks or even by means of political decree, interfere in the market thereby distorting it and curtailing free trade.

European Union. When the EEC came into existence in 1958 its purpose, ostensibly, was the creation of a European free market area. Since then, however, the purely economic basis of the EEC has been superseded by the political goal of a united Europe under a central European government. The EEC became the EC (European Community). Then with the signing of the Maastricht Treaty it became the European Union (see *EEC*).

Fiat money. Money created by government authority alone, usually of a substance that is of little value economically and thus not in itself suitable as a medium of exchange, e.g. paper. Because paper is available in abundant supply and cheap to produce governments can use paper currency to inflate the money supply at will. Obtaining gold, whether by means of mining it or trading for it, is considerably more difficult, and it is impossible to acquire in the quantities that modern governments require for their coffers. The printing of fiat money that is foisted on the economy by legal tender laws is a quick and easy way for governments to get their hands on the nation's wealth without using taxation. The Chinese, who experimented with various substances as forms of money, including sea shells, were the first to use paper currency. They were also the first to invent toilet paper, arguably a more beneficial contribution to the progress of civilisation.

Fiduciary issue. The amount of banknotes issued over and above the value of the precious metal reserves held by a bank. These notes functioned in the economy as money only because people believed that the bank issuing them was safe (i.e. solvent), when in fact it was not, since it could not redeem all the notes it issued. They were used in faith: the holders of the notes used them in faith and the banks issued them in faith. Hence the term fiduciary media (from the Latin *fides*, meaning *trust*). Originally the Bank Charter Act of 1844 permitted the Bank of England to issue fiduciary media to the value of £14 million. This fiduciary issue had to be backed by government securities (debt). With the abandonment of gold, however, the term has in a sense become meaningless since all our banknotes are fiduciary media (backed only by government debt).

Fiscal policy. Government taxation and expenditure policy. The term comes from the Latin word *fiscus*, meaning *purse*. Because government has grown so large and become the biggest economic actor in the economy—spending over 43 per cent of the GNP in 1993—fiscal policy, i.e. what the government taxes and spends its revenues on, can be used as a means of controlling the economy in accordance with government ideology as well as a means of funding legitimate government business (cf. *monetary policy*).

Fractional reserve banking. The practice of issuing more claims for money (e.g. banknotes, cheques, demand deposits) than there are reserves to meet those claims. Thus, if a bank has £1,000 of gold deposited in its vaults, it might issue banknotes to the value of £10,000, only £1,000 of which is backed by *hard money* (q.v.). The amount of money reserved to redeem the bank's notes is only a fraction of the total face value of the notes it has issued. It has, therefore, issued fraudulent banknotes (i.e. claims for money that it cannot honour) and is, as a consequence, insolvent. Most businesses in this condition would be declared bankrupt and the official receiver called in. A bank, however, operates in this condition all the time; insolvency is the very basis of the modern banking system. Today banknotes are not backed by gold or silver at all, and our coin is purely token coin. Our currency has become a *fiat currency* (see *fiat money*). Cash has effectively become small change in our economy and most of the money in circulation is *bank money* (q.v.). The reserves held by the banks consist mostly of Treasury bills and government securities with five years or less to maturity (i.e. government debt), commercial bills and local authority bills eligible for discount at the Bank of England (private and local authority debt), *company tax reserve certificates* (q.v.), and money at call with the London money market. The system operates basically by monetising debt, i.e. causing debt to circulate as money—hence R. S. Sayers' definition of banks as "institutions whose debts—usually referred to as 'bank deposits'—are commonly accepted in final settlement of other people's debts" (see Chapter Four).

GDP. The gross domestic product, i.e. the total value of the flow of goods and services produced in an economy over a twelve month period (see *GNP*).

Gilt-edged securities. Long- and medium-dated interest-bearing government bonds (IOUs) issued to raise funds for the government (not all of these government stocks mature however; some stocks, such as consols, are perpetual interest-bearing bonds that are not dated). It is largely by the issue of these bonds and Treasury bills (q.v.) that the government borrows the money to fund the deficit—i.e. the shortfall between government receipts and expenditure. It is often said that these bonds are gilt-edged because they are considered absolutely safe. This is misleading for two reasons: first, the reason these bonds are called gilt-edged has nothing to do with their supposed security, but rather with the fact that the issues of these government stocks were originally recorded in a ledger with gilt edges. Second, however, and more to the point, such securities are not necessarily safe, since changes in economic conditions subsequent to their issue can reduce the value of their yield or depress their market value to such an extent that the holder has to bear a capital loss if he wishes to sell. In the case of stocks that mature it is true that they are safe in the sense that they will be redeemed at face value when they mature, but again this may mean very little if governments in the meantime have pursued inflationary policies. Performance of the War Loan stock issued in 1917 at 5 per cent and converted in 1932 to 3½ per cent between the end of the 1940s and the beginning of the 1980s is a good example of the fact that gilt-edged stocks are not always safe (see p. 136f.).

GNP. The gross domestic product (*GDP*, q.v.) plus incomes earned from overseas investments, minus incomes earned in the domestic market by overseas investors.

Hard currency. Currency that is undervalued in international exchange and therefore for which there is a high demand relative to supply in the currency markets. For example, if sterling became undervalued against foreign currency, US dollars or Deutschmarks for instance, holders of these currencies would be able to buy more sterling with their dollars and Deutschmarks. This would encourage British exports and tourism in Britain. Sterling would be considered a hard currency under these conditions. If sterling became overvalued against these currencies, however, holders of US dollars and Deutschmarks would not be able to buy as much sterling with their dollars or Deutschmarks. The demand for sterling as a foreign currency would decline and British exports and holidays in Britain for Americans and Germans would become more expensive. Sterling would be a soft currency under these conditions. Imports from and holidays in the US and Germany would become more attractive to British citizens, however, since holders of sterling would be able to buy more dollars and Deutschmarks with their sterling. Hard currency should not be confused with *hard money* (q.v.), i.e. specie.

Hard money. Specie, e.g. gold and silver coins. The term hard money, as used in this book and by proponents of hard money economies, should not be confused with the often somewhat ambiguously used term *hard currency*.

Inflation. An expansion of the money supply (cf. *deflation*). An expansion of the money supply leads to an aggregate rise in the level of prices, other things being equal. Since there is more money chasing the same supply of goods prices rise to a higher level at which all the money circulating in the economy is used to purchase all the available goods. It is important to understand, therefore, that this increase in the aggregate level of prices is an effect of inflation. Inflation is not caused by retailers putting prices up or by the labour unions' demanding wage rises; these are the *effects* of inflation. Inflation in modern Western economies is caused by the monetary authorities, i.e. the government and the central bank (the Bank of England and the Treasury in the UK), and by the banks, which are allowed to profit from the practice of *fractional reserve banking* (q.v.). Today, however, the term "inflation" is usually used to mean a rise of the aggregate level of prices. It is important that the reader distinguish between this popular definition of inflation, i.e. *price* inflation, and the definition used in this book. Price inflation, i.e. rising prices, is an *effect* of inflation, i.e. growth in the money supply, other things being equal.

Prices may also increase as a result of an increase in the *velocity of circulation of money* (q.v.), but unless this is generated by public expectation of currency devaluation (during a period of high inflation for instance) it is not of great significance (see *quantity theory of money*).

Interest. The difference between the value placed on the possession of a good or the satisfaction of a want today and the possession of the same good or satisfaction of the same want at some future date. We all value the possession of something today greater than its possession at a future date, other things being equal. The difference between one's valuation of a good to be obtained at a future date and one's valuation of that same good if obtained in the present constitutes interest. People who borrow are prepared to pay to get the use of a sum of money in the present, which is of more value to them now than it would be in say a year's time when they have saved up. Those who lend money charge a rate of interest that makes the value of the sum repaid to them at a later date greater than the value of the principal at the time it was loaned out. Without this interest there would be no inducement for a creditor to lend out his money. In an inflationary economy interest may represent more than this however, since the currency is depreciating in value constantly. The market rate of interest may represent, therefore, not only interest proper (the *originary* rate of interest—see *originary interest*), but also a charge made in order to ensure that the sum less originary interest repaid by the borrower is equal in purchasing power to the principal at the time it was loaned out.

Invisibles. A term relating to the *balance of payments* (q.v.). Invisibles are services provided by UK residents to overseas residents and expenditure by UK residents on foreign services, e.g. banking services, insurance, tourism, shipping, profits earned overseas and interest payments.

Legal tender. Money that cannot legally be refused in settlement of debt (cf. *currency*).

Limited Liability. A status granted in law to joint-stock companies limiting the liability of a shareholder to the nominal value of his stock (i.e. the price he paid for the shares). If a company is declared bankrupt and the receiver is called in the shareholders may lose part or all of their investment since the company's assets will be sold to reimburse its creditors. But shareholders will not be expected or required by law to make good out of their own personal estates any shortfall between the company's debts and the proceeds from the sale of its assets should the latter prove insufficient to clear its debts. In that case the creditors themselves will have to bear the loss, not the shareholders.

Medium of exchange. See *money*.

Merchant banks. Banks that specialise in providing banking and financial services to industry for purposes of international trade and, since the end of World War Two, for domestic trade also.

Minimum lending rate (prior to March 1997) or *bank rate* (prior to October 1972) or *repo rate* (since March 1997). The minimum lending rate was rate of interest at which the Bank of England would rediscount *eligible paper* (q.v.) or lend against its security to the *discount market* (q.v.). Until August 1981, when it ceased to be continuously posted, the MLR was set every Friday by the Bank of England at a rate of ½ per cent above the average discount rate on Treasury bills rounded up to the nearest ¼ per cent. Since October 1981 an MLR has been announced only six times. When the Chancellor announces an increase in interest rates today, therefore, he usually refers to the commercial banks' *base rates*. But the banks are not legally obligated to raise their base rates in accordance with the Chancellor's wishes. Nevertheless, when the Chancellor announces an increase he can usually be fairly certain that the banks will fall in line. The means by which this increase in the banks' base rates is achieved is an indirect one however. If the Chancellor wishes base rates to rise he raises the rate of interest at which the Bank of England will act as lender of last resort to the banking system (this was the old MLR). This has the knock-on effect of inducing the commercial banks to raise their base rates, and therefore interest rates generally will rise. As already mentioned, the banks are not legally obligated to follow the Chancellor's lead, but due to the way that the banking system works an increase in the Bank of England's lender of last resort rate will push up interest rates generally simply because the banks would be penalised economically if they did not fall in line. Since March 1997 the minimum lending rate has been replaced by *repo rate* (q.v.), which is broadly equivalent to the old minimum lending rate, and the Bank of England deals directly with a much wider range of financial institutions than those previously represented by the London Discount Market Association. The repo rate is set monthly by the Monetary Policy Committee. See "The Modern Banking System" in Chapter Four.

Monetary policy. The attempt to control the economy by controlling the money supply. Cf. *fiscal policy*.

Monetisation of debt. A process by which a bank, or the government via the Bank of England and the Treasury's Debt Management Office, transforms its debts into money. For example, when a bank issues banknotes it creates debts (i.e. IOUs containing a promise to pay the bearer on demand a specified sum of money) that function in the economy in the same way that money functions, i.e. as a common medium of exchange. This practice is safe as long as the bank has specie stored in its vaults to the full value of the banknotes it issues. But if the bank issues extra banknotes over and above the value of the specie it holds it creates debts that it cannot redeem. If everyone holding these banknotes were to claim their money (e.g. gold or silver) at the same time there would not be enough stored in the bank's vaults to go round. These extra unbacked banknotes function in the economy in just the same way as any other banknote, since they are exactly the same as any of the bank's other notes. These unbacked notes are called fiduciary media (see *fiduciary issue*). By issuing fiduciary media, therefore, the bank monetises its debts, i.e. it prints unredeemable IOUs that function as money in the economy. This monetisation of debt is also inflationary since fiduciary media expands the supply of money in circulation.

Similarly, the government can monetise its debts by issuing securities that function in the modern banking system as reserve assets on the basis of which *bank money* (q.v.) can be created by the banks. Suppose, for example, that the government increases the amount of money it borrows by issuing extra *Treasury bills* (q.v.) that are bought by the banking sector. The banks will have to pay for these bills by drawing on their balances at the Bank of England. However, once the government has spent this money back into circulation it will be deposited by those who receive it in their bank accounts, or in the bank accounts of those with whom they trade, and will by this route find its way back into the banks' balances at the Bank of England. The banks' aggregate balances with the Bank of England, therefore, will ultimately remain unchanged as a result of the sale of the extra Treasury bills. However, Treasury bills, because of their liquidity, form an important part of the banks' eligible reserve assets, and any increase in the banks' holding of these bills will enable them to advance more loans to their customers. In other words the increase in Treasury bills held by the banks will enable them to create extra bank money. Since in the fractional reserve system the value of a bank's eligible reserve assets is only a fraction of the total value of the bank money it is able to create, the issue of these extra Treasury bills will enable the banks to create bank money the value of which is many times greater than their holding of extra Treasury bills. Thus, by issuing Treasury bills (government IOUs) the government is able to transform its debts into a form of near-money that the banks can hold as reserve assets and on the basis of which they can create bank money. This process of monetisation of the debts of banks and governments accounts for most of the *inflation* (q.v.) experienced in modern Western economies. See Chapter Four.

Money. The most marketable good, i.e. the good that the greatest number of people will accept in exchange for the widest variety of goods. There are four qualities that a good must have if it is to function efficiently as money: it must be (*a*) scarce, (*b*) easily portable, (*c*) easily divisible, and (*d*) durable. Because of its marketability money becomes a common medium of exchange and is able to provide the economy with a rational means of economic calculation (the price mechanism), which is essential for economic efficiency and progress. When this important function of money is corrupted or destroyed, through for instance government-controlled inflation of the money supply with fiat paper money (see *fiat money*), fiduciary media (see *fiduciary issue*) or *bank money* (q.v.), the results for the economy are disastrous: at the very least the use of capital is not kept at its optimum level (i.e. economic growth is retarded because capital is diverted from its most productive use to less productive uses), or is squandered and consumed on non-essentials rather than put to productive use. This results in a decrease in the rate of capitalisation and in economic depression, with the consequent lowering of general standards of living and the economic hardships that this entails. Yet such government-controlled manipulation of the money supply is one of the major means used by the political authorities to "manage" the economy. This explains the constant swing between booms and slumps (see *business cycle*).

Gold and silver, the commodities that have historically functioned as money throughout the world, are not used in domestic Western economies as forms of money today. This is due, however, not to gold and silver being unsuitable as such, but rather to the fact that government-created fiat money has been foisted upon the public by legal tender laws.

Modern economists find it increasingly difficult to define money because the forms of money in use consist mostly of token money, bank deposits, money substitutes and claims to money, which, through government-imposed restrictions on the use of *hard money* (q.v.) and the development of the *fractional reserve banking* system (q.v.), function in the economy in the same way that hard money used to function. The Bank of England defines money in the following way: narrow money (M_0, M_1 and M_2), and broad money (M_3, M_4, M_4c and M_5). M_0 consists of notes and coin in circulation (including notes and coin in the banks' tills) and the banks' operational balances at the Bank of England. M_1 consists of notes and coin in circulation with the public (but not in the banks' tills) plus private sector non-interest-bearing sterling sight (i.e. demand) bank deposits (this is the non-interest-bearing component of M_1), plus private sector interest-bearing sight bank deposits. M_2 consists of the non-interest-bearing component of M_1 plus private sector interest-bearing retail (e.g. high street) sterling bank deposits and private sector holdings of retail building society shares and deposits and National Savings Bank ordinary accounts. M_3 consists of M_1 plus private sector sterling time bank deposits and private sector holdings of sterling bank certificates of deposit. M_4 consists of M_3 plus private sector holdings of building society shares and deposits and sterling certificates of deposit in building societies, minus building society holdings of bank deposits and bank certificates of deposit, and notes and coin. M4c consists of M4 plus bank and building society deposits in foreign currencies. M5 consists of M4 plus holdings by the private sector (excluding building societies) of money market instruments (bank bills, Treasury bills, local authority deposits), certificates of tax deposit, and National Savings instruments (excluding certificates, SAYE and other long-term deposits). (Source: *Economic Progress Report* [HM Treasury, August 1988]; *Bank of England Quarterly Bulletin*, cited in John Sloman, *Economics* [Harvester Wheatsheaf, 1991], p. 668–670). The Bank of England's definition of money is in flux however. For example, in the May 1987 *Bank of England Quarterly Bulletin* money was defined in terms of M0, M1, M2, £M3, M3, M4 and M5, and it was proposed that after 20 May 1987 £M3 should be redesignated M3 and the existing M3 redesignated M3c, i.e. £M3 plus private-sector foreign currency deposits (p. 212). Not all these definitions are emphasised equally by the authorities. Prior to the late 1980s M1 and M3 used to be the definitions more commonly in use, but for various reasons these were dropped and today M0, M4 and M5 are the commonly used measures of the money supply.

Money market. The market for short-term debt, e.g. short-dated bills of exchange, Treasury bills and repos. The money market includes institutions and firms such as the banks, building societies, securities firms, discount market, accepting houses, bullion and foreign exchange markets.

National debt. If the government wishes to spend more than it raises by taxation it has to borrow the money to do so. The debt incurred in any given year is the public sector borrowing requirement (see *PSBR*). The total debt accumulated by the government in the current and previous years comprises the national debt. The national debt consists of (*a*) funded debt, e.g. consols and war loan stock, which are perpetual interest-bearing stocks that do not mature; (*b*) unfunded (or floating) debt, e.g. Treasury bills, and (*c*) other unfunded debt, e.g. medium- and long-dated securities, National Savings Certificates, and Premium Bonds.

Originary interest. The ratio between the value one places on the satisfaction of a want or the possession of a good in the present and the value one places on the satisfaction of the same want or possession of the same good at some time in the future. The *rate* of originary interest is determined by one's *time preference* (q.v.).

Originary interest is interest proper (see *interest*. See also p. 65ff. above. On the ethics of charging interest see Appendix B).

PSBR. The public sector borrowing requirement, i.e. the total amount of borrowing needed to fund the public sector *deficit* (q.v.) in any given year. The public sector includes central and local government, local authorities (health and education), social services, public corporations and nationalised industries. The PSBR for 1993 was nearly £46 billion. Without the proceeds of privatisation it would have been well over £51 billion.

PSDR. The public sector debt repayment. If total government income is greater than total government expenditure the government has a financial surplus and is able to repay some of the *national debt* (q.v.). If this surplus is generated by genuine growth in the economy—i.e. wealth creation leading to greater tax receipts for the government—it is beneficial for the economy since it permits tax rates to be lowered. This in turn stimulates the economy and leads to greater wealth creation. As a result government spending as a proportion of GNP can be reduced, again helping to strengthen the free market and promote economic growth. If, however, the surplus is generated by inflation, the economy suffers, since the growth of economic activity, which leads to increased tax revenues during the boom, is followed sooner or later by recession (cf. *business cycle*). The Thatcher government ran a PSDR in the late 1980s. This PSDR was achieved by a combination of factors: partly it was due to inflation—that is to say, it was made possible by the increased tax receipts generated by the redistribution of wealth that inflation produces and therefore was effectively a tax on capital not on wealth creation; partly it was due to the proceeds accruing from Thatcher's privatisation programme; and partly it was due to genuine economic growth. It is impossible to determine the precise extent to which genuine economic growth contributed to the PSDR, however, and to what extent it was made possible by inflation.

Quantity theory of money. The theory that fluctuations in the value of the monetary unit and hence changes in the aggregate level of prices are related to changes in the quantity of money in circulation. Other things being equal, therefore, any substantial variation in the latter will affect the value of the monetary unit and thus the aggregate level of prices in the economy (i.e. if the money supply is increased prices will rise; if the money supply is decreased prices will fall).

The quantity theory of money has been subject to much criticism. The usual argument raised against it is that decreases in the velocity of circulation of money will tend to cancel the effects of monetary expansion and therefore inflation of the money supply does not inevitably lead to rising prices. Although this is true theoretically, and even possible in the early period of an inflationary boom, it is largely irrelevant in an economy such as modern Britain, where continual inflation is a characteristic of economic life. Increases or decreases in the velocity of circulation of money are not usually significant unless the public expect some sort of economic crisis. If people expect price inflation, or a higher level of price inflation than they have been used to, this will lead to an *increase* in the velocity of circulation, not a decrease. Some economists call such an increase in the velocity of circulation the second stage of inflation (e.g. Hans Senholz, *Age of Inflation* [Spring Mills Pennsylvania: Libertarian Press, Inc., 1979], p. 65f.). Increasing velocity of circulation of money is thus usually a symptom of inflation. It occurs when people try to spend their money more quickly because the monetary unit is being devalued—i.e. its purchasing power is declining. Holding onto money in such circumstances will lead to impoverishment, hence the increase in the velocity of circulation. The argument that the quantity theory of money is flawed because it does not take into account the velocity of circulation is naïve and misses the point. Why would people borrow money in order to save it in an inflationary economy? In an inflationary economy banks are trying to increase loans to their customers (create bank money). People borrow money to spend it, not to save it. Velocity of circulation will decrease in a *deflationary* economy but not in an inflationary economy unless people are unaware of what is happening, which is sometimes the case in the early period of the cycle (cf. note 15 on p. 74). But if inflation continues and people realise what is happening velocity of circulation will begin to *increase* as people try to find some way to avoid the depreciation of their savings by spending their money. This will further contribute to rising price levels. An increase in the velocity of circulation is thus a feature of an inflationary economy. Once these facts are taken into consideration this criticism of the quantity theory of money loses its validity.

Recession. A period in which society readjusts to a situation in which there are less scarce resources and capital available in the economy after a period of inflation and the consequent waste of economic resources that it generates. See *business cycle*.

Rediscount. The purchase by the Bank of England of *eligible paper* (q.v.) from the *discount market* (q.v.).

Repo. "Repo" is short for "sale and repurchase agreement." A repo is defined by the Gilt Repo Code of Best Practice as "A transaction, carried out under an agreement, in which one party sells securities to another, and at the same time and as part of the same transaction, commits to repurchase equivalent securities on a specified future date, or at call, at a specified price." Since 1997 repos have been used by the Bank of England as a major instrument in its operations in the money market. The *repo rate* (i.e. the interest rate on repos) is broadly equivalent to the old *minimum lending rate* (q.v.).

Settlement banks (sometimes called "clearing banks"). The core commercial banks that operate the *clearing system* (q.v.), e.g. High Street banks such as Barclays, Lloyds. These banks have to hold deposits at the Bank of England. There are currently sixteen settlement banks in the UK. The new high street banks that were formerly building societies, e.g. the Halifax, are not settlement banks.

Slump. The latter part of the *business cycle* (q.v.) during which the economy has to readjust to a situation in which there are less scarce resources and capital available for the manufacture of essential and non-luxury goods due to the uneconomic and wasteful consumption of resources and capital during the boom period.

Tax reserve certificates. Non-negotiable securities in which companies and individuals can invest funds that have been set aside in anticipation of tax liabilities. These securities bear interest and can be cashed in or surrendered in payment of taxes when they fall due (the rate of interest paid out is lower when they are cashed in than when they are used in payment of taxes).

Time deposits. Bank deposits from which withdrawals can be made only after a period of notice has been given to the bank (e.g. deposit accounts).

Time preference. The extent of one's preference for the satisfaction of a want (or possession of a good) today rather than at some future date. Time preference gives rise to *originary interest* (q.v. See also *interest*).

Token money. Once upon a time (i.e. before 1914) the coin in circulation in Britain consisted of precious metals (e.g. gold and silver). As a result of the government's determination to get its hands on the nation's gold at the outbreak of World War One gold coin went out of circulation. Then in 1920 the silver coinage was debased to 50 per cent silver. Finally, in 1947 even the debased silver coinage went out of circulation and was replaced by cupro-nickel tokens. The metal content of these cupro-nickel coins is worth less than their face value and they are merely part of our fiat money system. Such coin is not money in the proper sense—i.e. the most marketable good— but rather token money, since it is virtually worthless in itself and is only accepted because it is *legal tender* (q.v. See also *money*).

Trade cycle. See *business cycle*.

Treasury bills. Short-dated government IOUs (issued usually for 91 days) that are sold and circulate at a discount prior to maturity. They are issued by the Treasury's Debt Management Office and are used by the Bank of England in its money market operations to influence interest rates and control the money supply in accordance with government policy. See pp. 113–132 above.

Usury. Another word for *interest* (q.v.). The term *interest* was originally used by the canonists of the twelfth century to denote the profits made on certain kinds of financial and credit transactions that were designed to circumvent the ban on usury but were considered legal. The term *usury* later came to be used of rates of interest that were considered exorbitant or illegal, and the term *interest* of rates that were legal and considered fair. The distinction is a fiction however, a piece of scholastic casuistry.

VAT. Value Added Tax, a sales tax in the European Union. It was introduced in the United Kingdom in 1973 as a result of Britain's joining the EEC (now the European Union). The current rate in the UK is 17½ per cent. Some goods are zero rated, much to the chagrin of the Euro-bureaucrats, since most member nations of the EU charge VAT on a wider range of goods than the British government does. British Chancellors of the Exchequer have periodically threatened the British public with charging VAT on goods that are not "vatable" or that are zero rated in the United Kingdom, e.g. food, books, children's clothing, domestic fuel etc. With the exception of VAT on domestic fuel, which came into force as a result of the 1993 Spring budget (though at a rate of 8 per cent not 17½ per cent), these threats have not materialised, but ever closer involvement with the European Union will make this situation increasingly anomalous. Imposition of VAT on domestic fuel is to be explained by the enormous deficit of £50 billion that the government anticipated it would be running in 1993 (in the event the actual figure was a mere £46 billion) rather than pressure from the European Union.

Velocity of circulation of money. The number of times a monetary unit exchanges hands over a given period. Increases or decreases in the velocity of circulation are unlikely to be significant unless they are caused by some sort of crisis, which might be precipitated, for example, by panic buying, or unless the public expects some drastic change, such as devaluation of the currency (e.g. rising prices caused by inflation). In the case of devaluation the velocity of circulation will increase due to people trying to spend their money before it is devalued. If there is deflation the velocity of circulation will decrease, since people will try to hold on to their money as long as possible to gain from its increasing value. Changes in the exchange value of money of this magnitude are unlikely, however, unless they are created by government abuse of the money supply. Unfortunately, such abuse of the money supply by the monetary authorities is common in modern Western economies, hence the continual inflation experienced during the past fifty years and the constant susceptibility of the economy to the trade cycle. The remedy for the problems associated with the latter, however, lies not with government measures aimed at controlling the velocity of circulation of money (i.e. the volume of purchases made by the public), but rather with abolition of the government's power to expand the money supply artificially and license other privileged institutions (e.g. banks) to expand the money supply artificially, since it is the abuse of this power that causes such problems in the first place (cf. *quantity theory of money*).

Visibles. A term relating to the *balance of payments* (q.v.). Visibles are physical goods that are exported or imported, e.g. motorcars, fridges, raw materials, semi-manufactured goods etc. Visibles do not include services such as banking, insurance and tourism, which are *invisibles* (q.v.).

Welfare economics. The branch of economics that studies the efficiency of markets and resource allocation and analyses the effects of economic policy in terms of improved social welfare.

BIBLIOGRAPHY

Anderson, B. L., and P. L. Cottrell, *Money and Banking in England: The Development of the Banking System 1694–1914* (Newton Abbott: David and Charles, 1974).

Aristotle, *Politics* (Oxford: Clarendon Press, 1905, translated by Benjamin Jowett).

The Bank of England (Bank of England, October 1992).

Bank of England Banking Act Report 1989/90 (Bank of England).

Bank of England Inflation Report, February 1993 (reprinted from the February 1993 *Bank of England Quarterly Bulletin*).

Bank of England operations in the sterling money market (Bank of England, October 1988).

Bank of England operations in the sterling money markets: operational notice (Bank of England, June 1999).

Bank of England Quarterly Bulletin, March 1982 (Bank of England).

Bank of England Quarterly Bulletin, December 1986 (Bank of England).

Bank of England Quarterly Bulletin, May 1987 (Bank of England).

Bank of England Quarterly Bulletin, November 1989 (Bank of England).

Bank of England Quarterly Bulletin, February 1990 (Bank of England).

Banking Act 1979: Annual Report by the Bank of England 1986/87 (Bank of England).

Banking Supervision (Bank of England, May 1993).

Bannock, Graham, R. E. Baxter and Ray Rees, *The Penguin Dictionary of Economics* (London: Allan Lane and New York: The Viking Press, [1972] 1979).

Barnes, R. J., *Fundamentals of Economics* (London: Butterworths, Second Edition 1967).

Barrois, G. A., "Debt, Debtor" in *The Interpreter's Dictionary of the Bible* (Nashville: Abingdon Press, 1962).

Barr, James, *Holy Scripture: Canon, Authority, Criticism* (Oxford: Clarendon Press, 1983).

Barrois, G. A., "Trade and Commerce" in *The Interpreter's Dictionary of the Bible* (Nashville: Abingdon Press, 1962).

Bauer, P. T., and B. S. Yamey, *The Economics of Underdeveloped Countries* (London: James Nisbet and Co. Ltd, 1957).

Bauer, P. T., *Economic Analysis and Policy in Underdeveloped Countries* (London: Routledge and Kegan Paul Ltd, [1957] 1966).

Bauer, P. T., *Indian Economic Policy and Development* (London: George Allen and Unwin Ltd, 1961).

Bauer, P. T., *Equality, The Third World and Economic Delusion* (London: Methuen, [1981] 1982).

Bauer, P. T., *Reality and Rhetoric: Studies in the Economics of Development* (London: Weidenfeld and Nicolson, 1984).

Baxter, Richard, *Chapters from A Christian Directory*, Selected by Jeannette Tawney with a preface by the Right Rev. Charles Gore, D.D. (London: G. Bell and Sons Ltd, 1925).

Begg, David, Stanley Fischer and Rudiger Dornbusch, *Economics* (London: McGraw-Hill Book Company, Third Edition, 1991).

Bennett, W. H., "Debt, Debtor" in James Hastings. ed., *A Dictionary of the Bible* (Edinburgh: T. and T. Clark, 1902).

Bennett, W. H., "Usury" in James Hastings. ed., *A Dictionary of the Bible* (Edinburgh: T. and T. Clark, 1902).

Berman, Harold J., *Law and Revolution: The Formation of the Western Legal Tradition* (Cambridge, Massachusetts: Harvard University Press 1983).

Black, John, *The Economics of Modern Britain: An Introduction to Macroeconomics* (Oxford: Martin Robertson, Third Edition 1982).

Blass, F. and A. Debrunner, *A Greek Grammar of the New Testament and Other Early Christian Literature* (Cambridge University Press/University of Chicago Press, 1961).

Blumenfeld, Samuel L., *The New Illiterates* (Boise, Idaho: The Paradigm Company, [1973] 1988).

Body, Richard, *Farming in the Clouds* (London: Temple Smith, 1984).

Böhm-Bawerk, Eugen von, *Capital and Interest* (South Holland, Illinois: Libertarian Press, 1959), 3 vols.

The Decades of Henry Bullinger (The Parker Society: Cambridge University Press, [1549] 1851), Vol. II.

Burckhardt, Jacob, *The Civilisation of the Renaissance in Italy* (New York: The New American Library of World Literature, 1961).

Burningham, David, *Economics* (Hodder and Stoughton, [1978] 1991).

John Calvin, *Commentaries on The Four Last Books of Moses Arranged in the Form of a Harmony* (Grand Rapids, Michigan: Eerdmans), 4 vols.

Calvin, John, *Calvin's Ecclesiastical Advice* (T. and T. Clark, 1991).

Capie, Forrest and Alan Webber, *A Monetary History of the United Kingdom, 1870–1982* (London: George Allen and Unwin, 1985), Vol. 1.

The Chancellor's Statement to the House of Commons on the Bank of England (HM Treasury, 20th May 1997).

Chandler, George, *Four Centuries of Banking as illustrated by the Bankers, Customers and Staff associated with the constituent banks of Martins Bank Limited*, Vol. 1, *The Grasshopper and the Liver Bird, Liverpool and London* (London: B. T. Batsford Ltd, 1964).

Chilton, David, *Productive Christians in an Age of Guilt Manipulators* (Tyler, Texas: Institute for Christian Economics, [1981] 1985).

Chrystal, Alec k., ed., *Government debt structure and monetary conditions: A conference organised by the Bank of England 18–19 June 1998* (Bank of England 1999).

Clapham, Sir John, *The Bank of England: A History* (Cambridge University Press, 1944), 2 vols.

Clapham, Sir John, *A Concise Economic History of Britain from the earliest Times to 1750* (Cambridge University Press, [1949] 1966).

Clark, H. B., *Biblical Law* (Portland, Oregon: Binfords and Mort, 1943).

Coinage Act, 1971, Chapter 24.

Cohn, Norman, *The Pursuit of the Millennium* (London: Temple Smith, [1957], 1970).

Davis, J. J., *Your Wealth in God's World: Does the Bible Support the Free Market* (Phillipsburg, New Jersey: Presbyterian and Reformed, 1984).

Day, A. C. L., *Outline of Monetary Economics* (Oxford: The Clarendon Press, [1957] 1960).

Debt Management Report 1999–2000 (HM Treasury, march 1999).

Defence (Finance) Regulations, 1939 *(made under the Emergency Powers (Defence) Acts, 1939 and 1940, printed as amended up to the 14th October, 1942) together with A classified list of Orders made under the Defence (Finance) Regulations, 1939, and in force on the 14th October, 1942* (HMSO, 1942).

Duncan, Alan and Dominic Hobson, *Saturn's Children: How the State Devours Liberty, Prosperity and Virtue* (London: Sinclair-Stevenson, 1995).

Economic and Monetary Union in Europe (Bank of England, May 1994)

Edersheim, Alfred, *Sketches of Jewish Social Life in the Days of Christ* (Grand Rapids, Michigan: Eerdmans, 1988).

Elniff, T. I., *The Guise of Every Graceless Heart: Human Autonomy in Puritan Thought and Practice* (Vallecito, California: Ross House Books, 1981).

Epstein, Rabbi Dr I., ed., *The Babylonian Talmud* (London: The Soncino Press).

Exchange Control Act, 1947, 10 and 11 Geo. 6. Ch. 14.

Exchange Control Act, 1947, EC 62, Dated 8 August 1968, Supplement No. 2, 1 April 1971.

Exchange Control Act, 1947, EC 62, Dated 16 April 1975, Supplement No. 1, 16 December 1977.

Exchange Control Act, 1947, EC 62, Dated 16 April 1975, Supplement No. 2, 12 September 1978.

Exchange Control Act, 1947, Notice to Authorised Banks and Authorised Dealers in Gold [EC 62] (Bank of England, 8th August 1968)

Exchange Control Act, 1947, Notice to Authorised Banks and Authorised Dealers in Gold [EC 62] (Bank of England, 16th April, 1975).

Exchange Control (Gold Coins Exemption) Order 1966, Aide Memoire for Coin Collectors (Bank of England, 27th April, 1966).

Exchange Control (Gold Coins Exemption) Order 1966, Aide Memoire for Coin Collectors (Bank of England, 8th August, 1968).

Exodus Rabbah (London: The Soncino Press, 1983, translated by Rabbi Dr S. M. Lehrman).

Financial Statistics, No. 140, December 1973; No. 182, December 1977; No. 248, December 1982; No. 381, January 1994 (London: HMSO).

"The First Year of the Gilt Repo Market," *Bank of England Quarterly Bulletin*, May 1997, Vol. 37, No. 2.

The Foreign Exchange Market (Bank of England, February 1993).

The Future of UK Government Cash Management: The New Framework (United Kingdom Debt Management Office, December 4, 1998).

Goodzwaard, Bob, *Capitalism and Progress* (Toronto: Wedge Publishing Foundation, 1979).

Gray, Simon and Glenn Hoggarth, *Introduction to Monetary Operations* (Centre for Central Banking Studies, Bank of England, 1996).

Gray, Simon, *Government Securities: Primary Issuance* (Centre for Central Banking Studies, Bank of England, 1997).

Green, Timothy, *The World of Gold* (London: Michael Joseph, 1968).

Green, Timothy, *The New World of Gold* (London: Weidenfeld and Nicolson, [1982] 1985).

Green, Timothy, *The Prospect for Gold: The View to the Year 2000* (London: Rosendale Press, 1987).

Gilt Repo Review 1997–1998 (HM Treasury).

Gilt Repo Review 1998–1999 (HM Treasury, July 1999).

Griffiths, Brian, *Morality and the Market Place* (London: Hodder and Stoughton, 1982).

Griffiths, Brian, *The Moral Basis of the Market Economy* (London: Conservative Political Centre, 1983).

Griffiths, Brian, *The Creation of Wealth* (London: Hodder and Stoughton, 1984).

Griffiths, Brian, *Monetarism and Morality* (London: Centre for Policy Studies, 1985).

Guide to United Kingdom Exchange Control (Bank of England, February, 1977).

Harrison, Peter, *The Bible, Protestantism and the Rise of Natural Science* (Cambridge University Press, 1998).

Harvey, J., *Modern Economics* (London: The MacMillan Press Ltd, [1969] 1978).

Hay, Donald, *Economics Today, A Christian Critique* (Apollos, Inter-Varsity Press, 1989).

Hayek, F. A., *The Road to Serfdom* (London: George Routledge and Sons Ltd, [1944] 1945).

Hayek, F. A., *Denationalisation of Money* (London: Institute of Economic Affairs, [1976] 1990. Hobart Paper [Special] 70).

Heslam, Peter S., *Creating A Christian Worldview: Abraham Kuyper's Lectures of Calvinism* (Eerdmans/Paternoster Press, 1998).

Hill, Christopher, *The Century of Revolution 1603–1714* (Edinburgh: Thomas Nelson and Sons Ltd, 1961).

Hill, Christopher, *Society and Puritanism in Pre-Revolutionary England* (London: Secker and Warburg, 1964).

Hoff, Trygve J. B., *Economic Calculation in the Socialist Society* (Indianapolis: Liberty Fund, [1949] 1981).

Hogarth, Glen, *Introduction to Monetary Policy* (Bank of England: Centre for Central Banking Studies, 1996)

Hogue, Arthur R., *Origins of the Common Law* (Indianapolis: Liberty Fund, [1966] 1985).

Holden, J. Milnes, *The History of Negotiable Instruments in English Law* (London: The Athlone Press, 1955).

Hoyle, Ken and Geoffrey Whitehead, *Money and Banking Made Simple* (London: Heinemann, 1982).

Howard, F. C., *Butterworths Annotated Legislation Service, Statutes Supplement No. 43: Exchange and Borrowing Control* (London: Butterworth and Co. Publishers Ltd, 1948).

The Inflation Target and Remit for the Monetary Policy Committee—background notes (HM Treasury, 13th June 1997).

Jaki, S. L., *The Road of Science and the Ways to God* (Edinburgh: Scottish Academic Press, 1978).

Jaki, S. L., *Science and Creation: From eternal cycles to an oscillating universe* (Edinburgh: Scottish Academic Press, Revised Edition, 1986).

Josephus, Flavius, *Against Apion* (Whiston's translation).

Josset, C. R., *Money in Great Britain and Ireland* (Newton Abbott: MacMillan and Charles, 1971).

Leff, Gordon, *Heresy in the Later Middle Ages: The Relation of Heterodoxy to Dissent c. 1250–1450* (Manchester University Press, 1967), 2 vols.

Leigh-Pemberton, Robin, *Speech given by The Rt Hon. Robin Leigh-Pemberton Governor of the Bank of England at the CBI Eastern Region Annual Dinner on Thursday 8 October 1992* (released as a Bank of England Press Notice on the same day).

Lipsey, Richard G., *An Introduction to Positive Economics* (London: Weidenfeld and Nicolson, 1963).

Lipsey, Richard G., and K. Alec Chrystal, *An Introduction to Positive Economics* (Oxford University Press, 1995 Eighth Edition).

Maccoby, Hyam, *Early Rabbinic Writings* (Cambridge University Press, 1988).

Mackay, James, *A History of Modern English Coinage: Henry VIII to Elizabeth II* (London and New York: Longman).

Marshall, B. V., *Comprehensive Economics* (London and New York: Longman, Second Edition 1967), 2 vols.

Meredith, H. O., *Economic History of England* (London: Sir Isaac Pitman and Sons Ltd, 1936).

Miller, Perry, *The New England Mind: From Colony to Province* (Cambridge, Massachusetts: Harvard University Press, 1953).

Mills, Paul S. and John R. Presley, *Islamic Finance: Theory and Practice* (Macmillan, 1999).

Mises, Ludwig von, *The Theory of Money and Credit* (London: Jonathan Cape, 1934. Indianapolis: Liberty Fund, 1981).

Mises, Ludwig von, *Socialism: An Economic and Sociological Analysis* (Indianapolis: Liberty Fund, [1936] 1969).

Mises, Ludwig von, *Omnipotent Government: The Rise of the Total State and Total War* (Spring Mills, PA: Libertarian Press, Inc., [1944] 1969).

Mises, Ludwig von, *Bureaucracy* (Spring Mills, PA: Libertarian Press, Inc., [1944] 1969).

Mises, Ludwig von, *Planned Chaos* (Irvington-on-Hudson, New York: The Foundation for Economic Education, [1947] 1972).

Mises, Ludwig von, *Human Action: A Treatise on Economics* (Chicago: Contemporary Books, Inc., Third Revised Edition 1966).

Money Market Operations (Bank of England, June 1987).

Monetary Policy in the United Kingdom (Bank of England, May 1991).

Mooney, S. C., *Usury, Destroyer of Nations* (Warsaw, OH: Theopolis, 1988).

Morris, Leon, *The Gospel According to Matthew* (Eerdmans/IVP, 1992).

Mumford, Lewis, *The Condition of Man* (Lodon: Secker and Warburg, 1944).

Murray, John, *Principles of Conduct: Aspects of Biblical Ethics* (London: The Tyndale Press, 1957).

North, Gary, *An Introduction to Christian Economics* (The Craig Press, 1973).

North, Gary, ed., *The Journal of Christian Reconstruction* (Vallecito, California: Chalcedon Foundation, 1975), Vol. II, No. 1, *Symposium on Christian Economics*.

North Gary, ed., *Foundations of Christian Scholarship* (Vallecito, California: Ross House Books, 1976).

North, Gary, *The Dominion Covenant: Genesis, An Economic Commentary on the Bible* (Tyler, Texas: Institute for Christian Economics, 1982), Vol. I.

North, Gary, *Honest Money* (Tyler, Texas: Dominion Press, 1986).

North, Gary, *Puritan Economic Experiments* (Tyler, Texas: Institute for Christian Economics, 1988).

North, Gary, *Tools of Dominion: The Case Laws of Exodus* (Tyler, Texas: Institute for Christian Economics, 1990).

Numbers Rabbah (London: The Soncino Press, 1983).

Ormerod, Paul, *The Death of Economics* (London: Faber and Faber, 1994).

Perks, Stephen C., *The Christian Philosophy of Education Explained* (Whitby: Avant Books, 1992).

Perks, Stephen C., *Christianity and Law: An Enquiry into the Influence of Christianity on the Development of English Common Law* (Whitby: Avant Books, 1993).

Perks, Stephen C., *A Defence of the Christian State: The Case Against Principled Pluralism and the Christian Alternative* (Taunton: Kuyper Foundation, 1998).

Perks, Stephen C., "Christianity as a Cult," in *Christianity and Society* (October, 1999), Vol, IX, No. 4.

Perks, Stephen C., "Christianity and the Rule of Law," in *The Salisbury Review* (Winter 1999), Vol. 18, No. 2.

Peterson, Mark A., *The Price of Redemption: The Spiritual Economy of Puritan New England* (Stanford, California: Stanford University Press, 1997).

Porter, E. C., "Proselyte" in James Hastings. ed., *A Dictionary of the Bible* (Edinburgh: T. and T. Clark, 1902).

Report of the Committee on the Working of the Monetary System Presented to Parliament by the Chancellor of the Exchequer by Command of Her Majesty August 1959 (HMSO, 1959) [the "Radcliffe Report"].

Quigley, Carroll, *Tragedy and Hope: A History of the World in Our Time* (New York: The Macmillan Company, 1966).

Ricardo, David, *The Principles of Political Economy and Taxation* (London: Everyman's Library [1821] 1965).

Robertson, H. M., *Aspects of the Rise of Economic Individualism, A Criticism of Max Weber and his School* (Cambridge University Press, 1933)

Roll, Eric, *A History of Economic Thought* (London: Faber and Faber Ltd, [1938] 1973).

Röpke, Wilhelm, *A Humane Economy: The Social Framework of the Free Market* (London: Oswald Wolff Publishers Ltd, 1960).

Rothbard, Murray N., *Power and Market: Government and the Economy* (Kansas City: Sheed Andrews and McMeel, Inc., [1970] 1977).

Rushdoony, R. J., *Politics of Guilt and Pity* (Fairfax, Virginia: Thoburn Press, [1970] 1978).

Rushdoony, R. J., *The Institutes of Biblical Law* (Presbyterian and Reformed Publishing Company, 1973).

Russell, Bertrand, "Logical Atomism" in A J. Ayer, *Logical Positivism* (The Free Press of Glencoe, 1959).

Ryken, Leland, *Worldly Saints: The Puritans as They Really Were* (Grand Rapids, Michigan: Zondervan, 1986).

Samuelson, Paul A., *Economics* (McGraw-Hill Kogakusha, Ltd, Tenth Edition 1976).

Sayers, R. S., *Modern Banking* (The Clarendon Press, Seventh Edition 1967).

Schluter, Michael, *The Old Testament Ban on Interest: Its Relevance for Reform of Britain's Industrial Structure in the 1980s* (Cambridge: The Jubilee Centre, 1984).

Schulter, Michael, *Family Roots or Mobility?* (Cambridge: Jubilee Centre Publications Limited, 1986).

Schoeck, Helmut, *Envy, A Theory of Social Behaviour* (London: Secker and Warburg, 1969).

Schumpeter, Joseph A., *Capitalism, Socialism and Democracy* (George Allen and Unwin, [1943] 1947).

Schumpeter, Joseph A., *History of Economic Analysis* (London: Allen and Unwin, [1954] 1982).

Seldon, Arthur, and F. G. Pennance, *Everyman's Dictionary of Economics* (London: J. M. Dent and Sons Ltd, [1965] 1969).

Settlement of Gilt Repo: Summary of the outcome of the work of the Gilt Repo Settlement Working Party (Bank of England).

Sennholz, Hans F., *Age of Inflation* (Belmont, Massachusetts: Western Islands, 1979).

Sennholz, Hans F., *Money and Freedom* (Spring Mills, PA: Libertarian Press, 1985).

Sloman, John, *Economics* (Harvester Wheatsheaf, 1991).

Smith, Vera C., *The Rationale of Central Banking and the Free Banking Alternative* (Indianapolis: Liberty Fund, [1936] 1990).

Stapley, Neil F., *The Stock Market, A Guide for the Private Investor* (Woodhead-Faulkner in association with Laing and Cruickshank, [1981] 1984).

Storkey, Alan, *A Christian Social Perspective* (Leicester: IVP, 1979).

Storkey, Alan, *Transforming Economics* (London: SPCK, 1986).

Taylor, E. L. Hebden, *Economics, Money and Banking* (Nutley: New Jersey, 1978).

Taylor, E. L. Hebden, "The Reconstruction of Modern Science in Terms of the Biblical Life-and-World View" in *Calvinism Today* (January 1993), Vol. III, No. 1.

Taxation of gold coins—status and prospects for change (London: World Gold Council), reprinted from *MBM-Metal Bulletin Monthly*, June 1990 (Metal Bulletin Journals Ltd).

Thomas, Hugh, *The Conquest of Mexico* (London: Hutchinson, 1993).

Turretin, Francis, *Institutes of Elenctic Theology* (New Jersey: Presbyterian and Reformed Publishing Company, 1994, translated by George Musgrave Giger), 3 vols.

United Kingdom National Accounts, 1993 Edition (London: HMSO).

Vieira, Edwin, Jr., *Pieces of Eight: The Monetary Powers and Disabilities of the United States, A Study in Constitutional Law* (New Jersey: Sound Dollar Committee, 1983).

Vieira, Edwin, Jr, *The Federal Reserve System: A Fatal Parasite on the American Body Politic* (Manassas, Virginia: National Alliance for Constitutional Money).

Vieira, Edwin, Jr, *Why Does the United States Need Constitutional Money? Six Questions on Monetary Reform* (Manassas, Virginia: National Alliance for Constitutional Money, Inc.

Vaux, Roland de, *Ancient Israel, Its Life and Institutions* (London: Darton, Longman and Todd, 1961).

Weber, Max, *General Economic History* (New Brunswick and London: Transaction Books, [1927] 1984).

Weber, Max, *The Protestant Ethic and the Spirit of Capitalism* (London: George Allen and Unwin, [1930] Counterpoint edition 1985).

Weber, Max, *Economy and Society: An Outline of Interpretive Sociology* (University of California Press, [1968] 1978), 2 vols.

West, E. G., *Education and the State: A Study in Political Economy* (Indianapolis: Liberty Fund, [1965] Third Revised Edition 1994).

West, E. G., *Education and the Industrial Revolution* (London: B. T. Batsford Ltd, 1975).

Westminster Confession of Faith, the Larger and Shorter Catechisms, with the Scripture Proofs at Large: together with The Sum of Saving Knowledge (Free Presbyterian Church of Scotland).

Winton, J. R., *A Dictionary of Economic Terms* (London: Routledge and Kegan Paul Ltd, [1905] 1962).

Wortabet, J., "Trade and Commerce" in James Hastings, ed., *A Dictionary of the Bible* (Edinburgh: T. and T. Clark, 1902).

INDEX OF SCRIPTURE REFERENCES

INDEX OF NAMES

SUBJECT INDEX

402   THE POLITICAL ECONOMY OF A CHRISTIAN SOCIETY

(laws—*cont.*)
233, 234, 243; Mosaic, 274, 283; natural, 246, 252; of nature, 218; negative, 209; Old Testament law(s), 253, 255, 277; and order, 204; positive, 209; recusancy laws, 232; rule of, 5, 15, 63, 151; of sabbatical release, 234; sacrificial law (of Old Testament), 296; seven laws of the Noachian covenant, 257; Sunday trading laws, 254; statute, 177; typological, 297, 298, 299; usury laws, 246; welfare laws, 285; Western, 225, 240
leasehold, 284
legal unpredictability, 92
legal predictability, 82, 83
legal system, 82
legal tender, 55, 56, 115, 117, 153, 156, 170, 172, 187, 192, 193, 195, 367; defined, 153
legal tender laws, 155, 171, 193; abolition of, 152–156, 157, 171, 172
Levellers, 89
Levites, 286
Liberal Democrat Party, 92
Liberation Theology, 326
licences, 17, 197
limited government, 15
limited liability, 113, 153, 156, 367; abolition of, 225, 228, 229, 233, 234, 243, 244; as a legal status, 236; company limited by guarantee, 226; private limited liability company, 226; public limited liability company, 226; reform of, 225–245
liquid asset ratio (see also *reserve asset ratio* and *liquidity ratio*) 118, 122, 133
liquid assets (see also *reserve assets*), 118, 122
liquidation, 226, 228, 230, 242
liquidity (see also *bank, liquidity*), 124, 125
liquidity position, 122, 130
liquidity ratio, 118–122
loan(s), 108, 113, 119, 121, 125, 126, 129, 130, 178, 182, 187, 231, 240, 246, 247, 250, 251, 252, 253, 260, 261, 264, 265, 267, 269, 272, 274, 280; charitable, 108, 240, 253, 259, 261, 262, 264, 266; cheap, 26, 136, 230; commercial, 107, 240, 241, 260, 265, 266, 268, 269, 274, 275, 278, 279, 281; consumer, 260; to foreigners by Hebrews, 248; interest-

(loans—*cont.*)
bearing, 268, 269; interest-free, 279; mercy, 107, 277; non-charitable, 107, 108, 260, 279; poor, 107, 253, 260; poverty, 261, 262, 268
lobbying groups, 198
London, 88, 104, 116
London Bullion Market Association (LBMA), 167
London Discount Market Association, 123
Long Parliament, 88
Lovedu, 148
low income groups, 27

Macroeconomics, 11, 12, 23–30, 49
Mafia, 75
magistrate(s) (see also *government* and *State*), 80, 83, 86, 150, 200, 201, 202, 246, 250, 254, 276, 277, 284, 289, 305; a minister of God's wrath, 150; a minister of public justice, 308; are servants of God, 200
Malaysia, 15
mammon(ism), 31, 84, 304
man: calling of, 218; commanded to work six days of the week, 219; consequences of his actions or failure to act, 236; created order a moral environment for, 219; a creative being, 63; put on the earth for a purpose, 222; fallen, 219; is a finite creature, 237; God's creature, 201; made in God's image, 63, 219; God's image bearer and vicegerent, 77; has a duty to serve and glorify God, 82; cannot sin without impunity, 220; liability of, 227, 238; and limited liability, 226, 227, 233; plight of before God, 310; his relationships with others under God's law, 262; binding authority of Scripture over, 249; sinful will of, 219; a sinner under the sentence of God's law, 227; will of God for, 303
mankind, 65, 77, 146, 309, 314, 315; God's calling upon, 150
manufacturers, 26, 34, 35, 36, 37, 39, 41, 58, 64, 110, 144; British, 39; domestic, 36, 39; foreign, 39, 40
management(s), 56, 227, 228, 229, 247
managerial revolution, 229
mass production, 53, 90